Webster's
Spanish-English
English-Spanish
Dictionary

Webster's
Spanish-English
English-Spanish
Dictionary

AMPRODUCTIONS

Published 2007 for AM Productions by Geddes & Grosset,
David Dale House, New Lanark ML11 9DJ, Scotland

© 2007 Geddes & Grosset

ISBN 978 1 84205 641 7

Printed and bound in India

Abbreviations/Abreviaturas

abrev	abbreviation	abreviatura
adj	adjective	adjectivo
adv	adverb	adverbio
art	article	artículo
auto	automobile	automóvil
aux	auxiliary	auxiliar
bot	botany	botánica
chem	chemistry	química
col	colloquial term	lengua familiar
com	commerce	comercio
compd	in compounds	usada en palabras compuestas
comput	computers	informática
conj	conjunction	conjunctión
dep	sport	deporte
excl	exclamation	exclamación
f	feminine noun	sustantrivo femenino
fam	colloquial term	lengua familiar
ferro	railway	ferrocarrilero
fig	figurative use	uso figurado
gr	grammar	gramática
imp	impersonal	impersonal
inform	computers	informática
interj	interjection	interjección
invar	invariable	invariable
irr	irregular	irregular
jur	law term	jurisprudencia
law	law term	jurisprudencia
ling	linguistics	lingüística
m	masculine noun	sustantivo masculino
mar	marine term	vocablo marítimo
mat, math	mathematics	matemáticas
med	medicine	medicina
mil	military term	lo militar
mus	music	música
n	noun	sustantivo
pej	pejorative	peyorativo
pl	plural	plural
pn	pronoun	pronombre

poet	poetical term	vocablo poético
prep	preposition	preposición
quim	chemistry	química
rad	radio	radio
rail	railway	ferrocarilero
sl	slang	argot
teat	theatre	teatro
tec	technology	téchnica, tecnologia
TV	television	televisión
vb	verb	verbo
vi	intransitive verb	verbo intransitivo
vr	reflexive verb	verbo reflexivo
vt	transitive verb	verbo transitivo

Spanish–English Dictionary

A

a *prep* to; in; at; according to; on; by; for; of.

abadía *f* abbey.

abajo *adv* under, underneath; below.

abalanzarse *vr* to rush forward.

abandonado/da *adj* derelict; abandoned; neglected.

abandonar *vt* to abandon; to leave:—~**se** *vr* ~ **a** to give oneself up to.

abarcar *vt* to include; to monopolize.

abarrotado/da *adj* packed.

abarrotar *vt* to tie down; (*mar*) to stow.

abastecer *vt* to purvey.

abatido/da *adj* dejected, low-spirited; abject.

abatimiento *m* low spirits *pl*, depression.

abatir *vt* to knock down; to humble.

abdicar *vt* to abdicate.

abdomen *m* abdomen.

abdominal *adj* abdominal.

abecedario *m* alphabet; spelling book, primer.

abeja *f* bee.

aberración *f* aberration.

abertura *f* aperture, chink, opening.

abeto *m* fir tree.

abierto/ta *adj* open; sincere; frank.

abismal *adj* abysmal.

abismo *m* abyss; gulf; hell.

ablandar *vt, vi* to soften.

abnegado/da *adj* selfless.

abogacía *f* legal profession.

abogado/a *m/f* lawyer; barrister.

abogar *vi* to intercede:—~ **por** to advocate.

abolir *vt* to abolish.

abollar *vt* to dent.

abonado/da *adj* paid-up:—*m/f* subscriber.

abonar *vt* to settle; to fertilize.

abono *m* payment; subscription; dung, manure.

aborrecer *vt* to hate, abhor.

abortar *vi* to miscarry; to have an abortion.

aborto *m* abortion; monster.

abotonar *vt* to button.

abovedado/da *adj* vaulted.

abrasar *vt* to burn; to parch:—~**se** *vr* to burn oneself.

abrazar *vt* to embrace; to surround; to contain.

abrazo *m* embrace.

abrebotellas *m invar* bottle opener.

abrelatas *m invar* can opener.

abreviar *vt* to abridge, cut short.

abridor *m* opener.

abrigar *vt* to shelter; to protect.

abrigo *m* shelter; protection; aid.

abril *m* April.

abrillantar *vt* to polish.

abrir *vt* to open; to unlock.

abrochar *vt* to button; to do up.

abrumar *vt* to overwhelm.

absolución *f* forgiveness, absolution.

absoluto/ta *adj* absolute.

absorber *vt* to absorb.

absorción *f* absorption; takeover.

absorto *adj* engrossed.

abstemio *adj* teetotal.

abstracción *f* abstraction.

abstracto/ta *adj* abstract.

abstraer *vt* to abstract:—~**se** *vr* to be absorbed.

absuelto/ta *adj* absolved.

absurdo *adj* absurd.

9

abuela *f* grandmother.
abuelo *m* grandfather.
abulia *f* lethargy.
abultado/da *adj* bulky, large, massive.
abultar *vt* to increase, enlarge:—*vi* to be bulky.
abundante *adj* abundant, copious.
aburrido/da *adj* boring, bored.
aburrir *vt* to bore, weary.
abusar *vt* to abuse.
acá *adv* here.
acabado/da *adj* perfect, accomplished; old.
acabar *vt* to finish, complete; to achieve:—~**se** *vr* to finish, expire.
academia *f* academy; literary society.
acaecer *vi* to happen.
acallar *vt* to quiet, hush; to soften, appease.
acalorado/da *adj* heated.
acampar *vt* (*mil*) to encamp.
acanalado/da *adj* grooved; fluted.
acaparar *vt* to monopolize; to hoard.
acariciar *vt* to fondle, caress.
acarrear *vt* to transport; to occasion.
acaso *m* chance:—*adv* perhaps.
acatarrarse *vr* to catch cold.
acceder *vi* to agree:—~ **a** to have access to.
accesible *adj* attainable; accessible.
acceso *m* access; fit.
accidentado/da *adj* uneven; hilly; eventful.
accidental *adj* accidental; casual.
accidente *m* accident.
acción *f* action, operation; share.
accionar *vt* to work.
accionista *m* shareholder.
acebo *m* holly tree.
acechar *vt* to lie in ambush for; to spy on.
aceite *m* oil.

aceituna *f* olive.
aceitunado/da *adj* olive-green.
aceleración *f* acceleration.
aceleradamente *adv* swiftly, hastily.
acelerar *vt* to accelerate; to hurry.
acento *m* accent.
aceptar *vt* to accept, admit.
acera *f* sidewalk.
acerca *prep* about, relating to.
acercar *vt* to move nearer:—~**se** *vr* ~ **a** to approach.
acero *m* steel.
acertar *vt* to hit; to guess right.
acertijo *m* riddle.
achacar *vt* to impute.
achaque *m* ailment; excuse; subject, matter.
achicar *vt* to diminish; to humiliate; to bale (out).
achicharrar *vt* to scorch; to overheat.
aciago/ga *adj* unlucky; ominous.
ácido *m* acid:—~**/da** *adj* acid, sour.
acierto *m* success; solution; dexterity.
aclamar *vt* to applaud, acclaim.
aclaración *f* clarification.
aclarar *vt* to clear; to brighten; to explain; to clarify.
acobardar *vt* to intimidate.
acodarse *vr* to lean.
acoger *vt* to receive; to welcome; to harbor:—~**se** *vr* to take refuge.
acogida *f* reception; asylum.
acometida *f* attack, assault.
acomodar *vt* to accommodate, arrange:—~**se** *vr* to comply.
acompañar *vt* to accompany; to join; (*mus*) to accompany.
acompasado/da *adj* measured; well-proportioned.
acondicionar *vt* to arrange; to condition.
acongojar *vt* to distress.

aconsejar *vt* to advise:—**~se** *vr* to take advice.

acontecer *vi* to happen.

acontecimiento *m* event, incident.

acoplar *vt* to couple; to fit; to connect.

acordar *vt* to agree; to remind:—**~se** *vr* to agree; to remember.

acorde *adj* harmonious:—*m* chord.

acordeón *m* accordion.

acorralar *vt* to round up; to intimidate.

acortar *vt* to abridge, shorten:—**~se** *vr* to become shorter.

acostar *vt* to put to bed; to lay down:—**~se** *vr* to go to bed; to lie down.

acostumbrar *vi* to be used to:—*vt* to accustom:—**~se** *vr* **~ a** to become used to.

acotar *vt* to set bounds to; to annotate.

ácrata *m/f* anarchist.

acreditar *vt* to guarantee; to assure; to authorize.

acreedor *m* creditor.

acribillar *vt* to riddle with bullets; to molest, torment.

acta *f* act:—**~s** *fpl* records *pl*.

actitud *f* attitude; posture.

actividad *f* activity; liveliness.

activo/va *adj* active; diligent.

acto *m* act, action; act of a play; ceremony.

actor *m* actor; plaintiff.

actriz *f* actress.

actuación *f* action; behavior; proceedings *pl*.

actual *adj* actual, present.

actualizar *vt* to update.

actuar *vt* to work; to operate:—*vi* to work; to act.

acuarela *f* watercolor.

acudir *vi* to go to; to attend; to assist.

acuerdo *m* agreement:—**de ~** OK.

acumular *vt* to accumulate, collect.

acurrucarse *vr* to squat; to huddle up.

adelantado/da *adj* advanced; fast.

adelantar *vt, vi* to advance, accelerate; to pass.

adelante *adv* forward(s):—*excl* come in!

adelanto *m* advance; progress; improvement.

adelgazar *vt* to make thin or slender; to discuss with subtlety.

además *adv* moreover, besides:—**~ de** besides.

adentro *adv* in; inside.

aderezar *vt* to dress, adorn; to prepare; to season.

adeudar *vt* to owe:—**~se** *vr* to run into debt.

adherir *vi:*—**~a** to adhere to; to espouse.

adiestrar *vt* to guide; to teach, to instruct.

adiós *excl* goodbye; hello.

adivinar *vt* to foretell; to guess.

admirar *vt* to admire; to surprise:—**~se** *vr* to be surprised.

admitir *vt* to admit; to let in; to concede; to permit.

admonición *f* warning.

adobar *vt* to dress; to season.

adobe *m* adobe, sun-dried brick.

adobo *m* dressing; pickle sauce.

adolecer *vi* to suffer from.

adolescencia *f* adolescence.

adónde *adv* where.

adoptar *vt* to adopt.

adoquín *m* paving stone.

adorar *vt* to adore; to love.

adormecer *vt* to put to sleep:—**~se** *vr* to fall asleep.

adornar *vt* to embellish, adorn.

adosado/da *adj* semi-detached.

adquirir *vt* to acquire.

adrede *adv* on purpose.

aduana *f* customs *pl.*

adueñarse *vr:*—~ **de** to take possession of.

adular *vt* to flatter.

adulterio *m* adultery.

adulto/ta *adj, m/f* adult, grown-up.

advenedizo *m* upstart.

advenimiento *m* arrival; accession.

adversidad *f* adversity; setback.

advertencia *f* warning, foreword.

advertir *vt* to notice; to warn.

aerodeslizador *m* hovercraft.

aeronave *f* spaceship.

aeropuerto *m* airport.

afán *m* hard work; desire.

afanar *vt* to harass; (*col*) to pinch:—~se *vr* to strive.

afear *vt* to deform, misshape.

afección *f* affection; fondness, attachment; disease.

afectar *vt* to affect, feign.

afectuoso/sa *adj* affectionate; moving; tender.

afeitar *vt:*—~se *vr* to shave.

aferrar *vt* to grapple, grasp, seize.

afianzar *vt* to strengthen; to prop up.

aficionado/da *adj* keen:—*m/f* lover, devotee; amateur.

afilado *adj* sharp.

afilar *vt* to sharpen, grind.

afín *m* related; similar.

afinar *vt* to tune; to refine.

afincarse *vr* to settle.

afirmar *vt* to secure, fasten; to affirm, assure.

aflicción *f* affliction, grief.

aflictivo/va *adj* distressing.

aflojar *vt* to loosen, slacken, relax.

aflorar *vi* to emerge.

afluente *adj* flowing:—*m* tributary.

afónico/ca *adj* hoarse; voiceless.

afortunado/da *adj* fortunate, lucky.

afrenta *f* outrage; insult.

afrontar *vt* to confront; to bring face to face.

afuera *adv* out, outside.

agacharse *vr* to stoop, squat.

agarradero *m* handle.

agarrar *vt* to grasp, seize:—~se *vr* to hold on tightly.

agasajar *vt* to receive and treat kindly; to regale.

agenciarse *vr* to obtain.

agenda *f* diary.

agente *m* agent; policeman.

ágil *adj* agile.

agilidad *f* agility, nimbleness.

agitar *vt* to wave; to move:—~se *vr* to become excited; to become worried.

aglomeración *f* crowd; jam.

agobiar *vt* to weigh down; to oppress; to burden.

agolparse *vr* to assemble in crowds.

agonía *f* agony.

agorar *vt* to predict.

agostar *vt* to parch.

agosto *m* August.

agotado/da *adj* exhausted; finished; sold out.

agotar *vt* to exhaust; to drain; to misspend.

agradable *adj* pleasant; lovely.

agradar *vt* to please, gratify.

agradecer *vt* to be grateful for; to thank.

agradecido/da *adj* thankful.

agrandar *vt* to enlarge; to exaggerate.

agrario/ria *adj* agrarian; agricultural.

agravante *f* further difficulty.

agraviar *vt* to wrong; to offend:—~**se** *vr* to be aggrieved; to be piqued.

agredir *vt* to attack.

agregar *vt* to aggregate, heap together; to collate; to appoint.

agreste *adj* rustic, rural.

agrícola *adj* farming *compd*.

agricultor/ra *m/f* farmer.

agrietarse *vr* to crack.

agrimensor *m* surveyor.

agrio *adj* sour, acrid; rough, craggy; sharp, rude, unpleasant.

agrupar *vt* to group, cluster; to crowd.

agua *f* water.

aguacate *m* avocado pear.

aguacero *m* cloudburst, downpour.

aguado/da *adj* watery.

aguafuerte *m* etching.

aguamarina *f* aquamarine (gem stone).

aguanieve *f* sleet.

aguantar *vt* to bear, suffer; to hold up.

aguardar *vt* to wait for.

aguarrás *f* turpentine.

agudo/da *adj* sharp; keen-edged; smart; fine; acute; witty; brisk.

aguijón *m* sting of a bee, wasp, etc; stimulation.

águila *f* eagle; genius.

aguileño/ña *adj* aquiline; sharpfeatured.

aguja *f* needle; spire; hand; magnetic needle; (*ferro*) points *pl*.

agujerear *vt* to pierce, bore.

agujero *m* hole.

ahí *adv* there.

ahijada *f* goddaughter.

ahijado *m* godson.

ahínco *m* earnestness; eagerness.

ahogar *vt* to smother; to drown; to suffocate; to oppress; to quench.

ahora *adv* now, at present; just now.

ahorrar *vt* to save; to avoid.

ahumar *vt* to smoke, cure (in smoke):—~**se** *vr* to fill with smoke.

ahuyentar *vt* to drive off; to dispel.

aire *m* air; wind; aspect; musical composition.

aislar *vt* to insulate; to isolate.

ajardinado/da *adj* landscaped.

ajedrez *m* chess.

ajedrezado/da *adj* chequered.

ajeno/na *adj* someone else's; foreign; ignorant; improper.

ajetreo *m* activity; bustling.

ajo *m* garlic.

ajorca *f* bracelet.

ajustar *vt* to regulate, adjust; to settle (a balance); to fit.

al = **a el**.

ala *f* wing; aisle; row, file; brim:—*m/f* winger.

alabar *vt* to praise; to applaud.

alacena *f* cupboard, closet.

alacrán *m* scorpion.

alambre *m* wire.

alameda *f* avenue; poplar grove.

álamo *m* poplar.

alargar *vt* to lengthen; to extend.

alarido *m* outcry, shout:—**dar** ~**s** to howl.

alarma *f* alarm.

alba *f* dawn.

albañil *m* mason, bricklayer.

albarán *m* invoice.

albaricoque *m* apricot.

albedrío *m* free will.

albergue *m* shelter:—~ **de juventud** youth hostel.

albóndiga *f* meatball.

albornoz *m* burnous:—~ **de bañio** bath robe.

alboroto *m* noise; disturbance, riot.

alborozo *m* joy.

albricias *fpl* good news *pl*.

albufera *f* lagoon.

álbum *m* album.

alcachofa *f* artichoke.

alcalde *m* mayor.

alcaldesa *f* mayoress.

alcantarilla *m* sewer; gutter.

alcanzar *vt* to reach; to get, obtain; to hit.

alcaparra *f* caper.

alcayata *f* hook.

alcázar *m* castle, fortress.

alcornoque *m* cork tree.

aldea *f* village.

aleatorio/ria *adj* random.

aleccionar *vt* to instruct; to train.

alegar *vt* to allege; to quote.

alegrar *vt* to cheer; to poke; to liven up:—**~se** *vr* to get merry.

alegre *adj* happy; merry, joyful; content.

alegría *f* happiness; merriment.

alejar *vt* to remove; to estrange:—**~se** *vr* to go away.

alemán/ana *adj*, *m/f* German:—*m* German language.

alentar *vt* to encourage.

alergia *f* allergy.

alero *m* gable-end; eaves *pl*.

alertar *vt* to alert.

aleta *f* fin; wing; flipper; fender.

alfabeto *m* alphabet.

alfarería *f* pottery.

alféizar *m* window sill.

alfiler *m* pin; clip; clothes pin.

alfombra *f* carpet; rug.

alga *f* (*bot*) seaweed.

algo *pn* something; anything:—*adv* somewhat.

algodón *m* cotton; cotton plant; cotton wool.

alguien *pn* someone, somebody; anyone, anybody.

alguno/na *adj* some; any; no:—*pn* someone, somebody.

alhaja *f* jewel.

aliado/da *adj* allied.

alianza *f* alliance, league; wedding ring.

alicates *mpl* pincers *pl*, nippers *pl*.

aliciente *m* attraction; incitement.

aliento *m* breath; respiration.

aligerar *vt* to lighten; to alleviate; to hasten; to ease.

alijo *m* lightening of a ship; alleviation; cache.

alimentar *vt* to feed, nourish:—**~se** *vr* to feed.

aliñar *vt* to adorn; to season.

alinear *vt* to arrange in line:—**~se** *vr* to line up.

alisar *vt* to plane; to polish; to smooth.

aliviar *vt* to lighten; to ease; to relieve, mollify.

allá *adv* there; over there; then.

allanar *vt* to level, flatten; to subdue; to burgle.

allí *adv* there, in that place.

alma *f* soul; human being.

almacén *m* warehouse, store; magazine.

almacenar *vt* to store (up).

almeja *f* clam.

almena *f* battlement.

almendra *f* almond.

almíbar *m* syrup.

almirez *m* mortar.

almizcle *m* musk.

almohada *f* pillow; cushion.

almorranas *fpl* hemorrhoids *pl*.

almuerzo *m* lunch.

alocado/da *adj* crazy; foolish; inconsiderate.

alojamiento *m* lodgings, rooming house; housing.

alpargata *f* rope-soled shoe.
alpinismo *m* mountaineering.
alquilar *vt* to let, rent; to hire.
alquitrán *m* tar, liquid pitch.
alrededor *adv* around.
alta *f* (*mil*) discharge from hospital.
altanero/ra *adj* haughty, arrogant, vain, proud.
altavoz *m* loudspeaker, amplifier.
alterar *vt* to alter, change; to disturb.
altercado *m* altercation, controversy; quarrel.
alterno/na *adj* alternate; alternating.
Alteza *f* Highness (title).
altibajos *mpl* ups and downs *pl*.
altitud *f* height; altitude.
altivo/va *adj* haughty, proud, high-flown.
alto/ta *adj* high; tall:—*m* height; story; highland; (*mil*) halt; (*mus*) alto:— ¡~!/¡~ ahí! *interj* stop!
altura *f* height; depth; mountain summit; altitude.
alubia *f* kidney bean.
alucinar *vt* to blind, deceive:—*vi* to hallucinate.
alumbrado *m* lighting; illumination.
alumbrar *vt* to light:—*vi* to give birth.
alumno/na *m/f* student, pupil.
alza *f* rise; sight.
alzar *vt* to raise, lift up:—~se *vr* to get up; to rise in rebellion.
ama *f* mistress, owner; housewife; foster mother.
amable *adj* kind, nice.
amagar *vt* to threaten; to shake one's fist at:—*vi* to feint.
amamantar *vt* to suckle.
amanecer *vi* to dawn:—**al** ~ at daybreak.
amanerado/da *adj* affected.

amansar *vt* to tame; to soften; to subdue:—~se *vr* to calm down.
amante *m/f* lover.
amapola *f* (*bot*) poppy.
amar *vt* to love.
amargo/ga *adj* bitter, acrid; painful:— *m* bitterness.
amarillo/lla *adj* yellow:—*m* yellow.
amarrar *vt* to moor; to tie, fasten.
amasar *vt* to knead; (*fig*) to arrange, settle; to prepare.
ámbar *m* amber.
ambiente *m* atmosphere; environment.
ambiguo/gua *adj* ambiguous; doubtful, equivocal.
ámbito *m* circuit, circumference; field; scope.
ambos/bas *adj, pn* both.
ambulante *adj* traveling.
ambulatorio *m* state-run clinic.
amenazar *vt* to threaten.
ameno/na *adj* pleasant; delicious; flowery (of language).
América *f* America:—~ **del Norte/del Sur** North/South America.
amianto *m* asbestos.
amiga *f* (female) friend.
amigo *m* friend; comrade; lover:— ~/**ga** *adj* friendly.
aminorar *vt* to diminish; to reduce.
amistad *f* friendship.
amistoso/sa *adj* friendly, cordial.
amo *m* owner; boss.
amoldar *vt* to mold; to adapt:—~se *vr* to adapt oneself.
amor *m* love; fancy; lover:—~ **mio** my love:—**por** ~ **de Dios** for God's sake:—~ **propio** self-love.
amortiguador *m* shock absorber.
amortizar *vt* to redeem, pay, liquidate, discharge (a debt).

amperio *m* amp.

ampliar *vt* to amplify, enlarge; to extend; to expand.

amplificador *m* amplifier.

amplio/lia *adj* ample, extensive.

ampolla *f* blister; ampoule.

amueblar *vt* to furnish.

anacoreta *m* anchorite, hermit.

anacronismo *m* anachronism.

añadir *vt* to add.

analfabeto/ta *adj* illiterate.

analgésico *m* painkiller.

análisis *m* analysis.

anaranjado/da *adj* orange-colored.

anarquía *f* anarchy.

ancho/cha *adj* broad, wide, large:—*m* breadth, width.

anchoa *f* anchovy.

anchura *f* width, breadth.

anciano/na *adj* old:—*m/f* old man/ woman.

ancla *f* anchor.

anclaje *m* anchorage.

andamiaje *m* scaffolding.

andar *vi* to go, walk; to fare; to act, proceed.

andén *m* sidewalk; (*ferro*) platform; quayside.

andrajo *m* rag.

anegar *vt* to inundate, submerge;.

añejo/ja *adj* old; stale, musty.

anexión *f* annexation.

anfibio/bia *adj* amphibious.

anfitrión/ona *m/f* host(ess).

ángel *m* angel.

angosto/ta *adj* narrow, close.

anguila *f* eel.

angula *f* elver.

angular *adj* angular:—**piedra** ~ *f* cornerstone.

ángulo *m* angle, corner.

angustia *f* anguish; heartache.

anhelar *vi* to gasp:—*vt* to long for.

anidar *vi* to nestle, make a nest; to dwell, inhabit.

añil *m* indigo plant; indigo.

anillo *m* ring.

ánima *f* soul.

animación *f* liveliness; activity.

animado/da *adj* lively.

animal *adj, m* animal.

animar *vt* to animate, liven up; to comfort; to revive:—~**se** *vr* to cheer up.

ánimo *m* soul; courage; mind; intention:—*excl* come on!

anís *m* aniseed; anisette.

aniversario/ria *adj* annual:—*m* anniversary.

ano *m* anus.

año *m* year.

anoche *adv* last night.

anochecer *vi* to grow dark:—*m* nightfall.

anónimo/ma *adj* anonymous.

añoranza *f* longing.

anormal *adj* abnormal.

anotar *vt* to comment, note.

anquilosamiento *m* paralysis.

ánsar *m* goose.

ansiar *vt* to desire.

ansiedad *f* anxiety.

antagónico/ca *adj* antagonistic; opposed.

antaño *adv* formerly.

ante *m* suede:—*prep* before; in the presence of; faced with.

anteanoche *adv* the night before last.

anteayer *adv* the day before yesterday.

antebrazo *m* forearm.

antelación *f*:—**con** ~ in advance.

antemano *adv*:—**de** ~ beforehand.

antena *f* feeler, antenna; aerial.

antepasado/da adj passed, elapsed:— ~s mpl ancestors pl.

anterior adj preceding; former.

antes prep, adv before:—conj before.

antibiótico m antibiotic.

anticiclón m anticyclone.

anticipar vt to anticipate; to forestall; to advance.

anticonceptivo m contraceptive.

anticongelante m antifreeze.

anticuado/da adj antiquated.

anticuerpo m antibody.

antiestético/ca adj unsightly.

antifaz m mask.

antiguamente adv in ancient times, of old.

antiguo/gua adj antique, old, ancient.

antipático/ca adj unpleasant.

antojo m whim, fancy; longing.

antorcha f torch; taper.

antro m (poet) cavern, den, grotto.

antropófago m cannibal.

antropología f anthropology.

anual adj annual.

anudar vt to knot; to join:—~se vr to get into knots.

anular vt to annul; to revoke; to cancel:—adj annular.

anunciar vt to announce; to advertise.

anuncio m advertisement.

anzuelo m hook; allurement.

apacible adj affable; gentle; placid, quiet.

apaciguar vt to appease; to pacify, calm.

apagar vt to put out; to turn off; to quench, extinguish.

apañar vt to grasp; to pick up; to patch:—~se vr to manage.

aparador m sideboard; store window.

aparato m apparatus; machine; radio or television set; ostentation, show; (med) bandage, dressing.

aparcamiento m parking lot.

aparcar vt, vi to park.

aparecer vi to appear:—~se vr to appear.

aparentar vt to look; to pretend; to deceive.

apariencia f outward appearance.

apartamento m flat, apartment.

apartar vt to separate, divide; to remove; to sort;.

aparte m aside; new paragraph:—adv apart, separately; besides; aside.

apasionado/da adj passionate; devoted; fond; biased.

apeadero m halt, stopping place; station.

apearse vr to dismount; to get down/ out/off.

apechugar vt to face up to.

apego m attachment, fondness.

apelar vi (jur) to appeal:—~ a to have recourse to.

apellido m surname; family name; epithet.

apenar vt to grieve; to embarrass:— ~se vr to grieve; to be embarrassed.

apenas adv scarcely, hardly:—conj as soon as.

apéndice m appendix, supplement.

apercibirse vr to notice.

aperitivo m aperitif; appetizer.

apero m agricultural implement.

apesadumbrar vt to sadden.

apestar vt to infect:—vi ~ a to stink of.

apetito m appetite.

apiadarse vr to take pity.

apilar vt to pile up:—~se vr to pile up.

apiñado/da adj crowded; pyramidal; pine-shaped.

apio m (*bot*) celery.

apisonadora f steamroller.

aplacar vt to appease, pacify:—~**se** vr to calm down.

aplastar vt to flatten, crush.

aplatanarse vr to get weary.

aplaudir vt to applaud; to extol.

aplauso m applause; approbation, praise.

aplazar vt to postpone.

aplicado/da adj studious; industrious.

aplicar vt to apply; to clasp; to attribute:—~**se** vr ~ **a** to devote oneself to.

aplique m wall light.

aplomo m self-assurance.

apocado/da adj timid.

apoderado/da adj powerful:—m proxy, attorney; agent.

apodo m nickname, sobriquet.

apogeo m peak.

apósito m (*med*) external dressing.

aposta adv on purpose.

apostar vt to bet, wager; to post soldiers:—vi to bet.

apóstol m apostle.

apoteosis f apotheosis.

apoyar vt to rest; to favor, patronize, support:—~**se** vr to lean.

apreciar vt to appreciate; to estimate, value.

aprecio m appreciation; esteem.

apremiante adj urgent.

aprender vt to learn:—~ **de memoria** to learn by heart.

aprensión f apprehension.

apresar vt to seize, grasp.

apresurar vt to accelerate, hasten, expedite:—~**se** vr to hurry.

apretar vt to compress, tighten; to constrain:—vi to be too tight.

aprisa adv quickly, swiftly; promptly.

aprobar vt to approve; to pass:—vi to pass.

apropiado/da adj appropriate.

aprovechar vt to use; to exploit; to profit from; to take advantage of:—vi to be useful; to progress:—~**se** vr ~ **de** to use; to take advantage of.

aproximar vt to approach:—~**se** vr to approach.

aptitud f aptitude, fitness, ability.

apto/ta adj apt; fit, able; clever.

apuesta f bet, wager.

apuñalar vt to stab.

apuntar vt to aim; to level, point at; to mark:—vi to begin to appear or show itself; to prompt (theater):—~**se** vr to score; to enrol.

apurado/da adj poor, destitute of means; exhausted; hurried.

aquél/~ la pn that (one):—~ **los/~ las** pl those (ones).

aquel/~la adj that:—~**los/~las** pl those.

aquello pn that.

aquí adv here; now.

árabe adj, m/f , m (*ling*) Arab, Arabic.

arado m plough.

araña f spider; chandelier.

arañar vt to scratch; to scrape; to corrode.

arancel m tariff.

arandela f washer.

arar vt to plough.

árbitro m arbitrator; referee; umpire.

árbol m tree; (*mar*) mast; shaft.

arbolado/da adj forested; wooded:—m woodland.

arbusto m shrub.

arca f chest, wooden box.

arcada f arch; arcade:—~**s** fpl retching.

arce m maple tree.

archivar *vt* to file.

arcilla *f* clay.

arco *m* arc; arch; fiddle bow; hoop:— **~iris** rainbow.

arder *vi* to burn, blaze.

ardilla *f* squirrel.

área *f* area.

arena *f* sand; grit; arena.

arenque *m* herring:—**~ ahumado** red herring.

argolla *f* large ring.

argucia *f* subtlety.

argumentar *vt, vi* to argue, dispute; to conclude.

árido/da *adj* dry; barren.

arisco/ca *adj* fierce; rude; intractable.

arlequín *m* harlequin, buffoon.

arma *f* weapon, arms.

armado/da *adj* armed; reinforced.

armador *m* shipowner; privateer; jacket, jerkin.

armar *vt* to man; to arm; to fit:—**~la** to kick up a fuss.

armario *m* wardrobe; cupboard.

armazón *f* chassis; skeleton; frame.

armonía *f* harmony.

armonizar *vt* to harmonize; to reconcile.

arnés *m* harness:—**~eses** *mpl* gear, trappings *pl*.

aro *m* ring; earring.

aroma *m* aroma, fragrance.

arpa *f* harp.

arpía *f* (*poet*) harpy, shrew.

arpillera *f* sackcloth.

arpón *m* harpoon.

arqueado/da *adj* arched, vaulted.

arquero *m* archer.

arquitectónico/ca *adj* architectural.

arrabal *m* suburb; slum.

arraigado *adj* deep-rooted; established.

arraigar *vi* to root; to establish:—*vt* to establish;.

arrancar *vt* to pull up by the roots; to pull out:—*vi* to start; to move.

arrasar *vt* to demolish, destroy.

arrastrar *vt* to drag:—*vi* to creep, crawl; to lead a trump at cards:— **~se** *vr* to crawl; to grovel.

arrebatar *vt* to carry off, snatch; to enrapture.

arrebato *m* fury; rapture.

arrecife *m* reef.

arreglar *vt* to regulate; to tidy; to adjust:—**~se** *vr* to come to an understanding.

arrellanarse *vr* to sit at ease; to make oneself comfortable.

arrendar *vt* to rent, let out, lease.

arrendatario/ria *m/f* tenant.

arrepentirse *vr* to repent.

arrestar *vt* to arrest; to imprison.

arriate *m* flowerbed; causeway.

arriba *adv* above, over, up; high, on high, overhead; aloft.

arribista *m/f* upstart.

arriendo *m* lease; farm rent.

arriesgado *adj* risky, dangerous; daring.

arriesgar *vt* to risk, hazard; to expose to danger:—**~se** *vr* to take a chance.

arrimar *vt* to approach, draw near; (*mar*) to stow (cargo):—**~se** *vr* to sidle up; to lean.

arrinconar *vt* to put in a corner; to lay aside.

arrodillarse *vr* to kneel down.

arrogante *adj* arrogant; haughty, proud; stout.

arrojar *vt* to throw, fling; to dash; to emit; to shoot, sprout:—**~se** *vr* to hurl oneself.

arrollar *vt* to run over; to defeat heavily.

arropar *vt* to clothe, dress:——**~se** *vr* to wrap up.

arroyo *m* stream; gutter.

arroz *m* rice.

arrozal *m* ricefield.

arrugar *vt* to wrinkle; to rumple; to fold:——**~ la frente** to frown:——**~se** *vr* to shrivel.

arruinar *vt* to demolish; to ruin:—— **~se** *vr* to go bankrupt.

arrullar *vt* to lull:—*vi* to coo.

artesanía *f* craftsmanship.

ártico/ca *adj* arctic, northern:—*m* **el A~** the Arctic.

articular *vt* to articulate; to joint.

artículo *m* article; clause; point; (*gr*) article; condition.

artífice *m* artisan; artist.

artificio *m* workmanship, craft; artifice, cunning trick.

artimaña *f* trap; cunning.

artista *m* artist; craftsman.

arzobispo *m* archbishop.

as *m* ace.

asa *f* handle; lever.

asado *m* roast meat; barbecue.

asaltar *vt* to assault; to storm (a position); to assail.

asamblea *f* assembly, meeting.

asar *vt* to roast.

ascender *vi* to be promoted; to rise:— *vt* to promote.

ascenso *m* promotion; ascent.

ascensor *m* elevator.

asco *m* nausea; loathing.

ascua *f* red-hot coal.

asear *vt* to clean; to tidy.

asedio *m* siege.

asegurar *vt* to secure; to insure; to affirm; to bail:——**~se** *vr* to make sure.

asentar *vt* to sit down; to affirm, assure; to note:—*vi* to suit.

asentir *vi* to acquiesce, concede.

aseo *m* cleanliness; neatness:——**~s** *mpl* rest room.

aséptico/ca *adj* germ-free.

asequible *adj* attainable; obtainable.

aserrar *vt* to saw.

aserrín *m* sawdust.

asesinar *vt* to assassinate; to murder.

asesorar *vt* to advise; to act as consultant:——**~se** *vr* to consult.

asfalto *m* asphalt.

asfixiar *vt* to suffocate:——**~se** *vr* to suffocate.

así *adv* so, thus, in this manner; like this; therefore; so that; also:——**~ que** so that; therefore:—**así/así** so-so; middling.

asiento *m* chair; bench, stool; seat; contract; entry; residence.

asignar *vt* to assign, attribute.

asignatura *f* subject; course.

asilo *m* asylum, refuge.

asimismo *adv* similarly, in the same manner.

asir *vt* to grasp, seize; to hold, grip:— *vi* to take root.

asistencia *f* audience; presence; assistance, help.

asistir *vi* to be present; to assist:—*vt* to help.

asma *f* asthma.

asno *m* ass.

asociación *f* association; partnership.

asolear *vt* to expose to the sun:——**~se** *vr* to sunbathe.

asomar *vi* to appear:——**~se** *vr* to appear, show up.

asombrar *vt* to amaze; to astonish:—— **~se** *vr* to be amazed; to get a fright.

aspa *f* cross; sail.

aspecto *m* appearance; aspect.

áspero/ra *adj* rough, rugged; craggy, knotty; horrid; harsh, hard; severe, austere; gruff.

aspiración *f* breath; pause.

asqueroso/sa *adj* disgusting.

asta *f* lance; horn; handle.

astilla *f* chip (of wood), splinter.

astillero *m* dockyard.

astral *adj* astral.

astro *m* star.

astrología *m* astrology.

astronomía *f* astronomy.

astucia *f* cunning, slyness.

astuto/ta *adj* cunning, sly; astute.

asumir *vt* to assume.

asunto *m* subject, matter; affair, business.

asustar *vt* to frighten:——**se** *vr* to be frightened.

atacar *vt* to attack.

atajo *m* short cut.

atañer *vi:*—— **a** to concern.

atar *vt* to tie; to fasten.

atardecer *vi* to get dark:—*m* dusk; evening.

atascar *vt* to jam; to hinder:——**se** *vr* to become bogged down.

ataúd *m* coffin.

atemorizar *vt* to frighten:——**se** *vr* to get scared.

atención *f* attention, heedfulness; civility; observance, consideration.

atender *vi* to be attentive:—*vt* to attend to; to heed, expect, wait for; to look at.

atenerse *vr:*—— **a** to adhere to.

atentamente *adv:*—**le saluda ~** yours faithfully.

atento/ta *adj* attentive; heedful; observing; mindful; polite, courteous, mannerly.

atenuar *vt* to diminish; to lessen.

ateo/a *adj, m/f* atheist.

aterciopelado/da *adj* velvety.

aterrar *vt* to terrify:——**se** *vr* to be terrified.

aterrizar *vi* to land.

aterrorizar *vt* to frighten, terrify.

atesorar *vt* to treasure *or* hoard up (riches).

atestado/da *adj* packed:—*m* affidavit.

atestiguar *vt* to witness, attest.

atiborrar *vt* to stuff:——**se** *vr* to stuff oneself.

ático *m* attic.

atinado/da *adj* wise; correct.

atizar *vt* to stir (the fire) with a poker; to stir up.

atlántico/ca *adj* atlantic.

atleta *m* athlete.

atletismo *m* athletics.

atomizador *m* spray.

átomo *m* atom.

atónito/ta *adj* astonished, amazed.

atontado/da *adj* stunned; silly.

atornillar *vt* to screw on; to screw down.

atosigar *vt* to poison; to harass; to oppress.

atracar *vt* to moor; to rob:——**se** *vr* **~ (de)** to stuff oneself (with).

atractivo/va *adj* attractive; magnetic:—*m* charm.

atraer *vt* to attract, allure.

atragantarse *vr* to stick in the throat, choke.

atrapar *vt* to trap; to nab; to deceive.

atrás *adv* backward(s); behind; previously:—**hacia ~** backward(s).

atrasar *vi* to be slow:—*vt* to postpone:——**~ el reloj** to put back a watch:——**se** *vr* to stay behind; to be late.

atravesado/da *adj* oblique; cross; perverse; mongrel; degenerate.

atravesar *vt* to cross; to pass over; to pierce; to go through:——~se *vr* to get in the way; to meddle.

atreverse *vr* to dare, venture.

atribuir *vt* to attribute, ascribe; to impute.

atril *m* lectern; bookrest.

atrio *m* porch; portico.

atrocidad *f* atrocity.

atropellar *vt* to trample; to run down; to hurry; to insult:——~se *vr* to hurry.

atroz *adj* atrocious, heinous; cruel.

atuendo *m* attire.

atún *m* tuna (fish).

aturdir *vt* to stun, confuse; to stupefy.

audaz *adj* audacious, bold.

audiencia *f* audience.

auge *m* boom; climax.

augurio *m* omen.

aula *f* lecture room.

aullar *vi* to howl.

aumentar *vt* to augment, increase; to magnify; to put up:—*vi* to increase; to grow larger.

aún *adv* even:——~ **asi** even so.

aunque *adv* though, although.

auricular *m* receiver:——~**es** *mpl* headphones *pl*.

aurora *f* dawn.

ausencia *f* absence.

ausente *adj* absent.

auspicio *m* auspice; prediction; protection.

austero/ra *adj* austere, severe.

auténtico/ca *adj* authentic.

autoadhesivo/va *adj* self-adhesive.

autobús *m* bus.

autocar *m* bus, coach.

autóctono/na *adj* native.

autodefensa *f* self-defense.

autodeterminación *f* self-determination.

autoescuela *f* driving school.

automovilismo *m* motoring; motor racing.

autónomo/ma *adj* autonomous.

autopista *f* motorway.

autopsia *f* post mortem, autopsy.

autor/ra *m/f* author; maker; writer.

autoridad *f* authority.

autorizar *vt* to authorize.

autorretrato *m* self-portrait.

autoservicio *m* self-service store; restaurant.

autostop *m* hitch-hiking.

autosuficiencia *f* self-sufficiency.

autovía *f* state highway.

auxiliar *vt* to aid, help, assist; to attend:—*adj* auxiliary.

aval *m* guarantee; guarantor.

avanzar *vt, vi* to advance.

avaricia *f* avarice.

avaro/ra *adj* miserly:—*m/f* miser.

ave *f* bird; fowl.

avecinarse *vr* to approach.

avellana *f* hazelnut.

avena *f* oats *pl*.

avenida *f* avenue.

aventajar *vt* to surpass, excel.

aventura *f* adventure; event, incident.

avergonzar *vt* to shame, abash:——~**se** *vr* to be ashamed.

avería *f* breakdown.

averiado/da *adj* broken down; out of order.

averiguar *vt* to find out; to inquire into; to investigate.

avestruz *m* ostrich.

aviación *f* aviation; air force.

avicultura *f* poultry farming.

avidez *f* covetousness.

avinagrado/da *adj* sour.

avión *m* airplane.
avioneta *f* light aircraft.
avisar *vt* to inform; to warn; to advise.
aviso *m* notice; warning; hint.
avispa *f* wasp.
avispado/da *adj* lively, brisk; vivacious.
¡ay! *excl* alas!; ow!:—**¡~ de mi!** alas!
poor me!
ayer *adv* yesterday.
ayuda *f* help, aid; support:—*m* deputy,
assistant.
ayudar *vt* to help, assist; to further.
ayunar *vi* to fast, abstain from food.

ayuntamiento *m* town/city hall.
azabache *m* jet.
azafata *f* air hostess.
azafrán *m* saffron.
azahar *m* orange or lemon blossom.
azar *m* fate:—**por ~** by chance:—
al~ at random.
azotar *vt* to whip, lash.
azotea *f* flat roof of a house.
azúcar *m* sugar.
azufre *m* sulfur, brimstone.
azul *adj* blue:—**~ celeste** sky blue.
azulejo *m* tile.

B

baba *f* dribble, spittle.
babero *m* bib.
babia *f:*—**estar en ~** to be absent-
minded *or* dreaming.
baca *f* (*auto*) luggage rack.
bacalao *m* cod.
bache *m* pothole.
bachillerato *m* baccalaureate.
bahía *f* bay.
bailar *vi* to dance.
bailarín/ina *m/f* dancer.
baja *f* fall; casualty.
bajada *f* descent; inclination; slope;
ebb.
bajamar *f* low tide.
bajar *vt* to lower, let down; to lessen;
to humble; to go/come down.
bajo/ja *adj* low; abject, despicable;
common; humble:—*prep* under,
underneath, below:—*adv* softly; qui-
etly:—*m* (*mus*) bass; low place.
bala *f* bullet.
balance *m* hesitation; balance sheet;
balance; rolling (of a ship).
balanza *f* scale; balance; judgement.

balar *vi* to bleat.
balcón *m* balcony.
balde *m* bucket:—**de ~** *adv* gratis, for
nothing:—**en ~** in vain.
baldío/dia *adj* waste; uncultivated.
baldosa *f* floor; tile; flagstone.
ballena *f* whale; whalebone.
balneario *m* spa.
baloncesto *m* basketball.
balonmano *m* handball.
balonvolea *m* volleyball.
balsa *f* balsa wood; pool; raft, float;
ferry.
bañador *m* swimsuit.
bañar *vt* to bathe; to dip; to coat (with
varnish):—**~se** *vr* to bathe; to swim.
bancarrota *f* bankruptcy.
banco *m* bench; work bench; bank.
banda *f* band; sash; ribbon; troop;
party; gang; touchline.
bandada *f* flock; shoal.
bandeja *f* tray, salver.
bandera *f* banner, standard; flag.
bando *m* faction, party; edict.
bandolero *m* bandit.

bañera f bath (tub).

baño m bath; dip; bathtub; varnish; crust of sugar; coating.

banqueta f three-legged stool; sidewalk.

banquete m banquet; formal dinner.

banquillo m dock.

bar m bar.

baraja f deck of cards.

barandilla f small balustrade, small railing.

barato/ta adj cheap:—**de** ~ gratis:— m cheapness; bargain sale.

barba f chin; beard:—~ **a** ~ face to face.

barbaridad f barbarity, barbarism; outrage.

bárbaro/ra adj barbarous; cruel; rude; rough.

barbecho m first ploughing, fallow land.

barbero m barber.

barbilampiño/ña adj clean-shaven; (fig) inexperienced.

barbilla f chin.

barca f boat.

barco m boat; ship.

barnis m varnish; glaze.

barómetro m barometer.

barquillo m wafer; cornet, cone.

barra m bar; rod; lever; French loaf; sandbank.

barraca f hut.

barranco m gully, ravine; (fig) great difficulty.

barrenar vt to drill, bore; (fig) to frustrate.

barrendero m sweeper, garbage man.

barrer vt to sweep.

barrera f barrier; turnpike, claypit.

barriga f abdomen; belly.

barril m barrel; cask.

barrio m area, district.

barro m clay, mud.

barrote m ironwork of doors, windows, tables; crosspiece.

barruntar vt to guess; to foresee; to conjecture.

bártulos mpl gear, belongings pl.

barullo m uproar.

basar vt to base:—~**se** vr ~ **en** to be based on.

báscula f scales pl.

base f base, basis.

básico/ca adj basic.

bastante adj sufficient, enough:—adv quite.

bastar vi to be sufficient, be enough.

bastidor m embroidery frame:—~**es** mpl scenery (on stage).

basto/ta adj coarse, rude, unpolished.

bastón m cane, stick; nightstick; (fig) command.

bastos mpl clubs pl (one of the four suits at cards).

basura f trash, garbage.

bata f bathrobe; overall; laboratory coat.

batalla f battle, combat; fight.

batata f sweet potato.

batería m battery; percussion.

batir vt to beat; to whisk; to dash; to demolish; to defeat.

baúl m trunk.

bautisar vt to baptize, christen.

baza f card-trick.

bazo m spleen.

beato/ta adj happy; blessed; devout:— m lay brother:—m/f pious person.

bebé m/f baby.

beber vt to drink.

bebida f drink, beverage.

beca f fellowship; grant, bursary, scholarship; sash; hood.

bedel *m* head porter; uniformed employee.

belén *m* nativity scene.

bélico/ca *adj* warlike, martial.

belladona *f* (*bot*) deadly nightshade.

belleza *f* beauty.

bello/lla *adj* beautiful; handsome; lovely; fine.

bellota *f* acorn.

bemol *m* (*mus*) flat.

bendecir *vt* to bless; to consecrate; to praise.

bendito/ta *adj* saintly; blessed; simple; happy.

beneficiar *vt* to benefit; to be of benefit to.

beneficio *m* benefit, advantage; profit; benefit night.

beneficioso/sa *adj* beneficial.

beneplácito *m* consent, approbation.

benévolo/la *adj* benevolent, kind-hearted.

benigno/na *adj* benign; kind; mild.

berberecho *m* cockle.

berenjena *f* eggplant.

bergantín *m* (*mar*) brig.

berrear *vi* to low, bellow.

berrinche *m* anger, rage, tantrum (applied to children).

berrinchudo/da *adj* bad-tempered.

berro *m* watercress.

berza *f* cabbage.

besar *vt* to kiss:—**~se** *vr* to kiss.

bestia *f* beast, animal; idiot.

besugo *m* sea bream.

betún *m* shoe polish.

biberón *m* feeding bottle.

bibliófilo/la *m/f* book-lover, book-worm.

bibliografía *f* bibliography.

biblioteca *f* library.

bicarbonato *m* bicarbonate.

bicho *m* small animal; bug:—**mal ~** villain.

bici *f* (*fam*) bike.

bicicleta *f* bicycle.

bidé *m* bidet.

bien *m* good, benefit; profit:—**~es** *mpl* goods *pl*, property; wealth:—*adv* well, right; very; willingly; easily:—**~ que** *conj* although:—**está ~** very well.

bienestar *m* well-being.

bienhechor/ra *m/f* benefactor.

bienvenida *f* welcome.

bifurcación *f* fork.

bigote *m* mustache; whiskers *pl*.

bilingüe *adj* bilingual.

bilis *f* bile.

billar *m* billiards *pl*.

billete *m* note, bill; ticket; (*ferro*) ticket:—**~ sencillo** single ticket:—**~ de ida y vuelta** return ticket.

biografía *f* biography.

biología *f* biology.

biombo *m* screen.

birlar *vt* to knock down at one blow; to pinch (*fam*).

bis *excl* encore.

bisabuela *f* great-grandmother.

bisabuelo *m* great-grandfather.

bisagra *f* hinge.

bisiesto *adj*:—**año' ~** leap year.

bisnieto/ta *m/f* great-grandson/ daughter.

bistec *m* steak.

bisturí *m* scalpel.

bisutería *f* costume jewelry.

bisco/ca *adj* cross-eyed.

biscocho *m* sponge cake; biscuit; ship's biscuit.

blanco/ca *adj* white; blank:—*m* whiteness; white person; blank, blank space; target (to shoot at).

blando/da *adj* soft, smooth; mild, gentle; (*fam*) cowardly.

blanquear *vt* to bleach; to whitewash; to launder (money).

blasfemar *vi* to blaspheme.

bledo *m:*—**no me importa un ~** I don't give a damn (*sl*).

blindado/da *adj* armor-plated; bullet-proof.

bloc *m* writing pad.

bloque *m* block.

bloquear *vt* to block; to blockade.

blusa *f* blouse.

bobada *f* folly, foolishness.

bobina *f* bobbin.

bobo/ba *m/f* idiot, fool; clown, funny man:—*adj* stupid, silly.

boca *f* mouth; entrance, opening; mouth of a river:—**~ en ~** *adv* by word of mouth:—**a pedir de ~** to one's heart's content.

bocacalle *f* entrance to a street.

bocadillo *m* sandwich, roll.

bocado *m* mouthful.

bocazas *m invar* big-mouth.

boceto *m* sketch; design; mock-up.

bochorno *m* sultry weather, scorching heat; blush.

bocina *f* (*mus*) trumpet; (*auto*) horn.

bocinar *vi* to sound a horn, hoot.

boda *f* wedding.

bodega *f* wine cellar; warehouse; bar.

bofetada *f* slap (in the face).

boina *f* beret.

boj *m* box, box tree.

bola *f* ball; marble; globe; (*fam*) lie, fib.

bolera *f* bowling alley.

bolero *m* bolero jacket; bolero dance.

boletín *m* bulletin; journal, review.

boleto *m* ticket.

boliche *m* jack at bowls; bowls, bowling alley; dragnet.

bolígrafo *m* (ballpoint) pen.

bollo *m* bread roll; lump.

bolo *m* ninepin; (large) pill.

bolsa *f* purse; bag; pocket; sac; stock exchange.

bolsillo *m* pocket; purse.

bomba *f* pump; bomb; surprise:—**dar a la ~** to pump:—**~ de gasolina** gas pump.

bombero *m* fireman.

bombilla *f* light bulb.

bombo *m* large drum.

bombón *m* chocolate.

bondad *f* goodness, kindness; courtesy.

bondadoso/sa *adj* good, kind.

boñiga *f* cow pat.

bonito *adj* pretty, nice-looking; pretty good, passable:—*m* tuna (fish).

boquerón *m* anchovy; large hole.

boquilla *f* mouthpiece of a musical instrument; nozzle.

borde *m* border; margin; (*mar*) board.

bordear *vi* (*mar*) to tack:—*vt* to go along the edge of; to flank.

bordillo *m* curb.

bordo *m* (*mar*) board of a ship.

boreal *adj* boreal, northern.

borracho/cha *adj* drunk, intoxicated; blind with passion:—*m/f* drunk, drunkard.

borrador *m* first draft; scribbling pad; eraser.

borrar *vt* to erase, rub out; to blur; to obscure.

borrasca *f* storm; violent squall of wind; hazard; danger.

borrico/ca *m/f* donkey, ass; blockhead.

borrón *m* blot, blur.

bosque *m* forest; wood.

bosquejo *m* sketch (of a painting); unfinished work.

bostezar *vi* to yawn; to gape.

bota *f* leather wine-bag; boot.

botánica *f* botany.

bote *m* bounce; thrust; tin, can; boat.

botella *f* bottle.

botijo *m* earthenware pitcher.

botín *m* high boot, half-boot; gaiter; booty.

botiquín *m* medicine chest.

botón *m* button; knob (of a radio etc); (*bot*) bud.

bóveda *f* arch; vault, crypt.

boxeo *m* boxing.

boya *f* (*mar*) buoy.

boyante *adj* buoyant, floating; (*fig*) fortunate, successful.

bozo *m* down (on the upper lip or chin); headstall (of a horse).

braga *f* sling, rope; nappy, diaper:— **~s** *fpl* breeches *pl*; panties *pl*.

bragueta *f* fly, flies *pl* (of pants/ trousers).

brasa *f* live coal:—**estar hecho una ~** to be very flushed.

bravío/vía *adj* ferocious, savage, wild; coarse.

bravo/va *adj* brave, valiant; bullying; savage, fierce; rough; sumptuous; excellent, fine:—*excl* well done!

braza *f* fathom.

brazo *m* arm; branch (of a tree); enterprise; courage:—**luchar a ~ par-tido** to fight hand-to-hand.

brea *f* pitch; tar.

brebaje *m* potion.

brecha *f* (*mil*) breach; gap, opening.

breva *f* early fig; early large acorn.

breve *m* papal brief:—*f* (*mus*) breve:— *adj* brief, short:—**en ~** shortly.

brezo *m* (*bot*) heather.

bribón/ona *adj* dishonest, rascally.

bricolaje *m* do-it-yourself.

brida *f* bridle; clamp, flange.

brigada *f* brigade; squad, gang.

brillante *adj* brilliant; bright, shining:— *m* diamond.

brillar *vi* to shine; to sparkle, glisten; to shine, be outstanding.

brincar *vi* to skip; to leap, jump; to gambol; to fly into a passion.

brindis *m invar* toast.

brío *m* spirit, dash.

brisca *f* card game.

broca *f* reel; drill; shoemaker's tack.

brocado *m* gold or silver brocade:— **~/da** *adj* embroidered, like brocade.

brocha *f* large brush:—**~ de afeitar** shaving brush.

broche *m* clasp; brooch; cufflink.

broma *f* joke.

bromear *vi* to joke.

bronca *f* row.

bronceado/da *adj* tanned:—*m* bronzing, suntan.

brotar *vi* (*bot*) to bud, germinate; to gush, rush out; (*med*) to break out.

bruces *adv:*—**a ~/de ~** face downward(s).

bruja *f* witch.

brújula *f* compass.

bruma *f* mist; (*mar*) sea mist.

bruñir *vt* to polish; to put rouge on.

brusco/ca *adj* rude; sudden; brusque.

brutal *adj* brutal, brutish:—*m* brute.

bruto *m* brute, beast:—**~/ta** *adj* stupid; gross; brutish.

bucal *adj* oral.

bucear *vi* to dive.

bucle *m* curl.

buen *adj* (*before m nouns*) good.

bueno/na *adj* good, perfect; fair; fit, proper; good-looking:—**¡buenos días!** good morning!:—**¡buenas tardes!** good afternoon:—**¡buenas noches!** good night!:—**¡~!** right!

buey *m* ox, bullock.

bufanda *f* scarf.

bufete *m* desk, writing-table; lawyer's office.

bufo/fa *adj* comic:—**opera ~a** *f* comic opera.

buhardilla *f* attic.

búho *m* owl; unsocial person.

buitre *m* vulture.

bujía *f* candle; spark plug.

bullicio *m* bustle; uproar.

bulto *m* bulk; tumor, swelling; bust; baggage.

buñuelo *m* doughnut; fritter.

buque *m* vessel, ship, tonnage, capacity (of a ship); hull (of a ship).

burbuja *f* bubble.

burdel *m* brothel.

burguesía *f* bourgeoisie.

burlar *vt* to hoax; to defeat; to play tricks on, deceive; to frustrate:—**~se** *vr* to joke, laugh at.

burro *m* ass, donkey; idiot; sawhorse.

bursátil *adj* stock exchange *compd*.

buscar *vt* to seek, search for; to look for; to hunt after:—*vi* to look, search, seek.

busilis *m* difficulty, snag.

busto *m* bust.

butaca *f* armchair; seat.

butano *m* butane.

butifarra *f* Catalan sausage.

butrón *m* burglary.

buzo *m* diver.

buzón *m* mailbox; conduit, canal; cover of a jar.

C

cabalgar *vi* to ride, go riding.

cabalgata *f* procession.

caballa *f* mackerel.

caballería *f* mount, steed; cavalry; cavalry horse; chivalry; knighthood.

caballero *m* knight; gentleman; rider, horseman.

caballete *m* ridge of a roof; painter's easel; trestle; bridge (of the nose).

caballo *m* horse; (at chess) knight; queen (in cards):—**a ~** on horseback.

cabecera *f* headboard; head; far end; pillow; headline; vignette.

cabecilla *m* ringleader.

cabello *m* hair.

caber *vi* to fit.

cabeza *f* head; chief, leader; main town, chief center.

cabida *f* room, capacity.

cabildo *m* chapter (of church); meeting of a chapter; corporation of a town.

cabina *f* cabin; telephone booth.

cabizbajo/ja, cabizcaido/da *adj* crestfallen; pensive, thoughtful.

cable *m* cable, lead, wire.

cabo *m* end, extremity; cape, headland; (*mar*) cable, rope.

cabra *f* goat.

cabrón *m* cuckold:—**¡~!** (*fam*) bastard! (*sl*).

cacahuete *m* peanut.

cacao *m* (*bot*) cacao tree; cocoa.

cacarear *vi* to crow; to brag, boast.

cacerola *f* pan, saucepan; casserole.

cachalote *m* sperm whale.

cacharro *m* pot.

cachivache *m* pot; piece of junk.

cachondo/da *adj* randy; funny.

cachorro/ra *m/f* puppy; cub.

caco *m* pickpocket; coward.

cada *adj invar* each; every.

cadáver *m* corpse, cadaver.

cadena *f* chain; series, link; radio or TV network.

cadera *f* hip.

caducar *vi* to become senile; to expire, lapse; to deteriorate.

caer *vi* to fall; to tumble down; to lapse; to happen; to die:—~**se** *vr* to fall down.

café *m* coffee; cafe, coffee house.

cafetera *f* coffee pot.

cagar *vi* (*fam*) to have a shit (*sl*).

caimán *m* caiman, alligator.

caja *f* box, case; casket; cashbox; cash desk; supermarket check-out:—~ **de ahorros** savings bank:—~ **de cambios** gearbox.

cajón *m* bureau; locker.

cal *f* lime:—~ **viva** quick lime.

calabacín *m* small marrow, zucchini.

calabaza *f* pumpkin, squash.

calamar *m* squid.

calar *vt* to soak, drench; to penetrate, pierce; to see through; to lower:—~**se** *vr* to stall (of a car).

calavera *f* skull; madcap.

calcar *vt* to trace, copy.

calcetín *m* sock.

calcio *m* calcium.

calcomanía *f* transfer.

calculadora *f* calculator.

calcular *vt* to calculate, reckon; to compute.

caldear *vt* to weld; to warm, heat up.

calderada *f* stew.

calderilla *f* small change.

caldo *m* stock; broth.

calefacción *f* heating.

calendario *m* calendar.

calentar *vt* to warm up, heat up:— ~**se** *vr* to grow hot; to dispute.

calidad *f* grade, quality, condition; kind.

cálido/da *adj* hot; (*fig*) warm.

caliente *adj* hot; fiery:—**en** ~ in the heat of the moment.

callado/da *adj* silent, quiet.

callar *vi*, ~**se** *vr* to be silent, keep quiet.

calle *f* street; road.

callejear *vi* to loiter about the streets.

callejón *m* alley.

callo *m* corn; callus:—~**s** *mpl* tripe.

calmante *m* (*med*) sedative.

calmar *vt* to calm, quiet, pacify:—*vi* to become calm.

calor *m* heat, warmth; ardor, passion.

calumnia *f* calumny, slander.

calvo/va *adj* bald; bare, barren.

calzado *m* footwear.

calzoncillos *mpl* underpants, shorts *pl*.

cama *f* bed:—**hacer la** ~ to make the bed.

cámara *f* hall; chamber; room; camera; cine camera.

camarada *m/f* comrade, companion.

camarera *f* waitress.

camarero *m* waiter.

camarón *m* shrimp, prawn.

camarote *m* berth, cabin.

cambalache *m* exchange, swap.

cambiar *vt* to exchange; to change:— *vi* to change, alter:—~**se** *vr* to move house.

cambio *m* change, exchange; rate of exchange; bureau de change.

camelar *vt* to flirt with.

camello *m* camel; drug dealer.

camilla f couch; cot; stretcher.

caminar vi to travel; to walk, go.

camino m road; way.

camión m truck.

camisa f shirt; chemise.

camisería f dry goods store.

camiseta f T-shirt; undershirt.

camisón m nightgown.

campamento m (mil) encampment.

campana f bell.

campanario m belfry.

campeón/ona m/f champion.

campesino/na, campestre adj rural.

campo m country; field; camp; ground; pitch.

caña f cane, reed; stalk; shinbone; glass of beer:—~ **dulce** sugar cane.

cañada f gully; glen; sheep-walk.

canal m channel, canal.

canalla f mob, rabble.

cáñamo m hemp.

canas fpl gray hair:—**peinar** ~ to grow old.

cañaveral m reedbed.

cancelar vt to cancel; to write off.

cancha f (tennis) court.

canción f song.

candado m padlock.

candilejas fpl footlights pl.

canela f cinnamon.

cangrejo m crab; crayfish.

canica f marble.

canilla f shinbone; arm-bone; tap of a cask; spool.

canjear vt to exchange.

cano/na adj gray-haired; whitehaired.

canoso/sa adj gray-haired; white-haired.

cansancio m tiredness, fatigue.

cansar vt to tire, tire out; to bore:—~**se** vr to get tired, grow weary.

cantante m/f singer.

cantar m song:—vt to sing; to chant:—vi to sing; to chirp.

cántaro m pitcher; jug:—**llover a** ~**s** to rain heavily, pour.

cantera f quarry.

cantidad f quantity, amount; number.

cantina f buffet, refreshment room; canteen; cellar; snack bar; bar.

canto m stone; singing; song; edge.

canuto m (fam) joint (sl), marijuana cigarette.

caño m tube, pipe; sewer.

cañón m tube, pipe; barrel; gun; canyon.

caoba f mahogany.

caos m chaos; confusion.

capa f cloak; cape; layer, stratum; cover; pretext.

capacidad f capacity; extent; talent.

capataz m foreman, overseer.

capaz adj capable; capacious, spacious, roomy.

capeo m challenging of a bull with a cloak.

caperuza f hood.

capirote m hood.

capital m capital; capital sum:—f capital, capital city:—adj capital; principal.

capítulo m chapter of a cathedral; chapter (of a book).

capó m (auto) hood.

capote m greatcoat; bullfighter's cloak.

capricho m caprice, whim, fancy.

captar vt to captivate; to understand; (rad) to tune in to, receive.

capturar vt to capture.

capucha f cap, cowl, hood of a cloak.

capullo m cocoon of a silkworm; rosebud.

cara f face; appearance:—~ **a** ~ face to face.

cárabe *m* amber.

caracol *m* snail; seashell; spiral.

carácter *m* character; quality; condition; hand-writing.

característico/ca *adj* characteristic.

caradura *m/f*:—**es un ~** he's got a nerve.

caramba *excl* well!

carámbano *m* icicle.

carambola *f* cannon (at billiards); trick.

caravana *f* trailer; queue; tailback (traffic).

carbón *m* coal; charcoal; carbon; carbon paper.

carboncillo *m* charcoal.

carbono *m* (*quim*) carbon.

carburador *m* carburettor.

carcajada *f* (loud) laugh.

cárcel *f* prison, penitentiary; jail.

carcoma *f* deathwatch beetle; woodworm; anxious concern.

cardenal *m* cardinal; cardinal bird; (*med*) bruise, weal.

cardo *m* thistle.

carecer *vi*:—**~ de** to want, lack.

cargar *vt* to load, burden; to charge:—*vi* to charge; to load (up); to lean.

cargo *m* burden, loading; employment, post; office; charge, care; obligation; accusation.

carguero *m* freighter.

caricia *f* caress.

caridad *f* charity.

caries *f* (*med*) tooth decay, caries.

cariño *m* fondness, tenderness; love.

carmesí *adj*, *m* crimson.

carmín *m* carmine; rouge; lipstick.

carne *f* flesh; meat; pulp (of fruit).

carné, carnet *m* driver's license:—**~ de identidad** identity card.

carnicería *f* butcher's (store); carnage, slaughter.

caro/ra *adj* dear; affectionate; dear, expensive:—*adv* dearly.

carpa *f* carp (fish); tent.

carpeta *f* table cover; folder, file, portfolio.

carpintero *m* carpenter.

carraca *f* carrack (ship); rattle.

carrera *f* career; course; race; run, running; route; journey:—**a ~ abierta,** at full speed.

carrete *m* reel, spool, bobbin.

carretera *f* highway.

carril *m* lane (of highway); furrow.

carrillo *m* cheek; pulley.

carro *m* cart; car.

carrocería *f* bodywork, coachwork.

carta *f* letter; map; document; playing card; menu:—**~ blanca** carte blanche:—**~ credencial** *o* **de creencia** credentials *pl*:—**~ certificada** registered letter:—**~ de crédito** credit card:—**~ verde** green card.

cartabón *m* square (tool).

cartel *m* placard; poster; wall chart; cartel.

cartera *f* satchel; purse, handbag; briefcase.

carterista *m/f* pickpocket.

cartero *m* mailman.

cartón *m* cardboard, pasteboard; cartoon.

casa *f* house; home; firm, company:—**~ de campo** country house:—**~ de moneda** mint:—**~ de huéspedes** boarding house, rooming house.

casar *vt* to marry; to couple; to abrogate; to annul:—**~se** *vr* to marry, get married.

cascabel *m* small bell; rattlesnake.

cascada *f* cascade, waterfall.

cascanueces *m invar* nutcracker.

cascar *vt* to crack, break into pieces; (*fam*) to beat:—**~se** *vr* to be broken open.

cáscara *f* rind, peel; husk, shell; bark.

casco *m* skull; helmet; fragment; shard; hulk (of a ship); crown (of a hat); hoof; empty bottle, returnable bottle.

cascote *m* rubble, fragment of material used in building.

caserío *m* country house; hamlet.

casero *m* landlord; janitor:—**~/ra,** *adj* domestic; household *compd*; home-made.

caset(t)e *m* cassette:—*f* cassetteplayer.

casi *adv* almost, nearly:—**~ nada** next to nothing:—**~ nunca** hardly ever, almost never.

caso *m* case; occurrence, event; hap, casuality; occasion; (*gr*) case:—**en ese ~** in that case:—**en todo ~** in any case:—**~ que** in case.

caspa *f* dandruff; scurf.

castaño *m* chestnut tree:—**~/na** *adj* chestnut(-colored), brown.

castañuela *f* castanet.

castellano *m* Castilian, Spanish.

castigar *vt* to castigate, punish; to afflict.

castillo *m* castle.

castizo/za *adj* pure, thoroughbred.

casto/ta *adj* pure, chaste.

castor *m* beaver.

castrar *vt* to geld, castrate; to prune; to cut the honeycombs out of (beehives).

casualidad *f* chance, accident.

cataplasma *f* poultice.

catar *vt* to taste; to inspect, examine; to look at; to esteem.

catarata *f* (*med*) cataract; waterfall.

catarro *m* catarrh; cold.

cátedra *f* professor's chair.

categoría *f* category; rank.

católico/ca *adj*, *m/f* catholic.

catorce *adj*, *m* fourteen.

catre *m* cot.

cauce *m* riverbed; (*fig*) channel.

caucho *m* rubber; tire.

caudal *m* volume, flow; property, wealth; plenty.

causa *f* cause; motive, reason; lawsuit:—**a ~ de** considering, because of.

causar *vt* to cause; to produce; to occasion.

cautela *f* caution, cautiousness.

cautivar *vt* to take prisoner in war; to captivate, charm.

cauto/ta *adj* cautious, wary.

cavar *vt* to dig up, excavate:—*vi* to dig, delve; to think profoundly.

caverna *f* cavern, cave.

cavidad *f* cavity, hollow.

cavilar *vt* to ponder, consider carefully.

cazador/ra *m/f* hunter; *m* huntsman:—**~ furtivo** poacher.

cazar *vt* to chase, hunt; to catch.

cazo *m* saucepan; ladle.

cazuela *f* casserole; pan.

cebada *f* barley.

cebar *vt* to feed (animals), fatten.

cebo *m* feed, food; bait, lure; priming.

cebolla *f* onion; bulb.

cebra *f* zebra.

cedazo *m* sieve, strainer.

ceder *vt* to hand over; to transfer, make over; to yield, give up:—*vi* to submit, comply, give in; to diminish, grow less.

cedro *m* cedar.

cédula *f* certificate; document; slip of paper; bill:—~ **de cambio** bill of exchange.

cegar *vi* to grow blind:—*vt* to blind; to block up.

ceja *f* eyebrow.

cejar *vi* to go backward(s); to slacken, give in.

celebrar *vt* to celebrate; to praise:—~ **misa** to say mass.

célebre *adj* famous, renowned; witty, funny.

celeste *adj* heavenly; sky-blue.

celestial *adj* heavenly; delightful.

celo *m* zeal; rut (in animals):—~**s** *mpl* jealousy.

celoso/sa *adj* zealous; jealous.

célula *f* cell.

cementerio *m* graveyard.

cena *f* supper.

cenar *vt* to have for dinner:—*vi* to have supper, have dinner.

cenegal *m* quagmire.

cenicero *m* ashtray.

ceniza *f* ashes *pl*:—**miércoles de ~** Ash Wednesday.

censo *m* census; tax; ground rent:—~ **electoral** electoral roll.

censurar *vt* to review, criticize; to censure, blame.

centella *f* lightning; spark.

centenar *m* hundred.

centeno *m* rye.

centésimo/ma *adj* hundredth:—*m* hundredth.

centígrado *m* centigrade.

centímetro *m* centimeter.

céntimo *m* cent.

centinela *f* sentry, guard.

central *adj* central:—*f* head office, headquarters; (telephone) exchange.

centro *m* center:—~ **comercial** shopping center.

centuplicar *vt* to increase a hundredfold.

ceñido/da *adj* tight-fitting; sparing, frugal.

ceñudo/da *adj* frowning, grim.

cepa *f* stock (of a vine); origin (of a family).

cepillo *m* brush; plane (tool).

cepo *m* branch, bough; trap; snare; poorbox.

cera *f* wax:—~**s** *fpl* honeycomb.

cerámica *f* pottery.

cerca *f* enclosure; fence:—~**s** *mpl* objects *pl* in the foreground of a painting:—*adv* near, at hand, close by:—~ **de** close, near.

cercano/na *adj* near, close by; neighboring, adjoining.

cerciorar *vt* to assure, ascertain, affirm:—~**se** *vr* to find out.

cerdo *m* pig, hog.

cerebro *m* brain.

cereza *f* cherry.

cerilla *f* wax taper; ear wax:—~**s** *fpl* matches, safety matches *pl*.

cero *m* nothing, zero.

cerrado/da *adj* closed, shut; locked; overcast, cloudy; broad (of accent).

cerrajero *m* locksmith.

cerrar *vt* to close, shut; to block up; to lock:—~ **la cuenta** to close an account:—~**se** *vr* to close; to heal; to cloud over:—*vi* to close, shut; to lock.

cerro *m* hill; neck (of an animal); backbone; combed flax or hemp:—**en ~** bareback.

cerrojo *m* bolt (of a door).

certamen *m* competition, contest.

certero *adj* accurate; well-aimed.

certeza, certidumbre f certainty.

certificado m certificate:—~/**da** adj registered (of a letter).

cerveza m beer.

cesar vt to cease, stop; to fire (sl); to remove from office:—vi to cease, stop; to retire.

cese m suspension; dismissal.

cesión f cession; transfer.

césped m grass; lawn.

cesta f basket, pannier.

chabola f shack.

chal m shawl.

chalado/da adj crazy.

chale(t) m detached house.

chaleco m vest.

champán m champagne.

champiñón m mushroom.

champú m shampoo.

chamuscar vt to singe, scorch.

chantaje m blackmail.

chapa f metal plate; panel; (auto) license plate.

chaparrón m heavy shower (of rain).

chapuza f badly done job.

chaqueta f jacket.

charco m pool, puddle.

charcutería f store selling pork meat products.

charlar vi to chat.

charlatán/ana m/f chatterbox.

charol m varnish; patent leather.

chasco m disappointment; joke, jest.

chasis m invar (auto) chassis.

chasquido m crack; click.

chatarra f scrap.

chato/ta adj flat, flattish; snub-nosed.

chaval/la m/f lad/lass.

chicle m chewing gum.

chico/ca adj little, small:—m/f boy/girl.

chiflado/da adj crazy.

chile m chilli pepper.

chillar vi to scream, shriek; to howl; to creak.

chimenea f chimney; fireplace.

china f pebble; porcelain, chinaware; China silk.

chincheta f thumbtack.

chino/na adj, m/f Chinese:—m Chinese language.

chirriar vi to hiss; to creak; to chirp.

chisme m tale; thingummyjig.

chispa f spark; sparkle; wit; drop (of rain); drunkenness.

chiste m funny story, joke.

chivo/va m/f billy/nanny goat.

chocar vi to strike, knock; to crash:—vt to shock.

chochear vi to dodder, be senile; to dote.

chocolate m chocolate.

chófer m driver.

chopo m (bot) black poplar.

chorizo m pork sausage.

chorro m gush; jet; stream:—**a ~s** abundantly.

chuchería f trinket.

chulear vi to brag.

chuleta f chop.

chulo m rascal; pimp.

chupar vt to suck; to absorb.

churro m fritter.

ciática f sciatica.

cicatriz f scar.

cicatrizar vt to heal.

ciclista m/f cyclist.

ciclo m cycle.

cicuta f (bot) hemlock.

ciego/ga adj blind.

cielo m sky; heaven; atmosphere; climate.

ciempiés m invar centipede.

cien adj, m a hundred.

ciénaga *f* swamp.

ciencia *f* science.

cieno *m* mud; mire.

cierto/ta *adj* certain, sure; right, correct:—**por ~** certainly.

ciervo *m* deer, hart, stag:—**~ volante** stag beetle.

cierzo *m* cold northerly wind.

cifra *f* number, numeral; quantity; cipher; abbreviation.

cigarra *f* cicada.

cigarro *m* cigar; cigarette.

cigüeña *f* stork; crank (of a bell).

cilindro *m* cylinder.

cima *f* summit; peak; top.

cimiento *m* foundation, groundwork; basis, origin.

cinc *m* zinc.

cincelar *vt* to chisel, engrave.

cinco *adj, m* five.

cincuenta *adj, m* fifty.

cine *m* cinema.

cínico/ca *adj* cynical.

cinta *f* band, ribbon; reel.

cintura *f* waist.

cinturón *m* belt, girdle; (*fig*) zone:—**~ de seguridad** seatbelt.

ciprés *m* cypress tree.

circo *m* circus.

circuito *m* circuit; circumference.

circular *adj* circular; circulatory:—*vt* to circulate:—*vi* (*auto*) to drive.

círculo *m* circle; (*fig*) scope, compass.

circunspecto/ta *adj* circumspect, cautious.

circunstancia *f* circumstance.

circunvalacion *f:*—**carretera de ~** bypass.

cirio *m* wax candle.

ciruela *f* plum:—**~ pasa** prune.

cirugía *f* surgery.

cisne *m* swan.

citar *vt* to make an appointment with; to quote; (*jur*) to summon.

ciudad *f* city; town.

ciudadano/na *m/f* citizen:—*adj* civic.

clamor *m* clamor, outcry; peal of bells.

clandestino/na *adj* clandestine, secret, concealed.

clara *f* egg-white.

claraboya *f* skylight.

clarear *vi* to dawn:—**~se** *vr* to be transparent.

clarín *m* bugle; bugler.

clarinete *m* clarinet:—*m/f* clarinetist.

claro/ra *adj* clear, bright, evident, manifest:—*m* opening; clearing (in a wood).

clase *f* class; rank; order.

clasificar *vt* to classify.

claudicar *vi* to limp; to act deceitfully; to back down.

claustro *m* cloister; faculty (of a university).

cláusula *f* clause.

clavar *vt* to nail.

clave *f* key; (*mus*) clef:—*m* harpsichord.

clavel *m* (*bot*) carnation.

clavicordio *m* clavichord.

clavícula *f* clavicle, collar bone.

clavija *f* pin, peg.

clavo *m* nail; corn (on the feet); clove.

clemente *adj* clement, merciful.

clérigo *m* priest; clergyman.

cliente *m/f* client.

clima *m* climate.

climatizado/da *adj* air-conditioned.

clínica *f* clinic; private hospital.

clip *m* paper clip.

cloaca *f* sewer.

coacción *f* coercion, compulsion.

coagular vt, ~**se** vr to coagulate; to curdle.

coartada f (jur) alibi.

coartar vt to limit, restrict, restrain.

cobalto m cobalt.

cobarde adj cowardly, timid.

cobaya f guinea pig.

cobertizo m small shed; shelter.

cobijar vt to cover; to shelter.

cobrar vt to recover:—~**se** vr (med) to come to.

cobre m copper; kitchen utensils pl; (mus) brass.

cocear vt to kick; (fig) to resist.

cocer vt to boil; to bake (bricks):—vi to boil; to ferment:—~**se** vr to suffer intense pain.

cochambroso/sa adj nasty; filthy, stinking.

coche m car; coach, carriage; pram, baby carriage:—(ferro) ~ **cama** sleeping car:—~ **restaurante** restaurant car.

cochino/na adj dirty, filthy; nasty:—m pig, hog.

cocina f kitchen; stove; cookery.

cocinero/ra m/f cook.

coco m coconut; bogeyman.

cocodrilo m crocodile.

codazo m blow given with the elbow.

codear vt, vi to elbow:—~**se** vr ~**se con** to rub shoulders with.

codiciar vt to covet, desire.

código m code; law; set of rules.

codillo m knee of a four-legged animal; angle; (tec) elbow (joint).

codo m elbow.

codorniz f quail.

coetáneo/nea adj contemporary.

coexistir vi to coexist.

cofia f (nurse's) cap.

cofradía f brotherhood, fraternity.

cofre m trunk.

coger vt to catch, take hold of; to occupy, take up:—~**se** vr to catch.

cogollo m heart of a lettuce or cabbage; shoot of a plant.

cogote m back of the neck.

cohecho m bribery.

coherencia f coherence.

cohete m rocket.

cohibido/da adj shy.

coincidir vi to coincide.

coito m intercourse, coitus.

cojear vi to limp, hobble; (fig) to go astray.

cojín m cushion.

cojo/ja adj lame, crippled.

col f cabbage.

cola f tail; queue; last place; glue.

colaborar vi to collaborate.

colada f wash, washing; (quím) bleach; sheep run.

colador m sieve.

colar vt to strain, filter:—vi to ooze:—~**se en** to get into without paying.

colcha f bedspread, counterpane.

colchón m mattress.

coleccionar vt to collect.

colecta f collection (for charity).

colectivo/va adj collective.

colega m/f colleague.

colegial m schoolboy.

colegiala f schoolgirl.

colegio m college; school.

colegir vt to collect; to deduce, infer.

cólera f bile; anger; fury, rage; cholera.

coleta f pigtail.

colgar vt to hang; to suspend; to decorate with tapestry:—vi to be suspended.

colibrí m hummingbird.

coliflor m cauliflower.

colina f hill.

colisión f collision; friction.

colmar vt to heap up:—vi to fulfill, realize.

colmena f hive, beehive.

colmillo m eyetooth; tusk.

colmo m height, summit; extreme:— **a ~** plentifully.

colocar vt to arrange; to place; to provide with a job:—**~se** vr to get a job.

collar m necklace; (dog) collar.

colono m colonist; farmer.

coloquio m conversation; conference.

color m color, hue; dye; rouge; suit (of cards).

colorado/da adj ruddy; red.

colorete m rouge.

columna f column.

columpio m swing, seesaw.

colza f (bot) rape; rape seed.

coma f (gr) comma:—m (med) coma.

comadreja f weasel.

comandante m commander.

comarca f territory, district.

combatir vt to combat, fight; to attack:—vi to fight.

combinar vi to combine.

combustible adj combustible:—m fuel.

comedia f comedy; play, drama.

comedido/da adj moderate, restrained.

comedor/ra m/f glutton:—m dining room.

comentar vt to comment on, expound.

comentario m comment, remark; commentary.

comenzar vi to commence, begin.

comer vt to eat; to take (a piece at chess):—vi to have lunch.

comercial adj commercial.

comercio m trade, commerce; business.

comestible adj eatable:—mpl **~s** food, foodstuffs pl.

cometa m comet:—f kite.

cometer vt to commit, charge; to entrust.

cómico/ca adj comic, comical.

comida f food; eating; meal; lunch.

comillas fpl quotation marks pl.

comino m cumin (plant or seed).

comisaría f police station; commissariat.

como adv as; like; such as.

cómo adv how?; why?:—excl what?

cómoda f bureau.

cómodo/da adj convenient; comfortable.

compacto/ta adj compact; close, dense.

compadecer vt to pity:—**~se** vr to agree with each other.

compaginar vt to arrange, put in order:—**~se** vr to tally.

compañero/ra m/f companion, friend; comrade; partner.

compañía f company.

comparar vt to compare.

compartimento m compartment.

compartir vt to share.

compás m compass; pair of compasses; (mus) measure, beat.

compatible adj:—**~ con** compatible with, consistent with.

compensar vt to compensate; to recompense.

competencia f competition, rivalry; competence.

competente adj competent; adequate.

compilar vt to compile.

compinche m pal, mate (sl).

complacencia f pleasure; indulgence.

complacer vt to please:—**~se** vr to be pleased with.

complejo m complex:—**~/ja** adj complex.

complementario/ria *adj* complementary.

complemento *m* complement.

completar *vt* to complete.

completo/ta *adj* complete; perfect.

complicar *vt* to complicate.

cómplice *m/f* accomplice.

complot *m* plot.

componer *vt* to compose; to constitute; to mend, repair; to strengthen, restore; to compose, calm:—~se *vr* ~se de to consist of.

comportamiento *m* behavior.

compostura *f* composition, composure; mending, repairing; discretion; modesty, demureness.

compota *f* stewed fruit.

comprar *vt* to buy, purchase.

comprender *vt* to include, contain; to comprehend, understand.

compresa *f* sanitary napkin.

comprimido *m* pill.

comprimir *vt* to compress; to repress, restrain.

comprobar *vt* to verify, confirm; to prove.

comprometer *vt* to compromise; to embarrass; to implicate; to put in danger:—~se *vr* to compromise oneself.

compuerta *f* hatch; sluice.

compuesto *m* compound:—~/ta *adj* composed; made up of.

compulsar *vt* to collate, compare; to make an authentic copy.

compungirse *vr* to feel remorseful.

comulgar *vt* to administer communion to:—*vi* to receive communion.

común *adj* common, usual, general:— *m* community; public:—**en** ~ in common.

comunicar *vt* to communicate:—~se *vr* to communicate (with each other).

comunidad *f* community.

con *prep* with; by:—~ **que** so then, providing that.

coñac *m* brandy, cognac.

cóncavo/va *adj* concave.

concebir *vt* to conceive:—*vi* to become pregnant.

conceder *vt* to give; to grant; to concede, allow.

concejal/la *m/f* member of a council.

concentrar *vt:*—~se *vr* to concentrate.

concepto *m* conceit, thought; judgement, opinion.

concernir *v imp* to regard, concern.

concertar *vt* to coordinate; to settle; to adjust; to agree; to arrange, fix up:—*vi* (*mus*) to harmonize, be in tune.

concesión *f* concession.

concha *f* shell; tortoise-shell.

conciencia *f* conscience.

concienciar *vt* to make aware:—~se *vr* to become aware.

concierto *m* concert; agreement; concerto:—**de** ~ in agreement, in concert.

conciliar *vt* to reconcile:—*adj* conciliar, council.

conciso/sa *adj* concise, brief.

concluir *vt* to conclude, end, complete; to infer, deduce:—~se *vr* to conclude.

concordar *vt* to reconcile, make agree:—*vi* to agree, correspond.

concordia *f* conformity, agreement.

concretar *vt* to make concrete; to specify.

concubina *f* concubine.

concurrido/da *adj* busy.

concursante *m/f* competitor.

concurso *m* crowd; competition; help, cooperation.

conde *m* earl, count.

condenable *adj* culpable.

condenar *vt* to condemn; to find guilty:—**~se** *vr* to blame oneself; to confess (one's guilt).

condensar *vt* to condense.

condescender *vi* to acquiesce, comply.

condición *f* condition, state; quality; status; rank; stipulation.

condimentar *vt* to flavor, season.

condolerse *vr* to sympathize.

condón *m* condom.

conducir *vt* to convey, conduct; to drive; to manage:—*vi* to drive:—**~ (a)** to lead (to):—**~se** *vr* to conduct oneself.

conducta *f* conduct, behavior; management.

conducto *m* conduit, pipe; drain; (*fig*) channel.

conductor/ra *m/f* conductor, guide; (*ferro*) guard; driver.

conectar *vt* to connect.

conejo *m* rabbit.

conexión *f* connection; plug; relationship.

confección *f* preparation; clothing industry.

conferencia *f* conference; telephone call.

confesar *vt* to confess; to admit.

confianza *f* trust; confidence; conceit; familiarity:—**en ~** confidential.

confiar *vt* to confide, entrust:—*vi* to trust.

configurar *vt* to shape, form.

confinar *vt* to confine:—*vi* **~ con** to border upon.

confirmar *vt* to confirm; to corroborate.

confiscar *vt* to confiscate.

confitería *f* sweet store.

confitura *f* preserve; jam.

conflicto *m* conflict.

conformar *vt* to shape; to adjust, adapt:—*vi* to agree:—**~se** *vr* to conform; to resign oneself.

conforme *adj* alike, similar; agreed:—*prep* according to.

confortar *vt* to comfort; to strengthen; to console.

confundir *vt* to confound, jumble; to confuse:—**~se** *vr* to make a mistake.

confusión *f* confusion.

congelado/da *adj* frozen:—*mpl* **~s** frozen food.

congelar *vt* to freeze:—**~se** *vr* to congeal.

congeniar *vi* to get on well.

congoja *f* anguish, distress, grief.

congraciarse *vr* to ingratiate oneself.

congregar(se) *vt* (*vr*) to assemble, meet, collect.

conjetura *f* conjecture, guess.

conjugar *vt* (*gr*) to conjugate; to combine.

conjunto/ta *adj* united, joint:—*m* whole; (*mus*) ensemble, band; team.

conjurar *vt* to exorcize:—*vi* to conspire, plot.

conmemorar *vt* to commemorate.

conmigo *pn* with me.

conmover *vt* to move; to disturb.

conmutador *m* switch.

conmutar *vt* (*jur*) to commute; to exchange.

connotar *vt* to imply.

cono *m* cone.

conocer *vt* to know, understand:— ~**se** *vr* to know one another.

conocimiento *m* knowledge, understanding; (*med*) consciousness; acquaintance; (*mar*) bill of lading.

conquistar *vt* to conquer.

consabido/da *adj* well-known; above-mentioned.

consagrar *vt* to consecrate.

consanguíneo/nea *adj* related by blood.

consecuencia *f* consequence; conclusion; consistency:—por ~ therefore.

consecuente *adj* consistent.

conseguir *vt* to attain; to get, obtain.

consejo *m* advice; council.

consentir *vt* to consent to; to allow; to admit; to spoil (a child).

conserje *m* doorman; janitor.

conservar *vt* to conserve; to keep; to preserve (fruit).

conservas *fpl* canned food.

conservatorio *m* (*mus*) conservatoire.

consideración *f* consideration; respect.

considerar *vt* to consider.

consigna *f* (*mil*) watchword; order, instruction; (*ferro*) left-luggage office.

consignar *vt* to consign, dispatch; to assign; to record, register.

consigo *pn* (*m*) with him; (*f*) with her; (*vd*) with you; (*refl*) with oneself.

consiguiente *adj* consequent.

consistente *adj* consistent; firm, solid.

consistir *vi*:—~ **en** to consist of; to be due to.

consola *f* control panel.

consolar *vt* to console, comfort, cheer.

consolidar *vt* to consolidate.

consonante *m* rhyme:—*f* (*gr*) consonant:—*adj* consonant, harmonious.

consorcio *m* partnership.

consorte *m/f* consort, companion, partner; accomplice.

conspirar *vi* to conspire, plot.

constante *adj* constant; firm.

constar *vi* to be evident, be certain; to be composed of, consist of.

constatar *vt* to note; to check.

consternar *vt* to dismay; to shock.

constipado/da *adj:*—**estar** ~ to have a cold.

constituir *vt* to constitute; to establish; to appoint.

construir *vt* to form; to build, construct; to construe.

consuegro/gra *m/f* father-in-law/ mother-in-law of one's son or daughter.

consuelo *m* consolation, comfort.

cónsul *m* consul.

consultar *vt* to consult, ask for advice.

consultor/ra *m/f* adviser, consultant.

consultorio *m* (*med*) consulting room, doctor's rooms.

consumar *vt* to consummate, finish; to carry out.

consumir *vt* to consume; to burn, use; to waste, exhaust:—~**se** *vr* to waste away, be consumed.

contabilidad *f* accounting; bookkeeping.

contacto *m* contact; (*auto*) ignition.

contado/da *adj:*—~**s** scarce, few:— *m* **pagar al** ~ to pay (in) cash.

contador *m* meter; counter in a cafe:—~/~**a** *m/f* accountant.

contagiar *vt* to infect:—~**se** *vr* to get infected.

contaminar *vt* to contaminate; to pollute; to corrupt.

contar *vt* to count, reckon; to tell:—*vi* to count:—~ **con** to rely upon.

contemplar *vt* to look at; to contemplate, consider; to meditate.

contemporáneo/nea *adj* contemporary.

contenedor *m* container.

contener *vt* to contain, hold; to hold back; to repress:—**~se** *vr* to control oneself.

contentar *vt* to content, satisfy; to please:—**~se** *vr* to be pleased or satisfied.

contento/ta *adj* glad; pleased; content:—*m* contentment; (*jur*) release.

contestador *m:*—**~ automatico** answering machine.

contestar *vt* to answer, reply; to prove, corroborate.

contienda *f* contest, dispute.

contigo *pn* with you.

contiguo/gua *adj* contiguous, close.

continente *m* continent, mainland:— *adj* continent.

contingencia *f* risk; contingency.

continuar *vt, vi* to continue.

continuo/nua *adj* continuous.

contorno *m* environs *pl*; contour, outline:—**en ~** round about.

contra *prep* against; contrary to; opposite.

contrabajo *m* (*mus*) double bass; bass guitar; low bass.

contrabando *m* contraband; smuggling.

contrachapado *m* plywood.

contradecir *vt* to contradict.

contraer *vt* to contract, shrink; to make (a bargain):—**~se** *vr* to shrink, contract.

contrahecho/cha *adj* deformed; hunchbacked; counterfeit, fake, false.

contralto *m* (*mus*) contralto.

contrapartida *f* (*com*) balancing entry.

contrapelo *adv:*—**a ~** against the grain.

contrapeso *m* counterpoise; counterweight.

contraproducente *adj* counterproductive.

contrariar *vt* to contradict, oppose; to vex.

contrariedad *f* opposition; setback; annoyance.

contrario/ria *m/f* opponent:—*adj* contrary, opposite:—**por el ~** on the contrary.

contrarrestar *vt* to return a ball; (*fig*) to counteract.

contraseña *f* countersign; (*mil*) watchword.

contrasentido *m* contradiction.

contrastar *vt* to resist; to contradict; to assay (metals); to verify (measures and weights):—*vi* to contrast.

contratar *vt* to contract; to hire, engage.

contratiempo *m* setback; accident.

contrato *m* contract, agreement.

contravenir *vi* to contravene, transgress; to violate.

contraventana *f* shutter.

contribución *f* contribution; tax.

contribuir *vt, vi* to contribute.

contrincante *m* competitor.

controlar *vt* to control; to check.

contumaz *adj* obstinate, stubborn; (*jur*) guilty of contempt of court.

contundente *adj* overwhelming; blunt.

contusión *f* bruise.

convalecer *vi* to recover from sickness, convalesce.

convencer *vt* to convince.

conveniencia *f* suitability; usefulness; agreement:—**~s** *fpl* property.

convenir *vi* to agree, suit.

convento *m* convent, nunnery; monastery.

conversar *vi* to talk, converse.

convicto/ta *adj* convicted (found guilty).

convidar *vt* to invite.

convocar *vt* to convoke, assemble.

convocatoria *f* summons; notice of a meeting.

conyugal *adj* conjugal, married.

cónyuge *m/f* spouse.

cooperar *vi* to cooperate.

coordinar *vt* to arrange, coordinate.

copa *f* cup; glass; top of a tree; crown of a hat:—~s *fpl* hearts *pl* (at cards).

copiar *vt* to copy; to imitate.

copla *f* verse; (*mus*) popular song, folk song.

copo *m* small bundle; flake of snow.

coquetear *vi* to flirt.

coraje *m* courage; anger, passion.

coral *m* coral; choir:—*adj* choral.

corazón *m* heart; core:—**de ~** willingly.

corazonada *f* inspiration; quick decision; presentiment.

corbata *f* tie.

corchete *m* clasp; hook and eye.

corcho *m* cork; float (for fishing); cork bark.

cordel *m* cord, rope; (*mar*) line.

cordero *m* lamb; lambskin; meek, gentle person.

cordial *adj* cordial, affectionate:—*m* cordial.

cordillera *f* range of mountains.

cordón *m* cord, string; lace; cordon.

cornada *f* thrust with a bull's horn.

coro *m* choir; chorus.

corona *f* crown; coronet; top of the head; crown (of a tooth); tonsure; halo.

coronilla *f* crown of the head.

corpiño *m* bodice.

corporal *adj* corporal.

corpulento/ta *adj* corpulent, bulky.

corral *m* yard; farmyard; corral; playpen.

correa *f* leather strap, thong; flexibility.

correcto/ta *adj* exact, correct.

corregir *vt* to correct, amend; to reprehend:—~**se** *vr* to reform.

correo *m* post, mail; courier; mailman:—**a vuelta de ~** by return of post:—~**s** *mpl* post office.

correr *vt* to run; to flow; to travel over; to pull (a drape):—*vi* to run, rush; to flow; to blow (applied to the wind):—~**se** *vr* to be ashamed; to slide, move; to run (of colors).

correspondencia *f* correspondence; communication; agreement.

corresponder *vi* to correspond; to answer; to be suitable; to belong; to concern:—~**se** *vr* to love one another.

corresponsal *m/f* correspondent.

corriente *f* current; course, progression; (electric) current:—*adj* current; common, ordinary, general; fluent; flowing, running.

corro *m* circle of people.

corroer *vt* to corrode, erode.

corromper *vt* to corrupt; to rot; to turn bad; to seduce; to bribe:—~**se** *vr* to rot; to become corrupted:—*vi* to stink.

cortacesped *m* lawn mower.

cortado *m* coffee with a little milk:—~**/ da** *adj* cut; sour; embarrassed.

cortar *vt* to cut; to cut off, curtail; to intersect; to carve; to chop; to cut (at cards); to interrupt:—~**se** *vr* to be ashamed or embarrassed; to curdle.

corte *m* cutting; cut; section; length (of cloth); style:—*f* (royal) court; capital (city):—**C~s** *fpl* Spanish Parliament.

cortejo *m* entourage; courtship; procession; lover.

cortés/esa *adj* courteous, polite.

cortesía *f* courtesy, good manners *pl*.

corteza *f* bark; peel; crust; (*fig*) outward appearance.

cortina *f* curtain.

corto/ta *adj* short; scanty, small; stupid; bashful:—**a la ~a** *o* **a la larga** sooner or later.

corzo/za *m/f* roe deer, fallow deer.

cosa *f* thing; matter; affair:—**no hay tal ~** nothing of the sort!

cosecha *f* harvest; harvest time:—**de su ~** of one's own invention.

coser *vt* to sew; to join.

cosquillas *fpl* tickling; (*fig*) agitation.

costa *f* cost, price; charge, expense; coast, shore:—**a toda ~** at all events.

costado *m* side; (*mil*) flank; side of a ship.

costal *m* sack, large bag.

costar *vt* to cost; to need.

coste *m* cost, expense.

costero/ra *adj* coastal; (*mar*) coasting.

costilla *f* rib; cutlet:—**~s** *fpl* back, shoulders *pl*.

costra *f* crust; (*med*) scab.

costumbre *f* custom, habit.

cotejar *vt* to compare.

cotidiano/na *adj* daily.

cotilla *m/f* gossip.

cotizar *vt* to quote:—**~se** *vr* **~ a** to sell at; to be quoted at.

coto *m* enclosure; reserve; boundary stone.

cotorra *f* small parrot; (*col*) chatterbox.

covacha *f* small cave, grotto.

coyuntura *f* joint, articulation; juncture.

coz *f* kick; recoil (of a gun); ebbing (of a flood); (*fig*) insult.

cráneo *m* skull.

crear *vt* to create, make; to establish.

crecer *vi* to grow, increase; to rise.

crecida *f* swell (of rivers).

creciente *f* crescent (moon); (*mar*) flood tide:—*adj* growing; crescent.

crecimiento *m* increase; growth.

crédito *m* credit; belief, faith; reputation.

creer *vt, vi* to believe; to think; to consider.

crema *f* cream; custard.

cremallera *f* zipper.

crepúsculo *m* twilight.

cresta *f* crest (of birds).

creyente *m/f* believer.

cría *f* breeding; young.

criadero *m* (*bot*) nursery; breeding place.

criadilla *f* testicle; small loaf; truffle.

crianza *f* breeding, rearing.

criar *vt* to create, produce; to breed; to breast-feed; to bring up.

criatura *f* creature; child.

crimen *m* crime.

criminal *adj, m/f* criminal.

crin *f* mane; horsehair.

crío/a *m/f* (*fam*) kid.

cripta *f* crypt.

crisis *f invar* crisis.

crisol *m* crucible; melting pot.

crispar *vt* to set on edge; to tense up.

cristal *m* crystal; glass; pane; lens.

cristalino/na *adj* crystalline.

cristalizar *vt* to crystallize.

cristiano/na *adj, m/f* Christian.

criterio *m* criterion.

crítica *m/f* criticism.

criticar *vt* to criticize.

croar *vi* to croak.

cromo *m* chrome.

crónica *f* chronicle; news report; feature.

crónico/ca *adj* chronic.

cronista *m/f* chronicler; reporter; columnist.

cronómetro *m* stopwatch.

cruce *m* crossing; crossroads.

crucero *m* cruiser; cruise; transept; crossing.

crucifijo *m* crucifix.

crucigrama *m* crossword.

crudo/da *adj* raw; green, unripe; crude; cruel; hard to digest.

cruel *adj* cruel.

crueldad *f* cruelty.

crujiente *adj* crunchy.

crujir *vi* to crackle; to rustle.

crustáceo *m* crustacean.

cruz *f* cross; tails (of a coin).

cruzar *vt* to cross; (*mar*) to cruise:—~**se** *vr* to cross; to pass each other.

cuaderno *m* notebook; exercise book; logbook.

cuadra *f* block; stable.

cuadrado/da *adj*, *m* square.

cuadrante *m* quadrant; dial.

cuadrar *vt*, *vi* to square; to fit, suit, correspond.

cuadrilátero/ra *adj*, *m* quadrilateral.

cuadrilla *f* party, group; gang, crew.

cuadro *m* square; picture, painting; window frame; scene; chart.

cuadrúpedo/da *adj* quadruped.

cuajar *vt* to coagulate; to thicken; to adorn; to set:—~**se** *vr* to coagulate, curdle; to set; to fill up.

cual *pn* which; who; whom:—*adv* as; like:—*adj* such as.

cuál *pn* which (one).

cualidad *f* quality.

cualquier *adj* any.

cualquiera *adj* anyone, anybody; someone, somebody; whoever; whichever.

cuando *adv* when; if; even:—*conj* since:—**de** ~ **en** ~ from time to time:—~ **más/**~ **mucho** at most, at best:—~ **menos** at least.

cuándo *adv* when:—¿**de cuándo acá?** since when?

cuánto *adj* what a lot of; how much?:—¿~**s?** how many?:—*pn*, *adv* how; how much; how many.

cuanto/ta *adj* as many as; as much as; all; whatever:—*adv* **en** ~ as soon as:—**en** ~ **a** as regards:—~ **más** moreover, the more as.

cuarenta *adj*, *m* forty.

cuaresma *f* Lent.

cuarto *m* fourth part; quarter; room, apartment; span:—~**s** *mpl* cash, money:—~**/ta** *adj* fourth.

cuarzo *m* quartz.

cuatro *adj*, *m* four.

cuatrocientos/tas *adj* four hundred.

cuba *f* cask; tub; (*fig*) drunkard.

cubierta *f* cover; deck of a ship; (*auto*) hood; tire; pretext.

cubierto *m* cover; shelter; place at table; meal at a fixed charge:—~**s** *mpl* cutlery, silverware.

cubo *m* cube; bucket; can:—~**de la basura** garbage can.

cubrir *vt* to cover; to disguise; to protect; to roof a building:—~**se** *vr* to become overcast.

cucaracha *f* cockroach.

cuchara *f* spoon.

cucharada *f* spoonful; ladleful.

cucharadita *f* teaspoonful.

cuchichear *vi* to whisper.

cuchillo *m* knife.

cuclillas *adv*:—**en** ~ squatting.

cuclillo m cuckoo; (fig) cuckold.
cuello m neck; collar.
cuenca m bowl, deep valley; hollow; socket of the eye.
cuenta f calculation; account; check, bill (in a restaurant); count, counting; bead; importance.
cuento m tale, story, narrative.
cuerda f rope; string; spring.
cuerdo/da adj sane; prudent, judicious.
cuerno m horn.
cuero m hide, skin, leather.
cuerpo m body; cadaver, corpse.
cuesta f slope, hill; incline:—**ir ~ abajo** to go downhill:—**~ arriba** uphill.
cuestión f question, matter; dispute; quarrel; problem.
cueva f cave; cellar.
cuidado m care, worry, concern; charge.
cuidar vt to care for; to mind, look after.
culebra f snake.
culo m backside; bum (sl); bottom.
culpa f fault, blame; guilt.
culpable adj culpable; guilty:—m/f culprit.
cultivar vt to cultivate.

culto/ta adj cultivated, cultured; refined, civilized:—m culture; worship.
cumbre f top, summit.
cumplir vt to carry out, fulfil; to serve (a prison sentence); to carry out (death penalty); to attain, reach (a certain age):—**~se** vr to be fulfilled; to expire, be up.
cuna f cradle.
cuña f wedge.
cuñado/da m/f brother/sister-inlaw.
cura m priest:—f cure; treatment.
curar vt to cure; to treat, dress (a wound); to salt; to dress; to tan.
curioso/sa adj curious:—m/f bystander.
currar vi (fam)to work.
curso m course, direction; year (at university); subject.
curtir vt to tan leather:—**~se** vr to become sunburned; to become inured.
curva f curve, bend.
custodia f custody, safekeeping, care; monstrance.
cutis m skin.
cutre adj (fam) mean, grotty.
cuyo/ya pn whose, of which, of whom.

D

dado m die (pl dice).
daga f dagger.
dama f lady, gentlewoman; mistress; queen; actress of principal parts.
damnificar vt to hurt, injure, damage.
dañar vt to hurt, injure; to damage.
dañino/na adj harmful; noxious; mischievous.

danza f dance.
dar vt to give; to supply, administer, afford; to deliver.
dátil m (bot) date.
dato m fact.
de prep of; from; for; by; on; to; with.
debajo adv under, underneath, below.
debatir vt to debate, argue, discuss.

debe *m* (*com*) debit:——~ **y haber** debit and credit.

deber *m* obligation, duty; debt:—*vt* to owe; to be obliged to:—*vi* **debe (de)** it must, it should.

debidamente *adv* justly, duly; exactly, perfectly.

débil *adj* feeble, weak; sickly; frail.

debilitar *vt* to debilitate, weaken.

decadencia *f* decay, decline.

decena *f* ten.

decencia *f* decency.

decepción *f* disappointment.

decidir *vt* to decide, determine.

décimo/ma *adj*, *m* tenth.

decir *vt* to say; to tell; to speak; to name.

decisión *f* decision; determination, resolution; sentence.

declamar *vi* to declaim; to harangue.

declarar *vt* to declare; to manifest; to expound; to explain; (*jur*) to decide:——~**se** *vr* to declare one's opinion:—*vi* to testify.

declinar *vi* to decline; to decay, degenerate:—*vt* (*gr*) to decline.

declive *m* slope; decline.

decorar *vt* to decorate, adorn; to illustrate.

decrecer *vi* to decrease.

decrépito/ta *adj* decrepit, worn out with age.

decretar *vt* to decree, determine.

dedal *m* thimble; very small drinking glass.

dedicar *vt* to dedicate, devote; to consecrate:——~**se** *vr* to apply oneself to.

dedo *m* finger; toe; small bit:——~ **meñique** little finger:——~ **pulgar** thumb:——~ **del corazón** middle finger:——~ **anular** ring finger.

deducir *vt* to deduce, infer; to allege in pleading; to subtract.

defecto *m* defect; defectiveness.

defectuoso/sa *adj* defective, imperfect, faulty.

defender *vt* to defend, protect; to justify, assert;to resist, oppose.

defensor/ra *m/f* defender, protector; lawyer, defense counsel.

deferir *vi* to defer; to yield (to another's opinion):—*vt* to communicate.

deficiente *adj* defective.

definir *vt* to define, describe, explain; to decide.

definitivo/va *adj* definitive; positive.

deformar *vt* to deform:——~**se** *vr* to become deformed.

deforme *adj* deformed; ugly.

defraudar *vt* to defraud, cheat; to usurp; to disturb.

defunción *f* death; funeral.

degenerar *vi* to degenerate.

degollar *vt* to behead; to destroy, ruin.

degradar *vt* to degrade:——~**se** *vr* to degrade or demean oneself.

degustar *vt* to taste.

dehesa *f* pasture.

dejadez *f* slovenliness, neglect.

dejar *vt* to leave, quit; to omit; to let; to permit, allow; to forsake; to bequeath; to pardon:——~ **de** to stop; to fail to:——~**se** *vr* to abandon oneself.

del *adj* of the (contraction of *de* and *el*).

delantal *m* apron.

delante *adv* in front; opposite; ahead:——~ **de** in front of; before.

delantero/ra *adj* front:—*m* forward.

delegar *vt* to delegate; to substitute.

deleitar *vt* to delight.

deletrear *vt* to spell; to examine; to conjecture.

delfín *m* dolphin; dauphin.

delgado/da *adj* thin; delicate, fine; light; slender, lean.

deliberadamente *adv* deliberately.

deliberar *vi* to consider, deliberate:— *vt* to debate; to consult.

delicado/da *adj* delicate, tender; faint; exquisite; delicious, dainty; slender, subtle.

delicioso/sa *adj* delicious; delightful.

delincuencia *f* delinquency.

delineante *m/f* draftsman/woman.

delirar *vi* to rave; to talk nonsense.

delito *m* offence; crime.

demacrado/da *adj* pale and drawn.

demandar *vt* to demand; to ask; to claim; to sue.

demarcar *vt* to mark out (limits).

demás *adj* other; remaining:—*pn* **los/las** ~ the others, the rest:— **estar** ~ to be over and above; to be useless or superfluous:—**por** ~ in vain.

demasiado/da *adj* too; excessive:— *adv* too, too much.

demencia *f* madness.

demoler *vt* to demolish; to destroy.

demonio *m* demon.

demorar *vt* to delay:—~**se** *vr* to be delayed:—*vi* to linger.

demostrar *vt* to prove, demonstrate; to manifest.

denegar *vt* to deny; to refuse.

denigrar *vt* to blacken; to insult.

denominar *vt* to name; to designate.

denotar *vt* to denote; to express.

denso/sa *adj* dense, thick; compact.

dentado/da *adj* toothed; indented.

dentadura *f* set of teeth.

dentífrico *m* toothpaste.

dentista *m/f* dentist.

dentro *adv* within:—*pn* ~ **de** in, inside.

denunciar *vt* to advise; to denounce; to report.

depender *vi:*—~ **de** to depend on, be dependent on.

dependiente *m* sales clerk:—*adj* dependent.

depilatorio *m* hair remover.

deponer *vt* to depose; to declare; to displace; to deposit.

deportar *vt* to deport.

deporte *m* sport.

deportista *m/f* sportsman/woman.

depositar *vt* to deposit; to confide; to put away for safekeeping.

depravación *f* depravity.

deprimir *vt* to depress:—~**se** *vr* to become depressed.

deprisa *adv* quickly.

depurar *vt* to cleanse, purify; to filter.

derecho/cha *adj* right; straight; just; perfect; certain:—*m* right, justice; law; just claim; tax, duty; fee:—*adv* straight.

derivar *vt, vi* to derive; (*mar*) to drift.

derogar *vt* to derogate, abolish; to reform.

derramar *vt* to drain off (water); to spread; to spill, scatter; to waste, shed:—~**se** *vr* to pour out.

derretir *vt* to melt; to consume; to thaw:—~**se** *vr* to melt.

derribar *vt* to demolish; to flatten.

derrochar *vt* to dissipate; to squander.

derrotar *vt* to destroy; to defeat.

derruir *vt* to demolish.

derrumbar *vt* to throw down:—~**se** *vr* to collapse.

desabrido/da *adj* tasteless, insipid; rude; unpleasant.

desacato *m* disrespect, incivility.

desacertado/da *adj* mistaken; unwise; inconsiderate.

desaconsejar *vt* to advise against.

desacostumbrado/da *adj* unusual.

desacuerdo *m* blunder; disagreement; forgetfulness.

desafiar *vt* to challenge; to defy.

desafinar *vi* to be out of tune.

desafuero *m* outrage; excess.

desagradable *adj* disagreeable, unpleasant.

desagradecido/da *adj* ungrateful.

desagüe *m* channel, drain; drainpipe; drainage.

desahogar *vt* to ease; to vent:—~**se** *vr* to recover; to relax.

desahuciar *vt* to cause to despair; to give up; to evict.

desajustar *vt* to make uneven; to unbalance:—~**se** *vr* to get out of order.

desalentar *vt* to put out of breath; to discourage.

desaliño *m* slovenliness; carelessness.

desalmado/da *adj* cruel, inhuman.

desalojar *vt* to eject; to move out:— *vi* to move out.

desamparar *vt* to forsake, abandon; to relinquish.

desangrar *vt* to bleed; to drain (a pond); (*fig*) to exhaust (one's means):—~**se** *vr* to lose a lot of blood.

desanimar *vt* to discourage:—~**se** *vr* to lose heart.

desaparecer *vi* to disappear.

desapercibido/da *adj* unnoticed.

desaprobar *vt* to disapprove; to condemn; to reject.

desaprovechado/da *adj* useless; unprofitable; backward; slack.

desaprovechar *vt* to waste, turn to a bad use.

desarmar *vt* to disarm; to disband (troops); to dismantle; (*fig*) to pacify.

desarraigar *vt* to uproot; to root out; to extirpate.

desarrollar *vt* to develop; to unroll; to unfold:—~**se** *vr* to develop; to be unfolded; to open.

desasosiego *m* restlessness; anxiety.

desastre *m* disaster; misfortune.

desatar *vt* to untie, loose; to separate; to solve:—~**se** *vr* to come undone; to break.

desatascar *vt* to unblock; to clear.

desatender *vt* to pay no attention to; to disregard.

desatinar *vi* to talk nonsense; to reel, stagger.

desatornillar *vt* to unscrew.

desayunar *vt* to have for breakfast:— ~**se** *vr* to breakfast:—*vi* to have breakfast.

desazón *f* disgust; uneasiness; annoyance.

desbarrar *vi* to talk nonsense.

desbordar *vt* to exceed:—~**se** *vr* to overflow.

descalabrado/da *adj* wounded on the head; imprudent.

descalificar *vt* to disqualify; to discredit.

descalzo/za *adj* barefooted; (*fig*) destitute.

descaminado/da *adj* (*fig*) misguided.

descansar *vt* to rest:—*vi* to rest; to lie down.

descansillo *m* landing.

descapotable *m* convertible.

descarado/da *adj* cheeky, barefaced.

descargar *vt* to unload, discharge:— ~**se** *vr* to unburden oneself.

descarriar *vt* to lead astray; to misdirect:—~**se** *vr* to lose one's way; to stray; to err.

descarrilar *vi* (*ferro*) to leave or run off the rails.

descartar *vt* to discard; to dismiss; to rule out.

descendencia *f* descent, offspring.

descender *vt* to take down:—*vi* to descend, walk down; to flow; to fall:—~ **de** to be derived from.

descenso *m* descent; drop.

descifrar *vt* to decipher; to unravel.

descollar *vi* to excel.

descolorido/da *adj* pale, colorless.

descomunal *adj* uncommon; huge.

desconcertar *vt* to disturb; to confound; to disconcert:—~**se** *vr* to be bewildered; to be upset.

desconectar *vt* to disconnect.

desconfiar *vi:*—~ **de** to mistrust, suspect.

descongelar *vt* to defrost.

desconocer *vt* to disown, disavow; to be totally ignorant of (a thing); not to know (a person); not to acknowledge (a favor received).

desconsuelo *m* distress; trouble; despair.

descontar *vt* to discount; to deduct.

descontento *m* dissatisfaction; disgust.

descortés/esa *adj* impolite, rude.

descoser *vt* to unseam; to separate:—~**se** *vr* to come apart at the seams.

descreído/da *adj* incredulous.

descremado/da *adj* skimmed.

describir *vt* to describe; to draw, delineate.

descuartizar *vt* to quarter; to carve.

descubrir *vt* to discover, disclose; to uncover; to reveal; to show:—~**se** *vr* to reveal oneself; to take off one's hat; to confess.

descuento *m* discount; decrease.

descuidado/da *adj* careless, negligent.

descuidar *vt* to neglect:—*vi* ~**se** *vr* to be careless.

desde *prep* since; after; from:—~ **luego** of course:—~ **entonces** since then.

desdén *m* disdain, scorn.

desdeñar *vt* to disdain, scorn:—~**se** *vr* to be disdainful.

desdentado/da *adj* toothless.

desdicha *f* misfortune, calamity; great poverty.

desdoblar *vt* to unfold, spread open.

desear *vt* to desire, wish; to require, demand.

desecar *vt* to dry up.

desechar *vt* to depreciate; to reject; to refuse; to throw away.

desecho *m* residue:—~**s** *mpl* trash.

desembarcar *vt* to unload, disembark:—*vi* to disembark, land.

desembolsar *vt* to pay out.

desempatar *vi* to hold a play-off.

desempeñar *vt* to redeem; to extricate from debt; to fulfil (any duty or promise); to acquit:—~**se** *vr* to get out of debt.

desempleo *m* unemployment.

desencadenar *vt* to unchain:—~**se** *vr* to break loose; to burst.

desencajar *vt* to disjoint; to dislocate; to disconnect.

desencanto *m* disenchantment.

desenchufar *vt* to unplug.

desenfado *m* ease; facility; calmness; relaxation.

desenfocado/da *adj* out of focus.

desenfreno *m* wildness; lack of self-control.

desengañar *vt* to disillusion:—~**se** *vr* to become disillusioned.

desenganchar *vt* to unhook; to uncouple.

desengrasar *vt* to take the grease off.

desenlace *m* climax; outcome.

desenredar vt to disentangle.

desenroscar vt to untwist; to unroll.

desentenderse vr to feign not to understand; to pass by without noticing.

desenterrar vt to exhume; to dig up.

desentonar vi to be out of tune; to clash.

desenvolver vt to unfold; to unroll; to decipher, unravel; to develop:— ~**se** vr to develop; to cope.

deseo m desire, wish.

desequilibrado/da adj unbalanced.

desertar vt to desert; (jur) to abandon (a cause).

desesperar vi, ~**se** vr to despair:—vt to make desperate.

desestabilizar vt to destabilize.

desfachatez f impudence.

desfalco m embezzlement.

desfallecer vi to get weak; to faint.

desfasado/da adj old-fashioned.

desfavorable adj unfavorable.

desfiladero m gorge.

desfilar vi (mil) to parade.

desfogarse vr to give vent to one's passion or anger.

desgana f disgust; loss of appetite; aversion, reluctance.

desgañitarse vr to scream, bawl.

desgarrar vt to tear; to shatter.

desgaste m wear (and tear).

desgracia f misfortune; disgrace; accident; setback.

desgreñado/da adj disheveled.

deshabitado/da adj deserted, uninhabited; desolate.

deshacer vt to undo, destroy; to cancel, efface; to rout (an army); to solve; to melt; to break up, divide; to dissolve in a liquid; to violate (a treaty); to diminish; to disband (troops):—~**se** vr to melt; to come apart.

deshelar vt to thaw:—~**se** vr to thaw, melt.

desheredar vt to disinherit.

deshidratar vt to dehydrate.

deshinchar vt to deflate:—~**se** vr to go flat, go down.

deshonesto/ta adj indecent.

deshonrar vt to affront, insult, defame; to dishonor.

deshuesar vt to rid of bones; to stone.

desidia f idleness, indolence.

desierto/ta adj deserted; solitary:—m desert; wilderness.

designar vt to design; to intend; to appoint; to express, name.

desigual adj unequal, unlike; uneven, craggy, cliffy.

desilusionar vt to disappoint:—~**se** vr to become disillusioned.

desinfectar vt to disinfect.

desinflar vt to deflate.

desinteresado/da adj disinterested; unselfish.

desistir vi to desist, cease.

desleal adj disloyal; unfair.

desleír vt to dilute; to dissolve.

deslenguado/da adj foul-mouthed.

desligar vt to untie; to separate.

deslizar vt to slip, slide; to let slip (a comment):—~**se** vr to slip; to skid; to flow softly; to creep in.

deslumbrar vt to dazzle; to puzzle.

desmayar vi to be dispirited or fainthearted:—~**se** vr to faint.

desmedido/da adj disproportionate.

desmemoriado/da adj forgetful.

desmentir vt to give the lie to:—~**se** vr to contradict oneself.

desmenuzar vt to crumble; to chip at; to fritter away; to examine minutely.

desmesurado/da adj excessive; huge; immeasurable.

desmoralizar *vt* to demoralize.

desnatado/da *adj* skimmed.

desnivel *m* unevenness of the ground.

desnudar *vt* to undress; to strip; to discover, reveal:—**~se** *vr* to undress.

desnutrido/da *adj* undernourished.

desobedecer *vt, vi* to disobey.

desocupar *vt* to vacate; to empty:— **~se** *vr* to retire from a business; to withdraw from an arrangement.

desodorante *m* deodorant.

desolado/da *adj* desolate, disconsolate.

desordenar *vt* to disorder; to untidy:— **~se** *vr* to get out of order.

desorganizar *vt* to disorganize.

desorientar *vt* to mislead; to confuse:—**~se** *vr* to lose one's way.

desovar *vi* to spawn.

despabilado/da *adj* watchful, vigilant; wide-awake.

despacho *m* dispatch, expedition; cabinet; office; commission; warrant, patent; expedient; smart answer.

despachurrar *vt* to squash, crush; to mangle.

despacio *adv* slowly, leisurely; little by little:—**¡~!** softly!, gently!

desparramar *vt* to disseminate, spread; to spill; to squander, lavish:—**~se** *vr* to be dissipated.

despavorido *adj* frightened.

despecho *m* indignation; displeasure; spite; dismay, despair; deceit; derision, scorn:—**a~ de** in spite of.

despectivo/va *adj* pejorative, derogatory.

despedir *vt* to discharge; to dismiss (from office); to see off:—**~se** *vr* **~ de** to say goodbye to.

despegar *vt* to unglue; to take off:— **~se** *vr* to come loose.

despegue *m* take-off.

despeinar *vt* to ruffle.

despejado/da *adj* sprightly, quick; clear.

despellejar *vt* to skin.

despensa *f* pantry, larder; provisions *pl*.

desperdiciar *vt* to squander.

desperdigar *vt* to separate; to scatter.

desperfecto *m* slight damage; flaw.

despertador *m* alarm clock.

despertar *vt* to wake up, rouse from sleep; to excite:—*vi* to wake up; to grow lively or sprightly:—**~se** *vr* to wake up.

despiadado/da *adj* heartless; merciless.

despido *m* dismissal.

despierto/ta *adj* awake; vigilant; fierce; brisk, sprightly.

despistar *vt* to mislead; to throw off the track:—**~se** *vr* to take the wrong way; to become confused.

desplazar *vt* to move; to scroll:— **~se** *vr* to travel.

desplegar *vt* to unfold, display; to explain, elucidate; (*mar*) to unfurl:— **~se** *vr* to open out; to travel.

desplomarse *vr* to fall to the ground; to collapse.

despoblar *vt* to depopulate; to desolate:—**~se** *vr* to become depopulated.

despojar *vt:*—**~ (de)** to strip (of); to deprive (of):—**~se** *vr* to undress.

desposar *vt* to marry, betroth:—**~se** *vr* to be betrothed or married.

desposeer *vt* to dispossess.

déspota *m* despot.

despreciar *vt* to offend; to despise.

desprender *vt* to unfasten, loosen; to separate:—**~se** *vr* to give way; to fall down; to extricate oneself.

despreocupado/da *adj* careless; unworried.

desprevenido/da *adj* unawares, unprepared.

desproporcionado/da *adj* disproportionate.

desprovisto/ta *adj* unprovided.

después *adv* after, afterwards; next.

despuntar *vt* to blunt:—*vi* to sprout; to dawn:—**al ~ del dia** at break of day.

desquiciar *vt* to upset; to discompose; to disorder.

desquite *m* recovery of a loss; revenge, retaliation.

destacamento *m* (*mil*) detachment.

destacar *vt* to emphasize; (*mil*) to detach (a body of troops):—**~se** *vr* to stand out.

destajo *m* piecework.

destapar *vt* to uncover; to open:—**~se** *vr* to be uncovered.

destartalado/da *adj* untidy.

destello *m* signal light; sparkle.

desteñir *vt* to discolor:—**~se** *vr* to fade.

desternillarse *vr:*—**~ de risa** to roar with laughter.

desterrar *vt* to banish; to expel, drive away.

destetar *vt* to wean.

destilar *vt, vi* to distil.

destinar *vt* to destine for, intend for.

destinatario/a *m/f* addressee.

destino *m* destiny; fate, doom; destination; office.

destornillador *m* screwdriver.

destreza *f* dexterity, cleverness, cunning, expertness, skill.

destrozar *vt* to destroy, break into pieces; (*mil*) to defeat.

destruir *vt* to destroy.

desvalido/da *adj* helpless; destitute.

desvalijar *vt* to rob; to burgle.

desván *m* garret.

desvanecer *vt* to dispel:—**~se** *vr* to grow vapid, become insipid; to vanish; to be affected with giddiness.

desvarío *m* delirium; giddiness; inconstancy, caprice; extravagance.

desvelar *vt* to keep awake:—**~se** *vr* to stay awake.

desventaja *f* disadvantage; damage.

desventura *f* misfortune; calamity.

desvergüenza *f* impudence; shamelessness.

desvestir *vt:*—**~se** *vr* to undress.

desviar *vt* to divert; to dissuade; to parry (at fencing):—**~se** *vr* to go off course.

detallar *vt* to detail, relate minutely.

detener *vt* to stop, detain; to arrest; to keep back; to reserve; to with-hold:—**~se** *vr* to stop; to stay.

detenidamente *adv* carefully.

detergente *m* detergent.

deteriorar *vt* to damage.

determinar *vt* to determine:—**~se** *vr* to decide.

detestar *vt* to detest, abhor.

detonar *vi* to detonate.

detrás *adv* behind; at the back, in the back.

deuda *f* debt; fault; offence.

devanar *vt* to reel; to wrap up.

devastar *vt* to devastate.

devengar *vt* to accrue.

devoción *f* devotion, piety; strong affection; ardent love.

devolver *vt* to return; to send back; to refund:—*vi* to be sick.

devorar *vt* to devour, swallow up.

día *m* day.

diablo *m* devil.

diablura *f* prank.

diana *f* (*mil*) reveille; bull's-eye.

diapositiva *f* transparency, slide.

diario *m* journal, diary; daily newspaper; daily expenses *pl:*—**~/ ria** *adj* daily.

diarrea *f* diarrhea.

dibujar *vt* to draw, design.

diccionario *m* dictionary.

dicha *f* happiness, good fortune:—**por~** by chance.

diciembre *m* December.

dictamen *m* opinion, notion; suggestion; judgement.

dictar *vt* to dictate.

diecinueve *adj, m* nineteen.

dieciocho *adj, m* eighteen.

dieciséis *adj, m* sixteen.

diecisiete *adj, m* seventeen.

diente *m* tooth; fang; tusk.

diestro/tra *adj* right; dexterous, skillful, clever; sagacious, prudent; sly, cunning:—*m* skillful fencer; halter; bridle.

dieta *f* diet, regimen; diet, assembly; daily salary of judges.

diez *adj, m* ten.

diezmar *vt* to decimate.

difamar *vt* to defame, libel.

diferencia *f* difference.

diferenciar *vt* to differentiate, distinguish:—**~se** *vr* to differ, distinguish oneself.

diferente *adj* different, unlike.

diferido/da *adj* recorded.

difícil *adj* difficult.

dificultad *f* difficulty.

difundir *vt* to diffuse, spread; to divulge:—**~se** *vr* to spread (out).

difunto/ta *adj* dead, deceased; late.

digerir *vt* to digest; to bear with patience; to adjust, arrange.

dignarse *vr* to condescend, deign.

digno/na *adj* worthy; suitable.

dilatado/da *adj* large; numerous; prolix; spacious, extensive.

dilatar *vt* to dilate, expand; to spread out; to defer, protract.

dilema *m* dilemma.

diligencia *f* diligence; affair, business; call of nature; stage coach.

dilucidar *vt* to elucidate, explain.

diluir *vt* to dilute.

diluviar *vi* to rain in torrents.

diminuto/ta *adj* minute, small.

dimitir *vt* to give up:—*vi* to resign.

dinamita *f* dynamite.

dinamo *f* dynamo.

dineral *m* large sum of money.

dinero *m* money.

dios *m* god.

diosa *f* goddess.

diplomado/da *adj* qualified.

dique *m* dam.

dirección *f* direction, guidance; administration; steering.

directo/ta *adj* direct, straight; apparent, evident; live.

director/ra *m/f* director; conductor; president; manager.

dirigir *vt* to direct; to conduct; to regulate, govern:—**~se** *vr* to go towards; to address oneself to.

discernir *vt* to discern, distinguish.

discípulo *m* disciple; scholar.

disco *m* disc; record; discus; light; face (of the sun or moon); lens (of a telescope).

díscolo/la *adj* ungovernable; peevish.

discordante *adj* dissonant, discordant.

discreción *f* discretion; acuteness of mind.

discrepar *vi* to differ.

discreto/ta *adj* discreet; ingenious; witty, eloquent.

disculpar *vt* to exculpate, excuse; to acquit, absolve:—**~se** *vr* to apologize; to excuse oneself.

discurrir vi to ramble about; to run to and fro; to discourse (on a subject):— vt to invent, contrive; to meditate.

discurso m speech; conversation; dissertation; space of time.

discutir vt, vi to discuss.

disecar vt to dissect; to stuff.

diseminar vt to scatter; to disseminate, propagate.

diseñar vt to draw; to design.

disentir vi to dissent, disagree.

disfrazar vt to disguise, conceal; to cloak, dissemble:—~**se** vr to disguise oneself as.

disfrutar vt to enjoy:—~**se** vr to enjoy oneself.

disgustar vt to disgust; to offend:— ~**se** vr to be displeased; to fall out.

disidente adj dissident:—m/f dissident, dissenter.

disimular vt to hide; to tolerate.

disipar vt to dissipate, disperse, scatter; to lavish.

dislocarse vr to be dislocated or out of joint.

disminuir vt to diminish; to decrease.

disolver vt to loosen, untie; to dissolve; to disunite; to melt, liquefy; to interrupt.

disparar vt to shoot, discharge, fire; to let off; to throw with violence:— vi to shoot, fire.

disparate m nonsense, absurdity, extravagance.

displicencia f displeasure; dislike.

disponer vt to arrange, prepare; to dispose.

disponible adj available; disposable.

dispositivo m device.

disputar vt to dispute, controvert, question:—vi to debate, argue.

disquete m floppy disk.

distancia f distance; interval; difference.

distante adj distant, far off.

distinguido/da adj distinguished, conspicuous.

distinguir vt to distinguish; to discern: —~**se** vr to distinguish oneself.

distinto/ta adj distinct, different; clear.

distraer vt to distract:—~**se** vr to be absent-minded, be inattentive.

distraído/da adj absent-minded, inattentive.

distribuir vt to distribute.

distrito m district; territory.

disturbio m riot; disturbance, interruption.

disuadir vt to dissuade.

diurno/na adj daily.

diva f prima donna.

divagar vt to digress.

divergencia f divergence.

diversidad f diversity; variety of things.

diversificar vt to diversify; to vary.

diversión f diversion; sport; amusement; (mil) diversion.

divertir vt to divert (the attention); to amuse, entertain; (mil) to draw off: —~**se** vr to amuse oneself.

dividir vt to divide; to disunite; to separate; to share out.

divieso m (med) boil.

divino/na adj divine, heavenly; excellent.

divorcio m divorce; separation, disunion.

divulgar vt to publish, divulge.

dobladillo m hem; turn-up.

doblar vt to double; to fold; to bend:—vi to turn; to toll:—~**se** vr to bend, bow, submit.

doble adj double; dual; deceitful:— **al**~ doubly:—m double.

doblegar vt to bend:——**se** vr to yield.

doblez m crease; fold; turn-up:—f duplicity.

doce adj, m twelve.

docena f dozen.

dócil adj docile, tractable.

doctor/ra m/f doctor.

documento m document; record.

dogma m dogma.

dólar m dollar.

doler vt, vi to feel pain; to ache:——**se** vr to feel for the sufferings of others; to complain.

dolor m pain; aching, ache; affliction.

domar vt to tame; to subdue, master.

domesticar vt to domesticate.

domicilio m domicile; home, abode.

dominar vt to dominate; to be fluent in:——**se** vr to moderate one's passions.

domingo m Sunday; (Christian) Sabbath.

donar vt to donate; to bestow.

donativo m contribution.

doncella f virgin, maiden; lady's maid.

donde relative adv where

¿dónde? interrogative adv where?:—¿**de dónde?** from where?

dondequiera adv wherever.

dorado/da adj gilt compd; golden:—m gilding.

dormir vi to sleep:——**se** vr to fall asleep.

dos adj, m two.

doscientos/tas adj pl two hundred.

dosis f invar dose.

dotado/da adj gifted.

drama m drama.

dramatizar vt to dramatize.

droga f drug; stratagem; artifice, deceit.

droguería f hardware store.

ducha f shower; (med) douche.

ducho/cha adj skilled, experienced.

dudar vt to doubt.

duelo m grief, affliction; mourning.

duende m elf, hobgoblin.

dueño/ña m/f owner; landlord/lady; employer.

dulce adj sweet; mild, gentle, meek; soft:—m sweet, candy.

dúo m (mus) duo, duet.

duodécimo/ma adj twelfth.

duplicar vt to duplicate; to repeat.

duradero/ra adj lasting, durable.

durante adv during.

durar vi to last, continue.

durazno m peach; peach tree.

dureza f hardness; harshness:——**de oido** hardness of hearing.

duro/ra adj hard; cruel; harsh, rough: —m five peseta coin:—adv hard.

E

e conj and (before words starting with i and hi).

ébano m ebony.

ebrio/ia adj drunk.

ebullición f boiling.

echar vt to throw; to add; to pour out; to mail:——**se** vr to lie down.

eco m echo.

económico/ca adj economic; cheap; thrifty; financial; avaricious.

ecuánime *adj* level-headed.

ecuménico/ca *adj* ecumenical; universal.

edad *f* age.

edición *f* edition; publication.

edificar *vt* to build, construct; to edify.

edificio *m* building; structure.

editar *vt* to edit; to publish.

educación *f* education; upbringing; (good) manners *pl*.

educar *vt* to educate, instruct; to bring up.

efectivamente *adv* exactly; really; in fact.

efecto *m* effect; consequence; purpose:—~**s** *mpl* effects *pl*, goods *pl*:—**en**~ in fact, really.

efectuar *vt* to effect, carry out.

eficaz *adj* efficient; effective.

eficiente *adj* efficient.

egoísta *m/f* self-seeker:—*adj* selfish.

eje *m* axle; axis.

ejecutar *vt* to execute, perform; to put to death; (*jur*) to distrain, seize.

ejecutivo/va *adj* executive:—*m/f* executive.

ejemplar *m* specimen; copy; example:—*adj* exemplary.

ejemplo *m* example:—**por**~ for example, for instance.

ejercer *vt* to exercise; *vi* to apply oneself to the functions of an office.

ejercicio *m* exercise.

ejercitar *vt* to exercise.

ejército *m* army.

el *art, m* the.

él *pn* he, it.

elaborar *vt* to elaborate.

elástico/ca *adj* elastic.

elección *f* election; choice.

eléctrico/ca *adj* electric, electrical.

electrocutar *vt* to electrocute.

electrodomesticos *mpl* (electrical) household appliances *pl*.

electrotecnia *f* electrical engineering.

elefante *m* elephant.

elegante *adj* elegant, fine.

elegir *vt* to choose, elect.

elemento *m* element:—~**s** *mpl* elements, rudiments, first principles *pl*.

elevar *vt* to raise; to elevate:—~**se** *vr* to rise; to be enraptured; to be conceited.

eliminar *vt* to eliminate, remove.

eliminatoria *f* preliminary (round).

ella *pn* she; it.

ello *pn* it.

elogiar *vt* to praise, eulogize.

eludir *vt* to elude, escape.

emanar *vi* to emanate.

embadurnar *vt* to smear, bedaub.

embalaje *m* packing, package.

embaldosar *vt* to pave with tiles.

embalse *m* reservoir.

embarazada *f* pregnant woman:—*adj* pregnant.

embarazoso/sa *adj* difficult; intricate, entangled.

embarcación *f* embarkation; any vessel or ship.

embarcar *vt* to embark:—~**se** *vr* to go on board; (*fig*) to get involved (in a matter).

embargo *m* embargo:—**sin**~ still, however.

embarque *m* embarkation.

embaucar *vt* to deceive; to trick.

embeber *vt* to soak; to saturate:—*vi* to shrink:—~**se** *vr* to be enraptured; to be absorbed.

embeleso *m* amazement, enchantment.

embellecer *vt* to embellish, beautify.

embestir *vt* to assault, attack.

emblanquecer *vt* to whiten:—**~se** *vr* to grow white; to bleach.

embobado/da *adj* amazed; fascinated.

émbolo *m* plunger; piston.

embolsar *vt* to put money into (a purse); to pocket.

emborrachar *vt* to intoxicate, inebriate:—**~se** *vr* to get drunk.

emboscada *f* (*mil*) ambush.

embotar *vt* to blunt:—**~se** *vr* to go numb.

embotellamiento *m* traffic jam.

embotellar *vt* to bottle (wine).

embozar *vt* to muffle (the face); (*fig*) to cloak, conceal.

embrague *m* clutch.

embriagar *vt* to intoxicate, inebriate; to transport, enrapture.

embrión *m* embryo.

embrollo *m* muddle.

embromar *vt* to tease; to cajole, wheedle.

embrujar *vt* to bewitch.

embrutecer *vt* to brutalize:—**~se** *vr* to become depraved.

embudo *m* funnel.

embustero/ra *m/f* impostor, cheat; liar:—*adj* deceitful.

embutido *m* sausage; inlay.

emerger *vi* to emerge, appear.

emigrar *vi* to emigrate.

eminente *adj* eminent, high; excellent, conspicuous.

emisora *f* broadcasting station.

emitir *vt* to emit; to issue; to broadcast.

emoción *f* emotion; feeling; excitement.

emocionar *vt* to excite; to move, touch.

emotivo/va *adj* emotional.

empacho *m* (*med*) indigestion.

empalagoso/sa *adj* cloying; tiresome.

empalmar *vt* to join.

empanada *f* (meat) pie.

empanar *vt* to cover with breadcrumbs.

empantanarse *vr* to get swamped; to get bogged down.

empapar *vt* to soak; to soak up:—**~se** *vr* to soak.

empapelar *vt* to paper.

empaquetar *vt* to pack, parcel up.

emparedado *m* sandwich.

emparrado *m* vine arbor.

empastar *vt* to paste; to fill (a tooth).

empatar *vi* to draw.

empedernido/da *adj* inveterate; heartless.

empedrado *m* paving.

empeine *m* instep.

empellón *m* push; heavy blow.

empeñar *vt* to pawn, pledge:—**~se** *vr* to pledge oneself to pay debts; to get into debt:—**~se en algo** to insist on something.

empeorar *vt* to make worse:—*vi* **~se** *vr* to grow worse.

empequeñecer *vt* to dwarf; (*fig*) to belittle.

empezar *vt* to begin, start.

emplazamiento *m* summons; location.

empleado/da *m/f* official; employee.

emplear *vt* to employ; to occupy; to commission.

empobrecer *vt* to reduce to poverty:—*vi* to become poor.

empollar *vt* to incubate; to hatch; (*fam*) to swot (up).

empolvar *vt* to powder; to sprinkle powder upon.

empotrado/da *adj* built-in.

emprender *vt* to embark on; to tackle; to undertake.

empresa *f* (*com*) company; enterprise, undertaking.

empujar *vt* to push; to press forward.

empujón *m* push; impulse:—**a~ones** in fits and starts.

emular *vt* to emulate, rival.

en *prep* in; for; on, upon.

enaguas *fpl* petticoat.

enamorado/da *adj* in love, lovesick.

enamorar *vt* to inspire love in:—**~se** *vr* to fall in love.

enano/na *adj* dwarfish:—*m* dwarf.

enardecer *vt* to fire with passion, inflame.

enarenar *vt* to fill with sand.

encabezar *vt* to head; to put a heading to; to lead.

encadenar *vt* to chain, link together; to connect, unite.

encajar *vt* to insert; to drive in; to encase; to intrude:—*vi* to fit (well).

encaje *m* lace.

encalar *vt* to whitewash.

encallar *vi* (*mar*) to run aground.

encaminar *vt* to guide, show the way: —**~se** *vr* ~ **a** to take the road to.

encandilar *vt* to dazzle.

encanecer *vi* to grow gray; to grow old.

encantado/da *adj* bewitched; delighted; pleased.

encantador/ra *adj* charming:—*m/f* magician.

encantar *vt* to enchant, charm; (*fig*) to delight.

encarcelar *vt* to imprison.

encarecimiento *m* price increase:— **con~** insistently.

encargado/da *adj* in charge:—*m/f* representative; person in charge.

encargar *vt* to charge; to commission.

encariñarse *vr:*—**~ con** to grow fond of.

encarnar *vt* to embody, personify.

encasillar *vt* to pigeonhole; to typecast.

encastillarse *vr* to refuse to yield.

encausar *vt* to prosecute.

encauzar *vt* to channel.

encebollado *m* casseroled beef or lamb and onions, seasoned with spice.

encenagado/da *adj* muddy, mudstained.

encendedor *m* lighter.

encender *vt* to kindle, light, set on fire; to inflame, incite; to switch on, to turn on:—**~se** *vr* to catch fire; to flare up.

encerado *m* blackboard.

encerar *vt* to wax; to polish.

encerrar *vt* to shut up, confine; to contain:—**~se** *vr* to withdraw from the world.

enchufar *vt* to plug in; to connect.

enchufe *m* plug; outlet, socket; connection; (*fam*) contact, connection.

encía *f* gum (of the teeth).

encierro *m* confinement; enclosure; prison, penitentiary; bull-pen; penning (of bulls).

encima *adv* above; over; at the top; besides:—**~ de** *prep* above; over; at the top of; besides.

encina *f* evergreen oak.

encinta *adj* pregnant.

enclenque *adj* weak, sickly:—*m* weakling.

encoger *vt* to contract, shorten; to shrink; to discourage:—**~se** *vr* to shrink; (*fig*) to cringe.

encolar *vt* to glue.

encolerizar vt to provoke, irritate:— ~**se** vr to get angry.

encomendar vt to recommend; to entrust:—~**se** vr ~ **a** to entrust oneself to; to put one's trust in.

encontrar vt to meet, encounter:—vr ~**se con** to run into:—vi to assemble, come together.

encrucijada f four way stop, intersection; junction.

encuadernar vt to bind (books).

encubierto/ta adj hidden, concealed.

encubrir vt to hide, conceal.

encuesta f inquiry; opinion poll.

encurtir vt to pickle.

endeble adj feeble, weak.

endemoniado/da adj possessed with the devil; devilish.

enderezar vt to straighten out; to set right:—~**se** vr to stand upright.

endeudarse vr to get into debt.

endosar vt to endorse.

endrino m blackthorn, sloe.

endulzar vt to sweeten; to soften.

endurecer vt to harden, toughen:— ~**se** vr to become cruel; to grow hard.

enebro m (bot) juniper.

enemistar vt to make an enemy:— ~**se** vr to become enemies; to fall out.

energía f energy, power, drive; strength of will.

energúmeno/na m/f (fam) madman/ woman.

enero m January.

enfadar vt to anger, irritate; to trouble:—~**se** vr to become angry.

énfasis m emphasis.

enfermar vi to fall ill:—vt to make sick; to weaken.

enfermedad f illness.

enfermero/ra m/f nurse.

enfermo/ma adj sick, ill:—m/f invalid, sick person; patient.

enfocar vt to focus; to consider (a problem).

enfoque m focus.

enfrentar vt to confront; to put face to face:—~**se** vr to face each other; to meet (two teams).

enfrente adv over against, opposite; in front.

enfriar vt to cool; to refrigerate:— ~**se** vr to cool down; (med) to catch a cold.

enfurecer vt to madden, enrage:— ~**se** vr to get rough (of the wind and sea); to become furious or enraged.

enfurruñarse vr to get sulky; to frown.

engañar vt to deceive, cheat:—~**se** vr to be deceived; to make a mistake.

enganchar vt to hook, hang up; to hitch up; to couple, connect; to recruit into military service:—~**se** vr (mil) to enlist.

engañoso/sa adj deceitful, artful, false.

engastar vt to set, mount.

engatusar vt to coax.

engendrar vt to beget, engender; to produce.

englobar vt to include.

engordar vt to fatten:—vi to grow fat; to put on weight.

engorroso/sa adj troublesome, cumbersome.

engranaje m gear; gearing.

engrasar vt to grease, lubricate.

engreído/da adj conceited, vain.

engullir vt to swallow; to gobble, devour.

enharinar vt to cover or sprinkle with flour.

enhebrar vt to thread.

enhorabuena f congratulations pl:—adv all right; well and good.

enhoramala interj good riddance!

enjalbegar vt to whitewash.

enjambre m swarm of bees; crowd, multitude.

enjuagar vt to rinse out; to wash out.

enjuiciar vt to prosecute, try; to pass judgement on, judge.

enlace m connection, link; relationship.

enladrillar vt to pave with bricks.

enlazar vt to join, unite; to tie.

enlodar vt to cover in mud; (fig) to stain.

enloquecer vt to madden, drive crazy:—vi to go mad.

enmarañar vt to entangle; to complicate; to confuse:—~se vr to become entangled; to get confused.

enmendar vt to correct; to reform; to repair, compensate for; to amend:—~se vr to mend one's ways.

enmohecer vt to make moldy; to rust:—~se vr to grow moldy or musty; to rust.

enmudecer(se) vt to silence:—~se vr to grow dumb; to be silent.

ennegrecer vt to blacken; to darken; to obscure.

enojar vt to irritate, make angry; to annoy; to upset; to offend:—~se vr to get angry.

enorgullecerse vr:—~ (de) to be proud (of).

enorme adj enormous, vast, huge; horrible.

enredadera f climbing plant; bindweed.

enredar vt to entangle, ensnare, confound, perplex; to puzzle; to sow discord among:—~se vr to get entangled; to get complicated; to get embroiled.

enrejado m trelliswork.

enrevesado/da adj complicated.

enriquecer vt to enrich; to adorn:—~se vr to grow rich.

enrojecer vt to redden:—vi to blush.

enrolar vt to recruit:—~se vr (mil) to join up.

enrollar vt to roll (up).

enroscar vt to twist:—~se vr to curl or roll up.

ensalada f salad.

ensalmo m enchantment, spell.

ensalzar vt to exalt, aggrandize; to exaggerate.

ensamblar vt to assemble.

ensañar vt to irritate, enrage:—~se con vr to treat brutally.

ensanchar vt to widen; to extend; to enlarge:—~se vr to expand; to assume an air of importance.

ensangrentar vt to stain with blood.

ensartar vt to string (beads, etc).

ensayar vt to test; to rehearse.

ensayo m test, trial; rehearsal of a play; essay.

enseñar vt to teach, instruct; to show.

ensimismarse vr to be or become lost in thought.

ensordecer vt to deafen:—vi to grow deaf.

ensuciar vt to stain, soil; to defile:—~se vr to wet oneself; to dirty oneself.

ensueño m fantasy; daydream; illusion.

entablar vt to board (up); to strike up (conversation).

entablillar vt (med) to put in a splint.

entallar *vt* to tailor (a suit):—*vi* to fit.

ente *m* organization; entity, being; (*fam*) odd character.

entender *vt, vi* to understand, comprehend; to remark, take notice (of); to reason, think:—**a mi ~** in my opinion:—**~se** *vr* to understand each other.

enterar *vt* to inform; to instruct:— **~se** *vr* to find out.

enternecer *vt* to soften; to move (to pity):—**~se** *vr* to be moved.

entero/ra *adj* entire, complete; perfect; honest; resolute:—**por ~** entirely, completely.

enterrar *vt* to inter, bury.

entidad *f* entity; company; body; society.

entierro *m* burial; funeral.

entonar *vt* to tune, intonate; to intone; to tone:—*vi* to be in tune:— **~se** *vr* to give oneself airs.

entonces *adv* then, at that time.

entornar *vt* to half close.

entorpecer *vt* to dull; to make lethargic; to hinder; to delay.

entrada *f* entrance, entry; (*com*) receipts *pl*; entree; ticket (for cinema, theater, etc).

entrampar *vt* to trap, snare; to mess up; to burden with debts:—**~se** *vr* get into debt.

entrañable *adj* intimate; affectionate.

entrañas *fpl* entrails *pl*, intestines *pl*.

entrar *vi* to enter, go in; to commence.

entre *prep* between; among(st); in:— **~ manos** in hand.

entrecejo *m* space between the eyebrows; frown.

entredicho *m* (*jur*) injunction:—**estar en ~** to be banned:—**poner en ~** to cast doubt on.

entregar *vt* to deliver; to hand over:—**~se** *vr* to surrender; to devote oneself.

entremeses *mpl* hors d'oeuvres.

entrenarse *vr* to train.

entrepierna *f* crotch.

entresuelo *m* entresol; mezzanine.

entretanto *adv* meanwhile.

entretejer *vt* to interweave.

entretela *f* interfacing, stiffening, interlining.

entretener *vt* to amuse; to entertain, divert; to hold up; to maintain:—**~se** *vr* to amuse oneself; to linger.

entrever *vt* to have a glimpse of.

entrevistar *vt* to interview:—**~se** *vr* to have an interview.

entristecer *vt* to sadden.

entrometer *vt* to put (one thing) between (others):—**~se** *vr* to interfere.

entumecido/da *adj* numb, stiff.

enturbiar *vt* to make cloudy; to obscure, confound:—**~se** *vr* to become cloudy; (*fig*) to get confused.

entusiasmar *vt* to excite, fill with enthusiasm; to delight.

enumerar *vt* to enumerate.

envalentonar *vt* to give courage to:— **~se** *vr* to boast.

envanecer *vt* to make vain; to swell with pride:—**~se** *vr* to become proud.

envaramiento *m* stiffness; numbness.

envasar *vt* to pack; to bottle; to can.

envase *m* packing; bottling; canning; container; package; bottle; can.

envejecer *vt* to make old:—*vi* **~se** *vr* to grow old.

envenenar *vt* to poison; to embitter.

envés *m* wrong side (of material).

enviar vt to send, transmit, convey, dispatch.

enviciar vt to vitiate, corrupt:—~**se** vr to get corrupted.

envidia f envy; jealousy.

envidiar vt to envy; to grudge; to be jealous of.

envilecer vt to vilify, debase:—~**se** vr to degrade oneself.

envío m (com) dispatch, remittance of goods; consignment.

enviudar vi to become a widower or widow.

envolver vt to involve; to wrap up.

enyesar vt to plaster; (med) to put in a plaster cast.

enzarzarse vr to get involved in a dispute; to get oneself into trouble.

épico/ca adj epic.

epígrafe f epigraph, inscription; motto; headline.

episodio m episode, installment.

época f epoch; period, time.

epopeya f epic.

equidad f equity, honesty; impartiality, justice.

equilibrar vt to balance; to poise.

equilibrio m balance, equilibrium.

equipaje m luggage; equipment.

equipar vt to fit out, equip, furnish.

equipararse vr:—~ **con** to be on a level with.

equipo m equipment; team; shift.

equitación f horsemanship; riding.

equitativo/va adj equitable; just.

equivaler vi to be of equal value.

equivocación f mistake, error; misunderstanding.

equivocar vt to mistake:—~**se** vr to make a mistake, be wrong.

equívoco/ca adj equivocal, ambiguous:—m equivocation; quibble.

era f era, age; threshing floor.

erario m treasury, public funds pl.

erguir vt to erect, raise up straight:— ~**se** vr to straighten up.

erial m fallow land.

erigir vt to erect, raise, build; to establish.

erizarse vr to bristle; to stand on end.

erizo m hedgehog:—~ **de mar** sea urchin.

ermita f hermitage.

erotismo m eroticism.

errar vi to be mistaken; to wander.

errata f misprint.

erre:—~ **que** ~ adv obstinately.

error m error, mistake, fault.

eructar vi to belch, burp.

esbelto/ta adj slim, slender.

esbirro m bailiff; henchman; killer.

esbozo m outline.

escabeche m pickle; pickled fish.

escabroso/sa adj rough, uneven; craggy; rude, risqué, blue.

escabullirse vr to escape, evade; to slip through one's fingers.

escafandra f diving suit; space suit.

escala f ladder; (mus) scale; stopover.

escalar vt to climb.

escalera f staircase; ladder.

escalfar vt to poach (eggs).

escalofriante adj chilling.

escalón m step of a stair; rung.

escama f (fish) scale.

escamar vt to scale, take off scales:— ~**se** vr to flake off; to become suspicious.

escamotear vt to swipe; to make disappear.

escampar vi to stop raining.

escándalo m scandal; uproar.

escaño m bench with a back; seat (parliament).

escapar *vi* to escape:—**~se** *vr* to get away; to leak (water, etc).

escaparate *m* store window; wardrobe.

escape *m* escape, flight; leak; exhaust (of motor).

escarabajo *m* beetle.

escaramuza *f* skirmish; dispute, quarrel.

escarbar *vt* to scratch (the earth as hens do); to inquire into.

escarcha *f* white frost.

escarlata *adj* scarlet.

escarlatina *f* scarlet fever.

escarmentar *vi* to learn one's lesson:—*vt* to punish severely.

escarola *f* (*bot*) endive.

escarpado/da *adj* sloped; craggy.

escaso/sa *adj* small, short, little; sparing; scarce; scanty.

escenario *m* stage; set.

escéptico/ca *adj* sceptic, sceptical.

esclarecer *vt* to lighten; to illuminate; to illustrate; to shed light on (problem, etc).

esclavo/va *m/f* slave; captive.

esclusa *f* sluice, floodgate.

escoba *f* broom, brush.

escocer *vt* to sting; to burn:—**~se** *vr* to chafe.

escoger *vt* to choose, select.

escolar *m/f* schoolboy/girl:—*adj* scholastic.

escollo *m* reef, rock.

escoltar *vt* to escort.

escombros *mpl* trash; debris.

esconder *vt* to hide, conceal:—**~se** *vr* to be hidden.

escondite *m* hiding place:—**juego de ~** hide-and-seek.

escoplo *m* chisel.

escorbuto *m* scurvy.

escote *m* low neck (of a dress).

escribir *vt* to write; to spell.

escrito *m* document; manuscript, text.

escritor/ra *m/f* writer, author.

escritorio *m* writing desk; office, study.

escrúpulo *m* doubt, scruple, scrupulousness.

escuchar *vt* to listen to, heed.

escudilla *f* bowl.

escudo *m* shield.

escudriñar *vt* to search, examine; to pry into.

escuela *f* school.

esculpir *vt* to sculpt.

escupir *vt* to spit.

escurreplatos *m invar* plate rack.

escurrir *vt* to drain; to drip:—**~se** *vr* to slip away; to slip, slide:—*vi* to wring out.

ese/esa *adj* that:—**esos/as** *pl* those.

ése/ésa *pn* that (one):—**ésos/as** *pl* those (ones).

esencial *adj* essential; principal.

esfera *f* sphere; globe.

esforzarse *vr* to exert oneself, make an effort.

esfuerzo *m* effort.

esfumarse *vr* to fade away.

esgrima *f* fencing.

esguince *m* (*med*) sprain.

eslabón *m* link of a chain; steel; shackle.

esmalte *m* enamel.

esmerado/da *adj* careful, neat.

esmeralda *m* emerald.

esmero *m* careful attention, great care.

eso *pn* that.

esos/as; ésos/as *pl* of **ese/a; ése/a.**

espabilar *vt* to wake up:—**~se** *vr* to wake up; (*fig*) to get a move on.

espaciar *vt* to spread out; to space (out).

espacio *m* space; (radio or TV) program.

espada *f* sword; ace of spades.

espalda *f* back, back-part:—~s *fpl* shoulders *pl*.

español/la *adj* Spanish:—*m/f* Spaniard:—*m* Spanish language.

espantajo *m* scarecrow; bogeyman.

espantar *vt* to frighten; to chase or drive away.

esparadrapo *m* adhesive tape.

esparcir *vt* to scatter; to divulge:— ~se *vr* to amuse oneself.

espárrago *m* asparagus.

espátula *f* spatula.

especia *f* spice.

especial *adj* special; particular:—**en ~** especially.

especie *f* species; kind, sort; matter.

especificar *vt* to specify.

espectáculo *m* spectacle; show.

espectador/ra *m/f* spectator.

especular *vt* to speculate.

espejismo *m* mirage.

espejo *m* mirror.

espeluznante *adj* horrifying.

esperanza *f* hope.

esperar *vt* to hope; to expect, wait for.

esperma *f* sperm.

espeso/sa *adj* thick, dense.

espesor *m* thickness.

espía *m/f* spy.

espiga *f* ear (of corn).

espigón *m* ear of corn; sting; (*mar*) breakwater.

espina *f* thorn; fishbone.

espinaca *f* (*bot*) spinach.

espinilla *f* shinbone.

espino *m* hawthorn.

espiral *adj, f* spiral.

espirar *vt* to exhale.

espíritu *m* spirit, soul; mind; intelligence:—**el E~ Santo** the Holy Ghost:—~s *pl* demons, hobgoblins *pl*.

espléndido/da *adj* splendid.

espliego *m* (*bot*) lavender.

espolón *m* spur (of a cock); spur (of a mountain range); sea wall; jetty; (*mar*) buttress.

espolvorear *vt* to sprinkle.

esponja *f* sponge.

espontáneo/nea *adj* spontaneous.

esposa *f* wife.

esposas *fpl* handcuffs *pl*.

esposo *m* husband.

espuma *f* froth, foam.

espumar *vt* to skim, take the scum off.

espumoso/sa *adj* frothy, foamy; sparkling (wine).

esputo *m* spit, saliva.

esqueje *m* cutting (of plant).

esquela *f* note, slip of paper.

esqueleto *m* skeleton.

esquema *m* scheme; diagram; plan.

esquí *m* ski; skiing.

esquina *f* corner, angle.

esquirol *m* blackleg.

esquivar *vt* to shun, avoid, evade.

esta *adj f* this:—~s *pl* these.

ésta *pn f* this:—~s *pl* these.

estable *adj* stable.

establecer *vt* to establish.

establo *m* stable.

estaca *f* stake; stick; post.

estación *f* season (of the year); station; railroad station, terminus:—~ **de autobuses** bus station:—~ **de servicio** service station.

estacionar *vt* to park; (*mil*) to station.

estadio *m* phase; stadium.

estado *m* state, condition.

Estados Unidos *mpl* United States (of America).

estafar *vt* to deceive, defraud.

estallar *vi* to crack; to burst; to break out.

estambre *m* stamen.

estamento *m* estate; body; layer; class.

estampa *f* print; engraving; appearance.

estampar *vt* to print.

estancar *vt* to check (a current); to monopolize; to prohibit, suspend:—**~se** *vr* to stagnate.

estancia *f* stay; bedroom; ranch; (*poet*) stanza.

estanco *m* tobacconist's (store):—**~/ca** *adj* watertight.

estándar *adj*, *m* standard.

estaño *m* tin.

estanque *m* pond, pool; reservoir.

estantería *f* shelves *pl,* shelving.

estar *vi* to be; to be (in a place).

estatua *f* statue.

este[1] *m* east;

este[2]**/ta** *adj* this:—**estos/tas** *pl* these.

estera *f* mat.

estéreo *adj invar, m* stereo.

estereotipo *m* stereotype.

estéril *adj* sterile, infertile.

esterlina *adj*:—**libra ~** pound sterling.

estético/ca *adj* esthetic:—*f* esthetics.

estiércol *m* dung; manure.

estilo *m* style; fashion; stroke (swimming).

estima *f* esteem.

estimar *vt* to estimate, value; to esteem; to judge; to think.

estimular *vt* to stimulate, excite; to goad.

estío *m* summer.

estipular *vt* to stipulate.

estirar *vt* to stretch out.

esto *pn* this.

estofado *m* stew.

estómago *m* stomach.

estopa *f* tow.

estorbar *vt* to hinder; (*fig*) to bother:—*vi* to be in the way.

estornudar *vi* to sneeze.

estos/as, éstos/tas *pl* of **este/ta, éste/ta.**

estrado *m* drawing room; stage, platform.

estrafalario/ria *adj* slovenly; eccentric.

estrago *m* ruin, destruction; havoc.

estrangular *vt* to strangle; (*med*) to strangulate.

estraperlo *m* black market.

estratagema *f* stratagem, trick.

estrato *m* stratum, layer.

estraza *f* rag:—**papel de ~** brown paper.

estrechar *vt* to tighten; to contract, constrain; to compress:—**~se** *vr* to grow narrow; to embrace:—**~ la mano** to shake hands.

estrecho *m* straits *pl*:—**~/cha** *adj* narrow, close; tight; intimate; rigid, austere; short (of money).

estrella *f* star.

estrellar *vt* to dash to pieces:—**~se** *vr* to smash; to crash; to fail.

estremecer *vt* to shake, make tremble:—**~se** *vr* to shake, tremble.

estrenar *vt* to wear for the first time; to move into (a house); to show (a movie) for the first time:—**~se** *vr* to make one's debut.

estreñido/da *adj* constipated.

estrépito *m* noise, racket; fuss.

estribillo *m* chorus.

estribo *m* buttress; stirrup; running board:—**perder los ~s** to fly off the handle (*fam*).

estribor m (mar) starboard.

estricto/ta adj strict; severe.

estrofa f (poet) verse, strophe.

estropajo m scourer.

estropear vt to spoil; to damage:—
~**se** vr to get damaged.

estructura f structure.

estruendo m clamor, noise; confusion, uproar; pomp, ostentation.

estuche m case (for scissors, etc);
sheath.

estudiar vt to study.

estufa f heater, fire.

estupefaciente m narcotic.

estupefacto adj speechless; thunder-
struck.

estupendo/da adj terrific, marvelous.

estúpido adj stupid.

etapa f stage; stopping place; (fig)
phase.

etcétera adv etcetera, and so on.

eterno/na adj eternal.

ético/ca adj ethical, moral.

etiqueta f etiquette; label.

evacuar vt to evacuate, empty.

evadir vt to evade, escape.

evaluar vt to evaluate.

evaporar vt to evaporate:—~**se** vr to
vanish.

eventual adj possible; temporary,
casual (worker).

evidente adj evident, clear.

evitar vt to avoid.

evolucionar vi to evolve.

ex adj ex.

ex profeso adv on purpose.

exacerbar vt to exacerbate; to irritate.

exacto/ta adj exact; punctual; accurate.

exagerar vt to exaggerate.

exaltar vt to exalt, elevate; to praise,
extol:—~**se** vr to get excited.

examen m exam, examination, test,
inquiry.

examinar vt to examine.

exasperar vt to exasperate, irritate.

excavar vt to excavate, dig out.

exceder vt to exceed, surpass, excel,
outdo.

excelente adj excellent.

excéntrico/ca adj eccentric.

excepto adv excepting, except (for).

exceso m excess.

excitar vt to excite:—~**se** vr to get
excited.

exclamar vt to exclaim, cry out.

excluir vt to exclude.

excremento m excrement.

excursión f excursion, trip.

excusa f excuse, apology.

excusado m bathroom.

excusar vt to excuse; to avoid:—~
de to exempt from:—~**se** vr to
apologize.

exento/ta adj exempt, free.

exhalar vt to exhale; to give off; to
heave (a sigh).

exhausto/ta adj exhausted.

exhibir vt to exhibit.

exhortar vt to exhort.

exhumar vt to disinter, exhume.

exigir vt to demand, require.

exiliado/da adj exiled:—m/f exile.

existir vi to exist, be.

éxito m outcome; success; (mus,etc)
hit:—**tener** ~ to be successful.

exorbitante adj exhorbitant, excessive.

exótico/ca adj exotic.

expandir vt to expand.

expatriarse vr to emigrate; to go into
exile.

expectativa f expectation; prospect.

expedición f expedition.

expediente *m* expedient; means; (*jur*) proceedings *pl*; dossier, file.

expedir *vt* to send, forward, dispatch.

expensas *fpl*:—**a ~ de** at the expense of.

experimentar *vt* to experience:—*vi* **~ con** to experiment with.

experto/ta *adj* expert; experienced.

expiar *vt* to atone for; to purify.

expirar *vi* to expire.

explayarse *vr* to speak at length.

explicar *vt* to explain, expound:— **~se** *vr* to explain oneself.

explorar *vt* to explore.

explotar *vt* to exploit; to run:—*vi* to explode.

exponer *vt* to expose; to explain.

exportar *vt* to export.

exposición *f* exposure; exhibition; explanation; account.

expresar *vt* to express.

expreso/sa *adj* express, clear, specific; fast (train).

exprimir *vt* to squeeze out.

expropriar *vt* to expropriate.

expulsar *vt* to expel, drive out.

éxtasis *m* ecstasy, enthusiasm.

extender *vt* to extend, stretch out:— **~se** *vr* to extend; to spread.

extenso/sa *adj* extensive.

extenuar *vt* to exhaust, debilitate.

exterior *adj* exterior, external:—*m* exterior, outward appearance.

exterminar *vt* to exterminate.

externo/na *adj* external, outer:—*m/f* day pupil.

extinguir *vt* to wipe out; to extinguish.

extintor *m* (fire) extinguisher.

extra *adj invar* extra; good quality:— *m/f* extra:—*m* bonus.

extraer *vt* to extract.

extrañar *vt* to find strange; to miss:— **~se** *vr* to be surprised; to grow apart.

extranjero/ra *m/f* stranger; foreigner:— *adj* foreign, alien.

extraño/ña *adj* foreign; rare; singular, strange, odd.

extraviar *vt* to mislead:—**~se** *vr* to lose one's way.

extremidad *f* extremity; brim; tip:— **~es** *fpl* extremities *pl*.

extremo/ma *adj* extreme, last:—*m* extreme, highest degree:—**en ~/por ~** extremely.

extrovertido/da *adj, m/f* extrovert.

exuberancia *f* exuberance; luxuriance.

F

fábrica *f* factory.

fabricar *vt* to build, construct; to manufacture; (*fig*) to fabricate.

fábula *f* fable; fiction; rumor, common talk.

fabuloso/sa *adj* fabulous, fictitious.

facción *f* (political) faction; feature.

fachada *f* facade, face, front.

fácil *adj* facile, easy.

facilitar *vt* to facilitate.

fácilmente *adv* easily.

factor *m* (*mat*) factor; (*com*) factor, agent.

factura *f* invoice.

facultativo/va *adj* optional:—*m/f* doctor, practitioner.

faena f task, job; hard work.

faisán m pheasant.

fajo m bundle; wad.

falaz adj deceitful, fraudulent; fallacious.

falda f skirt; lap; flap; train; slope, hillside.

fallar vt (jur) to pronounce sentence on, judge:—vi to fail.

fallecer vi to die.

falso/sa adj false, untrue; deceitful; fake.

falta f fault, defect; want; flaw, mistake;(dep) foul.

faltar vi to be wanting; to fail; not to fulfil one's promise; to need; to be missing.

fama f fame; reputation, name.

familia f family.

familiar adj familiar; homely, domestic:—m/f relative, relation.

famoso/sa adj famous.

fanfarrón m bully, braggart.

fango m mire, mud.

fantasía f fancy; fantasy; caprice; presumption.

fantasma f phantom, ghost.

fardo m bale, parcel.

farmacia f drugstore.

faro m (mar) lighthouse; (auto) headlamp; floodlight.

farola f street light.

fascículo m part, installment.

fascinar vt to fascinate; to enchant.

fase f phase.

fastidiar vt to annoy; to offend; to spoil.

fatal adj fatal; mortal; awful.

fatiga f weariness, fatigue.

fatuo/tua adj fatuous, stupid, foolish; conceited.

fauces fpl jaws pl, gullet.

favor m favor; protection; good turn.

favorecer vt to favor, protect.

fe f faith, belief.

febrero m February.

fecha f date (of a letter etc).

fecundar vt to fertilize.

felicitar vt to congratulate.

feliz adj happy, fortunate.

felpa f plush; toweling.

felpudo m doormat.

femenino/na adj feminine; female.

feo/ea adj ugly; bad, nasty.

feria f fair, rest day; village market.

fermentar vi to ferment.

feroz adj ferocious, savage; cruel.

ferretería f hardware store.

ferrocarril m railway.

fértil adj fertile, fruitful.

festejo m courtship; feast.

festivo/va adj festive, merry; witty:— **dia** ~ holiday.

feto m fetus.

fiable adj trustworthy; reliable.

fiambre m cold meat.

fianza f (jur) surety.

fiar vt to entrust, confide; to bail; to sell on credit:—~**se** vr to trust.

fibra f fibre.

ficha f token, counter (at games); (index) card.

fidelidad f fidelity; loyalty.

fideos mpl noodles pl.

fiebre f fever.

fiel adj faithful, loyal:—mpl **los** ~**es** the faithful pl.

fieltro m felt.

fiera f wild beast.

fiesta f party; festivity:—~**s** fpl vacations pl.

figura f figure, shape.

figurar *vt* to figure:—**~se** *vr* to fancy, imagine.

fijar *vt* to fix, fasten:—**~se** *vr* to become fixed:—**~se en** to notice.

fijo/ja *adj* fixed, firm; settled, permanent.

fila *f* row, line; (*mil*) rank:—**en ~** in a line, in a row.

filete *m* fillet; fillet steak.

filmar *vt* to film.

filo *m* edge, blade.

filosofía *f* philosophy.

filtro *m* filter.

fin *m* end; termination, conclusion; aim, purpose:—**al ~** at last:—**en ~** (*fig*) well then:—**por ~** finally, lastly.

finalmente *adv* finally, at last.

financiar *vt* to finance.

finca *f* land, property, real estate; country house; farm.

fingir *vt* to feign, fake:—**~se** *vr* to pretend to be:—*vi* to pretend.

fino/na *adj* fine, pure; slender; polite; acute; dry (of sherry).

firma *f* signature; (*com*) company.

firmamento *m* firmament, sky, heaven.

firme *adj* firm, stable, strong, secure; constant; resolute:—*m* road surface.

fiscal *adj* fiscal:—*m/f* district attorney.

fisco *m* treasury, exchequer.

fisgar *vt* to pry into.

física *f* physics.

flaco/ca *adj* lean, skinny; feeble.

flan *m* crème caramel.

flauta *f* (*mus*) flute.

flecha *f* arrow.

flequillo *m* fringe (of hair).

flete *m* (*mar*) freight; charter.

flexible *adj* flexible; compliant; docile.

flojo/ja *adj* loose; flexible; slack; lazy.

flor *f* flower.

florecer *vi* to blossom.

florero *m* vase.

flotador *m* float; rubber ring.

flotar *vi* to float.

fluctuar *vi* to fluctuate; to waver.

fluir *vi* to flow.

foco *m* focus; center; source; floodlight; (light)bulb.

fogón *m* stove; hearth.

fogoso/sa *adj* fiery; ardent, fervent; impetuous, boisterous.

folleto *m* pamphlet; folder, brochure.

follón *m* (*fam*) mess; fuss.

fomentar *vt* to encourage; to promote.

fondo *m* bottom; back; background; space:—**~s** *mpl* stock, funds *pl*, capital:—**a ~** perfectly, completely.

fontanero/ra *m/f* plumber.

forjar *vt* to forge; to frame; to invent.

forma *f* form, shape; pattern; (*med*) fitness; (*dep*) form; means, method:—**de ~ que** in such a manner that.

formación *f* formation; form, figure; education; training.

formar *vt* to form, shape.

fornido/da *adj* well-built.

forro *m* lining; book jacket.

fortuna *f* fortune; wealth.

forzar *vt* to force.

forzoso/sa *adj* indispensable, necessary.

fósforo *m* phosphorus:—**~s** *mpl* matches *pl*.

fotocopia *f* photocopy.

fotografía *f* photography; photograph.

fracasar *vi* to fail.

frágil *adj* fragile, frail.

fraguar *vt* to forge; to contrive:—*vi* to solidify, harden.

fraile *m* friar, monk.

frambuesa *f* raspberry.

francés/sa *adj* French:—*m* French language:—*m/f* Frenchman/woman.

frasco *m* flask.

frase *f* phrase.

fraternal *adj* fraternal, brotherly.

fraude *m* fraud, deceit; cheat.

frazada *f* blanket.

frecuencia *f* frequency.

fregar *vt* to scrub; to wash up.

freír *vt* to fry.

frenar *vt* to brake; (*fig*) to check.

frenesí *m* frenzy.

freno *m* bit; brake; (*fig*) check.

frente *f* front; face:—~ **a** ~ face to face:—**en** ~ opposite; (*mil*) front:—*m* forehead.

fresa *f* strawberry.

fresco/ca *adj* fresh; cool; new; ruddy:—*m* fresh air:—*m/f* (*fam*) shameless or impudent person.

fresno *m* ash tree.

frigorífico *m* fridge.

frijol *m* kidney bean.

frío/fría *adj* cold; indifferent:—*m* cold; indifference.

friso *m* frieze; wainscot.

frito/ta *adj* fried.

frívolo/la *adj* frivolous.

frondoso/sa *adj* leafy.

frontera *f* frontier.

frontón *m* (*dep*) pelota court; pelota.

frotar *vt* to rub.

fructificar *vi* to bear fruit; to come to fruition.

frugal *adj* frugal, sparing.

fruncir *vt* to pleat; to knit; to contract:—~ **las cejas** to knit the eyebrows.

frustrar *vt* to frustrate.

fruta *f* fruit:—~ **del tiempo** seasonal fruit.

frutal *m* fruit tree.

frutilla *f* strawberry.

fuego *m* fire.

fuente *f* fountain; spring; source; large dish.

fuera *adv* out(side); away:—~ **de** *prep* outside:—**i~!** out of the way!

fuerte *m* (*mil*) fortification, fort; forte:—*adj* vigorous, tough; strong; loud; heavy:—*adv* strongly; hard.

fuerza *f* force, strength; (*elec*) power; violence:—**a** ~ **de** by dint of:—~**s** *mpl* troops *pl*.

fugarse *vr* to escape, flee.

fugaz *adj* fleeting.

fullero *m* cardsharper, cheat.

fumar *vt, vi* to smoke.

función *f* function; duties *pl*; show, performance.

funcionar *vi* to function; to work (of a machine).

funcionario/ria *m/f* official; civil servant.

funda *f* case, sheath:—~ **de almohada** pillowcase.

fundar *vt* to found; to establish; to ground.

fundir *vt* to fuse; to melt; to smelt; (*com*) to merge; to bankrupt; (*elec*) to fuse, blow.

fúnebre *adj* mournful, sad; funereal.

furgoneta *f* pick-up (truck).

furioso/sa *adj* furious.

furtivo/va *adj* furtive.

fusible *m* fuse.

fusión *f* fusion; (*com*) merger.

fútbol *m* soccer.

futuro/ra *adj, m* future.

G

gabardina *f* gabardine; raincoat.

gabinete *m* (*pol*) cabinet, study; office (of solicitors, etc).

gafas *fpl* glasses *pl*, spectacles *pl*.

gafe *m* jinx.

gai (*fam*) *adj invar*, *m* gay (*sl*), homosexual.

gajo *m* segment (of orange).

galápago *m* tortoise.

galardón *m* reward, prize.

galbana *f* laziness, idleness.

galera *f* (*mar*) galley; wagon; galley (of type).

galería *f* gallery.

galgo *m* greyhound.

gallardo/da *adj* graceful, elegant; brave, daring.

galleta *f* biscuit.

gallina *f* hen:—*m/f* (*fig*) coward:—~ **ciega** blindman's buff.

gallo *m* cock.

gama *f* (*mus*) scale; (*fig*) range, gamut; doe.

gamba *f* shrimp.

gamberro/rra *m/f* hooligan.

gamuza *f* chamois.

gana *f* desire, wish; appetite; will, longing:—**de buena** ~ with pleasure, voluntarily:—**de mala** ~ unwillingly, with reluctance.

ganado *m* livestock, cattle *pl*:—~ **mayor** horses and mules *pl*:—~ **menor** sheep, goats and hogs *pl*.

ganar *vt* to gain; to win; to earn:—*vi* to win.

gancho *m* hook; crook.

gandul *adj*, *m/f* layabout.

ganga *f* bargain.

ganso/sa *m/f* gander; goose; (*fam*) idiot.

garabatear *vi*, *vt* to scrawl, scribble.

garaje *m* garage.

garantía *f* warranty, guarantee.

garbanzo *m* chickpea, garbanzo.

garbo *m* gracefulness, elegance; stylishness; generosity.

garganta *f* throat, gullet; instep; neck (of a bottle); narrow pass between mountains or rivers.

gárgara *f* gargling, gargle.

garra *f* claw; talon; paw.

garrafa *f* carafe; (gas) cylinder.

garrafal *adj* great, vast, huge.

garrotillo *m* (*med*) croup.

garrucha *f* pulley.

garza *f* heron.

gasa *f* gauze.

gaseoso/sa *adj* fizzy:—*f* lemonade.

gasoil *m* diesel (oil).

gasolina *f* gas.

gasolinera *f* gas station.

gastar *vt* to spend; to expend; to waste; to wear away; to use up:—~**se** *vr* to wear out; to waste.

gata *f* she-cat:—**a** ~**s** on all fours.

gato *m* cat; jack.

gavilán *m* sparrow hawk.

gavilla *f* sheaf of corn.

gaviota *f* seagull.

gazpacho *m* Spanish cold tomato soup.

gelatina *f* jelly; gelatine.

gemelo/la *m/f* twin.

gemir *vi* to groan, moan.

generación *f* generation; progeny, race.

general *m* general:—*adj* general:— **en** ~ generally, in general.

género *m* genus; kind, type; gender; cloth, material:—~**s** *mpl* goods, commodities *pl*.

generoso/sa *adj* noble, generous.

genio *m* nature, character; genius.

genital *adj* genital:—*mpl* **~es** genitals *pl*.

gente *f* people; nation; family.

gentileza *f* grace; charm; politeness.

genuino/na *adj* genuine; pure.

geografía *f* geography.

geología *f* geology.

geometría *f* geometry.

geranio *m* (*bot*) geranium.

gerente *m/f* manager; director.

germinar *vi* to germinate, bud.

gestión *f* management; negotiation.

gesto *m* face; grimace; gesture.

gigante *m* giant:—*adj* gigantic.

gilipollas *adj invar* (*fam*) stupid:—*m/f invar* wimp (*sl*).

gimnasia *f* gymnastics.

ginebra *f* gin.

ginecólogo/ga *m/f* gynecologist.

gira *f* trip, tour.

girar *vt* to turn around; to swivel:—*vi* to go round, revolve.

girasol *m* sunflower.

gitano/na *m/f* Gipsy.

glacial *adj* icy.

glándula *f* gland.

globo *m* globe; sphere; orb; balloon:—**~ aerostatico** air balloon.

glorieta *f* bower, arbor; traffic circle.

glosar *vt* to gloss; to comment on.

glotón/ona *m/f* glutton.

gobierno *m* government.

goce *m* enjoyment.

gol *m* goal.

golondrina *f* swallow.

golosina *f* dainty, titbit; sweet.

golpe *m* blow, stroke, hit; knock; clash; coup:—**de ~** suddenly.

goma *f* gum; rubber; elastic.

gordo/da *adj* fat, plump, big-bellied; first, main; (*fam*) enormous.

gorjear *vi* to twitter, chirp.

gorrión *m* sparrow.

gorro *m* cap; bonnet.

gorrón/ona *m/f* scrounger.

gota *f* drop; (*med*) gout.

gotera *f* leak.

gozar *vt* to enjoy, have, possess:—**~se** *vr* to enjoy oneself, rejoice.

gozne *m* hinge.

gozo *m* joy, pleasure.

grabado *m* engraving.

grabar *vt* to engrave; to record.

gracia *f* grace, gracefulness; wit:—**¡(muchas) ~s!** thanks (very much):—**tener ~** to be funny.

gracioso/sa *adj* graceful; beautiful; funny; pleasing:—*m* comic character.

grada *f* step of a staircase; tier, row:—**~s** *fpl* seats *pl* of stadium or theater.

grado *m* step; degree:—**de buen ~** willingly.

gráfico/ca *adj* graphic:—*m* diagram:—*f* graph.

grajo *m* rook.

gramo *m* gram(me).

gran *adj* = **grande**.

granada *f* pomegranate.

granate *m* garnet (precious stone).

grande *adj* great; big; tall; grand:—*m/f* adult.

grandioso/sa *adj* grand, magnificent.

granel *adv*:—**a ~** in bulk.

granizado *m* iced drink.

granizo *m* hail.

granja *f* farm.

grano *m* grain.

granuja *m/f* rogue; urchin.

grapa *f* staple; clamp.

grasa *f* suet, fat; grease.

gratis *adj* free.

grato/ta *adj* pleasant, agreeable.

gravamen *m* charge, obligation; nuisance; tax.

grave *adj* weighty, heavy; grave, important; serious.

gravilla *f* gravel.

gravoso/sa *adj* onerous, burdensome; costly.

graznar *vi* to croak; to cackle; to quack.

gremio *m* union, guild; society; company, corporation.

greña *f* tangle; shock of hair.

gresca *f* clatter; outcry; confusion; wrangle, quarrel.

grieta *f* crevice, crack, chink.

grifo *m* faucet, tap; gas station.

grillo *m* cricket; bud, shoot.

gripe *f* flu, influenza.

gris *adj* gray.

gritar *vi* to cry out, shout, yell.

grosella *f* redcurrant:—~ **negra** blackcurrant.

grosero/ra *adj* coarse; rude, badmannered.

grúa *f* crane (machine); derrick.

grueso/sa *adj* thick; bulky; large; coarse:—*m* bulk.

grulla *f* crane (bird).

gruñir *vi* to grunt; to grumble; to creak (of hinges, etc).

grupo *m* group.

gruta *f* grotto.

guadaña *f* scythe.

guante *m* glove.

guapo/pa *adj* good-looking; handsome; smart.

guardabosque *m* gamekeeper; ranger.

guardacostas *m invar* coastguard vessel.

guardaespaldas *m/f invar* bodyguard.

guardar *vt* to keep, preserve; to save (money); to guard:—~**se** *vr* to be on one's guard:—~**se de** to avoid, abstain from.

guardarropa *f* wardrobe; cloakroom.

guardia *f* guard; (*mar*) watch; care, custody:—*m/f* guard; police officer:—*m* (*mil*) guardsman.

guarecer *vt* to protect; to shelter:—~**se** *vr* to take refuge.

guarnecer *vt* to provide, equip; to reinforce; to garnish, set (in gold, etc); to adorn.

guasa *f* joke.

gubernativo/va *adj* governmental.

guía *m/f* guide:—*f* guidebook.

guiar *vt* to guide; (*auto*) to steer.

guijarro *m* pebble.

guiñar *vt* to wink.

guinda *f* cherry.

guindilla *f* chilli pepper.

guión *m* hyphen; script (of movie).

guisante *m* (*bot*) pea.

guisar *vt* to cook.

guitarra *f* guitar.

gula *f* gluttony.

gusano *m* maggot, worm.

gustar *vt* to taste; to sample:—*vi* to please, be pleasing:—**me gusta...** I like...

H

haba *f* bean.

haber *vt* to get, lay hands on; to occur:
—*v imp* **hay** there is, there are:—*v
aux* to have:——**~se** *vr* **habérselas
con uno** to have it out with somebody:—*m* income, salary; assets *pl*;
(*com*) credit.

hábil *adj* able, clever, skillful, dexterous, apt.

habitación *f* habitation, abode, rooming house, dwelling, residence; room.

habitar *vt* to inhabit, live in.

hábito *m* dress; habit, custom.

habitual *adj* habitual, customary.

hablar *vt, vi* to speak; to talk.

hacendoso/sa *adj* industrious.

hacer *vt* to make; to do; to put into
practice; to perform; to effect; to
prepare; to imagine; to force; (*mat*)
to amount to, make:—*vi* to act,
behave:——**~se** *vr* to become.

hacha *f* torch; ax, hatchet.

hacia *adv* toward(s); about:——**~ arriba/
abajo** up(wards)/ down(wards).

hada *f* fairy.

halagar *vt* to cajole, flatter.

halcón *m* falcon.

hallar *vt* to find; to meet with; to
discover:——**~se** *vr* to find oneself;
to be.

hambre *f* hunger; famine; longing.

harina *f* flour.

harto/ta *adj* full; fed up:—*adv* enough.

hasta *prep* up to; down to; until, as
far as:—*adv* even.

haya *f* beech tree.

hazaña *f* exploit, achievement.

hebilla *f* buckle.

hebra *f* thread; vein of minerals or
metals; grain of wood.

hebreo/ea *m/f, adj* Hebrew; Israeli:—
m Hebrew language.

hechizar *vt* to bewitch, enchant; to
charm.

hecho/cha *adj* made; done; mature;
ready-to-wear; cooked:—*m* action;
act; fact; matter; event.

hectárea *f* hectare.

helado/da *adj* frozen; glacial, icy;
astonished; astounded:—*m* ice
cream.

helar *vt* to freeze; to congeal; to astonish, amaze:——**~se** *vr* to be frozen; to
turn into ice; to congeal: —*vi* to
freeze; to congeal.

helecho *m* fern.

hélice *f* helix; propeller.

hembra *f* female.

heno *m* hay.

heredar *vt* to inherit.

hereje *m/f* heretic.

herir *vt* to wound, hurt; to beat, strike;
to affect, touch, move; to offend.

hermana *f* sister.

hermano *m* brother:——**~/na** *adj*
matched; resembling.

hermético/ca *adj* hermetic, airtight.

hermoso/sa *adj* beautiful, handsome,
lovely; large, robust.

héroe *m* hero.

herradura *f* horseshoe.

herrero *m* smith.

hervir *vt* to boil; to cook:—*vi* to boil;
to bubble; to seethe.

hiedra *f* ivy.

hiel *f* gall, bile.

hielo *m* frost; ice.

hierba *f* grass; herb.

hierro *m* iron.

hígado *m* liver; (*fig*) courage, pluck.

higiene f hygiene.

higo m fig.

hijo/ja m/f son/daughter; child; offspring.

hilera f row, line, file.

hilo m thread; wire.

hincar vt to thrust in, drive in.

hinchar vt to swell; to inflate; (fig) to exaggerate:—~**se** vr to swell; to become vain.

hinojo m (bot) fennel.

hipo m hiccups pl.

hipócrita adj hypocritical:—m/f hypocrite.

hipódromo m racetrack.

hipoteca f mortgage.

historia f history; tale, story.

historieta f short story; short novel; comic strip.

hocico m snout:—**meter el ~ en todo** to meddle in everything.

hogar m hearth, fireplace; (fig) house, home; family life.

hogaza f large loaf of bread.

hoguera f bonfire; blaze.

hoja f leaf; petal; sheet of paper; blade.

hojalata f tin (plate).

hojaldre f puff pastry.

hojear vt to turn the pages of.

hola excl hello!

holgado/da adj loose, wide, baggy; at leisure; idle, unoccupied; well-off.

hollín m soot.

hombre m man; human being.

hombro m shoulder.

homenaje m homage.

homicidio m murder.

hondo/da adj deep, profound.

honesto/ta adj honest; modest.

hongo m mushroom; fungus.

honor m honor.

honorario/ria adj honorary:—~**s** mpl fees pl.

honra f honor, reverence; selfesteem; reputation; integrity:—~**s funebres** pl funeral honors pl.

hora f hour; time.

horario/ria adj hourly, hour compd:—m schedule.

horchata f tiger-nut milk.

horma f mold, form.

hormiga f ant.

hormigón m concrete.

horno m oven; furnace.

horquilla f pitchfork; hairpin.

hórreo m granary.

horrible adj horrid, horrible.

horror m horror, fright; atrocity.

hortaliza f vegetable.

hospedar vt to put up, lodge; to entertain.

hospicio m orphanage; hospice.

hospital m hospital.

hostal m small hotel.

hostelería f hotel business or trade.

hostia f host; wafer; (fam) whack (sl), punch.

hostil adj hostile; adverse.

hotel m hotel.

hoy adv today; now, nowadays:—**de~ en adelante** from now on, henceforward.

hoyo m hole, pit; excavation.

hoz f sickle; gorge.

hucha f money-box.

hueco/ca adj hollow, concave; empty; vain, ostentatious:—m interval; gap, hole; vacancy.

huelga f strike.

huella f track, footstep.

huérfano/na adj, m/f orphan.

huerta f market garden; irrigated region.

hueso *m* bone; stone, core.
huésped/da *m/f* guest, lodger, roomer; inn-keeper.
huevo *m* egg.
huir *vi* to flee, escape.
humano/na *adj* human; humane, kind.
húmedo/da *adj* humid; wet; damp.
humilde *adj* humble.
humillar *vt* to humble; to subdue:—~**se** *vr* to humble oneself.

humo *m* smoke; fumes *pl.*
humor *m* mood, temper; humor.
hundir *vt* to submerge; to sink; to ruin:—~**se** *vr* to sink, go to the bottom; to collapse; to be ruined.
huraño/ña *adj* shy; unsociable.
hurtadillas *adv:*—**a** ~ by stealth.
hurtar *vt* to steal, rob.
husmear *vt* to scent; to pry into.

I

ictericia *f* jaundice.
ida *f* departure, going:—**(viaje de)** ~ outward journey:—~ **y vuelta** round trip:—~**s y venidas** comings and goings *pl.*
idea *f* idea; scheme.
ídem *pn* ditto.
idéntico/ca *adj* identical.
idioma *m* language.
idiota *m/f* idiot.
idóneo/nea *adj* suitable, fit.
iglesia *f* church.
ignorar *vt* to be ignorant of, not to know.
igual *adj* equal; similar; the same:—**al** ~ equally.
ilegal *adj* illegal, unlawful.
ileso/sa *adj* unhurt.
ilimitado/da *adj* unlimited.
iluminar *vt* to illumine, illuminate, enlighten.
ilusión *f* illusion; hope:—**hacerse** ~**ones** to build up one's hopes.
ilustre *adj* illustrious, famous.
imagen *f* image.
imaginar *vt* to imagine; to think up:—*vi* ~**se** *vr* to imagine.
imán *m* magnet.

imitar *vt* to imitate, copy; to counterfeit.
impaciente *adj* impatient.
impar *adj* odd.
imparcial *adj* impartial.
impedir *vt* to impede, hinder; to prevent.
impeler *vt* to drive, propel; to impel; to incite, stimulate.
impenetrable *adj* impenetrable, impervious; incomprehensible.
impenitente *adj* impenitent.
imperdible *m* safety pin.
imperdonable *adj* unforgivable.
imperfecto/ta *adj* imperfect.
impermeable *adj* waterproof:—*m* raincoat.
imperturbable *adj* imperturbable; unruffled.
implacable *adj* implacable, inexorable.
implicar *vt* to implicate, involve.
imponer *vt* to impose; to command:—~**se** *vr* to assert oneself; to prevail.
impopular *adj* unpopular.
importante *adj* important, considerable.
importar *vi* to be important, matter:—*vt* to import; to be worth.
importe *m* amount, cost.

importunar *vt* to bother, pester.

imposible *adj* impossible; extremely difficult; slovenly.

impostor/ra *m/f* impostor, fraud.

impotencia *f* impotence.

impracticable *adj* impracticable, unworkable.

impreciso/sa *adj* imprecise, vague.

imprenta *f* printing; press; printing office.

imprescindible *adj* essential.

impresión *f* impression; stamp; print; edition.

impresionar *vt* to move; to impress:— ~**se** *vr* to be impressed; to be moved.

imprevisto/ta *adj* unforeseen, unexpected.

imprimir *vt* to print; to imprint; to stamp.

improbable *adj* improbable, unlikely.

improvisar *vt* to extemporize; to improvise.

improviso/sa *adj*:—**de** ~ unexpectedly.

imprudente *adj* imprudent; indiscreet; unwise.

impúdico/ca *adj* shameless; lecherous.

impuesto/ta *adj* imposed:—*m* tax, duty.

impulso *m* impulse; thrust; (*fig*) impulse.

impune *adj* unpunished.

impuro/ra *adj* impure; foul.

inaccesible *adj* inaccessible.

inadvertido/da *adj* unnoticed.

inagotable *adj* inexhaustible.

inaguantable *adj* unbearable, intolerable.

inalterable *adj* unalterable.

inapreciable *adj* imperceptible; invaluable.

inaudito/ta *adj* unheard-of.

inaugurar *vt* to inaugurate.

incalculable *adj* incalculable.

incansable *adj* untiring, tireless.

incapaz *adj* incapable, unable.

incauto/ta *adj* incautious, unwary.

incendio *m* fire.

incentivo *m* incentive.

incertidumbre *f* doubt, uncertainty.

incierto/ta *adj* uncertain, doubtful.

incineración *f* incineration; cremation.

incitar *vt* to incite, excite.

inclemencia *f* inclemency, severity; inclemency (of the weather).

inclinar *vt* to incline; to nod, bow (the head):—~**se** *vr* to bow; to stoop.

incluir *vt* to include, comprise; to incorporate; to enclose.

incluso/sa *adj* included:—*adv* inclusively; even.

incógnito/ta *adj* unknown:—**de** ~ incognito.

incombustible *adj* incombustible, fireproof.

incómodo/da *adj* uncomfortable; annoying; inconvenient.

incomparable *adj* incomparable, matchless.

incompasivo *adj* unsympathetic.

incompleto/ta *adj* incomplete.

incomunicado/da *adj* isolated, cut off; in solitary confinement.

inconcebible *adj* inconceivable.

incondicional *adj* unconditional; whole-hearted; staunch.

inconfundible *adj* unmistakable.

inconsciente *adj* unconscious; thoughtless.

inconstante *adj* inconstant, variable, fickle.

incorporar *vt* to incorporate:—~**se** *vr* to sit up; to join (an organization), become incorporated.

incorrecto/ta *adj* incorrect.
incrédulo/la *adj* incredulous.
increíble *adj* incredible.
incremento *m* increment, increase; growth; rise.
inculcar *vt* to inculcate.
inculto/ta *adj* uncultivated; uneducated; uncouth.
incumbencia *f* obligation; duty.
incurable *adj* incurable; irremediable.
indagar *vt* to inquire into.
indebido/da *adj* undue; illegal, unlawful.
indeciso/sa *adj* hesitant; undecided.
indefenso/sa *adj* defenseless.
indemnizar *vt* to indemnify, compensate.
independiente *adj* independent.
indeterminado/da *adj* indeterminate; indefinite.
indicador *m* indicator; gage.
indicar *vt* to indicate.
índice *m* ratio, rate; hand (of a watch or clock); index, table of contents; catalog; forefinger, index finger.
indicio *m* indication, mark; sign, token; clue.
indiferencia *f* indifference, apathy.
indígena *adj* indigenous, native:—*m/f* native.
indignar *vt* to irritate; to provoke, tease:—~**se** *vr* ~ **por** to get indignant about.
indigno/na *adj* unworthy, contemptible, low.
indirecta *f* innuendo, hint.
indiscreción *f* indiscretion, tactlessness; gaffe.
individual *adj* individual; single (of a room):—*m* (*dep*) singles.
individuo *m* individual.

índole *f* disposition, nature, character; soft, kind.
indolente *adj* indolent, lazy.
indómito/ta *adj* untamed, ungoverned.
inducir *vt* to induce, persuade.
indudable *adj* undoubted; unquestionable.
indultar *vt* to pardon; to exempt.
industria *f* industry; skill.
inédito/ta *adj* unpublished; (*fig*) new.
ineficaz *adj* ineffective; inefficient.
inepto/ta *adj* inept, unfit, useless.
inercia *f* inertia, inactivity.
inerte *adj* inert; dull; sluggish, motionless.
inesperado/da *adj* unexpected, unforeseen.
inevitable *adj* unavoidable.
inexacto/ta *adj* inaccurate, untrue.
inexperto/ta *adj* inexperienced.
infame *adj* infamous.
infancia *f* infancy, childhood.
infantil *adj* infantile; childlike; children's.
infarto *m* heart attack.
infatigable *adj* tireless, untiring.
infectar *vt* to infect.
infeliz *adj* unhappy, unfortunate.
inferior *adj* inferior.
infernal *adj* infernal, hellish.
infiel *adj* unfaithful; disloyal; inaccurate.
infierno *m* hell.
infiltrarse *vr* to infiltrate.
ínfimo/ma *adj* lowest; of very poor quality.
infinidad *f* infinity; immensity.
infinito/ta *adj* infinite; immense.
inflamable *adj* inflammable.
inflar *vt* to inflate, blow up; (*fig*) to exaggerate.
inflexible *adj* inflexible.

influir *vt* to influence.

información *f* information; news; (*mil*) intelligence; investigation, judicial inquiry.

informal *adj* irregular, incorrect; untrustworthy; informal.

informar *vt* to inform; to reveal, make known:—**~se** *vr* to find out:—*vi* to report; (*jur*) to plead; to inform.

informática *f* computer science, information technology.

informe *m* report, statement; piece of information, account:—*adj* shapeless, formless.

infortunio *m* misfortune, ill luck.

infracción *f* infraction; breach, infringement.

infructuoso/sa *adj* fruitless, unproductive, unprofitable.

infundado/da *adj* groundless.

ingeniero/ra *m/f* engineer.

ingenio *m* talent; wit; ingenuity; engine:—**~ de azúcar** sugar mill.

ingenuo/nua *adj* naive.

ingerir *vt* to ingest; to swallow; to consume.

ingle *f* groin.

inglés/esa *adj* English:—*m* English language:—*m/f* Englishman/woman.

ingrato/ta *adj* ungrateful, thankless; disagreeable.

ingresar *vt* to deposit:—*vi* to come in.

inhabilitar *vt* to disqualify, disable.

inhabitable *adj* uninhabitable.

inhibir *vt* to inhibit; to restrain.

iniciar *vt* to initiate; to begin.

ininteligible *adj* unintelligible.

injertar *vt* to graft.

injuriar *vt* to insult, wrong.

injusto/ta *adj* unjust.

inmediaciones *fpl* neighborhood.

inmediatamente *adv* immediately, at once.

inmobiliario/ria *adj* real-estate *compd*:—*f* estate agency.

inmortal *adj* immortal.

inmóvil *adj* immovable, still.

inmueble *m* property:—*adj* **bienes ~s** real estate.

inmundo/da *adj* filthy, dirty; nasty.

inmune *adj* (*med*) immune; free, exempt.

innato/ta *adj* inborn, innate.

innecesario/ria *adj* unnecessary.

innegable *adj* undeniable.

innumerable *adj* innumerable, countless.

inocente *adj* innocent.

inodoro *m* washroom:—**~/ ra** *adj* odorless, without smell.

inofensivo/va *adj* harmless.

inolvidable *adj* unforgettable.

inoxidable *adj*:—**acero ~** stainless steel.

inquietar *vt* to worry, disturb:—**~se** *vr* to worry, get worried.

inquilino/na *m/f* tenant; roomer, lodger.

inquirir *vt* to inquire into, investigate.

inscribir *vt* to inscribe; to list, register.

insecto *m* insect.

insensato/ta *adj* senseless, stupid; mad.

insensible *adj* insensitive; imperceptible; numb.

inseparable *adj* inseparable.

insertar *vt* to insert.

inservible *adj* useless.

insignia *f* badge:—**~s** *fpl* insignia *pl*.

insinuar *vt* to insinuate:—**~se** *vr* **~ en** to worm one's way into.

insípido/da *adj* insipid.

insistir *vi* to insist.

insolación f (med) sunstroke.

insolencia f insolence, rudeness, effrontery.

insólito/ta adj unusual.

insolvente adj insolvent.

insomnio m insomnia.

insondable adj unfathomable; inscrutable.

insoportable adj unbearable.

inspeccionar vt to inspect; to supervize.

inspector/ra m/f inspector; superintendent.

inspirar vt to inspire; (med) to inhale.

instalar vt to install.

instantáneo/nea adj instantaneous:— f snap(shot):—**café ~** instant coffee.

instante m instant:—**al ~** immediately, instantly.

instigar vt to instigate.

instinto m instinct.

instructivo/va adj instructive; educational.

instrumento m instrument; tool, implement.

insuficiente adj insufficient, inadequate.

insulso/sa adj insipid; dull.

insultar vt to insult.

insuperable adj insuperable, insurmountable.

intacto/ta adj untouched; entire; intact.

integral adj integral, whole:—**pan ~** wholewheat bread.

intemperie f:—**a la ~** out in the open.

intencionado/da adj meaningful; deliberate.

intenso/sa adj intense, strong; deep.

intentar vt to try, attempt.

intercalar vt to insert.

intercambio m exchange, swap.

interés m interest; share, part; concern, advantage; profit.

interesar vt to be of interest to, interest:—**~se** vr **~ en** o **por** to take an interest in:—vi to be of interest.

interferir vt to interfere with; to jam (a telephone):—vi to interfere.

interfono m intercom.

interino/na adj provisional, temporary: —m/f temporary holder of a post; stand-in.

interior adj interior, internal:—m interior, inside.

intermedio/dia adj intermediate:—m interval.

interminable adj interminable, endless.

intermitente adj intermittent; m (auto) indicator.

internado m boarding school.

interno/na adj interior, internal:—m/f boarder.

interpretar vt to interpret, explain; (teat) to perform; to translate.

interrogación f interrogation; question mark.

interrogatorio m questioning; (jur) examination; questionnaire.

interrumpir vt to interrupt.

interruptor m switch.

intervenir vt to control, supervise; (com) to audit; (med) to operate on:—vi to participate; to intervene.

intestino/na adj internal, interior:—m intestine.

íntimo/ma adj internal, innermost; intimate, private.

intranquilo/la adj worried.

intransitable adj impassable.

intrépido/da adj intrepid, daring.

intrigar vt, vi to intrigue.

introducir vt to introduce; to insert.

introvertido/da *adj, m/f* introvert.

intruso/sa *adj* intrusive:—*m/f* intruder.

inundar *vt* to inundate, overflow; to flood.

inusitado/da *adj* unusual.

inútil *adj* useless.

inválido/da *adj* invalid, null and void: —*m/f* invalid.

invencible *adj* invincible.

invernadero *m* greenhouse.

inverosímil *adj* unlikely, improbable.

inverso/sa *adj* inverse; inverted; contrary.

invertir *vt* (*com*) to invest; to invert.

investigar *vt* to investigate; to do research into.

invierno *m* winter.

invitar *vt* to invite; to entice; to pay for.

invocar *vt* to invoke.

ir *vi* to go; to walk; to travel:—~**se** *vr* to go away, depart.

ira *f* anger, wrath.

iris *m* iris (eye):—**arco** ~ rainbow.

ironía *f* irony.

irracional *adj* irrational.

irreal *adj* unreal.

irreflexión *f* rashness, thoughtlessness.

irregular *adj* irregular; abnormal.

irremediable *adj* irremediable; incurable.

irresistible *adj* irresistible.

irreverente *adj* irreverent; disrespectful.

irrisorio/ria *adj* derisory, ridiculous.

irritar *vt* to irritate, exasperate; to stir up; to inflame.

isla *f* island, isle.

istmo *m* isthmus.

italiano/na *adj* Italian:—*m* Italian language:—*m/f* Italian.

itinerario *m* itinerary.

izquierdo/da *adj* left; left-handed:—*f* left; left(-wing).

J

jabalí *m* wild boar.

jabón *m* soap.

jaca *f* pony.

jacinto *m* hyacinth.

jadear *vi* to pant.

jaleo *m* racket, uproar.

jamás *adv* never:—**para siempre** ~ for ever.

jamón *m* ham:—~ **de York** cooked ham:—~ **serrano** cured ham.

jaque *m* check (at game of chess):— ~ **mate** checkmate.

jaqueca *f* migraine.

jarabe *m* syrup.

jardín *m* garden.

jarra *f* jug, jar, pitcher:—**en** ~**s, de** ~**s** with hands to the sides.

jaula *f* cage; cell for mad people.

jazmín *m* jasmin.

jefe *m* chief, head, leader:—(*ferro*) ~ **de tren** guard, conductor.

jerarquía *f* hierarchy.

jerigonza *f* jargon, gibberish.

jeringa *f* syringe.

jeroglífico/ca *adj* hieroglyphic:—*m* hieroglyph, hieroglyphic.

jersey *m* sweater, pullover.

jilguero *m* goldfinch.

jinete/ta *m/f* horseman/woman, rider.
jipijapa *m* straw hat.
jirón *m* rag, shred.
jornada *f* journey; day's journey; working day.
jornal *m* day's wage.
jornalero *m* (day) laborer.
joroba *f* hump:—*m/f* hunchback.
jota *f* jot, iota; Spanish dance.
joven *adj* young:—*m/f* youth; young woman.
jovial *adj* jovial, cheerful.
joya *f* jewel:—**s** *fpl* jewelry.
juanete *m* (*med*) bunion.
jubilar *vt* to pension off; to superannuate; to discard:—**se** *vr* to retire.
júbilo *m* joy, rejoicing.
judía *f* bean:—**verde** French bean.
judicial *adj* judicial.
judío/día *adj* Jewish:—*m/f* Jewish man/woman.
juego *m* play; amusement; sport; game; gambling.
jueves *m invar* Thursday.
juez *m/f* judge.

jugar *vt, vi* to play, sport, gamble.
jugo *m* sap, juice.
juguete *m* toy, plaything.
juicio *m* judgement, reason; sanity; opinion.
julio *m* July.
junco *m* (*bot*) rush; junk (Chinese ship).
junio *m* June.
junta *f* meeting; assembly; congress; council.
juntar *vt* to join; to unite:—**se** *vr* to meet, assemble; to draw closer.
junto/ta *adj* joined; united; near; adjacent:—**s** together:—*adv* **todo** ~ all at once.
jurar *vt, vi* to swear.
jurídico/ca *adj* lawful, legal; juridical.
justicia *f* justice; equity.
justificante *m* voucher; receipt.
justo/ta *adj* just; fair, right; exact, correct; tight:—*adv* exactly, precisely; just in time.
juventud *f* youthfulness, youth; young people *pl*.
juzgado *m* tribunal; court.

K

kilogramo *m* kilogram(me).
kilómetro *m* kilometer.

kiosco *m* kiosk.

L

la *art f* the:—*pn* her; you; it.
labio *m* lip; edge.
labor *f* labor, task; needlework; farmwork; ploughing.

laborioso/sa *adj* laborious; hardworking.
labrar *vt* to work; to carve; to farm; (*fig*) to bring about.

laca f lacquer; hairspray.

lacio/cia adj faded, withered; languid; lank (hair).

lacrar vt to seal (with sealing wax).

lactancia f lactation; breast-feeding.

lácteo/tea adj:—**productos** ~**s** dairy products.

ladera f slope.

ladino/na adj cunning, crafty.

lado m side; faction, party; favor, protection; (mil) flank:—**al** ~ **de** beside:—**poner a un** ~ to put aside:—**por todos** ~**s** on all sides.

ladrar vt to bark.

ladrillo m brick.

ladrón/ona m/f thief, robber.

lagar m wine press.

lagartija f (small) lizard.

lagarto m lizard.

lago m lake.

lágrima f tear.

laguna f lake; lagoon; gap.

laico/ca adj lay.

lamentar vt to be sorry about; to lament, regret:—vi ~**se** vr to lament, complain; to mourn.

lamer vt to lick, lap.

lámina f plate, sheet of metal; engraving.

lámpara f lamp.

lana f wool.

lancha f barge, lighter; launch.

langosta f locust; lobster.

lanzar vt to throw; (dep) to bowl, pitch; to launch, fling; (jur) to evict.

lápida f flat stone, tablet.

lápiz m pencil; mechanical pencil.

largamente adv for a long time.

largo/ga adj long; lengthy, generous; copious:—**a la** ~**a** in the end, eventually.

las art fpl the:—pn them; you.

lascivo/va adj lascivious; lewd.

láser m laser.

lástima f compassion, pity; shame.

lastimar vt to hurt; to wound; to feel pity for:—~**se** vr to hurt oneself.

lastre m ballast.

lata f tin; tin can; (fam) nuisance.

latido m (heart)beat.

latifundio m large estate.

latir vi to beat, palpitate.

latitud f latitude.

latón m brass.

latoso/sa adj annoying; boring.

laúd f lute (musical instrument).

laudable adj laudable, praiseworthy.

laurel m (bot) laurel; reward.

lavabo m washbasin; washroom.

lavadora f washing machine.

lavanda f lavender.

lavar vt to wash; to wipe away:—~**se** vr to wash oneself.

laxante m (med) laxative.

lazarillo m:—**perro** ~ guide dog.

lazo m knot; bow; snare, trap; tie; bond.

le pn him; you; (dativo) to him; to her; to it; to you.

leal adj loyal; faithful.

lebrel m greyhound.

lección f reading; lesson; lecture; class.

leche f milk.

lecho m bed; layer.

lechón m sucking pig.

lechuga f lettuce.

lechuza f owl.

leer vt, vi to read.

legado m bequest, legacy; legate.

legal adj legal; trustworthy.

legaña f sleep (in eyes).

legislar vt to legislate.

legítimo/ma adj legitimate, lawful; authentic.

legumbres *fpl* pulses *pl*.
lejano/na *adj* distant, remote; far.
lejía *f* bleach.
lejos *adv* at a great distance, far off.
lelo/la *adj* stupid, ignorant:—*m/f* idiot.
lema *m* motto; slogan.
leña *f* firewood, kindling.
lencería *f* linen, drapery.
lengua *f* tongue; language.
lenguado *m* sole.
lenguaje *m* language.
lente *m/f* lens.
lenteja *f* lentil.
lentilla *f* contact lens.
lento/ta *adj* slow.
león *m* lion.
leopardo *m* leopard.
leotardos *mpl* tights, pantihose.
lesión *f* wound; injury; damage.
letal *adj* mortal, deadly.
letanía *f* litany.
letargo *m* lethargy.
letra *f* letter; handwriting; printing type; draft of a song; bill, draft:—~s *fpl* letters *pl*, learning.
letrero *m* sign; label.
leucemia *f* leukemia.
levadura *f* yeast; brewer's yeast.
levantar *vt* to raise, lift up; to build; to elevate; to hearten, cheer up:—~se *vr* to get up; to stand up.
levante *m* Levant; east; east wind.
levantisco *adj* turbulent, restless.
leve *adj* light; trivial.
léxico *m* vocabulary.
ley *f* law; standard (for metal).
leyenda *f* legend.
liar *vt* to tie, bind; to confuse.
libélula *f* dragonfly.
liberal *adj* liberal, generous:—*m/f* liberal.
libertad *f* liberty, freedom.

libra *f* pound:—~ **esterlina** pound sterling.
libre *adj* free; exempt; vacant.
librería *f* book store.
libreta *f* notebook:—~ **de ahorros** savings book.
libro *m* book.
licencia *f* license; licentiousness.
licenciado/da *adj* licensed:—*m/f* graduate.
lícito/ta *adj* lawful, fair; permissible.
líder *m/f* leader.
liebre *f* hare.
lienzo *f* linen; canvas; face or front of a building.
liga *f* suspender; birdlime; league; coalition; alloy.
ligar *vt* to tie, bind, fasten:—~se *vr* to commit oneself:—*vi* to mix, blend; (*fam*) to pick up.
ligero/ra *adj* light, swift; agile; superficial.
liguero *m* suspender belt.
lijar *vt* to smooth, sandpaper.
lima *f* file.
límite *m* limit, boundary.
limón *m* lemon.
limosna *f* alms *pl*, charity.
limpiar *vt* to clean; to cleanse; to purify; to polish; (*fig*) to clean up.
linaza *f* linseed.
lince *m* lynx.
lindar *vi* to be adjacent.
lindo/da *adj* pretty; lovely.
línea *f* line; cable; outline.
lino *m* flax.
linterna *f* lantern, lamp; torch.
lío *m* bundle, parcel; (*fam*) muddle, mess.
liquidar *vt* to liquidate; to settle (accounts).
líquido/da *adj* liquid.

lirio *m* (*bot*) iris.

lirón *m* dormouse; (*fig*) sleepyhead.

liso/sa *adj* plain, even, flat, smooth.

lisonja *f* adulation, flattery.

lista *f* list; register; catalog; menu.

listo/ta *adj* ready; smart, clever.

litera *f* berth; bunk, bunk bed.

litigio *m* lawsuit.

litoral *adj* coastal:—*m* coast.

litro *m* liter (measure).

liviano/na *adj* light; fickle; trivial.

llama *f* flame; llama (animal).

llamar *vt* to call; to name; to summon; to ring up, telephone:—*vi* to knock at the door; to ring up, telephone:—**~se** *vr* to be named.

llano/na *adj* plain; even, level, smooth; clear, evident:—*m* plain.

llanta *f* (wheel) rim; tire; inner (tube).

llanura *f* evenness, flatness; plain, prairie.

llave *f* key:—**~ maestra** master key.

llegar *vi* to arrive:—**~ a** to reach:—**~se** *vr* to come near, approach.

llenar *vt* to fill; to cover; to fill out (a form); to satisfy, fulfil:—**~se** *vr* to gorge oneself.

llevar *vt* to take; to wear; to carry; to convey, transport; to drive; to lead; to bear:—**~se** *vr* to carry off, take away.

llorar *vt, vi* to weep, cry.

llover *vi* to rain.

lluvia *f* rain.

lo *pn* it; him; you:—*art* the.

lobo *m* wolf.

lóbulo *m* lobe.

local *adj* local:—*m* place, site.

loco/ca *adj* mad:—*m/f* mad person.

locutor/ra *m/f* (*rad*) announcer; (*TV*) newsreader.

lodo *m* mud, mire.

lograr *vt* to achieve; to gain, obtain.

lombarda *f* red cabbage.

lombriz *f* worm.

lomo *m* loin; back (of an animal); spine (of a book):—**llevar** *o* **traer a ~** to carry on the back.

lona *f* canvas.

loncha *f* slice; rasher.

longaniza *f* pork sausage.

longitud *f* length; longitude.

loro *m* parrot.

los *art mpl* the:—*pn* them; you.

losa *f* flagstone.

lote *m* lot; portion.

loza *f* crockery.

lucero *m* morning star, bright star.

luchar *vi* to struggle; to wrestle.

luciérnaga *f* glowworm.

lucir *vt* to light (up); to show off:—*vi* to shine:—**~se** *vr* to make a fool of oneself.

luego *adv* next; afterward(s):—**desde ~** of course.

lugar *m* place, spot; village; reason:—**en ~ de** instead of, in lieu of.

lúgubre *adj* lugubrious; sad, gloomy.

lujo *m* luxury; abundance.

lujuria *f* lust.

lumbre *f* fire; light.

luna *f* moon; glass plate for mirrors; lens.

lunar *m* mole, spot:—*adj* lunar.

lunes *m invar* Monday.

lupa *f* magnifying glass.

lupanar *m* brothel.

luto *m* mourning (dress); grief.

luz *f* light.

M

maceta *f* flowerpot.

machacar *vt* to pound, crush:—*vi* to insist, go on.

macho *adj* male; (*fig*) virile:—*m* male; (*fig*) he-man.

macizo/za *adj* massive; solid:—*m* mass, chunk.

madera *f* wood; lumber.

madrastra *f* stepmother.

madre *f* mother; womb.

madreselva *f* honeysuckle.

madriguera *f* burrow; den.

madrugar *vi* to get up early; to get ahead.

maduro/ra *adj* ripe, mature.

maestro *m* master; teacher:—~/ **tra** *adj* masterly, skilled; principal.

magia *f* magic.

magisterio *m* teaching; teaching profession; teachers *pl*.

magnetofón, magnetófono *m* tape recorder.

magnífico/ca *adj* magnificent, splendid.

mago/ga *m/f* magician.

magullar *vt* to bruise; to damage; to bash (*sl*).

mahometano/na *m/f, adj* Muslim.

maíz *m* maize, Indian corn.

majadero/ra *adj* dull; silly, stupid:—*m* idiot.

majo/ja *adj* nice; attractive; smart.

majuelo *m* vine newly planted; hawthorn.

mal *m* evil; hurt; harm, damage; misfortune; illness:—*adj* (before masculine nouns) bad.

malcriado/da *adj* rude, ill-behaved; naughty; spoiled.

maldad *f* wickedness.

maldecir *vt* to curse.

maldito/ta *adj* wicked; damned, cursed.

malecón *m* pier.

maleducado/da *adj* bad-mannered, rude.

malestar *m* discomfort; (*fig*) uneasiness; unrest.

maleta *f* suitcase; (*auto*) trunk.

maleza *f* weeds *pl*; thicket.

malgastar *vt* to waste, ruin.

malhablado/da *adj* foul-mouthed.

malhechor/ra *m/f* malefactor; criminal.

malhumorado/da *adj* cross, badtempered.

malla *f* mesh, network:—~**s** *fpl* leotard.

malo/la *adj* bad, ill; wicked:—*m/f* villain.

maltratar *vt* to ill-treat, abuse, mistreat.

malva *f* (*bot*) mallow.

malvado/da *adj* wicked, villainous.

mama *f* teat; breast.

mamá *f* (*fam*) mum, mummy.

mamar *vt, vi* to suck.

mamífero *m* mammal.

manada *f* flock, herd; pack; crowd.

manantial *m* source, spring; origin.

manchar *vt* to stain, soil.

manco/ca *adj* one-armed; onehanded; maimed; faulty.

mancomunidad *f* union, fellowship; community; (*jur*) joint responsibility.

mandar *vt* to command, order; to bequeath; to send.

mandarina *f* tangerine.

mandíbula *f* jaw.

mandil *m* apron.

manera *f* manner, way; fashion; kind.

manga *f* sleeve; hose.

mango *m* handle; mango.

manguera *f* hose; pipe.

maní *m* peanut.

manifestación *f* manifestation; show; demonstration; mass meeting.

manifestar *vt* to manifest, declare.

maniobrar *vt* to maneuvre; to handle.

manipular *vt* to manipulate.

maniquí *m* dummy:—*m/f* model.

manivela *f* crank.

mano *f* hand; hand (of clock, etc); foot, paw (of animal); coat (of paint); lot, series; hand (at game):—**a ~** by hand:—**a ~s llenas** liberally, generously.

manojo *m* handful, bunch.

manopla *f* wash cloth; mitten; gauntlet.

manosear *vt* to handle; to mess up.

manso/sa *adj* tame; gentle, soft.

manta *f* blanket.

manteca *f* fat:—**~ de cerdo** lard.

mantel *m* tablecloth.

mantener *vt* to maintain, support; to nourish; to keep:—**~se** *vr* to hold one's ground; to support oneself.

mantequilla *f* butter.

manzana *f* apple.

manzanilla *f* camomile; camomile tea; manzanilla sherry.

maña *f* handiness, dexterity, cleverness, cunning; habit, custom; trick.

mañana *f* morning:—*adv* tomorrow.

mapa *m* map.

maquillar *vt* to make up:—**~se** *vr* to put on make-up.

máquina *f* machine; (*ferro*) engine; camera; (*fig*) machinery; plan, project.

maquinilla *f:*—**~ de afeitar** razor.

maquinista *m* (*ferro*) train driver; operator; (*mar*) engineer.

mar *m/f* sea.

maravilla *f* wonder.

marca *f* mark; stamp; make, brand.

marcar *vt* to mark; to dial; to score; to record; to set (hair):—*vi* to score; to dial.

marchar *vi* to go; to work:—**~se** *vr* to go away.

marco *m* frame; framework; (*dep*) goalposts *pl*.

marea *f* tide.

marear *vt* (*mar*) to sail, navigate; to annoy, upset:—**~se** *vr* to feel sick; to feel faint; to feel dizzy.

marfil *m* ivory.

margarita *f* daisy.

margen *m* margin; border:—*f* bank (of river).

marido *m* husband.

marinero/ra *adj* sea *compd*; seaworthy:—*m* sailor.

marioneta *f* puppet.

mariposa *f* butterfly.

mariquita *f* ladybird.

marisco *m* shellfish *pl*.

mármol *m* marble.

marrano *m* hog, boar.

marrón *adj* brown.

martes *m invar* Tuesday.

martillo *m* hammer.

marzo *m* March.

mas *adv* but, yet.

más *adv* more; most; besides, moreover:—**a ~ tardar** at latest:—**sin ~ ni ~** without more ado.

masa *f* dough, paste; mortar; mass.

mascar *vt* to chew.

máscara *m/f* masked person:—*f* mask.

mascullar *vt* to mumble, mutter.

mástil *m* (*mar*) mast.

mastín *m* mastiff.

mata f shrub; sprig, blade; grove, group of trees; mop of hair.

matadero m slaughterhouse.

matar vt to kill; to execute; to murder:—~**se** vr to kill oneself, commit suicide.

matasellos m invar postmark.

mate m checkmate:—adj matt.

material adj material, physical:—m equipment, materials pl.

maternidad f motherhood.

matinal adj morning compd.

matiz m shade of color; shading.

matrícula f register, list; (auto) registration number; license plate.

matrimonio m marriage, matrimony.

matriz f matrix; womb; mold, form.

maullar vi to mew.

mayo m May.

mayor adj main, chief; (mus) major; biggest; eldest; greater, larger; elderly:—m chief, boss; adult:—**al por ~** wholesale:—~**es** mpl forefathers.

mayoría f majority, greater part:—~ **de edad** coming of age.

mayúsculo/la adj (fig) tremendous:—f capital letter.

mazo m bunch; club, mallet; bat.

mazorca f ear of corn.

me pn me; to me.

mear vi (fam) to pee, piss (sl).

mecanógrafo/fa m/f typist.

mecer vt to rock; to dandle (a child).

mechar vt to lard; to stuff.

mechón m lock of hair; large bundle of threads or fibres.

media f stocking; sock; average.

medianoche f midnight.

mediante prep by means of.

mediar vi to intervene; to mediate.

medicamento m medicine.

médico/ca adj medical:—m/f doctor.

medida f measure.

medio/dia adj half:—**a medias** partly:—m middle; average; way, means; medium.

mediodía m noon, midday.

medir vt to measure:—~**se** vr to be moderate.

medrar vi to grow, thrive, prosper; to improve.

médula f marrow; essence, substance; pith.

medusa f jellyfish.

mejilla f cheek.

mejillón m mussel.

mejor adj, adv better; best.

mejorar vt to improve, ameliorate; to enhance:—vi to improve; (med) to recover, get better:—~**se** vr to improve, get better.

melenudo/da adj long-haired.

melindroso/sa adj prudish, finicky.

mella f notch in edged tools; gap.

mellizo/za adj, m/f twin.

melocotón m peach.

meloso/sa adj honeyed; mellow.

membrete m letter head.

membrillo m quince; quince tree.

memoria f memory; report; record:—~**s** fpl memoirs pl.

mendigar vt to beg.

menear vt to move from place to place; (fig) to handle:—~**se** vr to move; to shake; to sway.

menguante f waning.

meñique m little finger.

menor m/f young person, juvenile:—adj less; smaller; minor:—**al por ~** retail.

menos adv less; least:—**a lo ~** o **por lo ~** at least:—prep except; minus.

menospreciar vt to undervalue; to despise, scorn.

mensaje m message.

mensual *adj* monthly.

menta *f* mint.

mente *f* mind; understanding.

mentecato/ta *adj* silly, stupid:—*m/f* idiot.

mentir *vt* to feign; to pretend:—*vi* to lie.

mentira *f* lie, falsehood.

menudo/da *adj* small; minute; petty, insignificant:—**a ~** frequently, often.

mercader *m* dealer, trader.

mercado *m* market; marketplace.

mercancía *f* commodity:—**~s** *fpl* goods *pl*, merchandise.

mercurio *m* mercury.

merecer *vt* to deserve, merit.

meridional *adj* southern.

merienda *f* (light) tea; afternoon snack; picnic.

merluza *f* hake.

mermelada *f* jam.

mero *m* pollack (fish):—**~/ra** *adj* mere, pure.

mes *m* month.

mesa *f* table; desk; plateau:—**~ redonda** round table.

mestizo/za *adj* of mixed race; cross-bred:—*m/f* half-caste.

meta *f* goal; finish.

metal *m* metal; (*mus*) brass; timbre (of voice).

meter *vt* to place, put; to insert, put in; to involve; to make, cause:—**~se** *vr* to meddle, interfere.

método *m* method.

metro *m* meter; subway.

mezclar *vt* to mix:—**~se** *vr* to mix; to mingle.

mezquino/na *adj* mean; smallminded, petty; wretched.

mezquita *f* mosque.

mi *adj* my.

mí *pn* me; myself.

miedo *m* fear, dread.

miel *f* honey.

miembro *m* member.

mientras *adv* meanwhile:—*conj* while; as long as.

miércoles *m invar* Wednesday.

mierda *f* (*fam*) shit (*sl*).

miga *f* crumb:—**~s** *fpl* fried bread-crumbs *pl*.

mijo *m* (*bot*) millet.

mil *m* one thousand.

milagro *m* miracle, wonder.

milésimo/ma *adj, m* thousandth.

milímetro *m* millimeter.

milla *f* mile.

millión *m* million.

mimar *vt* to spoil, pamper.

mimbre *m* wicker.

mimo *m* caress; spoiling; mime.

mina *f* mine; underground passage.

minero/ra *m/f* miner.

minifalda *f* miniskirt.

mínimo/ma *adj* minimum.

minoría *f* minority.

minucioso/sa *adj* meticulous; very detailed.

minúsculo/la *adj* minute:—*f* small letter.

minusválido/da *adj* (physically) handicapped:—*m/f* (physically) handicapped person.

minuto *m* minute.

mío/mía *adj* mine.

miope *adj* short-sighted.

mirar *vt* to look at; to observe; to consider:—*vi* to look:—**~se** *vr* to look at oneself; to look at one another.

mirlo *m* blackbird.

misa *f* mass:—**~ del gallo** midnight mass.

miserable *adj* miserable; mean; squalid (place); (*fam*) despicable:— *m/f* rotter.

misericordia *f* mercy.

mismo/ma *adj* same; very.

mitad *f* half; middle.

mitin *m* (political) rally.

mixto/ta *adj* mixed.

mobiliario *m* furniture.

mochila *f* backpack.

mochuelo *m* red owl.

moco *m* snot (*sl*), mucus.

moda *f* fashion, style.

modales *mpl* manners *pl*.

modelo *m* model, pattern.

módico/ca *adj* moderate.

modificar *vt* to modify.

modisto/ta *m/f* dressmaker.

modo *m* mode, method, manner.

modorra *f* drowsiness.

mofarse *vr*:—~ **de** to mock, scoff at.

moflete *m* fat cheek.

moho *m* rust; mold, mildew.

mojar *vt* to wet, moisten:—~**se** *vr* to get wet.

mojón *m* landmark.

molde *m* mold; pattern; model.

moler *vt* to grind, pound; to tire out; to annoy, bore.

molestar *vt* to annoy, bother; to trouble:—*vi* to be a nuisance.

molino *m* mill.

momentáneo/nea *adj* momentary.

momento *m* moment.

momia *f* mummy.

mondadientes *m invar* toothpick.

mondar *vt* to clean; to cleanse; to peel:—~**se** *vr* ~ **de risa** (*fam*) to split one's sides laughing.

mondo/da *adj* clean; pure:—~ **y lirondo** bare, plain; pure and simple.

moneda *f* money; currency; coin.

monja *f* nun.

mono/na *adj* lovely; pretty; nice:— *m/f* monkey; ape:—*mpl* dungarees *pl*; overalls *pl*.

monstruo *m* monster.

montaje *m* assembly; decor (of theater); montage.

montaña *f* mountain.

montar *vt* to mount, get on (a bicycle, horse, etc); to assemble, put together; to overlap; to set up (a business); to beat, whip (in cooking): —*vi* to mount; to ride:—~ **a** to amount to.

monte *m* mountain; woodland:—~ **alto** forest:—~ **bajo** scrub.

montón *m* heap, pile; mass:—**a ~ones,** abundantly, by the score.

montura *f* mount; saddle.

monzón *m* monsoon.

mora *f* blackberry.

morado/da *adj* violet, purple.

morcilla *f* blood sausage.

mordaz *adj* biting, scathing; pungent.

mordaza *f* gag; clamp.

morder *vt* to bite; to nibble; to corrode, eat away.

moreno/na *adj* brown; swarthy; dark-skinned.

morir *vi* to die; to expire; to die down:—~**se** *vr* to die; (*fig*) to be dying.

morisco/ca *adj* Moorish.

moroso/sa *adj* slow, sluggish; (*com*) slow to pay up.

morral *m* haversack.

morro *m* snout; nose (of plane, etc).

morsa *f* walrus.

mortal *adj* mortal; fatal, deadly.

mosca *f* fly.

mosquearse *vr* (*fam*) to get cross; (*fam*) to take offence.

mosquitero *m* mosquito net.

mosquito *m* gnat, mosquito.

mostaza *f* mustard.

mosto *m* must, grape juice.

mostrador *m* counter.

mostrar *vt* to show, exhibit; to explain:—~**se** *vr* to appear, show oneself.

mote *m* nickname.

motivo *m* motive, cause, reason.

moto (*fam*), **motocicleta** *f* motorcycle.

motor *m* engine, motor.

mover *vt* to move; to shake; to drive; (*fig*) to cause:—~**se** *vr* to move; (*fig*) to get a move on.

móvil *adj* mobile, movable; moving:— *m* motive.

mozo/za *adj* young:—*m/f* youth, young man/girl; waiter/waitress.

muchacho/a *m/f* boy/girl:—*f* maid, maidservant.

mucho/cha *adj* a lot of, much:—*adv* much, a lot; long.

mudar *vt* to change; to shed:—~**se** *vr* to change one's clothes; to change house:—*vi* to change;

mudo/da *adj* dumb; silent, mute.

mueble *m* piece of furniture:—~**s** *mpl* furniture.

mueca *f* grimace, funny face.

muela *f* tooth, molar.

muelle *m* spring; regulator; quay.

muérdago *m* (*bot*) mistletoe.

muerte *f* death.

mujer *f* woman.

mulato *adj* mulatto.

muleta *f* crutch.

mullido/da *adj* soft; springy.

mulo/la *m/f* mule.

multa *f* fine, penalty.

mundial *adj* worldwide; world *compd*.

mundo *m* world.

muñeca *f* wrist; child's doll.

municipio *m* town council; municipality.

murciélago *m* bat.

murmullo *m* murmur, mutter.

murmurar *vi* to murmur; to gossip.

muro *m* wall.

músculo *m* muscle.

museo *m* museum.

musgo *m* moss.

música *f* music.

muslo *m* thigh.

mustio/tia *adj* parched, withered; sad, sorrowful.

mutuo/tua *adj* mutual, reciprocal.

muy *adv* very; too; greatly:—~ **ilustre** most illustrious.

N

nabo *m* turnip.

nácar *m* mother-of-pearl, nacre.

nacer *vi* to be born; to bud, shoot (of plants); to rise; to grow.

nacimiento *m* birth; nativity.

nada *f* nothing:—*adv* no way, not at all, by no means.

nadar *vi* to swim.

nadie *pn* nobody, no one.

nafta *f* gas.

nalgas *fpl* buttocks *pl*.

naranja *f* orange.

nariz *f* nose.

narrar *vt* to narrate, tell.

nata *f* cream.

natillas *fpl* custard.

naturaleza *f* nature.

naufragar *vi* to be shipwrecked; to suffer ruin in one's affairs.

náutica *f* navigation.

navaja *f* penknife; razor.

nave *f* ship; nave; warehouse.

navegar *vt, vi* to navigate; to sail; to fly.

Navidad *f* Christmas.

nebuloso/sa *adj* misty; cloudy; nebulous; foggy; hazy; drizzling:—*f* nebula.

neceser *m* toilet bag; holdall.

necesitar *vt* to need:—*vi* to want, to need.

necio/cia *adj* ignorant; stupid, foolish; imprudent.

nefasto/ta *adj* unlucky.

negado/da *adj* incapable, unfit.

negar *vt* to deny; to refuse:—*~se vr* **~ a hacer** to refuse to do.

negocio *m* business, affair; transaction; firm; place of business.

negro/gra *adj* black:—*m* black:—*m/f* Black.

nene *m*, **nena** *f* baby.

neto/ta *adj* neat, pure; net.

neumático/ca *adj* pneumatic:—*m* tire.

neutro/tra *adj* neutral; neuter.

nevar *vi* to snow.

nevera *f* icebox.

ni *conj* neither, nor.

nido *m* nest; hiding place.

niebla *f* fog; mist.

nieta *f* granddaughter.

nieto *m* grandson.

nieve *f* snow.

niña *f* little girl; pupil, (of eye).

ningún, **ninguno/na** *adj* no:—*pn* nobody; none; not one; neither.

niño/ña *adj* childish:—*m/f* child; infant:—**desde ~** from infancy, from a child:—*m* boy.

nitidez *f* clarity; brightness; sharpness.

nivel *m* level; standard; height:—**a ~** perfectly level.

no *adv* no; not:—*excl* no!

no obstante *adv* nevertheless, notwithstanding.

noche *f* night; evening; darkness:— **~ buena** Christmas Eve:—**~ vieja** New Year's Eve:—**ibuenas ~s!** good night!

noción *f* notion, idea.

nocivo/va *adj* harmful.

nogal *m* walnut tree.

nombrar *vt* to name; to nominate; to appoint.

nombre *m* name; title; reputation.

nómina *f* list; (*com*) payroll.

non *adj* odd, uneven:—*m* odd number.

nor(d)este *adj* northeast, northeastern:—*m* northeast.

nórdico/ca *adj* northern; Nordic.

noria *f* water wheel; big wheel.

noroeste *adj* northwest, northwestern:—*m* northwest.

norte *adj* north, northern:—*m* north; (*fig*) rule, guide.

nos *pn* us; to us; for us; from us; to ourselves.

nosotros/tras *pn* we; us.

nostalgia *f* homesickness.

notar *vt* to note; to mark; to remark:—*~se vr* to be obvious.

noticia *f* information; note:—*~s fpl* news.

noticiario *m* newsreel; news bulletin.

notificar *vt* to notify, inform.

novato/ta *adj* inexperienced:—*m/f* beginner.

novecientos/tas *adj* nine hundred.

novedad *f* novelty; modernness; newness; piece of news; change.

noveno/na *adj* ninth.

noventa *adj, m* ninety.

novia *f* bride; girlfriend; fiancée.

noviembre *m* November.

novio *m* bridegroom; boyfriend; fiancé.

nube *f* cloud.

nublado/da *adj* cloudy:—*m* storm cloud.

nuca *f* nape (of the neck); scruff of the neck.

nudillo *m* knuckle.

nudo *m* knot.

nuera *f* daughter-in-law.

nuestro/tra *adj* our:—*pn* ours.

nueve *m, adj* nine.

nuevo/va *adj* new; modern; fresh:—*f* piece of news:—**¿que hay de ~?** is there any news?, what's new?

nuez *f* nut; walnut; Adam's apple:— **~ moscada** nutmeg.

número *m* number; cipher.

nunca *adv* never.

nutria *f* otter.

nutrir *vt* to nourish; to feed.

Ñ

ñato/ta *adj* snub-nosed.

ñoño/ña *adj* insipid; spineless; silly.

ñoñeria *f* insipidness.

O

o *conj* or; either.

obedecer *vt* to obey.

obeso/sa *adj* obese, fat.

objetar *vi* to object.

objeto *m* object; aim.

obligar *vt* to force:—**~se** *vr* to bind oneself.

obra *f* work; building, construction; play:—**por ~ de** thanks to.

obrero/ra *adj* working; labor *compd:* —*m/f* worker; laborer.

obsequiar *vt* to lavish attention on:— **~con** to present with.

observar *vt* to observe; to notice.

obstáculo *m* obstacle, impediment.

obstinarse *vr* to be obstinate:—**~ en** to persist in.

obstruir *vt* to obstruct:—**~se** *vr* to be blocked up, be obstructed.

obtener *vt* to obtain; to gain.

ocasión *f* occasion, opportunity.

ocasionar *vt* to cause, occasion.

occidente *m* occident, west.

océano *m* ocean.

ochenta *m, adj* eighty.

ocho *m, adj* eight.

ochocientos *m, adj* eight hundred.

ocio *m* leisure; pastime.

octavilla *f* pamphlet.

octavo/va *adj* eighth.

octubre *m* October.

ocultar *vt* to hide, conceal.

ocupar *vt* to occupy; to hold (office):—**~se** *vr* **~ de**, **~ en** to concern oneself with; to look after.

ocurrencia *f* event; bright idea.

ocurrir *vi* to occur, happen.

odiar *vt* to hate:—**~se** *vr* to hate one another.

oeste *adj* west, western:—*m* west.

ofender *vt* to offend; to injure:—**~se** *vr* to be vexed; to take offence.

oficina f office.

oficio m employment, occupation; ministry; function; trade, business.

ofrecer vt to offer; to present; to exhibit:—~**se** vr to offer oneself; to occur, present itself.

oído m hearing; ear.

oír vt, vi to hear; to listen (to).

ojal m buttonhole.

ojalá conj if only!, would that!

ojear vt to eye, view; to glance.

ojera f bag under the eyes.

ojo m eye; sight; eye of a needle; arch of a bridge.

ola f wave.

oler vt to smell, scent:—vi to smell:— ~ **a** to smack of.

olfato m sense of smell.

olivo m olive tree.

olla f pan; stew:—~ **exprés**, ~ **a presion** pressure cooker.

olmo m elm tree.

olor m smell, odor; scent.

olvidar vt to forget.

ombligo m navel.

once m, adj eleven.

onda f wave.

opaco/ca adj opaque; dark.

opinar vt to think:—vi to give one's opinion.

oponer vt to oppose:—~**se** vr to be opposed:—~ **a** to oppose.

oposición f opposition:—~**ones** fpl public examinations pl.

oprimir vt to oppress; to crush; to press; to squeeze.

optar vt to choose, elect.

optativo/va adj optional.

óptimo/ma adj best.

opuesto/ta adj opposite; contrary; adverse.

orar vi to pray.

ordenado/da adj methodical; tidy.

ordenador m computer.

ordenanza f order; statute, ordinance; ordination.

ordenar vt to arrange; to order; to ordain:—~**se** vr to take holy orders.

ordeñar vt to milk.

oreja f ear.

orgullo m pride, haughtiness.

oriental adj oriental, eastern.

orientar vt to orient; to point; to direct; to guide:—~**se** vr to get one's bearings; to decide on a course of action.

orificio m orifice; mouth; aperture.

orilla f limit, border, margin; edge (of cloth); shore.

orín m rust.

orina f urine.

orinal m chamber pot.

oro m gold; ~**s** mpl diamonds pl (cards).

ortiga f (bot) nettle.

oruga f (bot) caterpillar.

orzuelo m (med) stye.

os pn you; to you.

osa f she-bear:—**O~ Mayor/Menor** Great/Little Bear.

osar vi to dare, venture.

oscuro/ra adj obscure; dark.

oso m bear:—~ **blanco** polar bear.

ostentar vt to show:—vi to boast, brag.

ostra f oyster.

otoño m fall, autumn.

otorgar vt to concede; to grant.

otorrino/na, otorrinolaringólogo/ ga m/f ear, nose and throat specialist.

otro/tra adj another; other.

oveja f sheep.

ovillo m ball of wool.

óvulo m ovum.

oxidar vt to rust:—~**se** vr to go rusty.

oyente m/f listener, hearer.

P

pacificar *vt* to pacify, appease.

pacotilla *f:*—**de** ~ third-rate; cheap.

pactar *vt* to covenant; to contract; to stipulate.

padecer *vt* to suffer; to sustain (an injury); to put up with.

padrastro *m* stepfather.

padre *m* father:—~**s** *mpl* parents *pl.*

pagar *vt* to pay; to pay for; (*fig*) to repay:—*vi* to pay.

página *f* page.

pago *m* payment; reward.

país *m* country; region.

paisaje *m* landscape.

paisano/na *adj* of the same country:—*m/f* fellow countryman/woman.

paja *f* straw; (*fig*) trash.

pájaro *m* bird; sly, acute fellow.

pajita *f* (drinking) straw.

pala *f* spade, shovel.

palabra *f* word:—**de** ~ by word of mouth.

paladar *m* palate; taste, relish.

palanca *f* lever.

palangana *f* basin.

palco *m* box (in a theater).

paleto/ta *m/f* rustic.

pálido/da *adj* pallid, pale.

palillo *m* small stick; toothpick:—~**s** *mpl* chopsticks *pl.*

paliza *f* beating, thrashing.

palma *f* palm tree; palm of the hand; palm leaf.

palmada *f* slap, clap:—~**s** *fpl* clapping of hands, applause.

palmera *f* palm tree.

palo *m* stick; cudgel; blow given with a stick; post; mast; bat; suit (at cards):—~**s** *mpl* masting.

paloma *f* pigeon, dove:—~ **torcaz** ring dove:—~ **zorita** wood pigeon.

palomilla *f* moth; wing nut; angle iron.

palpar *vt* to feel, touch.

palta *f* avocado (pear).

pámpano *m* vine branch.

pan *m* bread; loaf; food in general.

pana *f* corduroy.

pañal *m* diaper, nappy.

pandereta *f* tambourine.

pandilla *f* group; gang; clique.

paño *m* cloth; piece of cloth; duster, rag.

pantalla *f* screen; lampshade.

pantalón *m,* **pantalones** *mpl* trousers, pants *pl.*

pantano *m* marsh; reservoir; obstacle, difficulty.

pantorrilla *f* calf (of the leg).

pañuelo *m* handkerchief.

panza *f* belly, paunch.

papá *m* (*fam*) dad, pop.

papada *f* double chin.

papel *m* paper; writing; part, role (in a play):—~ **de estraza** brown paper: —~ **sellado** stamped paper.

papeleo *m* red tape.

paperas *fpl* mumps.

paquete *m* packet; parcel; package tour.

par *adj* equal; alike; even:—*m* pair; couple; peer:—**sin** ~ matchless.

para *prep* for; to, in order to; towards.

parabrisas *m invar* windshield.

paracaídas *m invar* parachute.

parada *f* halt; suspension; pause; stop; shutdown; stopping place:—~ **de autobús** bus stop.

parado/da *adj* motionless; at a standstill; stopped; standing (up); unemployed.

paraguas *m invar* umbrella.

parar *vi* to stop, halt:—*vt* to stop, detain:—**sin ~** instantly, without delay:—**~se** *vr* to stop, halt; to stand up.

parecer *m* opinion, advice, counsel; countenance, air, mien:—*vi* to appear; to seem:—**~se** *vr* **~ a** to resemble.

parecido/da *adj* resembling, like.

pared *f* wall:—**~ medianera** party wall.

pareja *f* pair, couple, brace.

pariente/ta *m/f* relative, relation.

parir *vt* to give birth to:—*vi* to give birth.

paro *m* strike; unemployment.

párpado *m* eyelid.

parra *f* vine raised on stakes or nailed to a wall.

párrafo *m* paragraph.

parrilla *f* grill; grille.

parte *m* message; report:—*f* part; side; party:—**de ocho dias a esta ~** within these last eight days:—**de ~ a ~** from side to side, through and through.

partera *f* midwife.

particular *adj* particular, special:—*m* private individual; particular matter or subject treated upon.

partida *f* departure; party; item in an account; parcel; game.

partido *m* party; match; team.

partir *vt* to part; to divide, separate; to cut; to break:—*vi* to depart:—**~se** *vr* to break (in two, etc).

parvulario *m* nursery school.

pasa *f* raisin.

pasadizo *m* narrow passage; narrow, covered way.

pasado/da *adj* past; bad; overdone; out of date:—**~ mañana** the day after tomorrow:—**la semana pasada** last week:—*m* past.

pasaje *m* passage; fare; passengers *pl*.

pasajero/ra *adj* transient; transitory; fugitive:—*m/f* traveler; passenger.

pasamanos *m invar* (hand)rail; bannister.

pasar *vt* to pass; to surpass; to suffer; to strain; to dissemble:—*vi* to pass; to happen:—**~se** *vr* to go over (to another party); to go bad or off.

pasarela *f* footbridge; gangway.

pasatiempo *m* pastime, amusement.

Pascua *f* Passover; Easter.

pasear *vt* to walk:—*vi* **~se** *vr* to walk; to walk about.

pasmar *vt* to amaze; to numb; to chill:—**~se** *vr* to be astonished.

paso *m* pace, step; passage; manner of walking; flight of steps; accident:— (*ferro*) **~ a nivel** grade crossing:—**al ~** on the way, in passing.

pasta *f* paste; dough; pastry; (*fam*) dough:—**~s** *fpl* pastries *pl*; pasta: **—~ de dientes** toothpaste.

pastel *m* cake; pie; crayon (for drawing).

pastilla *f* bar (of soap); tablet, pill.

pastor *m* shepherd; pastor.

pata *f* leg (of animal or furniture); foot: **—meter la ~** to put one's foot in it.

patata *f* potato.

patear *vt* to kick; to stamp on.

patillas *fpl* sideburns *pl*.

patín *m* skate; runner.

patinar *vi* to skate; to skid; (*fam*) to blunder.

patio *m* courtyard; playground.

pato *m* duck.

patoso/sa *adj* (*fam*) clumsy.

patraña *f* lie.

patrocinar *vt* to sponsor; to back, support.

patrón/ona *m/f* boss, master/mistress; landlord/lady; patron saint:—*m* pattern.

patronal *adj*:—**la clase ~** management.

patrulla *f* patrol.

paulatino/na *adj* gradual, slow.

pausar *vi* to pause.

pauta *f* guideline.

pavo *m* turkey:—**~ real** peacock.

pavor *m* dread, terror.

payaso/sa *m/f* clown.

payo/ya *m/f* non-Gipsy (for a Gipsy).

paz *f* peace; tranquillity, ease.

peaje *m* toll.

peana *f* pedestal; footstool.

peatón *m* pedestrian.

peca *f* freckle; spot.

pecado *m* sin.

pecho *m* chest; breast(s) (*pl*); teat; (*fig*) courage, valor:—**dar el ~ a** to suckle:—**tomar a ~** to take to heart.

pechuga *f* breast of a fowl; (*fam*) bosom.

pedazo *m* piece, bit.

pedernal *m* flint.

pediatra *m/f* pediatrician.

pedicuro/ra *m/f* chiropodist.

pedir *vt* to ask for; to petition; to beg; to order; to need; to solicit:—*vi* to ask.

pedo *m* (*fam*) fart (*sl*):—**tirarse un ~** to fart (*sl*).

pegamento *m* glue.

pegar *vt* to cement; to join, unite; to beat:—**~ fuego a** to set fire to:—*vi* to stick; to match:—**~se** *vr* to intrude; to steal in.

pegatina *f* sticker.

peinar *vt* to comb; to style.

peine *m* comb.

pelar *vt* to cut (hair); to strip off (feathers); to peel:—**~se** *vr* to peel off; to have one's hair cut.

peldaño *m* step (of a flight of stairs).

pelear *vt* to fight, combat:—**~se** *vr* to scuffle.

pelele *m* dummy; man of straw.

película *f* film, thin covering; movie.

peligro *m* danger, peril; risk.

pelirrojo/ja *m/f* redhead:—*adj* red-haired.

pellejo *m* skin; hide, pelt; peel; wine skin; oilskin; drunkard.

pellizcar *vt* to pinch.

pelo *m* hair; pile; flaw (in precious stones).

pelota *f* ball.

peluca *f* wig.

peluquería *f* hairdresser's/barber's premises.

pelusa *f* bloom (on fruit); fluff.

pena *f* punishment, pain:—**a duras ~s** with great difficulty or trouble.

pendiente *f* slope, declivity:—*m* earring:—*adj* pending; unsettled.

pene *m* penis.

penetrante *adj* deep; sharp; piercing; searching; biting.

penique *m* penny.

penoso/sa *adj* painful.

pensar *vi* to think.

pensativo/va *adj* pensive, thoughtful.

pensión *f* guest-house; pension.

penúltimo/ma *adj* penultimate, last but one.

penumbra *f* half-light.

penuria f penury, poverty, neediness, extreme want.

peña f rock, large stone.

peón m (day) laborer; foot soldier; pawn (at chess).

peor adj, adv worse:—~ **que** ~ worse and worse.

pepino m cucumber.

pepita f kernel; pip.

pequeño/ña adj little, small; young.

pera f pear.

percatarse vr:—~ **de** to notice.

percha f coat hook; coat hanger; perch.

percibir vt to receive; to perceive, comprehend.

perder vt to lose; to waste; to miss:— ~**se** vr to go astray; to be lost; to be spoiled.

perdiz f partridge.

perdón m pardon; mercy:—¡~! sorry!

perdonar vt to pardon, forgive; to excuse.

perdurar vi to last; to still exist.

perecedero/ra adj perishable.

peregrino/na adj (fig) strange:—m pilgrim.

perejil m parsley.

pereza f laziness, idleness.

perfil m profile.

perforar vt to perforate; to drill; to punch a hole in:—vi to drill.

perfume m perfume.

pergamino m parchment.

periódico/ca adj periodical:—m newspaper.

periodista m/f journalist.

peripecia f vicissitude; sudden change.

periquito m budgie.

perito/ta adj skillful, experienced: —m/f expert; skilled worker; technician.

perjudicar vt to prejudice, damage; to injure, hurt.

perjurar vi to perjure, swear falsely; to swear.

perla f pearl:—**de** ~**s** fine.

permanecer vi to stay; to continue to be.

permiso m permission, leave, license.

permitir vt to permit, allow.

permutar vt to exchange, permute.

pernera f trouser leg.

perno m bolt.

pernoctar vi to spend the night.

pero m kind of apple:—conj but, yet.

perogrullada f truism, platitude.

perol m large metal pan.

perro m dog.

perseguir vt to pursue; to persecute; to chase after.

perseverar vi to persevere, persist.

persiana f (Venetian) blind.

persistir vi to persist.

persona f person:—**de** ~ **a** ~ from person to person.

personaje m celebrity; character.

persuadir vt to persuade:—~**se** vr to be persuaded.

pertenecer vi:—~ **a** to belong to; to appertain, concern.

pértiga f long pole or rod.

pertinaz adj pertinacious; obstinate.

pertinente adj relevant; appropriate.

perturbar vt to perturb, disturb.

pervertir vt to pervert; to corrupt.

pesa f weight.

pesadez f heaviness, weight; gravity; slowness; peevishness, fretfulness; trouble; fatigue.

pesadilla f nightmare.

pesado/da adj peevish; troublesome; cumbersome; tedious; heavy, weighty.

pesar m sorrow, grief; repentance:— **a ~ de** in spite of, not withstanding:—vi to weigh; to repent:—vt to weigh.

pescado m fish (in general).

pescar vt to fish for, catch (fish):—vi to fish.

pescuezo m neck.

pésimo/ma adj very bad.

peso m weight, heaviness; balance scales pl.

pesquisa f inquiry, examination.

pestaña f eyelash.

pestañear vi to blink.

pestillo m bolt.

petróleo m crude oil, petroleum.

pez m fish:—f pitch.

pezón m nipple.

pezuña f hoof.

piadoso/sa adj pious; mild; merciful; moderate.

piar vi to squeak; to chirp.

pibe/ba m/f boy/girl.

picado/da adj pricked; minced, chopped; bad (tooth); cross.

picante adj hot, spicy; racy.

picaporte m doorhandle; latch.

picar vt to prick; to sting; to mince; to nibble:—vi to prick; to sting; to itch:—~se vr to be piqued; to take offence; to be moth-eaten; to begin to rot.

pícaro/ra adj roguish; mischievous, malicious; sly:—m/f rogue, knave.

pico m beak; bill, nib; peak; pick-ax.

pie m foot; leg; basis; trunk (of trees); foundation; occasion:—**a ~** on foot.

piedad f piety; mercy, pity.

piedra f stone.

piel f skin; hide; peel.

pienso m fodder.

pierna f leg (human).

pieza f piece; room.

pila f battery; trough; font; sink; pile, heap:—**nombre de ~** first name.

píldora f pill.

pileta f basin; swimming pool.

pimentón m paprika.

pimienta f pepper.

pimiento m pepper, pimiento.

piña f pineapple; fir cone; group.

pincel m paintbrush.

pinchar vt to prick; to puncture.

pincho m thorn; snack.

ping-pong m table tennis.

pino m (bot) pine.

piñón m pine nut; pinion.

pintar vt to paint; to picture; to describe; to exaggerate:—vi to paint; (fam) to count, to be important:— **~se** vr to put on make-up.

pintura f painting.

pinza f claw; clothes pin; pincers pl: —**~s** fpl tweezers pl.

piojo m louse; troublesome hangeron.

pipa f pipe; sunflower seed.

pipí m (fam):—**hacer ~** to have to go (wee-wee).

piquete m prick, jab; hole; (mil) squad.

piragua f canoe.

piropo m compliment; flattery.

pisar vt to tread, trample; to stamp on (the ground); to hammer down: —vi to tread, walk.

piscina f swimming pool.

piso m apartment; tread, trampling; floor, sidewalk; floor, story.

pisotear vt to trample, tread under foot.

pista f trace, footprint; clue.

pita f (bot) agave.

pitar vt to blow; to whistle at:—vi to whistle; to toot one's horn; to smoke.

pito m whistle; horn.

pizarra *f* slate.

pizca *f* mite; pinch.

placa *f* plate; badge.

placer *m* pleasure; delight:—*vt* to please.

plan *m* plan; design; plot; scheme.

plancha *f* plate; iron; gangway.

planear *vt* to plan:—*vi* to glide.

planicie *f* plain.

planificación *f* planning:—~ **familiar** family planning.

plano/na *adj* plain, level, flat:—*m* plan; ground plot, map:—~ **inclinado** (*ferro*) dead level.

plantación *f* plantation.

plantar *vt* to plant; to fix upright; to strike or hit (a blow); to found; to establish:—~**se** *vr* to stand upright.

plantilla *f* personnel; insole of a shoe.

plata *f* silver; plate (wrought silver); cash:—**en** ~ briefly.

plátano *m* banana; plane tree.

plateado/da *adj* silvered; plated.

platicar *vi* to converse.

platillo *m* saucer:—~**s** *mpl* cymbals *pl*: —~ **volador**/~ **volante** flying saucer.

platino *m* platinum:—~**s** *mpl* contact points *pl*.

plato *m* dish; plate.

playa *f* beach.

playera *f* T-shirt:—~**s** *fpl* sneakers *pl*.

plaza *f* square; place; office, employment; room; seat.

plazo *m* term; installment; expiry date.

plegar *vt* to fold; to crease.

pleito *m* contract, bargain; dispute, controversy, debate; lawsuit.

plenilunio *m* full moon.

pleno/na *adj* full; complete:—*m* plenum.

pliego *m* sheet of paper.

pliegue *m* fold; pleat.

plisado/da *adj* pleated:—*m* pleating.

plomero *m* plumber.

plomo *m* lead:—**a** ~ perpendicularly.

pluma *f* feather, plume.

población *f* population; town.

pobre *adj* poor.

poco/ca *adj* little, scanty; (*pl*) few:— *adv* little:—~ **a** ~ gently; little by little:—*m* small part; little.

podar *vt* to prune.

poder *m* power, authority; command; force:—*vi* to be able to; to possess the power of doing or performing.

podrido/da *adj* rotten, bad; (*fig*) rotten.

poesía *f* poetry.

polea *f* pulley; (*mar*) tackle-block.

polideportivo *m* sports center.

polilla *f* moth.

pollera *f* skirt.

pollo *m* chicken.

polo *m* pole; ice lolly; polo; polo neck.

polvo *m* powder, dust.

pólvora *f* gunpowder.

pomada *f* cream, ointment.

pomelo *m* grapefruit.

pómez *f*:—**piedra** ~ pumice stone.

pompa *f* pomp; bubble.

pómulo *m* cheekbone.

poner *vt* to put, place; to put on; to impose; to lay (eggs):—~**se** *vr* to oppose; to set (of stars); to become.

poniente *m* west; west wind.

ponzoña *f* poison.

popa *f* (*mar*) poop, stern.

por *prep* for; by; about; by means of; through; on account of.

porción *f* part, portion; lot.

porfiar *vt* to dispute obstinately; to persist in a pursuit.

pormenor *f* detail.

poro *m* pore.

porque *conj* because; since; so that.

porquería *f* nastiness, foulness; brutishness, rudeness; trifle; dirty action.

porrón *m* spouted wine jar.

portada *f* portal, porch; frontispiece.

portaequipajes *m invar* trunk (in car); baggage rack.

portarse *vr* to behave.

portátil *adj* portable.

portavoz *m/f* spokesman/woman.

porte *m* transportation (charges *pl*); deportment, demeanor, conduct.

portero *m* porter, gatekeeper.

porvenir *m* future.

posar *vi* to sit, pose:—*vt* to lay down (a burden):—~**se** *vr* to settle; to perch; to land.

posdata *f* postcript.

poseer *vt* to hold, possess.

posesivo/va *adj* possessive.

posibilitar *vt* to make possible; to make feasible.

poso *m* sediment, dregs *pl*.

posponer *vt* to postpone.

postal *adj* postal:—*f* postcard.

poste *m* post, pillar.

postergar *vt* to leave behind; to postpone.

posterioridad *f*:—**con ~** subsequently, later.

postigo *m* wicket; postern; shutter.

postizo/za *adj* artificial (not natural):— *m* wig.

postrar *vt* to humble, humiliate:— ~**se** *vr* to prostrate oneself.

postre *m* dessert.

postura *f* posture, position; attitude; bet, wager; agreement, convention.

potable *adj* drinkable.

potaje *m* pottage; drink made up of several ingredients; medley of various useless things.

potro/ra *m/f* colt; foal.

pozo *m* well.

practicar *vt* to practice.

práctico/ca *adj* practical; skillful, experienced.

prado *m* lawn; meadow.

precaver *vt* to prevent; to guard against.

preceder *vt* to precede, go before.

preciado/da *adj* esteemed, valued.

precinto *m* seal.

precio *m* price; value.

precioso/sa *adj* precious; (*fam*) beautiful.

precisamente *adv* precisely; exactly.

precisar *vt* to compel, oblige; to need.

preciso/sa *adj* necessary, requisite; precise, accurate; abstracted.

precoz *adj* precocious.

precursor/ra *m/f* harbinger, forerunner.

predecir *vt* to foretell.

predicar *vt* to preach.

predilecto/ta *adj* darling, favorite.

predisponer *vt* to predispose; to prejudice.

predominar *vi* to predominate, prevail.

preferir *vt* to prefer.

pregón *m* proclamation; hue and cry.

preguntar *vt* to ask; to question; to demand; to inquire.

prejuicio *m* prejudgement; preconception; prejudice.

premiar *vt* to reward, remunerate.

premura *f* pressure, haste, hurry.

preñada *adj* pregnant.

prenda *f* pledge; garment; sweetheart; person or thing dearly loved: —~**s** *fpl* accomplishments, talents *pl*.

prender *vt* to seize, catch, lay hold of; to imprison:—~**se** *vr* to catch fire: —*vi* to take root.

prensar *vt* to press.

preocupar(se) *vt* (*vr*) to worry.

preparar *vt* to prepare:——**se** *vr* to be prepared.

prepucio *m* foreskin.

presa *f* capture, seizure; dike, dam.

presagio *m* omen.

prescindir *vi*:——**de** to do without; to dispense with.

presenciar *vt* to attend; to be present at; to witness.

presentar *vt* to present; to introduce; to offer; to show:——**se** *vr* to present oneself; to appear; to run (as candidate); to apply.

presentir *vt* to have a premonition of.

preservativo *m* condom, sheath.

presidiario *m* convict.

presilla *f* clip; loop (in clothes).

presión *f* pressure, pressing.

presionar *vt* to press; (*fig*) to put pressure on.

preso/sa *m/f* prisoner.

prestar *vt* to lend.

presto/ta *adj* quick; prompt; ready:——*adv* soon; quickly.

presumir *vt* to presume, conjecture:——*vi* to be conceited.

presunto/ta *adj* supposed; socalled.

presupuesto *m* presumed cost; budget.

pretender *vt* to claim; to try, attempt.

pretendiente *m* pretender; suitor.

pretexto *m* pretext; pretence, excuse.

prevalacer *vi* to prevail; to triumph; to take root.

prevenir *vt* to prepare; to foresee, know in advance; to prevent; to warn:——**se** *vr* to be prepared; to be predisposed.

prever *vt* to foresee, forecast.

previo/via *adj* previous.

previsión *f* foresight, prevision; forecast.

prima *f* bonus; (female) cousin.

primario/ria *adj* primary.

primavera *f* spring (the season).

primer(o)/ra *adj* first; prior; former:——*adv* first; rather, sooner.

primicias *f* first fruits *pl*.

primo/ma *m* cousin.

primogénito/ta *adj, m/f* first-born.

príncipe *m* prince.

principiante *m* beginner, learner.

principio *m* beginning, commencement; principle.

pringoso/sa *adj* greasy; sticky.

prisa *f* speed; hurry; urgency; promptness.

prismáticos *mpl* binoculars *pl*.

privación *f* deprivation, want.

privado/da *adj* private; particular.

proa *f* (*mar*) prow.

probador *m* fitting room.

probar *vt* to try; to prove; to taste:——*vi* to try.

probeta *f* test tube.

procedente *adj* reasonable; proper:——~ **de** coming from.

procesador *m*:——~ **de textos** word processor.

procesar *vt* to put on trial.

procurar *vt* to try; to obtain; to produce.

prodigar *vt* to waste, lavish.

producir *vt* to produce; (*jur*) to produce as evidence:——**se** *vr* to come about; to arise; to be made; to break out.

proeza *f* prowess, valor, bravery.

profanar *vt* to profane, desecrate.

profesor/ra *m/f* teacher.
prófugo *m* fugitive.
profundo/da *adj* profound.
programa *m* program(me).
prohibir *vt* to prohibit, forbid; to hinder.
prójimo *m* fellow creature; neighbor.
prole *f* offspring, progeny; race.
prolijidad *f* prolixity; minute attention to detail.
prólogo *m* prolog.
promedio *m* average; middle.
prometer *vt* to promise; to assure:—~se *vr* to become engaged.
promiscuo/cua *adj* promiscuous; confusedly mingled.
promover *vt* to promote, advance; to stir up.
promulgar *vt* to promulgate, publish.
pronosticar *vt* to predict, foretell; to conjecture.
pronto/ta *adj* prompt; ready:—*adv* promptly.
pronunciamiento *m* (*jur*) publication; insurrection, sedition.
pronunciar *vt* to pronounce; to deliver:—~se *vr* to rebel.
propaganda *f* propaganda; advertising.
propagar *vt* to propagate.
propasar *vt* to go beyond, exceed.
propenso/sa *adj* prone, inclined.
propiamente *adv* properly; really.
propiciar *vt* to favor; to cause.
propiedad *f* property, possessions *pl*; right of property; propriety.
propina *f* tip.
propio/pia *adj* proper; own; typical; very.
proponer *vt* to propose.
proporcionar *vt* to provide.

propósito *m* aim, purpose:—**a** ~ on purpose.
propuesta *f* proposal, offer; representation.
propulsar *vt* to propel; (*fig*) to promote.
prórroga *f* prolongation; extension; extra time.
prorrumpir *vi* to break forth, burst forth.
prosa *f* prose.
proscrito/ta *adj* banned.
proseguir *vt* to continue:—*vi* to continue, go on.
prospección *f* exploration; prospecting.
prosperar *vi* to prosper, thrive.
proteger *vt* protector.
protestar *vt* to protest; to make public declaration (of faith):—*vi* to protest.
provecho *m* profit; advantage.
proveedor/ra *m/f* purveyor, supplier.
provenir *vi* to arise, originate; to issue.
provocar *vt* to provoke; to lead to; to excite.
próximamente *adv* soon.
próximo/ma *adj* next; neighboring; close, nearby.
proyectar *vt* to throw; to cast; to screen; to plan.
prueba *f* proof; reason; argument; token; experiment; essay; attempt; relish, taste.
púa *f* sharp point, prickle; shoot; pick.
pubertad *f* puberty.
publicar *vt* to publish; to make public.
publicidad *f* publicity; advertising.
público/ca *adj* public:—*m* public; audience; crowd.

puchero *m* pot; stew.

púdico/ca *adj* chaste, pure.

pudiente *adj* rich, opulent.

pudor *m* bashfulness.

pudrir *vt* to rot, putrefy:——**~se** *vr* to decay, rot.

pueblo *m* people *pl;* town, village; population; populace.

puente *m* bridge.

puerco/ca *adj* nasty; filthy, dirty; rude, coarse:——*m* pig, hog:——**~ espín** porcupine.

pueril *adj* childish; puerile.

puerro *m* leek.

puerta *f* door; doorway; gateway:—— **~ trasera** back door.

puerto *m* port, harbor; haven; pass.

pues *adv* then; therefore; well:——**¡~!** well, then.

puesto *m* place; particular spot; post, employment; barracks *pl;* stand.

púgil *m* boxer.

pujante *adj* powerful, strong; robust; stout, strapping.

Pulga *f* flea:——**tener malas ~s** to be easily piqued; to be ill-tempered.

pulgada *f* inch.

pulgar *m* thumb.

pulir *vt* to polish; to put the last touches to.

pulmón *m* lung.

pulpa *f* pulp; soft part (of fruit).

pulpería *f* small grocery store.

pulpo *m* octopus.

pulsar *vt* to touch; to play; to press.

pulsera *f* bracelet.

pulso *m* pulse; wrist; firmness or steadiness of the hand.

pulular *vi* to swarm.

pulverizador *m* spray gun.

puna *f* (*med*) mountain sickness.

puñado *m* handful.

puñal *m* dagger.

puño *m* fist; handful; wrist-band; cuff; handle.

punta *f* point; end; trace.

puntada *f* stitch.

puntal *m* prop, stay; buttress.

puntapié *m* kick.

puntería *f* aiming.

puntiagudo/da *adj* sharp-pointed.

puntilla *f* narrow lace edging:——**de ~s** on tiptoe.

punto *m* point; end; spot; stitch; full stop.

puntual *adj* punctual; exact; reliable.

punzada *f* prick; sting; pain; compunction.

punzante *adj* sharp.

pupila *f* pupil (of eye).

puro/ra *adj* pure; mere; clear; genuine.

púrpura *f* purple.

purulento/ta *adj* purulent.

puta *f* whore.

Q

que *pn* that; who; which; what:——*conj* that; than.

¿qué? *adj* what?; which?:——*pn* what?; which?.

quebrantar *vt* to break; to crack; to burst; to pound, grind; to violate; to fatigue; to weaken.

quedar *vi* to stay:——**~se** *vr* to remain.

quedo/da *adj* quiet, still:—*adv* softly, gently.

quejarse *vr* to complain of.

quemar *vt* to burn; to kindle:—**~se** *vr* to be parched with heat; to burn oneself:—*vi* to be too hot.

querella *f* charge; dispute; complaint.

querer *vt* to want; to desire; to will; to love:—*m* will, desire.

querido/da *adj* dear, beloved:—*m/f* darling; lover:—**~ mio, ~da mia** my dear, my love, my darling.

queso *m* cheese.

quicio *m* hook, hinge (of a door).

quien *pn* who; whom.

¿quién? *pn* who?; whom?.

quienquiera *adj* whoever.

quieto/ta *adj* still, peaceable.

quilla *f* keel.

química *f* chemistry.

quina *f* Peruvian bark, quinine.

quince *adj, m* fifteen; fifteenth.

quincena *f* fortnight.

quinientos/tas *adj* five hundred.

quinta *f* country house; levy, drafting of soldiers.

quinto *adj* fifth:—*m* fifth; drafted soldier.

quiosco *m* bandstand; news stand.

quirúrgico/ca *adj* surgical.

quiste *m* cyst.

quitamanchas *m invar* stain remover.

quitanieves *m invar* snowplough.

quitar *vt* to take away, remove; to take off; to relieve; to annul:—**~se** *vr* to take off (clothes, etc); to withdraw.

quitasol *m* parasol.

quizá/quizás *adv* perhaps.

R

rábano *m* radish.

rabia *f* rage, fury.

rabo *m* tail.

racha *f* gust of wind:—**buena/mala ~** spell of good/bad luck.

racimo *m* bunch of grapes.

radiografía *f* x-ray.

ráfaga *f* gust; flash; burst.

raído/da *adj* scraped; worn-out; impudent.

raíz *f* root; base, basis; origin:—**bienes raices** *mpl* landed property.

raja *f* splinter, chip (of wood); chink, fissure.

rajatabla *f:*—**a ~** *adv* strictly.

rallar *vt* to grate.

rama *f* branch (of tree, of family).

ramo *m* branch (of tree).

rampa *f* ramp.

rana *f* frog.

rancho *m* grub; ranch; small farm.

rancio/cia *adj* rank; rancid.

ranura *f* groove; slot.

rapar *vt* to shave; to plunder.

rapaz/za *adj* rapacious:—*m/f* young boy/girl.

rápido/da *adj* quick, rapid, swift.

rapiña *f* robbery.

raptar *vt* to kidnap.

raquítico/ca *adj* stunted; (*fig*) inadequate.

raro/ra *adj* rare, scarce; extraordinary.

ras *m:*—**a ~ de** level with:—**a ~ de tierra** at ground level.

rascacielos *m invar* skyscraper.

rascar *vt* to scratch, scrape.

rasgar *vt* to tear, rip.

rasgo *m* dash, stroke; grand or magnanimous action:—**~s** *mpl* features *pl*.

rasguño *m* scratch.

raso *m* satin; glade:—**~/sa** *adj* plain; flat:—**al ~** in the open air.

raspa *f* beard (of an ear of corn); backbone (of fish); stalk (of grapes); rasp.

raspar *vt* to scrape, rasp.

rastrear *vt* to trace; to inquire into:— *vi* to skim along close to the ground (of birds).

rastrillo *m* rake.

rastro *m* track; rake; trace.

rata *f* rat.

ratificar *vt* to ratify, confirm.

rato *m* moment:—**a ~s perdidos** in leisure time.

ratón *m* mouse.

raya *f* stroke; line; part; frontier; ray (fish); roach (fish).

rayar *vt* to draw lines on; to cross out; to underline; to cross; to rifle.

rayo *m* ray, beam (of light).

raza *f* race, lineage; quality; crack, fissure.

razonar *vi* to reason; to discourse, talk.

reaccionar *vi* to react.

real *adj* real, actual; royal:—*m* (*mil*) camp.

realidad *f* reality; sincerity.

realizador/ra *m/f* producer (in TV, etc).

realzar *vt* to raise, elevate; to emboss; to heighten.

reanimar *vt* to cheer, encourage; to reanimate.

reanudar *vt* to resume.

rebaja *f* abatement; deduction:—**~s** *fpl* sale.

rebanada *f* slice.

rebaño *m* flock (of sheep), herd (of cattle).

rebasar *vt* to exceed.

rebatir *vt* to resist; to parry, ward off; to refute; to repress.

rebeca *f* cardigan.

rebelarse *vr* to revolt; to rebel; to resist.

rebosar *vi* to run over, overflow; to abound.

rebotar *vt* to bounce; to clinch; to repel:—*vi* to rebound.

rebozar *vt* to wrap up; to fry in batter or breadcrumbs.

rebuznar *vi* to bray.

recado *m* message; errand.

recaída *f* relapse.

recalcar *vt* to stress, emphasize.

recalentar *vt* to heat again; to overheat.

recambio *m* spare; refill.

recapacitar *vt* to reflect.

recargar *vt* to overload; to recharge; to charge again.

recatado/da *adj* prudent; circumspect; modest.

recaudar *vt* to gather; to obtain; to recover.

recelo *m* dread; suspicion, mistrust.

receta *f* recipe; prescription.

rechazar *vt* to refuse; to repulse; to contradict.

recibir *vt* to receive, accept; to let in; to go to meet:—**~se** *vr* **~ de** to qualify as.

recibo *m* receipt.

recién *adv* recently, lately.

reciente *adj* recent; new, fresh; modern.

recio/cia *adj* stout; strong, robust; coarse, thick; rude; àrduous, rigid:—

adv strongly, stoutly:—**hablar** ~ to talk loud.

recipiente *m* container.

reclamación *f* claim; reclamation; protest.

recluir *vt* to shut up.

reclutar *vt* to recruit.

recobrar *vt* to recover:—~**se** *vr* to recover (from sickness).

recodo *m* corner or angle jutting out.

recoger *vt* to collect; to take back; to get; to gather; to shelter; to compile:—~**se** *vr* to take shelter or refuge; to retire; to withdraw from the world.

recompensa *f* compensation; recompense, reward.

reconfortar *vt* to comfort.

reconocer *vt* to recognize; to examine closely; to acknowledge; to consider; (*mil*) to reconnoiter.

reconstituyente *m* tonic.

reconversión *f:*—~ **industrial** industrial rationalization.

recopilar *vt* to compile.

recordar *vt* to remember; to remind:—*vi* to remember.

recorrer *vt* to run over, peruse; to cover.

recortar *vt* to cut out.

recostar *vt* to lean, recline:—~**se** *vr* to lie down.

recoveco *m* cubby hole; bend.

recreo *m* recreation; playtime (school).

recta *f* straight line.

rectángulo/la *adj* rectangular:—*m* rectangle.

rectitud *f* straightness; rectitude; justness, honesty; exactitude.

recto/ta *adj* straight; right; just, honest:—*m* rectum.

rector/ra *m/f* superior of a community or establishment; rector (of a university); curate, rector:—*adj* governing.

recuadro *m* box; inset.

recuento *m* inventory.

recuerdo *m* souvenir; memory.

recuperar *vt* to recover:—~**se** *vr* to recover (from sickness).

recurrir *vi:*—~ **a** to resort to.

red *f* net; network; snare.

redactar *vt* to draft; to edit.

redada *f:*—~ **policial** police raid.

redimir *vt* to redeem; to ransom.

redoblar *vt* to redouble; to rivet.

redondo/da *adj* round; complete.

reducir *adj* to reduce; to limit:—~**se** *vr* to diminish.

redundancia *f* superfluity, redundancy, excess.

reembolso *m* reimbursement; refund:—**contra** ~ C.O.D.

referir *vt* to refer, relate, report:—~**se** *vr* to refer or relate to.

refinado/da *adj* refined; subtle, artful.

reflejar *vt* to reflect.

reflejo *m* reflex; reflection.

reflujo *m* reflux, ebb:—**flujo y** ~ the tides *pl*.

reformar *vt* to reform; to correct; to restore:—~**se** *vr* to mend; to have one's manners reformed or corrected.

reforzar *vt* to strengthen, fortify; to encourage.

refrán *m* proverb.

refrescar *vt* to refresh:—~**se** *vr* to get cooler; to go out for a breath of fresh air:—*vi* to cool down.

refriega *f* affray, skirmish, fray.

refrigerador *m*, **refrigeradora** *f* refrigerator, fridge.

refuerzo *m* reinforcement.

refugiar vt to shelter:—~**se** vr to take refuge.

refunfuñar vi to snarl; to growl; to grumble.

regadera f watering can.

regalar vt to give (as present); to give away; to pamper; to caress.

regaliz m licorice.

regalo m present, gift; pleasure; comfort.

regañadientes:—a ~ adv reluctantly.

regañar vt to scold:—vi to growl; to grumble; to quarrel.

regar vt to water, irrigate.

regata f irrigation ditch; regatta.

regatear vt (com) to bargain over; to be mean with:—vi to haggle; to dribble (in sport).

regazo m lap.

regentar vt to rule; to govern.

régimen m regime, management; diet; (gr) rules pl of verbs.

registrar vt to survey; to inspect, examine; to record, enter in a register:—~**se** vr to register; to happen.

regla f rule, ruler; period.

reglamentar vt to regulate.

regocijar vt to gladden:—~**se** vr to rejoice.

regordete adj chubby, plump.

regresar vi to return, go back.

reguero m small rivulet; trickle of spilt liquid; drain, gutter.

regular vt to regulate, adjust:—adj regular; ordinary.

rehén m hostage.

rehuir vt to avoid.

rehusar vt to refuse, decline.

reimpresión f reprint.

reina f queen.

reincidir vi:—~ **en** to relapse into, fall back into.

reino m kingdom, reign.

reintegrar vt to reintegrate, restore: —~**se** vr to be reinstated or restored.

reír(se) vi (vr) to laugh.

reiterar vt to reiterate, repeat.

reivindicar vt to claim.

reja f ploughshare; lattice, grating.

rejoneador m mounted bullfighter.

relación f relation; relationship; report; account.

relajar vt to relax, slacken:—~**se** vr to relax.

relamerse vr to lick one's lips; to relish.

relámpago m flash of lightning.

relatar vt to relate, tell.

relato m story; recital.

relegar vt to relegate; to banish, exile.

relente m evening dew.

relieve m relief; (fig) prominence.

relinchar vi to neigh.

reliquia f residue, remains pl; (saintly) relic.

rellano m landing (of stairs).

rellenar vt to fill up; to stuff.

reloj m clock; watch.

relucir vi to shine, glitter; to excel, be brilliant.

relumbrar vi to sparkle, shine.

remachar vt to rivet; (fig) to drive home.

remache m rivet; clinch; obstinacy.

remanente m remainder; (com) balance; surplus.

remanso m stagnant water; quiet place.

remar vi to row.

rematar vt to terminate, finish; to sell off cheaply:—vi to end.

remedar vt to copy, imitate; to mimic.

remediar *vt* to remedy; to assist, help; to free from danger; to avoid.

remesa *f* shipment; remittance.

remilgado/da *adj* prim; affected.

remitente *m* sender.

remojar *vt* to steep; to dunk.

remolacha *f* beet.

remolcar *vt* to tow.

remordimiento *m* remorse.

remoto/ta *adj* remote, distant; far.

remover *vt* to stir; to move around.

remozar *vt* to rejuvenate; to renovate.

renacer *vi* to be born again; to revive.

renacuajo *m* tadpole.

rendija *f* crevice, crack, cleft.

rendir *vt* to subject, subdue:——**se** *vr* to yield; to surrender; to be tired out.

renegar *vt* to deny; to disown; to detest, abhor:——*vi* to apostatize; to blaspheme, curse.

renglón *m* line; item.

reñir *vt, vi* to wrangle, quarrel; to scold, chide.

renombre *m* renown.

renovar *vt* to renew; to renovate; to reform.

renta *f* income; rent; profit.

reo *m* offender, criminal.

reparar *vt* to repair; to consider, observe; to parry:——*vi* ~ **en** to notice; to pass (at cards).

repartir *vt* to distribute; to deliver.

repasar *vt* to revise; to check; to mend.

repente:——**de** ~ *adv* suddenly.

repercutir *vi* to reverberate; to rebound.

repetir *vt, vi* to repeat.

repiquetear *vt* to ring merrily.

repisa *f* pedestal, stand; shelf; windowsill.

repleto/ta *adj* replete, very full.

replicar *vi* to reply.

repoblar *vt* to repopulate; to reafforest.

repollo *m* cabbage.

reponer *vt* to replace; to restore:——**se** *vr* to recover lost health or property.

reportaje *m* report, article.

reposar *vi* to rest, repose.

repostería *f* confectioner's (store).

reprender *vt* to reprimand.

represa *f* dam; lake.

representar *vt* to represent; to play on the stage; to look (age).

reprimir *vt* to repress; to check; to contain.

reprobable *adj* reprehensible.

reprochar *vt* to reproach.

repuesto *m* supply; spare part.

repugnancia *f* reluctance; repugnance; disgust.

requerir *vt* to intimate, notify; to request; to require, need; to summon.

requesón *m* cottage cheese.

requiebro *m* endearing expression.

res *f* head of cattle.

resabio *m* (unpleasant) aftertaste; vicious habit, bad custom.

resaca *f* surge, surf; (*fig*) backlash; (*fam*) hangover.

resaltar *vi* to rebound; to jut out; to be evident; to stand out.

resbaladizo/za *adj* slippery.

resbalar(se) *vi* (*vr*) to slip, slide.

rescindir *vt* to rescind, annul.

rescoldo *m* embers *pl*, cinders *pl*.

resecarse *vr* to dry up.

reseña *f* review; account.

resentirse *vr:*—— **de** to suffer:—— **con** to resent.

reservar *vt* to keep; to reserve:——**se** *vr* to preserve oneself; to keep to oneself.

resfriado *m* cold.

resguardar *vt* to preserve, defend:—
~**se** *vr* to be on one's guard.

residir *vi* to reside, dwell.

residuo *m* residue, remainder.

resistir *vt* to resist, oppose; to put up
with:—*vi* to resist; to hold out.

resol *m* glare (of the sun).

resollar *vi* to wheeze; to take breath.

resolver *vt* to resolve, decide; to analyse:
—~**se** *vr* to resolve, determine.

resoplar *vi* to snore; to snort.

resorte *m* spring.

respaldo *m* backing; endorsement;
back of a seat.

respetar *vt* to respect; to revere.

respingo *m* start; jump.

respiradero *m* vent, breathing hole;
rest, repose.

respirar *vi* to breathe.

resplandecer *vi* to shine; to glisten.

resplandor *m* splendor, brilliance.

responder *vt* to answer:—*vi* to
answer; to correspond:—~ **de** to
be responsible for.

responso *m* prayer for the dead.

respuesta *f* answer, reply.

resquemor *m* resentment.

restablecer *vt* to re-establish:—~**se**
vr to recover.

restallar *vi* to crack; to click.

restar *vt* to subtract, take away:—*vi*
to be left.

restaurar *vt* to restore.

restituir *vt* to restore; to return.

resto *m* remainder, rest.

restregar *vt* to scrub, rub.

restringir *vt* to restrict, limit; to
restrain.

resuelto/ta *adj* resolute, determined;
prompt.

resultar *vi* to be; to turn out; to
amount to.

resumir *vt* to abridge; to summarize.

retahíla *f* range, series.

retal *m* remnant.

retar *vt* to challenge.

retener *vt* to retain, keep back.

retentiva *f* memory.

retirar *vt* to withdraw, retire; to
remove:—~**se** *vr* to retire, retreat;
to go to bed.

reto *m* challenge; threat, menace.

retocar *vt* to retouch; to mend; to
finish off (work).

retoñar *vi* to sprout.

retorcer *vt* to twist; to wring.

retozar *vi* to frisk, skip.

retraído/da *adj* shy.

retransmitir *vt* to broadcast; to relay;
to retransmit.

retraso *m* delay; slowness; back-
wardness; lateness:—(*ferro*) **el tren
ha tenido** ~ the train is overdue or
late.

retrato *m* portrait, effigy.

retrete *m* lavatory.

retribuir *vt* to repay.

retroceder *vi* to go backwards, fly
back; to back down.

retrovisor *m* rear-view mirror.

retumbar *vi* to resound, jingle.

reúma *f* rheumatism.

reunir *vt* to reunite; to unite:—~**se**
vr to gather, meet.

revancha *f* revenge.

revelar *vt* to reveal; to develop (pho-
tographs).

reventar *vi* to burst, crack; to explode; to toil, drudge.

reverdecer *vi* to grow green again; to revive.

revés *m* back; wrong side; disappointment, setback.

revisar *vt* to revise, review.

revisor *m* inspector; ticket collector.

revista *f* review, revision; magazine.

revolcarse *vr* to wallow.

revolotear *vi* to flutter.

revoltijo *m* confusion, disorder.

revoltoso/sa *adj* rebellious, unruly.

revolver *vt* to move about; to turn around; to mess up; to revolve; ~**se** *vr* to turn round; to change (of the weather).

revuelta *f* turn; disturbance, revolt.

rey *m* king; king (in cards or chess).

rezagar *vt* to leave behind; to defer:—~**se** *vr* to remain behind.

rezar *vi* to pray, say one's prayers.

rezumar *vt* to ooze, leak.

ría *f* estuary.

riada *f* flood.

ribera *f* shore, bank.

rico/ca *adj* rich; delicious; lovely; cute.

riego *m* irrigation.

rienda *f* rein of a bridle:—**dar ~ suelta** to give free rein to.

riesgo *m* risk, danger.

rifa *f* raffle, lottery.

rígido/da *adj* rigid, inflexible; severe.

riguroso/sa *adj* rigorous.

rimar *vi* to rhyme.

rímel, rimmel *m* mascara.

riña *f* quarrel, dispute.

rincón *m* (inside) corner.

rinoceronte *m* rhinoceros.

riñón *m* kidney.

río *m* river, stream.

riqueza *f* riches *pl,* wealth.

risa *f* laugh, laughter.

risco *m* steep rock.

ritmo *m* rhythm.

rizo *m* curl; ripple (on water).

robar *vt* to rob; to steal; to break into.

roble *m* oak tree.

robusto/ta *adj* robust, strong.

roca *f* rock.

rociar *vt* to sprinkle; to spray.

rocío *m* dew.

rodaja *f* slice.

rodaje *m* filming:—**en ~** (*auto*) running in.

rodear *vi* to make a detour:—*vt* to surround, enclose.

rodilla *f* knee:—**de ~s** on one's knees.

rodillo *m* roller; rolling pin.

roer *vt* to gnaw; to corrode.

rogar *vt, vi* to ask for; to beg, entreat; to pray.

rojizo/za *adj* reddish.

rojo/ja *adj* red; ruddy.

rol *m* list, roll, catalog; role.

rollo *m* roll; coil.

romería *f* pilgrimage.

romero *m* (*bot*) rosemary.

rompecabezas *m invar* riddle; jigsaw.

romper *vt* to break; to tear up; to wear out; to break up (land):—*vi* to break (of waves); to break through.

ron *m* rum.

roña *f* scab, mange; grime; rust.

roncar *vi* to snore; to roar.

ronco/ca *adj* hoarse; husky; raucous.

ronda *f* night patrol; round (of drinks, cards, etc).

ronronear *vi* to purr.

ropa *f* clothes *pl*; clothing; dress.

rosa *f* rose; birthmark.

rosado/da *adj* pink; rosy.

rosca *f* thread (of a screw); coil, spiral.

rosquilla *f* doughnut.

rostro *m* face.

roto/ta *adj* broken, destroyed; debauched.

rótula *f* kneecap; ball-and-socket joint.

rotulador *m* felt-tip pen.

rótulo *m* inscription; label, ticket; placard, poster.

rotundo/da *adj* round; emphatic.

rozar *vt* to rub; to chafe; to nibble (the grass); to scrape; to touch lightly.

rubio/bia *adj* fair-haired, blond(e):— *m/f* blond/blonde.

rudimento *m* principle; beginning:— ~**s** *mpl* rudiments *pl*.

rudo/da *adj* rough, coarse; plain, simple; stupid.

rueda *f* wheel; circle; slice, round.

ruedo *m* rotation; border, selvage; arena, bullring.

ruego *m* request, entreaty.

rufián *m* pimp, pander; lout.

rugir *vi* to roar, bellow.

rugoso/sa *adj* wrinkled.

ruido *m* noise, sound; din, row; fuss.

ruin *adj* mean, despicable; stingy.

ruina *f* ruin, collapse; downfall, destruction:—~**s** *fpl* ruins *pl*.

ruiseñor *m* nightingale.

rulo *m* curler.

rumbo *m* (*mar*) course, bearing; road, route, way; course of events, pomp, ostentation.

rumboso/sa *adj* generous, lavish.

rústico/ca *adj* rustic:—*m/f* peasant.

ruta *f* route, itinerary.

rutina *f* routine; habit.

S

sábado *m* Saturday; (jewish) Sabbath.

sábana *f* sheet; altar cloth.

sabañón *m* chilblain.

sabelotodo *m/f invar* know-all.

saber *vt* to know; to be able to; to find out, learn; to experience:—*vi* ~ **a** to taste of:—*m* learning, knowledge.

sabiduría *f* learning, knowledge; wisdom.

sabio/bia *adj* sage, wise:—*m/f* sage, wise person.

sablazo *m* sword wound; (*fam*) sponging, scrounging.

sabor *m* taste, savor, flavor.

sabroso/sa *adj* tasty, delicious; pleasant; salted.

sabueso *m* bloodhound.

sacacorchos *m invar* corkscrew.

sacapuntas *m invar* pencil sharpener.

sacar *vt* to take out, extract; to get out; to bring out (a book etc); to take off (clothes); to receive, get; (*dep*) to serve.

sacerdote *m* priest.

saco *m* bag, sack; jacket.

sacudir *vt* to shake, jerk; to beat, hit.

sagaz *adj* shrewd, clever, sagacious.

sagrado/da *adj* sacred, holy.

sal *f* salt.

sala *f* large room; (*teat*) house, auditorium; public hall; (*jur*) court; (*med*) ward.

salado/da *adj* salted; witty, amusing.

salario *m* salary.

salchicha *f* sausage.

salchichón *m* (salami-type) sausage.

saldo *m* settlement; balance; remainder:—**~s** *mpl* sale.

salida *f* exit, way out; leaving, departure; production, output; (*com*) sale; sales outlet.

saliente *adj* projecting; rising; (*fig*) outstanding.

salir *vi* to go out, leave; to depart, set out; to appear; to turn out, prove:—**~se** *vr* to escape, leak.

salmo *m* psalm.

salmonete *m* red mullet.

salmuera *f* brine.

salón *m* living room, lounge; public hall.

salpicadero *m* dashboard.

salpicar *vt* to sprinkle, splash, spatter.

salsa *f* sauce.

saltamontes *m invar* grasshopper.

saltar *vt* to jump, leap; to skip, miss out:—*vi* to leap, jump; to bounce; (*fig*) to explode, blow up.

saltimbanqui *m/f* acrobat.

salubre *adj* healthy.

salud *f* health.

saludar *vt* to greet; (*mil*) to salute.

salvado *m* bran.

salvaguardar *vt* to safeguard.

salvaje *adj* savage.

salvar *vt* to save; to rescue; to overcome; to cross, jump across; to cover, travel; to exclude:—**~se** *vr* to escape from danger.

salvavidas *adj invar:*—**bote/chaleco/cinturón ~** lifeboat/life preserver/life belt.

salvia *f* (*bot*) sage.

salvo/va *adj* safe:—*adv* save, except (for).

San *adj* Saint (as title).

saña *f* anger, passion.

sanar *vt, vi* to heal.

sandalia *f* sandal.

sandez *f* folly, stupidity.

sandía *f* watermelon.

sangre *f* blood:—**a ~ fria** in cold blood:—**a ~ y fuego** without mercy.

sangriento/ta *adj* bloody, bloodstained, gory; cruel.

sano/na *adj* healthy, fit; intact, sound.

sapo *m* toad.

saquear *vt* to ransack, plunder.

sarampión *m* measles.

sarna *f* itch; mange; (*med*) scabies.

sarpullido *m* (*med*) rash.

sarro *m* (*med*) tartar.

sarta *f* string of beads, etc; string, row.

sartén *f* frying pan.

sastre *m* tailor.

satisfacer *vt* to satisfy; to pay (a debt):—**~se** *vr* to satisfy oneself; to take revenge.

sauce *m* (*bot*) willow.

saúco *m* (*bot*) elder.

savia *f* sap.

sazonar *vt* to ripen; to season.

se *pn reflexivo* himself; herself; itself; yourself; themselves; yourselves; each other; one another; oneself.

se(p)tiembre *m* September.

sebo *m* fat, grease.

secano *m* dry, arable land which is not irrigated.

secar *vt* to dry:—**~se** *vr* to dry up; to dry oneself.

seco/ca *adj* dry; dried up; skinny; cold (of character); brusque, sharp; bare.

secuestrar *vt* to kidnap; to confiscate.

sed *f* thirst:—**tener ~** to be thirsty.

seda *f* silk.

sedal *m* fishing line.

sede *f* see; seat; headquarters.

sediento/ta *adj* thirsty; eager.

seducir *vt* to seduce; to bribe; to charm, attract.

segar *vt* to reap, harvest; to mow.

seguido/da *adj* continuous; successive; long-lasting:—*adv* straight (on); after; often.

seguir *vt* to follow, pursue; to continue:—*vi* to follow; to carry on:—**~se** *vr* to follow, ensue.

según *prep* according to.

segundo/da *adj* second:—*m* second (of time).

seguro/ra *adj* safe, secure; sure, certain; firm, constant:—*adv* for sure:—*m* safety device; insurance; safety, certainty.

seis *adj, m* six; sixth.

seiscientos/tas *adj* six hundred.

seísmo *m* earthquake.

sello *m* seal; stamp.

seleccionar *vt* to select, chose, pick.

selectivo *adj* selective.

selva *f* forest.

semáforo *m* traffic lights *pl;* signal.

semana *f* week.

sembrar *vt* to sow; to sprinkle, scatter.

semejante *adj* similar, like:—*m* fellow man.

semestral *adj* half-yearly.

semilla *f* seed.

sémola *f* semolina.

sempiterno/na *adj* everlasting.

seña *f* sign, mark, token; signal; (*mil*) password:—**~s** *fpl* address.

señal *f* sign, token; symptom; signal; landmark; (*com*) deposit.

señalar *vt* to stamp, mark; to signpost; to point out; to fix, settle:—**~se** *vr* to distinguish oneself, excel.

sencillo/lla *adj* simple; natural; unaffected; single.

senda *f,* **sendero** *m* path, trail.

seno *m* bosom; lap; womb; hole, cavity; sinus:—**~s** *mpl* breasts *pl.*

señor *m* man; gentleman; master; Mr; sir.

señora *f* lady; Mrs; madam; wife.

señorita *f* Miss; young lady.

señorito *m* young gentleman; rich kid.

sensación *f* sensation, feeling; sense.

sensato/ta *adj* sensible.

sensible *adj* sensitive; perceptible, appreciable; regrettable.

sentado/da *adj* sitting, seated; sedate; settled.

sentar *vt* to seat; (*fig*) to establish:—*vi* to suit:—**~se** *vr* to sit down.

sentido *m* sense; feeling; meaning:—**~/da** *adj* regrettable; sensitive.

sentir *vt* to feel; to hear; to perceive; to sense; to suffer from; to regret, be sorry for:—**~se** *vr* to feel; to feel pain; to crack (of walls, etc):—*m* opinion, judgement.

separar *vt* to separate:—**~se** *vr* to separate; to come away, come apart; to withdraw.

septentrional *adj* north, northern.

séptimo/ma *adj* seventh.

sepultar *vt* to bury, inter.

sequía *f* dryness; thirst; drought.

séquito *m* retinue, suite; group of supporters; aftermath.

ser *vi* to be; to exist:—~ **de** to come from; to be made of; to belong to:—*m* being.

serenata *f* (*mus*) serenade.

sereno *m* night watchman:—~/**na** *adj* serene, calm, quiet.

serie *f* series; sequence.

serio/ria *adj* serious; grave; reliable.

serpentear *vi* to wriggle; to wind, snake.

serpiente *f* snake.

serranía *f* range of mountains; mountainous country.

serrar *vt* to saw.

serrín *m* sawdust.

servicial *adj* helpful, obliging.

servilleta *f* napkin, serviette.

servir *vt* to serve; to wait on:—*vi* to serve; to be of use; to be in service:—~**se** *vr* to serve oneself, help oneself; to deign, please; to make use of.

sesenta *m, adj* sixty; sixtieth.

seso *m* brain.

sestear *vi* to take a nap.

seta *f* mushroom.

setecientos/tas *adj* seven hundred.

setenta *adj, m* seventy.

setiembre *m* September.

seto *m* fence; enclosure; hedge.

severo/ra *adj* severe, strict; grave, serious.

sexto/ta *adj, m* sixth.

si *conj* whether; if.

sí *adv* yes; certainly; indeed:—*pn* oneself; himself; herself; itself; yourself; themselves; yourselves; each other; one another.

siderúrgico/ca *adj* iron and steel *compd*:—*f* **la siderúrgica** the iron and steel industry.

sidra *f* cider.

siempre *adv* always; all the time; ever; still:—~ **jamás** for ever and ever.

sien *f* temple (of the head).

sierra *f* saw; range of mountains.

siete *adj, m* seven.

sigilo *m* secrecy.

sigla *f* acronym; abbreviation.

siglo *m* century.

significado *m* significance, meaning.

significativo/va *adj* significant.

signo *m* sign, mark.

siguiente *adj* following, successive, next.

silbar *vt, vi* to hiss; to whistle.

silencio *m* silence:—i~! silence! quiet!

silla *f* chair; saddle; seat:—~ **de ruedas** wheelchair.

silo *m* silo; underground wheat store.

silueta *f* silhouette; outline; figure.

silvestre *adj* wild, uncultivated; rustic.

símbolo *m* symbol.

simio *m* ape.

simpático/ca *adj* pleasant; kind.

simpatizar *vi*:—~ **con** to get on well with.

simular *vt* to simulate.

sin *prep* without.

sindicato *m* trade(s) union; syndicate.

sinfín *m*:—**un** ~ **de** a great many.

singular *adj* singular; exceptional; peculiar, odd.

siniestro/tra *adj* left; (*fig*) sinister:—*m* accident.

sino *conj* but; except; save; only:—*m* fate.

sinsabor *m* unpleasantness; disgust.

sinuoso/sa *adj* sinuous; wavy; winding.

sinvergüenza *m/f* rogue.

siquiera *conj* even if, even though:— *adv* at least.

sitio *m* place; spot; site, location; room, space; job, post; (*mil*) siege, blockade.

situar *vt* to place, situate; to invest:— **~se** *vr* to be established in place or business.

smoking *m* tuxedo.

sobaco *m* armpit, armhole.

sobar *vt* to handle, soften; to knead; to massage, rub hard; to rumple (clothes); to fondle.

soberbia *f* pride, haughtiness; magnificence.

sobornar *vt* to suborn, bribe.

sobrante *adj* remaining:— *m* surplus, remainder.

sobrar *vt* to exceed, surpass:— *vi* to be more than enough; to remain, be left.

sobre *prep* on; on top of; above, over; more than; besides:— *m* envelope.

sobrecargar *vt* to overload; (*com*) to surcharge.

sobredosis *f* overdose.

sobreentender *vt* to deduce:— **~se** *vr* **se sobreentiende que** . . . it is implied that.

sobrellevar *vt* to carry; to tolerate.

sobremesa *f*:— **de ~** immediately after dinner.

sobrenombre *m* nickname.

sobrepasar *vt* to surpass.

sobresalto *m* start, scare; sudden shock.

sobrevenir *vi* to happen, come unexpectedly; to supervene.

sobrevivir *vi* to survive.

sobrevolar *vt* to fly over.

sobrino/na *m/f* nephew/niece.

sobrio/ria *adj* sober, frugal.

socarrón/ona *adj* sarcastic; ironic(al).

socavar *vt* to undermine.

socio/cia *m/f* associate, member.

socorrista *m/f* first aider; lifeguard.

socorro *m* help, aid, assistance, relief.

soez *adj* dirty, obscene.

sofá *m* sofa.

soga *f* rope.

soja *f* soya.

sol *m* sun; sunshine, sunlight.

solamente *adv* only, solely.

solapa *f* lapel.

solar *m* building site; piece of land; ancestral home of a family:— *adj* solar.

soldado *m/f* soldier:— **~ raso** private.

soldar *vt* to solder; to weld; to unite.

soledad *f* solitude; loneliness.

soler *vi* to be accustomed to, be in the habit of.

solicitar *vt* to ask for, seek; to apply for (a job); to canvass for; to chase after, pursue.

solidario/ria *adj* joint; mutually binding.

soliloquio *m* soliloquy, monologue.

solista *m/f* soloist.

solitario/ria *adj* solitary:— *m* solitaire:— *m/f* hermit.

sollozar *vi* to sob.

solo *m* (*mus*) solo:— **~la** *adj* alone, single:— **a solas** alone, unaided.

sólo *adv* only.

solomillo *m* sirloin.

soltar *vt* to untie, loosen; to set free, let out:— **~se** *vr* to get loose; to come undone.

soltero/ra *m/f* bachelor/single woman:— *adj* single, unmarried.

soltura *f* looseness, slackness; agility, activity; fluency.

solucionar vt to solve; to resolve.

sombra f shade; shadow.

sombrero m hat.

sombrilla f parasol.

sombrío/bría adj shady, gloomy; sad.

somero/ra adj superficial.

someter vt to conquer (a country); to subject to one's will; to submit; to subdue:—**~se** vr to give in, submit.

somnífero m sleeping pill.

sonar vt to ring:—vi to sound; to make a noise; to be pronounced; to be talked of; to sound familiar:—**~se** vr to blow one's nose.

soñar vt, vi to dream.

sondeo m sounding; boring; (fig) poll.

soneto m sonnet.

sonido m sound.

sonreír(se) vi (vr) to smile.

sonrisa f smile.

sonrojarse vr to blush.

sonsacar vt to wheedle; to cajole; to obtain by cunning.

sopa f soup; sop.

sopetón m:—**de ~** suddenly.

soplar vt to blow away, blow off; to blow up, inflate:—vi to blow, puff.

soplón/ona m/f telltale.

soportal m portico.

soportar vt to suffer, tolerate; to support.

sorber vt to sip; to inhale; to swallow; to absorb.

sorbete m sherbet; iced fruit drink.

sordo/da adj deaf; silent, quiet:—m/f deaf person.

sorprender vt to surprise.

sorteo m draw; raffle.

sortija f ring; ringlet, curl.

sortilegio m sorcery.

sosegar vt to appease, calm:—vi to rest.

soso/sa adj insipid, tasteless; dull.

sospechar vt to suspect.

sostén m support; bra; sustenance.

sostener vt to sustain, maintain:—**~se** vr to support or maintain oneself; to contrive, remain.

sota f knave (at cards).

sótano m basement, cellar.

su pn his, her, its, one's; their; your.

suave adj smooth, soft; delicate; gentle; mild, meek.

subalterno/na adj secondary; auxiliary.

subasta f auction.

subcampeón/ona m/f runner-up.

subestimar vt to underestimate.

subir vt, vi to raise, lift up; to go up; to climb, ascend, mount; to increase, swell; to get in, get on, board; to rise (in price).

súbito/ta adj sudden, hasty; unforeseen.

sublevar vt to excite (a rebellion); to incite (a revolt):—**~se** vr to revolt.

submarino/na adj underwater:—m submarine.

subrayar vt to underline.

subsanar vt to excuse; to mend, repair; to overcome.

subsidio m subsidy, aid; benefit, allowance.

su(b)stancia f substance.

su(b)straer vt to remove; (mat) to subtract:—**~se** vr to avoid; to withdraw.

subterráneo/nea adj subterranean; underground:—m underground passage; (ferro) underground (railway).

suburbio m slum quarter; suburbs pl.

subvencionar vt to subsidize.

sucedáneo/nea adj substitute:—m substitute (food).

suceder *vt* to succeed, inherit:—*vi* to happen.

suceso *m* event; incident.

sucesor/ra *m/f* successor; heir.

sucio/cia *adj* dirty, filthy; obscene; dishonest.

sucursal *f* branch (office).

sudar *vt, vi* to sweat.

sudeste *adj* southeast, southeastern:—*m* southeast.

sudoeste *adj* southwest, southwestern:—*m* southwest.

suegra *f* mother-in-law.

suegro *m* father-in-law.

suela *f* sole of the shoe.

sueldo *m* wages *pl,* salary.

suelo *m* ground; floor; soil, surface.

suelto/ta *adj* loose; free; detached; swift:—*m* loose change.

sueño *m* sleep; dream.

suero *m* (*med*) serum; whey.

suerte *f* fate, destiny, chance, lot, fortune, good luck; kind, sort.

sufrir *vt* to suffer; to bear, put up with; to support.

sugerir *vt* to suggest.

sujetador *m* fastener; bra.

sujetar *vt* to fasten, hold down; to subdue; to subject:—**~se** *vr* to subject oneself.

sujeto/ta *adj* fastened, secure; subject, liable:—*m* subject; individual.

sumamente *adv* extremely.

sumar *vt* to add, add up; to collect, gather:—*vi* to add up.

sumergir *vt* to submerge, sink; to immerse.

sumidero *m* sewer, drain.

suministrar *vt* to supply, furnish.

sumiso/sa *adj* submissive, docile.

sumo/ma *adj* great, extreme; highest, greatest:—**a lo ~** at most.

súper *f* four-star (gas).

superar *vt* to surpass; to overcome; to exceed, go beyond.

superficial *adj* superficial; shallow.

superficie *f* surface; area.

superintendente *m/f* superintendent, supervisor; floorwalker.

superior *adj* superior; upper; higher; better:—*m/f* superior.

supermercado *m* supermarket.

superviviente *m/f* survivor:—*adj* surviving.

suplente *m/f* substitute.

suplicar *vt* to beg (for), plead (for); to beg; to plead with.

suplicio *m* torture.

suplir *vt* to supply; to make good, make up for; to replace.

suponer *vt* to suppose:—*vi* to have authority.

suprimir *vt* to suppress; to abolish; to remove; to delete.

supuesto *m* assumption:—**~/ta** *adj* supposed:—**~ que** *conj* since, granted that.

sur *adj* south, southern:—*m* south; south wind.

surco *m* furrow; groove.

surgir *vi* to emerge; to crop up.

surtido *m* assortment, supply.

surtir *vt* to supply, furnish, provide:—*vi* to spout, spurt.

suscitar *vt* to excite, stir up.

susodicho/cha *adj* above-mentioned.

suspender *vt* to suspend, hang up; to stop; to fail (an exam etc).

suspicaz *adj* suspicious, mistrustful.

suspirar *vi* to sigh.

sustentar *vt* to sustain; to support, nourish.

susto *m* fright, scare.

sustraer *vt* to take away; to subtract.

susurrar *vi* to whisper; to murmur; to rustle:—**~se** *vr* to be whispered about.

sutil *adj* subtle; thin; delicate; very soft; keen, observant.

suyo/ya *adj* his; hers; theirs; one's; his; her; its own; one's own; their own:—**de ~** per se:—**los ~s** *mpl* his own, near friends, relations, family, supporters.

T

tabaco *m* tobacco; (*fam*) cigarettes *pl.*

tabique *m* thin wall; partition wall.

tabla *f* board; shelf; plank; slab; index of a book; bed of earth in a garden.

tablero *m* plank, board; chessboard; dashboard; bulletin board; gambling den.

taburete *m* stool.

tacaño/ña *adj* mean, stingy; crafty.

tachar *vt* to find fault with; to erase.

tachuela *f* tack, nail.

tácito/ta *adj* tacit, silent; implied.

taco *m* stopper, plug; heel (of a shoe); wad; book of coupons; billiard cue.

tacón *m* heel.

tacto *m* touch, feeling; tact.

tahona *f* bakery.

taimado/da *adj* sly, cunning, crafty.

tajo *m* cut, incision; cleft, sheer drop; working area; chopping block.

tal *adj* such:—**con ~ que** provided that:—**no hay ~** no such thing.

taladro *m* drill; borer, gimlet.

talante *m* mood; appearance; aspect; will.

talar *vt* to fell (trees); to desolate.

talega *f,* **talego** *m* bag; bagful.

talla *f* raised work; sculpture; stature, size; measure (of anything); hand, draw, turn (at cards).

tallar *vt* to cut, chop; to carve in wood; to engrave; to measure.

taller *m* workshop, laboratory.

tallo *m* shoot, sprout.

talón *m* heel; receipt; cheque.

tamaño *m* size, shape, bulk.

tambalearse *vr* to stagger, waver.

también *adv* also, as well; likewise; besides.

tambor *m* drum; drummer; eardrum.

tamiz *m* fine sieve.

tampoco *adv* neither, nor.

tan *adv* so.

tanto *m* certain sum or quantity; point; goal:—**~/ta** *adj* so much, as much; very great:—*adv* so much, as much; so long, as long.

tapar *vt* to stop up, cover; to conceal, hide.

tapia *f* wall.

tapicería *f* tapestry; upholstery; upholsterer's (store).

tapiz *m* tapestry; carpet.

tapón *m* cork, plug, bung.

taquigrafía *f* shorthand.

taquilla *f* booking office; takings *pl.*

tardar *vi* to delay; to take a long time; to be late.

tarde *f* afternoon; evening:—*adv* late.

tarea *f* task.

tarima *f* platform; step.

tarjeta *f* card; visiting card:—**~ postal** postcard.

tarro *m* pot.

tarta *f* cake.

tartamudear *vi* to stutter, stammer.

tarugo *m* wooden peg or pin.

tasar *vt* to appraise, value.

tatarabuelo/la *m/f* great-great-grand-father/mother.

tataranieto/ta *m/f* great-great-grand-son/daughter.

tatuaje *m* tattoo; tattooing.

taurino/na *adj* bullfighting *compd*.

taza *f* cup; basin of a fountain.

te *pn* you.

té *m* (*bot*) tea.

teatro *m* theater, playhouse.

tebeo *m* comic.

techo *m* roof; ceiling.

tecla *f* key (of an organ, piano, etc).

técnico/ca *adj* technical.

tedio *m* boredom; dislike, abhor-rence.

tejado *m* roof covered with tiles.

tejer *vt* to weave.

tejo *m* quoit; yew tree.

tejón *m* badger.

tela *f* cloth; material.

telaraña *f* cobweb.

telefax *m invar* fax; fax (machine).

televisor *m* television set.

telón *m* curtain, drape.

tema *m* theme.

temblar *vi* to tremble.

temer *vt* to fear, doubt:—*vi* to be afraid.

temerario/ria *adj* rash.

temible *adj* dreadful, terrible.

témpano *m* ice-floe.

templado/da *adj* temperate, tem-pered.

templar *vt* to temper, moderate, cool; to tune:—**~se** *vr* to be mod-erate.

temple *m* temperature; tempera; tem-perament; tuning:—**al ~** painted in distemper.

temporada *f* time, season; epoch, period.

temprano/na *adj* early, anticipated:—*adv* early; very early, prematurely.

tenaz *adj* tenacious; stubborn.

tenaza(s) *f* (*pl*) tongs *pl*, pincers *pl*.

tender *vt* to stretch out; to expand; to extend; to hang out; to lay:—**~se** *vr* to stretch oneself out.

tendero/ra *m/f* shop-keeper.

tendón *m* tendon, sinew.

tenebroso/sa *adj* dark, obscure.

tenedor *m* holder, keeper, tenant; fork.

tener *vt* to have; to take; to hold; to possess:—**~se** *vr* to stand upright; to stop, halt; to resist; to adhere.

tenia *f* tapeworm.

teñir *vt* to tinge, dye.

tensar *vt* to tauten; to draw.

tentar *vt* to touch; to try; to tempt; to attempt.

tentempié *m* (*fam*) snack.

tenue *adj* thin; tenuous, slender.

terapia *f* therapy.

tercer(o)/ra *adj* third:—*m* (*jur*) third party.

tercio/cia *adj* third:—*m* third part.

terciopelo *m* velvet.

terco/ca *adj* obstinate.

tergiversar *vt* to distort.

terminante *adj* decisive; categorical.

terminar *vt* to finish; to end; to ter-minate:—*vi* to end; to stop.

termo *m* flask.

ternero/ra *m/f* calf; veal; heifer.

ternilla *f* gristle.

ternura *f* tenderness.

terrado *m* terrace.

terrateniente *m/f* landowner.

terraza *f* balcony; (flat) roof; terrace (in fields).

terremoto *m* earthquake.

terreno/na *adj* earthly, terrestrial:—*m* land, ground, field.

terrón *m* clod of earth; lump:—**~ones** *mpl* landed property.

terror *m* terror, dread.

terso/sa *adj* smooth, glossy.

tertulia *f* club, assembly, circle.

tesorero *m* treasurer.

tesoro *m* treasure; exchequer.

testamento *m* will, testament.

testar *vt, vi* to make one's will.

testarudo/da *adj* obstinate.

testificar *vt* to attest, witness.

testigo *m* witness, deponent.

teta *f* breast.

tetera *f* teapot.

tetilla *f* nipple; teat (of a bottle).

tétrico/ca *adj* gloomy, sullen, surly.

tez *f* complexion, hue.

ti *pn* you; yourself.

tía *f* aunt; (fam) bird.

tibio/bia *adj* lukewarm.

tiburón *m* shark.

tiempo *m* time; term; weather; (gr) tense; occasion, opportunity; season.

tienda *f* tent; awning; tilt; shop.

tierno/na *adj* tender.

tierra *f* earth; land, ground; native country.

tieso/sa *adj* stiff, hard, firm; robust; valiant; stubborn.

tiesto *m* earthen pot.

tigre *m* tiger.

tijeras *fpl* scissors *pl*.

tilde *f* tilde (ñ).

tilo *m* lime tree.

timar *vt* to con; to swindle.

timbre *m* stamp; bell; timbre; stamp duty.

tímido/da *adj* timid; cowardly.

timón *m* helm, rudder.

tímpano *m* ear-drum; small drum.

tina *f* tub; bath (tub).

tinieblas *fpl* darkness; shadows *pl*.

tino *m* skill; judgement, prudence.

tinta *f* ink; tint, dye; color.

tinte *m* tint, dye; dry cleaner's.

tinto/ta *adj* dyed:—*m* red wine.

tío *m* uncle; (fam) guy.

tiovivo *m* merry-go-round.

tipico/ca *adj* typical; characteristic; picturesque; traditional; regional.

tipo *m* type; norm; pattern; guy.

tiquismiquis *m invar* fussy person.

tira *f* abundance; strip.

tirachinas *m invar* slingshot.

tirado/da *adj* dirt-cheap; (fam) very easy:—*f* cast; distance; series; edition.

tirano/na *m/f* tyrant.

tirante *m* joist; stay; strap; brace:—*adj* taut, extended, drawn.

tirar *vt* to throw; to pull; to draw; to drop; to tend, aim at:—*vi* to shoot; to pull; to go; to tend to.

tirita *f* (sticking) plaster.

tiritar *vi* to shiver.

títere *m* puppet; ridiculous little fellow.

titubear *vi* to stammer; to stagger; to hesitate.

titular *adj* titular:—*m/f* occupant:—*m* headline:—*vt* to title:—**~se** *vr* to obtain a title.

tiza *f* chalk.

tiznar *vt* to stain; to tarnish.

tizón *m* half-burnt wood.

toalla *f* towel.

tobillo *m* ankle.

tobogán *m* toboggan; roller-coaster; slide.

tocadiscos m invar record player.
tocado m headdress, headgear.
tocar vt to touch; to strike; (mus) to play; to ring (a bell):—vi to belong; to concern; to knock; to call; to be a duty or obligation.
tocino m bacon.
todavía adv even; yet, still.
todo/da adj all, entire; every:—pn everything, all:—m whole.
todopoderoso/sa adj almighty.
toldo m awning; parasol.
tomar vt to take; to seize, grasp; to understand; to interpret, perceive; to drink; to acquire:—vi to drink; to take.
tomavistas m invar cine-camera.
tomillo m thyme.
tomo m bulk; tome; volume.
tonada f tune, melody.
tonel m cask, barrel.
tonelada f ton; (mar) tonnage duty.
tónico/ca adj tonic, strengthening:— m tonic:—f tonic (water); (mus) tonic; (fig) keynote.
tontería f foolery, nonsense.
tonto/ta adj stupid, foolish.
topar vt to run into; to find.
topo m mole; stumbler.
toquilla f head-scarf; shawl.
tórax m thorax.
torbellino m whirlwind.
torcer vt to twist, curve; to turn; to sprain:—~se vr to bend; to go wrong:—vi to turn off.
torcido/da adj oblique; crooked.
tordo m thrush:—~/da adj speckled black and white.
torear vt to avoid; to tease:—vi to fight bulls.
tormenta f storm, tempest.

tornar vt to return; to restore:—~se vr to become:—vi to return:—~ a hacer to do again.
tornasolado adj iridescent; shimmering.
torneo m tournament.
tornillo m screw.
torno m winch; revolution.
toro m bull.
toronja f grapefruit.
torpe adj dull, heavy; stupid.
torre f tower; turret; steeple.
torrefacto/ta adj roasted.
torta f cake; (fam) slap.
tortilla f omelet; pancake.
tortuga f tortoise; turtle.
tos f cough.
tosco/ca adj coarse; ill-bred, clumsy.
toser vi to cough.
tostado/da adj parched; sunburnt; light-yellow; light-brown.
tostar vt to toast, roast.
total m whole, totality:—adj total, entire:—adv in short.
tóxico/ca adj toxic:—m poison.
trabajar vt to work, labor; to persuade; to push:—vi to strive.
trabalenguas m invar tongue twister.
trabar vt to join, unite; to take hold of; to fetter, shackle.
tracción f traction:—~ delantera/ trasera front-wheel/rear-wheel drive.
traducir vt to translate.
traer vt to bring, carry; to attract; to persuade; to wear; to cause.
traficar vi to trade, do business, deal.
tragaluz m skylight.
tragaperras m o f invar slot machine.
tragar vt to swallow; to swallow up.

trago *m* drink; gulp; adversity, misfortune.

traicionar *vt* to betray.

traje *m* suit; dress; costume.

trajinar *vt* to carry:—*vi* to bustle about; to travel around.

trama *f* plot; weft, woof.

tramitar *vt* to transact; to negotiate; to handle.

tramo *m* section; piece of ground; flight of stairs.

tramoya *f* scene, theatrical decoration; trick.

trampa *f* trap, snare; trapdoor; fraud.

trampolín *m* trampoline; diving board.

tramposo/sa *adj* deceitful, swindling.

tranca *f* bar, crossbeam.

trance *m* danger; last stage of life; trance.

tranquilizar *vt* to calm; to reassure.

tranquilo/la *adj* tranquil, calm, quiet.

transbordador *m* ferry.

transbordo *m* transfer:—**hacer ~** to change (trains).

transcurrir *vi* to pass; to turn out.

transeúnte *adj* transitory:—*m* passerby.

transigir *vi* to compromise.

tránsito *m* passage; transition; road, way; change; removal; death of holy or virtuous persons.

transmitir *vt* to transmit; to broadcast.

transparente *adj* transparent; seethrough.

transpirar *vt* to perspire; to transpire.

tranvía *m* tram.

trapo *m* rag, tatter.

tráquea *f* windpipe.

tras *prep* after, behind.

trascender *vi* to smell; to come out:— **~ de** to go beyond.

trasegar *vt* to move about; to decant.

trasero/ra *adj* back:—*m* bottom.

trasfondo *m* background.

trasgredir *vt* to contravene.

trashumante *adj* migrating.

trasladar *vt* to transport; to transfer; to postpone; to transcribe, copy:— **~se** *vr* to move.

trasnochar *vi* to watch, sit up the whole night.

traspasar *vt* to remove, transport; to transfix, pierce; to return; to exceed (the proper bounds); to transfer.

traste *m* fret (of a guitar):—**dar al ~ con algo** to ruin something.

trastero *m* lumber room.

trastienda *f* back room behind a shop.

trasto *m* piece of junk; useless person.

trastornar *vt* to overthrow, overturn; to confuse:—**~se** *vr* to go crazy.

trastrocar *vt* to invert (the order of).

tratar *vt* to traffic, trade; to use; to treat; to handle; to address; **~se** *vr* to treat each other.

trato *m* treatment; manner, address; trade, traffic; conversation; (*com*) agreement.

través *m* (*fig*) reverse:—**de** *o* **al ~** across, crossways:—**a ~ de** *prep* across; over; through.

travesía *f* crossing; cross-street; trajectory; (*mar*) side wind.

travieso/sa *adj* restless, uneasy, fidgety; lively; naughty.

trayecto *m* road; journey, stretch; course.

trazar *vt* to plan out; to project; to trace.

trébedes *fpl* trivet, tripod.

trébol *m* trefoil, clover.

trece *adj, m* thirteen; thirteenth.

trecho *m* space, distance of time or place:—**a ~s** at intervals.

tregua *f* truce, cessation of hostilities.

treinta *adj, m* thirty.

tremendo/da *adj* terrible, formidable; awful, grand.

tren *m* train, retinue; show, ostentation; (*ferro*) train:—**~ de gran velocidad** fast *or* express train:—**~ de mercancías** freight train.

trenza *f* braid (in hair), plaited silk.

trepar *vi* to climb; to crawl.

tres *adj, m* three.

tresillo *m* three-piece suite; (*mus*) triplet.

tricotar *vi* to knit.

trigésimo/ma *adj, m* thirtieth.

trigo *m* wheat.

trillado/da *adj* beaten; trite, hackneyed:—**camino ~** common routine.

trinar *vi* to trill, quaver; to be angry.

trinchar *vt* to carve, divide (meat).

trineo *m* sled.

trino *m* trill.

tripa *f* gut, intestine:—**~s** *fpl* guts; tripe.

tripulación *f* crew.

tripular *vt* to man; to drive.

tris *m invar:*—**estar en un ~ de** to be on the point of.

triste *adj* sad, mournful, melancholy.

triturar *vt* to reduce to powder; to grind, pound.

triza *f:*—**hacer ~s** to smash to bits; to tear to shreds.

trocar *vt* to exchange.

trompa *f* trumpet; proboscis; large top.

trompazo *m* heavy blow; accident.

trompeta *f* trumpet:—*m* trumpeter.

tronar *vi* to thunder; to rage.

tronco *m* trunk; log of wood; stock.

tropel *m* confused noise; hurry; bustle, confusion; heap; crowd:—**en ~** in a tumultuous and confused way.

tropezar *vi* to stumble:—*vt* to meet accidentally.

trotamundos *m invar* globetrotter.

trotar *vi* to trot.

trozo *m* piece.

trucha *f* trout.

truco *m* knack; trick.

trueno *m* thunderclap.

trueque *m* exchange.

truncar *vt* to truncate, maim.

tu *adj* your.

tú *pn* you.

tubería *f* pipe; pipeline.

tubo *m* tube.

tuerca *f* nut.

tumba *f* tomb.

tumbar *vt* to knock down:—*vi* to fall down:—**~se** *vr* to lie down to sleep.

tumbona *f* easy chair; beach chair.

tunda *f* beating.

tupido/da *adj* dense.

turbar *vt* to disturb, trouble:—**~se** *vr* to be disturbed.

turbio/bia *adj* muddy; troubled.

turno *m* turn; shift; opportunity.

turrón *m* nougat (almond cake).

tutear *vt* to address as 'tu'.

tutor *m* guardian, tutor.

tuyo/ya *adj* yours:—**~s** *pl* friends and relations of the party addressed.

U

u *conj* or (instead of *o* before an *o* or *ho*).

ubicar *vt* to place:—**~se** to be located.

ufanarse *vr* to boast.

últimamente *adv* lately.

ultimar *vt* to finalize; to finish.

último/ma *adj* last; latest; bottom; top.

ultrajar *vt* to outrage; to despise; to abuse.

ultramar *adj, m* overseas.

ultramarinos *mpl* groceries.

umbral *m* threshold.

un/una *art* a, an:—*adj, m* one (for **uno**).

uña *f* nail; hoof; claw, talon.

ungir *vt* to anoint.

ungüento *m* ointment.

únicamente *adv* only, simply.

único/ca *adj* only; singular, unique.

unidad *f* unity; unit; conformity; union.

unificar *vt* to unite.

unir *vt* to join, unite; to mingle; to bind, tie:—**~se** *vr* to associate.

uno *m* one:—**~/una** *adj* one; sole, only:—**~ a otro** one another:—**~ a ~** one by one:—**a una** jointly together.

untar *vt* to anoint; to grease; (*fam*) to bribe.

urbanidad *f* urbanity, politeness.

urbanismo *m* town planning.

urbanización *f* housing estate.

urdir *vt* to warp; to contrive.

urgencia *f* urgency; emergency; need, necessity.

urinario/ria *adj* urinary:—*m* urinal.

urna *f* urn; ballot box.

urraca *f* magpie.

usado/da *adj* used; experienced; worn.

usar *vt* to use, make use of; to wear:—**~se** *vr* to be used.

usted *pn* you.

usuario *m* user.

útero *m* uterus, womb.

util *adj* useful, profitable:—*m* utility.

utilizar *vt* to use; to make useful.

uva *f* grape.

V

vaca *f* cow; beef.

vacaciones *fpl* vacation; holidays *pl*.

vacante *adj* vacant:—*f* vacancy.

vaciar *vt* to empty, clear; to mold:—*vi* to fall, decrease (of waters):—**~se** *vr* to empty.

vacilar *vi* to hesitate; to falter; to fail.

vacío/cía *adj* void, empty; unoccupied; concave; vain; presumptuous:—*m* vacuum; emptiness.

vacuna *f* vaccine.

vacuno/na *adj* bovine, cow *compd*.

vagar *vi* to rove or loiter about; to wander.

vago/ga *adj* vagrant; restless; vague.

vagón *m* (*ferro*) wagon; carriage:—**~ de mercancías** goods wagon.

vaho *m* steam, vapor.

vaina *f* pod, husk.

vaivén *m* fluctuation, instability; giddiness.

vajilla *f* crockery.

vale m OK; promissory note, IOU.

valer vi to be valuable; to be deserving; to cost; to be valid; to be worth; to produce; to be current:—vt to protect, favor; to be worth; to be equivalent to:—~**se** vr to employ, make use of; to have recourse to.

valiente adj robust, vigorous; valiant, brave; boasting.

valija f suitcase.

valioso/sa adj valuable.

valla f fence; hurdle; barricade.

valle m valley.

valor m value; price; validity; force; power; courage, valor.

valorar vt to value; to evaluate.

vals m invar waltz.

valsar vi to waltz

válvula f valve.

vanidoso/sa adj vain, showy; haughty; conceited.

vano/na adj vain; useless, frivolous; arrogant; futile:—**en** ~ in vain.

vapor m vapor, steam; breath.

vaquero m cow-herd:—~/**ra** adj belonging to a cowman:—~**s** mpl jeans pl.

vara f rod; pole, staff; stick.

variar vt to vary; to modify; to change:—vi to vary.

varices fpl varicose veins pl.

varilla f small rod; curtain rod; spindle, pivot.

vario/ria adj varied, different; vague; variegated:—~**s** pl some; several.

varón m man, male.

vasco/ca adj, m/f Basque.

vasija f vessel.

vaso m glass; vessel; vase.

vástago m bud, shoot; offspring.

vasto/ta adj vast, huge.

vaticinar vt to divine, foretell.

vatio m watt.

vecindad f inhabitants of a place; neighborhood.

vecino/na adj neighboring; near:—m neighbor, inhabitant.

veinte adj, m twenty.

veintena f twentieth part; score.

vejar vt to vex; to humiliate.

vejez f old age.

vejiga f bladder.

vela f watch; watchfulness; nightguard; candle; sail:—**hacerse a la** ~ to set sail.

velar vi to stay awake; to be attentive: —vt to guard, watch.

velero/ra adj swift-sailing.

veleta f weather cock.

vello m down; gossamer; short downy hair.

velo m veil; pretext.

velocidad f speed; velocity.

vena f vein.

venado m deer; venison.

vencer vt to defeat; to conquer, vanquish:—vi to win; to expire.

vendaje m bandage, dressing for wounds.

vendaval m gale.

vender vt to sell.

vendimia f grape harvest; vintage.

vendimiar vt to harvest, gather; to profit from (something).

veneno m poison, venom.

venerar vt to venerate, worship.

vengar vt to revenge, avenge:—~**se** vr to take revenge.

venida f arrival; return; overflow of a river.

venidero/ra adj future:—~**s** mpl posterity.

venir *vi* to come, arrive; to follow, succeed; to happen; to spring from:—**~se** *vr* to ferment.

venta *f* sale.

ventaja *f* advantage.

ventana *f* window; window shutter; nostril.

ventilar *vt* to ventilate; to fan; to discuss.

ventisca *f*, **ventisco** *m* snowstorm.

ventosidad *f* flatulence.

ventura *f* happiness; luck, chance, fortune:—**por ~** by chance.

ver *vt* to see, look at; to observe; to visit:—*vi* to understand; to see:—**~se** *vr* to be seen; to be conspicuous; to find oneself:—**~se con uno** to have a bone to pick with someone:—*m* sense of sight; appearance.

veraneo *m* summer vacation.

verano *m* summer.

veras *fpl* truth, sincerity:—**de ~** in truth, really.

veraz *adj* truthful.

verbena *f* fair; dance.

verdad *f* truth, veracity; reality; reliability.

verdadero/ra *adj* true; real; sincere.

verde *m, adj* green.

verdura *f* verdure; vegetables *pl*, greens *pl*.

vereda *f* path, trail; sidewalk.

vergüenza *f* shame; bashfulness; confusion.

verificar *vt* to check, verify:—**~se** *vr* to happen.

verruga *f* wart.

vertedero *m* sewer, drain; tip.

verter *vt* to pour; to spill; to empty:—*vi* to flow.

vértice *m* vertex, zenith; crown (head).

vertiente *f* slope; waterfall, cascade.

vertiginoso/sa *adj* giddy.

vespertino/na *adj* evening *compd*.

vestíbulo *m* vestibule, lobby.

vestido *m* dress; clothes *pl*.

vestir *vt* to put on; to wear; to dress; to adorn; to cloak, disguise:—*vi* to dress:—**~se** to get dressed.

vestuario *m* clothes *pl*; uniform; vestry; changing room.

veta *f* vein (in mines, wood, etc); streak; grain.

veteado/da *adj* veined; striped:—*m* veining; streaks.

veterano/na *adj* experienced, practiced:—*m* veteran, old soldier.

veterinaría *f* veterinary medicine.

veterinario/ria *m/f* veterinary surgeon.

vez *f* time; turn; return:—**cada ~** each time:—**una ~** once:—**a veces** sometimes, by turns.

veza *f* (*bot*) vetch.

vía *f* way; road, route; mode, manner, method; (*ferro*) railway line.

viajante *m* sales representative.

viajar *vi* to travel.

víbora *f* viper.

vibrar *vt, vi* to vibrate.

vicio *m* vice.

vid *f* (*bot*) vine.

vida *f* life.

vídeo *m* video.

vidriera *f* stained-glass window; shop window.

vidrio *m* glass.

vieira *f* scallop.

viejo/ja *adj* old; ancient, antiquated.

viento *m* wind; air.

vientre *m* belly.

viernes *m invar* Friday:—**V ~ Santo** Good Friday.

viga *f* beam; girder.

vigente *adj* in force.

vigésimo/ma *adj, m* twentieth.
vigía *f* (*mar*) lookout:—*m* watchman.
vigilar *vt* to watch over:—*vi* to keep watch.
vil *adj* mean, sordid, low; worthless; infamous; ungrateful.
vilipendiar *vt* to despise, revile.
villancico *m* Christmas carol.
vilo:—**en** ~ *adv* in the air; in suspense.
vinagre *m* vinegar.
vincular *vt* to link.
viñedo *m* vineyard.
vino *m* wine:—~ **tinto** red wine.
violar *vt* to rape; to violate; to profane.
violentar *vt* to force.
violento/ta *adj* violent; forced; absurd; embarrassing.
violeta *f* violet.
violón *m* double bass.
virar *vi* to swerve.
viril *adj* virile, manly.
virtud *f* virtue.
viruela *f* smallpox.
visa *f,* **visado** *m* visa.
viscoso/sa *adj* viscous, glutinous.
visillos *mpl* net curtains *pl*.
visión *f* sight, vision; fantasy.
visitar *vt* to visit.
vislumbrar *vt* to catch a glimpse of; to perceive indistinctly.
visón *m* mink.
víspera *f* eve; evening before:—~**s** *pl* vespers.
vista *f* sight, view; vision; eyesight; appearance; looks *pl;* prospect; intention; (*jur*) trial:—*m* customs officer.
vistazo *m* glance.
vistoso/sa *adj* colorful, attractive, lively.
vitalicio/cia *adj* for life.
vitorear *vt* to shout, applaud.

vitrina *f* showcase.
viudo/a *f* widower, widow.
vivaz *adj* lively.
víveres *mpl* provisions.
vivero *m* nursery (for plants); fish farm.
vivienda *f* housing; flat, apartment.
viviente *adj* living.
vivir *vt* to live through; to go through:—*vi* to live; to last.
vivo/va *adj* alive; lively:—**al** ~ to the life; very realistically.
vocablo *m* word, term.
vocal *f* vowel:—*m/f* member (of a committee):—*adj* vocal, oral.
vociferar *vt* to shout; to proclaim in a loud voice:—*vi* to yell.
volante *adj* flying:—*m* (*auto*) steering wheel; note; pamphlet; shuttlecock.
volar *vi* to fly; to pass swiftly (of time); to rush, hurry:—*vt* to blow up, explode.
volcán *m* volcano.
volcar *vt* to upset, overturn; to make giddy; to empty out; to exasperate:—~**se** *vr* to tip over.
volquete *m* tipcart; dump truck.
voltear *vt* to turn over; to overturn:—*vi* to roll over, tumble.
voltereta *f* tumble; somersault.
voluble *adj* unpredictable; fickle.
volumen *m* volume; size.
voluntad *f* will, willpower; wish, desire.
volver *vt* to turn (over); to turn upside down; to turn inside out:—*vi* to return, go back:—~**se** *vr* to turn around.
vórtice *m* whirlpool.
vos *pn* you.
vosotros/tras *pn pl* you.
votar *vi* to vow; to vote.
voz *f* voice; shout; rumor; word, term.

vuelo *m* flight; wing; projection of a building; ruffle, frill:—**cazar al ~** to catch in flight:—**~ chárter** charter flight.

vuelta *f* turn; circuit; return; row of stitches; cuff; change; bend, curve; reverse, other side; return journey.

vuestro/tra *adj* your:—*pn* yours.

WXYZ

xenofobia *f* xenophobia.

xilófono *m* xylophone.

y *conj* and.

ya *adv* already; now; immediately; at once; soon:—*conj* **~ que** since, seeing that:—**¡~!** of course!, sure!

yacimiento *m* deposit.

yate *m* yacht, sailing boat.

yedra *f* ivy.

yegua *f* mare.

yema *f* bud; leaf; yolk:—**~ del dedo** tip of the finger.

yerno *m* son-in-law.

yeso *m* gypsum; plaster:—**~ mate** plaster of Paris.

yo *pn* I:—**~ mismo** I myself.

yodo *m* iodine.

yogur *m* yogurt.

yunque *m* anvil.

yute *m* jute.

zafiro *m* sapphire.

zaguán *m* porch, hall.

zalamero/ra *adj* flattering:—*m/f* wheedler.

zamarra *f* sheepskin (jacket).

zambullirse *vr* to plunge into water, dive.

zampar *vt* to gobble down; to put away hurriedly:—**~se** *vr* to thrust oneself suddenly into any place; to crash, hurtle.

zanahoria *f* carrot.

zancada *f* stride.

zancudo/da *adj* long legged:—*m* mosquito.

zángano *m* drone; idler, slacker.

zanja *f* ditch, trench.

zapata *f* boot:—**~ de freno** (*auto*) brake shoe.

zapatilla *f* slipper; pump (shoe); (*dep*) trainer, training shoe.

zapato *m* shoe.

zarandear *vt* to shake vigorously.

zarcillo *m* earring; tendril.

zarpar *vi* to weigh anchor.

zarza *f* bramble.

zarzuela *f* Spanish light opera.

zócalo *m* plinth, base; baseboard.

zona *f* zone; area, belt.

zopenco/ca *adj* dull, very stupid.

zoquete *m* block; crust of bread; (*fam*) blockhead.

zorro/a *m* fox; cunning person.

zozobrar *vi* (*mar*) to founder; to capsize; (*fig*) to fail; to be anxious.

zueco *m* wooden shoe; clog.

zumbar *vt* to hit:—**~se** *vr* to hit each other:—*vi* to buzz.

zumo *m* juice.

zurcir *vt* to darn; (*fig*) to join, unite; to hatch (lies).

zurdo/da *adj* left; left-handed.

zurrar *vt* (*fam*) to flog, lay into; (*fig*) to criticize harshly.

English–Spanish Dictionary

A

a *art* un, uno, una:—*prep* a, al, en.

abandon *vt* abandonar, dejar.

abash *vt* avergonzar, causar confusión,

abbey *n* abadía *f.*

abbot *n* abad *m.*

abbreviate *vt* abreviar, acortar.

abbreviation *n* abreviatura *f.*

abdicate *vt* abdicar; renunciar.

abdication *n* abdicación *f;* renuncia *f.*

abdomen *n* abdomen, bajo vientre *m.*

abduct *vt* secuestrar.

aberration *n* error *m;* aberración *f.*

abet *vt:*—**to aid and ~** ser cómplice de.

abide *vt* soportar, sufrir.

ability *n* habilidad, capacidad.

ablaze *adj* en llamas.

able *adj* capaz, hábil.

able-bodied *adj* robusto/ta, vigoroso/sa.

ably *adv* con habilidad.

abnormal *adj* anormal.

abnormality *n* anormalidad *f.*

aboard *adv* a bordo.

abode *n* domicilio *m.*

abolish *vt* abolir, anular.

abolition *n* abolición, anulación *f.*

abominable *adj* abominable.

abomination *n* abominación *f.*

aboriginal *adj* aborigen.

abort *vi* abortar.

abortion *n* aborto *m.*

abound *vi* abundar.

about *prep* acerca de, acerca.

above *prep* encima.

aboveboard *adj* legitimo/ma.

abrasion *n* abrasión *f.*

abrasive *adj* abrasivo/va.

abroad *adv* en el extranjero.

abrupt *adj* brusco/ca.

abscess *n* absceso *m.*

abscond *vi* esconderse; huirse.

absence *n* ausencia *f.*

absent *adj* ausente.

absentee *n* ausente *m.*

absent-minded *adj* distraído/da.

absolute *adj* absoluto/ta.

absorb *vt* absorber.

abstain *vi* abstenerse.

abstinence *n* abstinencia *f.*

abstinent *adj* abstinente.

abstract *adj* abstracto/ta:—*n* extracto *m.*

abstraction *n* abstracción *f.*

absurd *adj* absurdo/da.

abundance *n* abundancia *f.*

abundant *adj* abundante.

abuse *vt* abusar; maltratar.

abusive *adj* abusivo/va, ofensivo/va.

abysmal *adj* abismal.

abyss *n* abismo *m.*

acacia *n* acacia *f.*

academic *adj* académico/ca.

academy *n* academia *f.*

accede *vi* acceder.

accelerate *vt* acelerar.

accelerator *n* acelerador *m.*

accent *n* acento *m;* tono *m.*

accentuate *vt* acentuar.

accept *vt* aceptar; admitir.

acceptable *adj* aceptable.

acceptance *n* aceptación *f.*

access *n* acceso *m;* entrada *f.*

accessible *adj* accesible.

accession *n* aumento.

accessory *n* accesorio *m.*

accident n accidente m; casualidad f.

acclaim vt aclamar, aplaudir.

accommodate vt alojar; complacer.

accommodation n alojamiento m.

accompany vt acompañar.

accomplice n cómplice m.

accomplish vt efectuar, completar.

accord n acuerdo, convenio m.

accordance n:—**in ~ with** de acuerdo con.

according prep segun, conforme.

accordion n (mus) acordeón m.

account n cuenta f.

accountability n responsabilidad f.

accountancy n contabilidad f.

accountant n contable, contador m.

accrue vi resultar, provenir.

accumulate vt acumular; amontonar.

accuracy n exactitud f.

accurate adj exacto/ta.

accursed adj maldito/ta.

accuse vt acusar; culpar.

accustom vt acostumbrar.

ache n dolor m:—vi doler.

achieve vt realizar; obtener.

achievement n realización f.

acid adj ácido/da; agrio/ria:—n ácido m.

acknowledge vt reconocer, confesar.

acne n acne m.

acorn n bellota f.

acoustics n acústica f.

acquaint vt informar, avisar.

acquaintance n conocimiento m; conocido m.

acquire vt adquirir.

acquisition n adquisición

acquit vt absolver.

acquittal n absolución f.

acre n acre m.

acrid adj acre.

acrimony n acrimonio m.

across adv de través.

action n acción f.

activate vt activar.

active adj activo/va.

activity n actividad f.

actor n actor m.

actress n actriz f.

actual adj real; efectivo/va.

actuary n actuario de seguros m.

acumen n agudeza f.

acute adj agudo/da; ingenioso/sa.

ad n aviso m.

adage n proverbio m.

adamant adj inflexible.

adapt vt adaptar.

adaptor n adaptador m.

add vt añadir, agregar:—**to ~ up** sumar.

adder n culebra f; víbora f.

addict n drogadicto m.

addiction n dependencia f.

addition n adición f.

additional adj adicional.

additive n aditivo m.

address vt dirigir:—n dirección f.

adenoids npl vegetaciones adenoideas fpl.

adept adj hábil.

adequacy n suficiencia f.

adequate adj adecuado/da; suficiente.

adhere vi adherir.

adhesion n adhesión f.

adhesive adj pegajoso/sa.

adhesiveness n adhesividad f.

adieu adv adiós:—n despedida f.

adjacent adj adyacente, contiguo/gua.

adjective n adjetivo m.

adjoining adj contiguo/gua.

adjournment n prorroga f.

adjudicate vt adjudicar.

adjust *vt* ajustar, acomodar.
adjustable *adj* ajustable.
adjustment *n* ajustamiento *m*.
ad lib *vt* improvisar.
administer *vt* administrar.
administration *n* administración *f.*
administrative *adj* administrativo/va.
admirable *adj* admirable.
admiral *n* almirante *m*.
admire *vt* admirar.
admirer *n* admira/a *m/f.*
admission *adj* entrada *f.*
admit *vt* admitir.
admittance *n* entrada *f.*
admittedly *adj* de acuerdo que.
admonish *vt* amonestar.
ad nauseam *adv* hasta el cansancio.
adolescence *n* adolescencia *f.*
adopt *vt* adoptar.
adorable *adj* adorable.
adore *vt* adorar.
adorn *vt* adornar.
adrift *adv* a la deriva.
adult *adj* adulto/ta.
adulterate *vt* adulterar, corromper.
adulterer *n* adultero *m*.
adultery *n* adulterio *m*.
advance *vt* avanzar; promover.
advantage *n* ventaja *f.*
advantageous *adj* ventajoso/sa.
adventure *n* aventura *f.*
adventurous *adj* intrépido/da.
adverb *n* adverbio *m*.
adversary *n* adversario enemigo *m*.
adversity *n* calamidad *f;* infortunio *m*.
advertise *vt* anunciar.
advertisement *n* aviso *m*.
advice *n* consejo *m;* aviso *m*.
advisability *n* prudencia *f.*
advise *vt* aconsejar; avisar.
advocacy *n* defensa *f.*

advocate *n* abogado *m;* protector *m*.
aerial *n* antena *f.*
aerobics *npl* aerobic *m*.
aerometer *n* areómetro *m*.
aerosol *n* aerosol *m*.
afar *adv* lejos, distante.
affair *n* asunto *m;* negocio *m*.
affect *vt* conmover; afectar.
affection *n* cariño *m*.
affidavit *n* declaración jurada *f.*
affiliate *vt* afiliar.
affiliation *n* afiliación *f.*
affinity *n* afinidad *f.*
affirm *vt* afirmar, declarar.
affirmation *n* afirmación *f.*
affirmative *adj* afirmativo/va.
affix *vt* pegar:—*n* (*gr*) afijo *m*.
afflict *vt* afligir.
affliction *n* aflicción *f;* dolor *m*.
affluence *n* opulencia *f.*
affluent *adj* opulento/ta.
affray *n* asalto *m;* tumulto *m*.
aflame *adv* en llamas.
afloat *adv* flotante, a flote.
afore *prep* antes:—*adv* primero.
afraid *adj* espantado/da.
afresh *adv* de nuevo, otra vez.
after *prep* después.
afterbirth *n* secundinas *fpl.*
after-effects *npl* consecuencias *fpl.*
afterlife *n* vida venidera *f.*
aftermath *n* consecuencias *fpl.*
afternoon *n* tarde *f.*
aftershave *n* aftershave *m*.
aftertaste *n* resabio *m*.
afterwards *adv* después.
again *adv* otra vez.
against *prep* contra.
agate *n* ágata *f.*
age *n* edad *f;* vejez *f.*
agency *n* agencia *f.*
agenda *n* orden del día *m*.

agent n agente m.

aggrandizement n engrandecimiento m.

aggravate vt agravar, exagerar.

aggregate n agregado m.

aggregation n agregación f.

aggression n agresión f.

aggressor n agresor m.

aggrieved adj ofendido/da.

aghast adj horrorizado/da.

agile adj ágil; diestro/tra.

agitate vt agitar.

ago adv pasado.

agonizing adj atngustioso.

agony n agonía f.

agree vt convenir:—vi estar de acuerdo/da.

agreeable adj agradable; amable.

agreement n acuerdo m.

agriculture n agricultura f.

ah! excl iah! iay!

ahead adv más allá, delante de otro.

aid vt ayudar, socorrer.

AIDS n SIDA m.

ail vt afligir, molestar.

ailment n dolencia, indisposición f.

aim vt apuntar aspirar a; intentar.

air n aire m:—vt airear; ventilar.

air balloon n globo aerostático m.

airborne adj aerotransportado/da.

air-conditioning n climatización f.

aircraft n avión m.

air force n fuerzas aéreas fpl.

airline n línea aérea f.

airmail n:—by ~ por avión,

airplane n avión m.

airport n aeropuerto m.

airstrip n pista de aterrizaje f.

airy adj bien ventilado/da.

aisle n nave de una iglesia f.

akin adj parecido/da.

alabaster n alabastro m.

alarm n alarma f:—vt alarmar; inquietar.

alas adv desgraciadamente.

albeit conj aunque.

album n album m.

alchemy n alquimia f.

alcohol n alcohol m.

alcoholic adj alcohólico/ca:—n alcoholizado m.

alcove n nicho m.

alder n aliso m.

ale n cerveza f.

alert adj vigilante; alerto/ta.

algae npl alga f.

algebra n álgebra f.

alias adj alias.

alibi n (law) coartada f.

alien adj ajeno/na.

alienate vt enajenar.

alight vi apearse.

align vt alinear.

alike adj semejante, igual.

alive adj vivo/va, viviente; activo/va.

alkali n álcali m.

alkaline adj alcalino/na.

all adj todo/da.

allay vt aliviar.

allegation n alegación f.

allege vt alegar; declarar.

allegiance n lealtad, fidelidad f.

allegorical adj alegórico/ca.

allegory n alegoría f.

allergy n alergia f.

alley n callejuela f.

alliance n alianza f.

allied adj aliado/da.

alligator n caimán m.

allocate vt repartir.

allot vt asignar.

allow vt conceder; permitir; dar.

allowance n concesión f.

alloy n liga, mezcla f.

allspice *n* pimienta de Jamaica *f.*
allude *vt* aludir.
allure *n* fascinación *f.*
allusion *n* alusión *f.*
allusive *adj* alusivo/va.
alluvial *adj* aluvial.
ally *n* aliado *m:—vt* aliar.
almanac *n* almanaque *m.*
almighty *adj* omnipotente, todopoderoso/sa.
almond *n* almendra *f.*
almost *adv* casi; cerca de.
aloft *prep* arriba.
alone *adj* solo.
along *adv* a lo largo.
aloof *adv* lejos.
alphabet *n* alfabeto *m.*
alphabetical *adj* alfabético/ca.
alpine *adj* alpino/na.
already *adv* ya.
also *adv* también, además.
altar *n* altar *m.*
altarpiece *n* retablo *m.*
alter *vt* modificar.
alteration *n* alteración *f.*
alternate *adj* alterno/na:—*vt* alternar, variar.
alternator *n* alternador *m.*
alternative *n* alternativa *f.*
although *conj* aunque, no obstante.
altitude *n* altitud, altura *f.*
altogether *adv* del todo.
aluminum *n* aluminio *m.*
always *adv* siempre, constantemente.
a.m. *adv* de la mañana.
amalgam *n* amalgama *f.*
amalgamate *vt vi* amalgamar(se).
amaryllis *n* (*bot*) amarillas *f.*
amass *vt* acumular, amontonar.
amateur *n* aficionado *m.*
amateurish *adj* torpe.
amaze *vt* asombrar.

amazon *n* amazona *f.*
ambassador *n* embajador *m.*
amber *n* ámbar *m.*
ambidextrous *adj* ambidextro/tra.
ambiguity *n* ambigüedad, duda *f.*
ambiguous *adj* ambiguo:—**~ly** *adv* ambiguamente.
ambition *n* ambición *f.*
amble *vi* andar sin prisa.
ambulance *n* ambulancia *f.*
ambush *n* emboscada *f.*
amenable *adj* sensible.
amend *vt* enmendar.
amendment *n* enmienda *f.*
amends *npl* compensación *f.*
amenities *npl* comodidades *fpl.*
America *n* América *f.*
amethyst *n* amatista *f.*
amiable *adj* amable.
amiableness *n* amabilidad *f.*
amiably *adv* amablemente.
amicable *adj* amigable.
amid(st) *prep* entre, en medio de.
amiss *adv:—***something's ~** pasa algo malo.
ammonia *n* amoníaco *m.*
ammunition *n* municiones *fpl.*
amnesia *n* amnesia *f.*
amnesty *n* amnistía *f.*
amoral *adv* amoral.
amorous *adj* amoroso/sa.
amount *n* importe *m;* cantidad *f.*
amp(ere) *n* amperio *m.*
amphibian *n* anfibio *m.*
amphibious *adj* anfibio/bia.
amphitheater *n* anfiteatro *m.*
ample *adj* amplio/lia.
ampleness *n* amplitud, abundancia *f.*
amplifier *n* amplificador *m*
amplify *vt* ampliar, extender.
amplitude *n* amplitud, extensión *f.*
amputate *vt* amputar.

amuse vt entretener, divertir.
amusement n diversión f.
amusing adj divertido/da.
an art un, uno, una.
anachronism n anacronismo m.
anemia n anemia f.
anesthetic n anestesia f.
analogy n analogía f.
analyse vt analizar.
anarchy n anarquía f.
anatomical adj anatómico/ca.
anatomy n anatomía f
ancestor n:—~s pl antepasados mpl.
ancestral adj hereditario/ria.
ancestry n raza, alcurnia f.
anchor n ancla f:—vi anclar.
anchovy n anchoa f.
ancient adj antiguo.
and conj y, e.
anecdote n anécdota f
anemone n (bot) anémona f
angel n ángel m
anger n cólera f:—vt enojar, irritar.
angle n ángulo m:—vt pescar concana.
anglicism n anglicismo m.
angry adj enojado/da.
anguish n ansia, angustia f
angular adj angular.
animal n adj animal m.
animation n animación f
aniseed n anís m **ankle** n tobillo m.
annals n anales mpl.
annex vt anejar:—n anejo m.
annihilate vt aniquilar.
annihilation n aniquilación f.
anniversary n aniversario m.
annotate vi anotar.
announce vt anunciar, publicar.
announcement n anuncio m.
annoy vt molestar.
annual adj anual.

annunciation n anunciación f
anoint vt untar, ungir.
anomaly n anomalía, irregularidad f.
anon adv más tarde.
anonymity n anonimato m.
anonymous adj anónimo/ma.
anorexia n anorexia f.
another adj otro/tra.
answer vt responder.
answering machine n contestador automático m.
ant n hormiga f.
antagonize vt provocar.
antarctic adj antártico/ca.
antelope n antílope m.
antenna npl antena f.
anterior adj anterior, precedente.
anthem n himno m.
anthology n antología f.
anthropology n antropología f
antibiotic n antibiótico m.
antibody n anticuerpo m.
Antichrist n Anticristo m.
anticipate vt anticipar, prevenir.
anticipation n anticipación f.
antidote n antídoto m.
antipodes npl antípodas fpl
antiquarian n anticuario m.
antiquated adj antiguo/gua.
antiquity n antigüedad f.
antiseptic adj antiséptico/ca.
antler n cuerna f.
anvil n yunque m.
anxiety n ansiedad, ansia f.
anxious adj ansioso/sa.
any adj pn cualquier, cualquiera; alguno, alguna
apart adv aparte, separadamente.
apartment n departamento m.
apathy n apatía f.
ape n mono m.

apologize *vt* disculpar.

apology *n* apología, defensa *f.*

apostrophe *n* apóstrofe *m.*

appall *vt* espantar, aterrar.

apparatus *n* aparato *m.*

apparent *adj* evidente, aparente.

apparition *n* aparición, visión *f.*

appeal *vi* apelar.

appear *vi* aparecer.

appease *vt* aplacar.

append *vt* anejar.

appendicitis *n* apendicitis *f.*

appendix *n* apéndice *m.*

appetite *n* apetito *m.*

applaud *vi* aplaudir.

apple *n* manzana *f.*

appliance *n* aparato *m.*

applicable *adj* aplicable.

applicant *n* aspirante, candidato *m.*

application *n* aplicación *f*; solicitud *f.*

applied *adj* aplicado/da.

apply *vt* aplicar.

appoint *vt* nombrar.

appointment *n* cita *f*; nombramiento *m.*

apportion *vt* repartir.

appraisal *n* estimación *f.*

appraise *vt* tasar; estimar.

appreciate *vt* apreciar; agradecer.

apprehend *vt* arrestar.

apprehension *n* aprensión *f.*

apprehensive *adj* aprensivo/va.

apprentice *n* aprendiz *m.*

approach *vt vi* aproximar(se).

appropriate *vt* apropiarse de:—*adj* apropiado/da.

approve (of) *vt* aprobar.

April *n* abril *m.*

apron *n* delantal *m.*

apse *n* ábside *m.*

apt *adj* apto/ta, idóneo/nea.

aptitude *n* aptitud *f.*

aquarium *n* acuario *m.*

Aquarius *n* Acuario *m.*

aqueduct *n* acueducto *m.*

arable *adj* labrantío/tía.

arbitrate *vt* arbitrar.

arcade *n* galería *f.*

arch *n* arco *m.*

archeology *n* arqueología *f.*

archaic *adj* arcaico/ca.

archbishop *n* arzobispo *m.*

archer *n* arquero *m.*

architect *n* arquitecto/ta *m/f.*

architecture *n* arquitectura *f.*

archives *npl* archivos *mpl.*

arctic *adj* ártico/ca.

area *n* área *f*; espacio *m.*

arena *n* arena *f.*

arguably *adv* posiblemente.

argue *vi* discutir.

argument *n* argumento *m*, controversia *f.*

arid *adj* árido/da, estéril.

aridity *n* sequedad *f.*

Aries *n* Aries *m.*

arise *vi* levantarse.

aristocracy *n* aristocracia *f.*

arithmetic *n* aritmética *f.*

ark *n* arca *f.*

arm *n* brazo *m*; arma *f.*

armament *n* armamento *m.*

armchair *n* sillón *m.*

armor *n* armadura *f.*

armpit *n* sobaco *m.*

army *n* ejercito *m.*

aroma *n* aroma *m.*

around *prep* alrededor de.

arouse *vt* despertar; excitar.

arraign *vt* acusar.

arraignment *n* acusación *f*; proceso criminal *m.*

arrange vt organizar.

arrangement n colocación f; arreglo.

arrant adj consumado/da.

array n serie f.

arrears npl resto de una deuda m; atraso m.

arrest n arresto m:—vt detener, arrestar.

arrival n llegada f.

arrive vi llegar.

arrogance n arrogancia, presunción f.

arrogant adj arrogante, presuntuoso/ sa:—**~ly** adv arrogantemente.

arrogate vt arrogarse.

arrogation n arrogación f.

arrow n flecha f.

arsenal n (mil) arsenal m; (mar) atarazana, armeríaf.

arsenic n arsénico m.

art n arte m.

arterial adj arterial.

artery n arteria f.

artful adj ingenioso/sa.

art gallery n pinacoteca f.

arthritis n artritis f.

artichoke n alcachofa f.

article n articulo m.

articulate vt articular.

artifice n artificio m.

artillery n artillería f.

artisan n artesano/na m/f.

artist n artista m.

artistry n habilidad f.

artless adj sencillo, simple.

artlessness n sencillez f.

as conj como; mientras.

asbestos n asbesto m.

ascend vi ascender, subir.

ascribe vt atribuir.

ash n (bot) fresno m; ceniza f

ashamed adj avergonzado/da.

ashtray n cenicero m.

Ash Wednesday n miércoles de ceniza m.

ask vt pedir, rogar, preguntar por.

askew adv de lado.

asleep adj dormido/da.

asparagus n espárrago m.

aspect n aspecto m.

aspen n álamo temblón m.

asphalt n asfalto m.

asphyxia n (med) asfixia f.

asphyxiate vt asfixiar.

asphyxiation n asfixia f.

aspiration n aspiración f.

aspire vi aspirar, desear.

aspirin n aspirina f.

ass n asno m:—**she ~** burra f.

assassin n asesino m.

assassinate vt asesinar.

assault n asalto m.

assemble vt reunir, convocar.

assembly n asamblea f.

assert vt sostener, mantener.

assess vt valorar.

assessment n valoración f.

assets npl bienes mpl.

assign vt asignar.

assimilate vt asimilar.

assist vt asistir, ayudar.

assistance n asistencia f.

assistant n asistente, ayudante m.

associate vt asociar.

association n asociación, sociedad f.

assortment n surtido m.

assume vt asumir; suponer.

assurance n seguro m.

assure vt asegurar.

asterisk n asterisco m.

asthma n asma f.

asthmatic adj asmático/ca.

astonish vt pasmar, sorprender.

astringent *adj* astringente.
astrologer *n* astrólogo/ga *m/f.*
astrology *n* astrología *f.*
astronaut *n* astronauta *m/f.*
astronomer *n* astrónomo *m.*
astronomy *n* astronomía *f.*
astute *adj* astuto/ta.
asylum *n* asilo, refugio *m.*
at *prep* a; en.
atheism *n* ateísmo *m.*
atheist *n* ateo *m*, atea *f.*
athlete *n* atleta *m/f.*
atlas *n* atlas *m.*
atmosphere *n* atmósfera *f.*
atom *n* átomo *m.*
atomic *adj* atómico/ca.
atrocious *adj* atroz.
atrocity *n* atrocidad, enormidad *f.*
attach *vt* adjuntar.
attaché *n* agregado *m.*
attack *vt* atacar; acometer.
attempt *vt* intentar; probar, experimentar.
attend *vt* servir; asistir.
attendant *n* sirviente *m.*
attention *n* atención *f;* cuidado *m.*
attentive *adj* atento/ta; cuidadoso/sa.
attest *vt* atestiguar.
attic *n* desván *m;* guardilla *f.*
attorney *n* abogado *m.*
attract *vt* atraer.
attraction *n* atracción *f;* atractivo *m.*
auburn *adj* moreno/na, castaño/ña.
auction *n* subasta *f.*
auctioneer *n* subastador/a.
audacious *adj* audaz.
audible *adj* perceptible al oído.
audience *n* audiencia *f.*
audit *n* auditoría *f.*
augment *vt* aumentar, acrecentar.
August *n* agosto *m.*

august *adj* augusto/a.
aunt *n* tia *f.*
au pair *n* au pair *f.*
aura *n* aura *f.*
auspicious *adj* propicio/cia.
austere *adj* austero/ra, severo/ra;
authentic *adj* auténtico/ca.
authenticate *vt* autenticar.
authenticity *n* autenticidad *f.*
author *n* autor *m;* escritor *m.*
authorization *n* autorización *f.*
authorize *vt* autorizar.
authority *n* autoridad *f.*
auto *n* carro, coche *m.*
autograph *n* autógrafo *m.*
automatic *adj* automático/ca.
autonomy *n* autonomía *f.*
autopsy *n* autopsia *f.*
auxiliary *adj* auxiliar, asistente.
available *adj* disponible.
avalanche *n* alud *m.*
avarice *n* avaricia *f.*
avenue *n* avenida *f.*
avert *vt* desviar, apartar.
aviary *n* pajarera *f.*
avoid *vt* evitar, escapar.
await *vt* aguardar.
awake *vt* despertar.
award *vt* otorgar:—*n* premio *m.*
aware *adj* consciente; vigilante.
away *adv* ausente, fuera.
awe *n* miedo, temor *m.*
awful *adj* tremendo/da; horroroso/sa.
awhile *adv* un rato, algún tiempo.
awkward *adj* torpe, rudo/da.
awning *n* (*mar*) toldo *m.*
awry *adv* oblicuamente, torcidamente.
axe *n* hacha *f.*
axiom *n* axioma *m.*
axis *n* eje *m.*
axle *n* eje *m.*

B

baboon n cinocéfalo m.

baby n niño pequeño m.

bachelor n soltero m; bachiller m.

back n dorso m.

backbone n hueso dorsal, espinazo m.

backer n partidario/ria m.

backgammon n juego de chaquete o tablas m.

background n fondo m.

backlash n reacción f.

backpack n mochila f.

backside n trasero m.

backward adj tardo/da, lento/ta.

bacon n tocino m.

bad adj mal, malo.

badge n señal f; símbolo m.

badger n tejón m.

badminton n bádminton m.

baffle vt confundir.

bag n saco m; bolsa f.

baggage n bagaje, equipaje m.

bail n fianza, caución (juratoria) f.

bailiff n alguacil m.

bake vt cocer en horno.

bakery n panadería f.

baking powder n levadura f.

balance n balanza f; equilibrio m.

balcony n balcón m.

bald adj calvo/va.

ball n bola f; pelota f; baile m.

ballad n balada f.

ballerina n bailarina f.

ballet n ballet m.

balloon n globo m.

ballpoint (pen) n bolígrafo m.

balm, balsam n bálsamo m.

balustrade n balaustrada f.

bamboo n bambú m.

ban n prohibición f.

banal adj vulgar.

banana n plátano m.

band n faja f; cuadrilla f.

bandage n venda f.

bandit n bandido/da m/f.

bang n golpe m.

bangle n brazalete m.

banister(s) n(pl) pasamanos m.

banjo n banjo m.

bank n orilla (de río) f; montón de tierra m; banco m.

bank account n cuenta de banco f.

bankrupt adj insolvente.

banner n bandera f.

banquet n banquete m.

baptize vt bautizar.

bar n bar m; barra f.

barbecue n barbacoa f.

barber n peluquero m.

bare adj desnudo/da, descubierto/ta.

barely adv apenas.

bargain n ganga f.

barge n barcaza f.

bark n corteza f.

barley n cebada f.

barn n granero.

barometer n barómetro m.

baron n barón m.

barracks npl cuartel m.

barrel n barril m.

barren adj estéril, infructuoso/sa.

barrier n barrera f; obstáculo m.

barter vi baratar.

base n fondo m; base f; basa f.

baseball n béisbol m.

basement n sótano m.

basic adj básico/ca.

basin n jofaina, bacía f.

basis n base f; fundamento m.

basket n cesta, canasta f.

basketball *n* baloncesto *m.*

bastard *n, adj* bastardo/da *m/f.*

bat *n* murciélago *m.*

batch *n* serie *f.*

bath *n* baño *m.*

bathe *vt* (*vi*) bañar(se).

bathing suit *n* traje de baño *m.*

bathroom *n* (cuarto de) baño *m.*

baths *npl* piscina *f.*

battery *n* batería *f.*

battle *n* combate *m.*

bawdy *adj* indecente.

bay *n* bahía *f*; laurel.

bazaar *n* bazar *m.*

be *vi* ser; estar.

beach *n* playa, orilla *f.*

beacon *n* almenara *f.*

beagle *n* sabueso *m.*

beak *n* pico *m.*

beam *n* rayo de luz *m*; travesaño *m.*

bean *n* haba *f.*

beansprouts *npl* brotes de soja *mpl.*

bear *vt* llevar alguna cosa como carga; sostener; soportar.

bear *n* oso *m.*

beard *n* barba *f.*

bearer *n* portador/a *m/f.*

beast *n* bestia *f.*

beat *vt* golpear; tocar (un tambor).

beatify *vt* beatificar, santificar.

beautiful *adj* hermoso/sa, bello.

beauty *n* hermosura, belleza *f.*

because *conj* porque, a causa de.

bed *n* cama *f.*

bedroom *n* dormitorio *m.*

bee *n* abeja *f.*

beech *n* haya *f.*

beef *n* carne de vaca *f.*

beefburger *n* hamburguesa *f.*

beefsteak *n* bistec *m.*

beeline *n* línea recta *f.*

beer *n* cerveza *f.*

beetle *n* escarabajo *m.*

befall *vi* suceder, acontecer.

before *adv, prep* antes de; delante.

beg *vt* mendigar.

beggar *n* mendigo/ga *m/f.*

begin *vt vi* comenzar, empezar.

beginning *n* principio *m.*

begrudge *vt* envidiar.

behave *vi* comportarse.

behind *prep* detrás; atrás.

beige *adj* color beige.

belch *vi* eructar.

belief *n* fe, creencia *f.*

believe *vt* creer.

believer *n* creyente, fiel.

bell *n* campana *f.*

bellows *npl* fuelle *m.*

belly *n* vientre *m*; panza *f.*

belong *vi* pertenecer.

beloved *adj* querido/da, amado/da.

below *adv, prep* debajo, inferior; abajo.

belt *n* cinturón, cinto *m.*

bench *n* banco *m.*

bend *vt* encorvar, inclinar, plegar.

beneath *adv, prep* debajo, abajo.

benefit *n* beneficio *m*; utilidad *f*; provecho *m.*

benevolence *n* benevolencia *f.*

benevolent *adj* benévolo.

benign *adj* benigno/na.

bent *n* inclinación *f.*

bereave *vt* privar.

bereavement *n* perdida *f.*

beret *n* boina *f.*

berry *n* baya *f.*

beset *vt* acosar.

beside(s) *prep* al lado de; excepto.

best *adj* mejor.

bestial *adj* bestial, brutal.

bestow *vt* dar, conferir.

bestseller *n* bestseller *m.*

bet *n* apuesta *f*.
betray *vt* traicionar.
betroth *vt* contraer esponsales.
betting *n* juego *m*.
between *prep* entre, en medio de.
beverage *n* bebida *f*.
beware *vi* guardarse.
bewitch *vt* encantar, hechizar.
beyond *prep* más allá.
bias *n* propensión.
bib *n* babador *m*.
Bible *n* Biblia *f*.
bibliography *n* bibliografía *f*.
bicycle *n* bicicleta *f*.
bid *vt* mandar, ordenar; ofrecer.
biennial *adj* bienal.
bifocals *npl* anteojos bifocales *mpl*.
big *adj* grande, lleno/na.
bigamist *n* bígamo/ma *m/f*.
bigamy *n* bigamia *f*.
bigot *n* fanático/ca *m/f*.
bike *n* bici *f*.
bikini *n* bikini *m*.
bile *n* bilis *f*.
bilingual *adj* bilingüe.
bill *n* pico de ave *m*; billete.
billboard *n* cartelera *f*.
billet *n* alojamiento *m*.
billfold *n* cartera.
billiards *npl* billar *m*.
billion *n* billón *f*.
bin *n* cubo de la basura *m*.
binder *n* encuadernador/a *m/f*.
bingo *n* bingo *m*.
binoculars *npl* prismáticos *mpl*.
biographer *n* biógrafo/fa *m/f*.
biography *n* biografía *f*.
biological *adj* biológico/ca.
biology *n* biología *f*.
birch *n* abedul *m*.
bird *n* ave *f*; pájaro *m*.
birth *n* nacimiento *m*.

birthday *n* cumpleaños *m invar*.
biscuit *n* bizcocho *m*.
bishop *n* obispo *m*.
bit *n* bocado *m*; pedacito *m*.
bitch *n* perra *f*.
bite *vt* morder; picar.
bitter *adj* amargo/ga.
bitumen *n* betún *m*.
bizarre *adj* raro/ra.
blab *vi* chismear.
black *adj* negro/gra, oscuro/ra.
blackberry *n* zarzamora *f*.
blackbird *n* mirlo *m*.
blackboard *n* pizarra *f*.
blackmail *n* chantaje *m*:—*vt* chantajear.
blacksmith *n* herrero *m*.
bladder *n* vejiga *f*.
blade *n* hoja *f*; filo *m*.
blame *vt* culpar.
blameless *adj* inocente.
blank *adj* blanco/ca.
blanket *n* manta *f*.
blaspheme *vt* blasfemar, jurar.
blasphemy *n* blasfemia *f*.
blatant *adj* obvio.
blaze *n* llama *f*.
bleed *vi, vt* sangrar.
blemish *vt* manchar.
bless *vt* bendecir.
blessing *n* bendición *f*.
blight *vt* arruinar.
blind *adj* ciego/ga.
blink *vi* parpadear.
bliss *n* felicidad (eterna) *f*.
blister *n* ampolla *f*.
blitz *n* bombardeo aéreo *m*.
blizzard *n* huracán *m*.
bloated *adj* hinchado/da.
blob *n* gota *f*.
bloc *n* bloque *m*.
block *n* bloque *m*; obstáculo *m*.

blockade *n* bloqueo *m:—vt* bloquear.
blond *adj* rubio/bia.
blood *n* sangre *f.*
blood group *n* grupo sanguíneo *m.*
blood poisoning *n* envenenamiento de la sangre. *m.*
blood pressure *n* presión de sangre *f.*
blood sausage *n* morcilla *f.*
blood test *n* análisis de sangre *m.*
blood transfusion *n* transfusion de sangre *f.*
bloom *n* flor *f*; (*also* fig):—*vi* florecer.
blossom *n* flor *f.*
blot *vt* manchar.
blotchy *adj* muy manchado/da.
blouse *n* blusa *f.*
blow *vi* soplar; sonar.
blubber *n* grasa de ballena *f.*
blue *adj* azul.
bluebell *n* campanilla *f.*
blueprint *n* (*fig*) anteproyecto *m.*
blunder *n* desatino *m.*
blunt *adj* obtuso/sa; grosero/ra.
blush *n* rubor *m*; sonrojo *m.*
boar *n* verraco *m:—***wild** ~ jabalí *m.*
board *n* tabla *f*; mesa *f.*
boarder *n* pensionista *m.*
boarding card *n* tarjeta de embarque *f.*
boast *vi* jactarse.
boat *n* barco *m.*
bobsleigh *n* bob *m.*
bodice *n* corsé *m.*
body *n* cuerpo *m*; individuo *m*; gremio *m.*
body-building *n* culturismo *m.*
bodyguard *n* guardaespaldas *m.*
boil *vi* hervir; bullir.
bold *adj* ardiente, valiente; audaz.
bolt *n* cerrojo *m.*
bomb *n* bomba *f.*
bond *n* ligadura *f*; vinculo *m.*

bondage *n* esclavitud, servidumbre *f.*
bone *n* hueso *m.*
bonfire *n* hoguera *f.*
bonny *adj* bonito/ta.
bonus *n* cuota, prima *f.*
book *n* libro *m.*
bookcase *n* armario para libros *m.*
bookmarker *n* registro *m.*
bookstore *n* librería *f.*
boom *n* trueno *m.*
boon *n* presente, regalo *m.*
booth *n* barraca, cabaña *f.*
booty *n* botín *m*; presa *f*; saqueo *m.*
border *n* orilla *f*; borde *m.*
borderline *n* frontera *f.*
bore *vt* taladrar; barrenar; fastidiar.
boredom *n* aburrimiento *m.*
borrow *vt* pedir prestado/da.
bosom *n* seno, pecho *m.*
boss *n* jefe *m*; patrón/ona *m/f.*
botany *n* botánica *f.*
botch *vt* chapuzar.
both *adj* ambos.
bother *vt* preocupar; fastidiar.
bottle *n* botella *f.*
bottom *n* fondo *m.*
bough *n* brazo del árbol *m*; ramo *m.*
boulder *n* canto rodado *m.*
bounce *vi* rebotar.
bound *n* limite *m*; salto *m.*
boundary *n* limite *m*; frontera *f.*
bouquet *n* ramillete de flores *m.*
bourgeois *adj* burgués.
bout *n* ataque *m.*
bow *vt* encorvar, doblar.
bow *n* arco *m.*
bowels *npl* intestinos *mpl.*
bowl *n* taza; bola *f.*
bow tie *n* pajarita *f.*
box *n* caja, cajita *f.*
boxer *n* boxeador *m.*
boxing *n* boxeo *m.*

box office *n* taquilla *f.*

boy *n* muchacho *m;* niño *m.*

boycott *vt* boicotear:—*n* boicot *m.*

boyfriend *n* novio *m.*

bra *n* sujetador *m.*

bracelet *n* brazalete *m.*

bracket *n* puntal *m;* paréntesis *m.*

brag *n* jactancia *f:*—*vi* jactarse.

braid *n* pliegue *m,* trenza *f:*—*vt* trenzar.

brain *n* cerebro *m.*

brake *n* freno *m:*—*vt vi* frenar.

bran *n* salvado *m.*

branch *n* ramo *m;* rama *f.*

brand *n* marca *f.*

brandy *n* coñac *m.*

brass *n* latón *m.*

brassiere *n* sujetador *m.*

brave *adj* bravo/va, valiente.

bravery *n* valor *m.*

brawl *n* pelea *f.*

brazier *n* brasero *m.*

breach *n* rotura *f.*

bread *n* pan *m.*

breadth *n* anchura *f.*

break *vt* romper; quebrantar.

breakage *n* rotura *f.*

breakfast *n* desayuno *m:*—*vi* desayunar.

breast *n* pecho, seno *m.*

breastbone *n* esternón *m.*

breath *n* aliento *m,* respiración *f;* soplo de aire *m.*

breathe *vt vi* respirar; exhalar.

breathtaking *adj* pasmoso/sa.

breed *n* casta, raza *f.*

breeze *n* brisa *f.*

brevity *n* brevedad, concisión *f.*

brew *vt* hacer; tramar, mezclar.

bribe *n* cohecho, soborno *m.*

bribery *n* cohecho, soborno *m.*

bric-a-brac *n* baratijas *fpl.*

brick *n* ladrillo *m.*

bricklayer *n* albañil *m.*

bride *n* novia *f.*

bridegroom *n* novio *m.*

bridesmaid *n* madrina de boda *f.*

bridge *n* puente *m/f.*

brief *adj* breve, conciso/sa, sucinto/ta.

briefcase *n* cartera *f.*

brigade *n* (*mil*) brigada *f.*

bright *adj* claro/ra, luciente, brillante.

brighten *vt* pulir, dar lustre.

brilliant *adj* brillante.

bring *vt* llevar, traer.

brisk *adj* vivo/va, alegre, jovial; fresco/ca.

brisket *n* pecho (de un animal) *m.*

briskly *adj* vigorosamente.

bristle *n* cerda, seta *f:*—*vi* erizarse.

bristly *adj* cerdoso/sa, lleno/na de cerdas.

brittle *adj* quebradizo, frágil.

broach *vt* comenzar a hablar de.

broad *adj* ancho.

broadcast *n* emisión *f.*

broadcasting *n* radiodifusión *f.*

broaden *vt vi* ensanchar(se).

broadly *adv* anchamente.

broad-minded *adj* tolerante.

brocade *n* brocado *m.*

broccoli *n* brécol *m.*

brochure *n* folleto *m.*

broil *vt* asar a la parrilla.

broken *adj* roto/ta.

broker *n* corredor/a *m/f.*

bronchial *adj* bronquial.

bronchitis *n* bronquitis *f.*

bronze *n* bronce *m.*

brooch *n* broche *m.*

brook *n* arroyo *m.*

broom *n* hiniesta *f;* escoba *f.*

broth *n* caldo *m.*

brothel *n* burdel *m.*

brother n hermano m.
brother-in-law n cuñado m.
brow n caja f; frente f; cima f.
browbeat vt intimidar.
brown adj moreno/na; castaño/ña.
browse vt ramonear.
bruise vt magullar.
brunette n morena f.
brunt n choque m.
brush n cepillo m; escobilla f.
brusque adj brusco/ca.
Brussels sprout n col de Bruselas f.
brutal adj brutal.
brutality n brutalidad f.
brute n bruto m.
bubble n burbuja f.
bubblegum n chicle m.
bucket n cubo, pozal m.
buckle n hebilla f.
bucolic adj bucólico/ca.
bud n pimpollo, botón m:—vi brotar.
Buddhism n Budismo m.
buddy n compañero m.
budge vi moverse.
budgerigar n periquito m.
budget n presupuesto m.
buff n entusiasta m.
buffalo n búfalo m.
buffet n buffet m.
buffoon n bufón, chocarrero m.
bug n chinche m.
bugle(horn) n trompa de caza f.
build vt edificar; construir.
building n edificio m; construc- ción f.
bulb n bulbo m; cebolla f.
bulge vi combarse:—n bombeo m.
bulk n masa f; volumen m.
bulky adj grueso/sa, grande.
bull n toro m.
bulldog n dogo m.
bulldozer n aplanadora f.

bullet n bala f.
bullfight n corrida de toros f.
bullfighter n toreo m.
bullfighting n los toros mpl.
bullion n oro o plata en barras m o f.
bullock n novillo capado m.
bullring n plaza de toros f.
bully n valentón m:—vt tiranizar.
bumblebee n abejorro m.
bump n hinchazón f.
bun n bollo m; mono m.
bunch n ramo m.
bundle n fardo m, haz m.
bung n tapón m.
bungalow n bungalow m.
bunk n litera f.
bunker n refugio m; bunker m.
burden n carga f:—vt cargar.
bureau n armario m; escritorio m.
bureaucracy n burocracia f.
burglar n ladrón m.
burial n enterramiento m; exequias fpl.
burial place n cementerio m.
burly adj corpulento/ta, fornido/da.
burn vt quemar, abrasar, incendiar:— vi arder:—n quema dura f.
burner n quemador m; mechero m.
burning adj ardiente.
burrow n conejera f.
bursar n tesorero m.
burse n bolsa, lonja f.
burst vi reventar; abrirse.
bury vt enterrar, sepultar; esconder.
bus n autobús m.
bush n arbusto, espinal m.
busily adv diligentemente, apresurada- mente.
business n asunto m; negocios mpl.
businessman n hombre de nego- cios m.
bust n busto m.

bus-stop n parada de autobuses f.

bustle vi hacer ruido.

busy adj ocupado/da; entrometido/da.

busybody n entrometido m.

but conj pero; mas.

butcher n carnicero m.

butcher's (shop) n carnicería f.

butler n mayordomo m.

butter n mantequilla f.

buttercup n (bot) ranúnculo m.

butterfly n mariposa f.

buttocks npl posaderas fpl.

button n botón m.

buttonhole n ojal m.

buttress n estribo m; apoyo m.

buxom adj frescachona.

buy vt comprar.

buzz n susurro, zumbido m:—vi zumbar.

buzzard n ratonero común m.

buzzer n timbre m.

by prep por; a, en; de; cerca, al lado de.

bypass n carretera de circunvalación f.

by-product n derivado m.

bystander n mirador m.

byte n (comput) byte m.

byword n proverbio, refrán m.

C

cab n taxi m.

cabbage n berza, col f.

cabin n cabaña.

cabinet n consejo á ministros m; gabinete m.

cable n (mar) cable m.

cable car n teleférico m.

cactus n cacto m.

cadaver n cadáver m.

cadet n cadete m.

cadge vt mangar.

cafeteria n cantina f.

cage n jaula f.

cake n bollo m; tortita f.

calculate vt calcular.

calculator n calculadora f.

calendar n calendario m.

calf n ternero m.

call vt llamar, nombrar.

calligraphy n caligrafía f.

callous adj calloso/sa.

calm n calma, tranquilidad.

calorie n caloría f.

Calvinist n calvinista m.

camel n camello m.

cameo n camafeo m.

camera n máquina fotográfica f.

camomile n manzanilla f.

camouflage n camuflaje m.

camp n campo m.

campaign n campana f.

camping n camping m.

campsite n camping m.

can vi poder:—n lata f.

canal n estanque m; canal m.

cancel vt cancelar; anular.

cancer n cáncer m.

Cancer n Cáncer m (signo del zodiaco).

candid adj cándido/da, sencillo/lla.

candle n candela f; vela f.

candlestick n candelero m.

candy n caramelo m.

cane n cana f; bastón m.

cannabis *n* canabis *f.*
cannibal *n* caníbal *m.*
cannibalism *n* canibalismo *m.*
cannon *n* cañón *m.*
canoe *n* canoa *f.*
canon *n* canon *m*; regla *f.*
can opener *n* abrelatas *m invar.*
canopy *n* dosel, pabellón *m.*
canter *n* medio galope *m.*
canvas *n* cañamazo *m.*
canyon *n* cañón *m.*
cap *n* gorra *f.*
capability *n* capacidad *f.*
capable *adj* capaz.
cape *n* cabo, promontorio *m.*
capital *adj* capital; principal.
capitalism *n* capitalismo *m.*
Capitol *n* Capitolio *m.*
capitulate *vi* capitular.
Capricorn *n* Capricornio *m* (signo del zodiaco).
capsule *n* cápsula *f.*
captain *n* capitán *m.*
captivate *vt* cautivar.
capture *n* captura *f*; presa *f.*
car *n* coche, carro *m*; vagón *m.*
carafe *n* garrafa *f.*
caramel *n* caramelo *m.*
carat *n* quilate *m.*
carbohydrates *npl* hidratos de carbono *mpl.*
carcass *n* cadáver *m.*
card *n* naipe *m*; carta *f.*
cardboard *n* cartón *m.*
cardinal *adj* cardinal, principal.
care *n* cuidado *m*; solicitud *f.*
career *n* carrera *f.*
caress *n* caricia *f.*
caretaker *n* portero *m.*
cargo *n* cargamento de navío *m.*
caricature *n* caricatura *f.*
carnal *adj* carnal; sensual.

carnation *n* clavel *m.*
carnival *n* carnaval *m.*
carpenter *n* carpintero *m.*
carpentry *n* carpintería *f.*
carpet *n* alfombra *f.*
carrier *n* portador *m.*
carrot *n* zanahoria *f.*
carry *vt* llevar, conducir.
cart *n* carro *m*; carreta *f.*
cartilage *n* cartílago *m.*
carton *n* caja *f.*
cartoon *n* dibujo animado *m.*
carve *vt* cincelar.
carving *n* escultura *f.*
case *n* caja *f*; maleta *f.*
cash *n* dinero contante *m.*
cashmere *n* cachemira *f.*
cask *n* barril, tonel *m.*
casserole *n* cazuela *f.*
cassette *n* cassette *m.*
cassock *n* sotana *f.*
castanets *npl* castañetas *fpl.*
castaway *n* réprobo *m.*
caste *n* casta *f.*
castigate *vt* castigar.
castle *n* castillo *m.*
castrate *vt* castrar.
castration *n* capadura *f.*
casual *adj* casual.
cat *n* gato *m*; gata *f.*
catalog(ue) *n* catalogo *m.*
cataract *n* cascada *f*; catarata *f.*
catarrh *n* catarro *m*; reuma *f.*
catastrophe *n* catástrofe *f.*
catch *vt* coger.
catchphrase *n* lema *m.*
catechism *n* catecismo *m.*
categorize *vt* clasificar.
category *n* categoría *f.*
caterpillar *n* oruga *f.*
cathedral *n* catedral *f.*
catholic *adj, n* católico *m.*

Catholicism n catolicismo m.
cattle n ganado m.
cauliflower n coliflor f.
cause n causa f; razón f; motivo m.
causeway n arrecife m.
caustic adj, n cáustico m.
cauterize vt cauterizar.
caution n prudencia.
cavalry n caballería f.
cave n caverna f.
caviar n caviar m.
cease vt parar, suspender.
cedar n cedro m.
cede vt ceder.
ceiling n techo m.
celebrate vt celebrar.
celery n apio m.
celibacy n celibato m.
cell n celdilla f; célula f; cueva f.
cellar n sótano m.
cellophane n celofán m.
cement n cemento.
cemetery n cementerio m.
cenotaph n cenotafio m.
censor n censor m.
census n censo m.
cent n centavo m.
center n centro m.
centigrade n centígrado m.
centiliter n centilitro m.
centimeter n centímetro m.
centipede n escolopendra f.
central adj central.
centralize vt centralizar.
century n siglo m.
ceramic adj cerámico/ca.
ceremony n ceremonia f.
certain adj cierto/ta, evidente.
certificate n certificado, testimonio m.
certify vt certificar, afirmar.
cervical adj cervical.

chaffinch n pinzón m.
chain n cadena f.
chair n silla f.
chamber n cámara f.
chameleon n camaleón m.
champagne n champaña m.
championship n campeonato m.
chance n ventura, suerte f; oportunidad f.
chancellor n canciller m.
change vt cambiar.
channel n canal m.
chant n canto (llano) m.
chaos n caos m.
chapel n capilla f.
chaplain n capellán m.
chapter n capitulo m.
character n carácter m.
charcoal n carbón de leña m.
charge vt cargar; acusar, imputar.
charity n caridad.
charlatan n charlatán/tana m/f.
charm n encanto m.
charter flight n vuelo charter m.
chauffeur n chófer m.
chauvinist n machista m.
cheap adj barato/ta.
cheat vt engañar, defraudar.
check n cheque m.
checkmate n mate m.
checkout n caja f.
cheek n mejilla f.
cheese n queso m.
chef n jefe de cocina m.
chemical adj químico/ca.
chemist n químico m.
cheroot n puro m.
cherry n cereza f.
cherub n querubín m.
chess n ajedrez m.
chest n pecho m.
chestnut n castaña f.

chew *vt* mascar, masticar.
chewing gum *n* chicle *m*.
chicken *n* pollo *m*.
chickenpox *n* varicela *f*.
chickpea *n* garbanzo *m*.
chief *adj* principal.
chilblain *n* sabañón *m*.
child *n* niño *m*; niña *f*.
childhood *n* infancia, niñez *f*.
children *npl de* **child** niños *mpl*.
chimney *n* chimenea *f*.
chimpanzee *n* chimpancé *m*.
chin *n* barbilla *f*.
chiropodist *n* pedicuro *m*.
chirp *vi* chirriar.
chlorine *n* cloro *m*.
chloroform *n* cloroformo *m*.
chocolate *n* chocolate *m*.
choice *n* elección, preferencia *f*.
choir *n* coro *m*.
choke *vt* sofocar.
cholera *n* cólera *m*.
choose *vt* escoger, elegir.
chop *vt* tajar, cortar:—*n* chuleta *f*.
chore *n* faena *f*.
Christ *n* Cristo *m*.
christen *vt* bautizar.
Christianity *n* cristianismo *m*; cristiandad *f*.
Christmas *n* Navidad *f*.
chrome *n* cromo *m*.
chronicle *n* crónica *f*.
chronological *adj* cronológico/ca.
chubby *adj* gordo/da.
chunk *n* trozo *m*.
church *n* iglesia *f*.
churchyard *n* cementerio *m*.
cider *n* sidra *f*.
cigar *n* cigarro *m*.
cigarette *n* cigarrillo *m*.
cinder *n* carbonilla *f*.
cinema *n* cine *m*.

cinnamon *n* canela *f*.
circle *n* circulo *m*.
circumcize *vt* circuncidar.
circumcision *n* circuncisión *f*.
circumference *n* circunferencia *f*; circuito *m*.
circumflex *n* acento circunflejo *m*.
circumstance *n* circunstancia.
circus *n* circo *m*.
cistern *n* cisterna *f*.
cite *vt* citar.
citizen *n* ciudadano *m*.
city *n* ciudad *f*.
civic *adj* cívico/ca.
civil *adj* civil, cortés.
civilization *n* civilización *f*.
clairvoyant *n* clarividente *m/f*.
clam *n* almeja *f*.
clammy *adj* viscoso/sa.
clamor *n* clamor *m*.
clan *n* familia, tribu, raza *f*.
clandestine *adj* clandestino/na.
clap *vt* aplaudir.
claret *n* clarete *m*.
clarify *vt* clarificar, aclarar.
clarinet *n* clarinete *m*.
clarity *n* claridad *f*.
class *n* clase *f*; orden *f*.
classic(al) *adj* clásico/ca:—*n* autor clásico *m*.
classify *vt* clasificar.
classmate *n* compañero de clase *m*.
classroom *n* aula *f*.
clause *n* cláusula *f*.
claw *n* garra *f*.
clay *n* arcilla *f*.
clean *adj* limpio/pia; casto/ta:—*vt* limpiar.
cleanse *vt* limpiar, purificar; purgar.
clear *adj* claro/ra.
clemency *n* clemencia *f*.
clement *adj* clemente, benigno/na.

clergy n clero m.
clerical adj clerical, eclesiástico/ca.
clerk n dependiente m; oficinista m.
clever adj listo/ta; hábil.
client n cliente m/f.
cliff n acantilado m.
climate n clima m.
climax n clímax m.
climb vt escalar, trepar.
cling vi colgar, adherirse.
clinic n clínica f.
clip vt cortar.
clique n camarilla f.
cloak n capa f.
cloakroom n guardarropa m.
clock n reloj m.
clog n zueco m.
cloister n claustro, monasterio m.
close vt cerrar; concluir, terminar.
closet n armario m.
close-up n primer plano m.
clot n grumo m; embolia f.
cloth n paño m.
clothe vt vestir.
clothes npl ropa f.
clothes pin n pinza f.
cloud n nube f.
clout n tortazo m.
clove n clavo m.
clover n trébol m.
clown n payaso m.
coach n autocar, autobús m.
coagulate vt coagular, cuajar.
coal n carbón m.
coalition n coalición, confederación f.
coarse adj basto/ta; grosero/ra.
coast n costa f.
coastguard n guardacostas m invar.
coat n chaqueta f; abrigo m.
coat hanger n percha f.
cobbler n zapatero m.

cobweb n telaraña f.
cocaine n cocaína f.
cock n gallo m; macho m.
cockle n caracol de mar m.
cockpit n cabina f.
cockroach n cucaracha f.
cocktail n cóctel m.
cocoa n coco m; cacao m.
coconut n coco m.
cod n bacalao m.
code n código m.
cod-liver oil n aceite de hígado de bacalao m.
coffee n café m.
coffer n cofre m; caja f.
coffin n ataúd m.
cog n diente (de rueda) m.
cognac n coñac m.
cogwheel n rueda dentada f.
cohabit vi cohabitar.
coherence n coherencia f.
cohesion n coherencia f.
cohesive adj cohesivo.
coil n rollo m.
coin n moneda f.
coincide vi coincidir.
coke n coque m.
colander n colador, pasador m.
cold adj frío/ría.
cold sore n herpes labial m.
coleslaw n ensalada de col f.
colic n cólico m.
collaborate vt cooperar.
collapse vi hundirse.
collapsible adj plegable.
collar n cuello m.
collarbone n clavícula f.
collate vt comparar.
collateral adj colateral.
colleague n colega m.
collect vt recoger; coleccionar.
collection n colección f; compilación f.

college n colegio m.
collide vi chocar.
colloquial adj familiar.
collusion n colusión f.
colon n dos puntos mpl; (med) colon m.
colonel n (mil) coronel m.
colonial adj colonial.
colonize vt colonizar.
colony n colonia f.
color n color m.
colossal adj colosal.
colt n potro m.
column n columna f.
columnist n columnista m.
coma n coma f.
comatose adj comatoso/sa.
comb n peine m:—vt peinar.
combat n combate m.
combination n combinación f.
combine vt combinar.
combustion n combustión f.
come vi venir.
comedy n comedia f.
comet n cometa f.
comfort n confort m.
comfortable adj cómodo/da.
comma n (gr) coma f.
command vt comandar.
commemorate vt conmemorar; celebrar.
commence vt, vi comenzar.
commencement n principio m.
commend vt encomendar.
commensurate adj proporcionado/da.
comment n comentario m.
commentator n comentador m.
commerce n comercio m.
commercial adj comercial.
commiserate vt compadecer.
commission n comisión f.

commit vt cometer.
committee n comité m.
commodity n comodidad f.
common adj común.
commotion n tumulto m.
communicate vt comunicar.
communion n comunión f.
communism n comunismo m.
community n comunidad f.
commute vt conmutar.
compact adj compacto/ta.
compact disc n disco compacto m.
companion n compañero/ra.
company n compañía, sociedad f.
compare vt comparar.
compartment n compartimiento m.
compass n brújula f.
compassion n compasión f.
compatriot n compatriota m.
compensate vt compensar.
compensation n compensación f.
compère n presentador m.
compete vi concurrir.
competent adj competente.
competition n competencia f.
competitor n competidor, rival m.
compilation n compilación f.
complain vi quejarse, lamentarse.
complement n complemento m.
complex adj complejo/ja.
complexion n tez f; aspecto m.
complicate vt complicar.
component adj componente.
compose vt componer.
composer n autor m.
composite adj compuesto/ta.
composition n composición f.
comprehend vt comprender, contener; entender.
compress vt comprimir.
comprise vt comprender.
compromise n compromiso m.

compulsive *adj* compulsivo/va.
computer *n* ordenador *m*.
comrade *n* camarada.
con *vt* estafar:—*n* estafa *f*.
concave *adj* cóncavo/va.
conceal *vt* ocultar, esconder.
concede *vt* conceder.
conceit *n* concepto *m*, capricho *m*.
conceive *vt* concebir, comprender.
concentrate *vt* concentrar.
concept *n* concepto *m*.
conception *n* concepción *f*.
concern *vt* concernir, importar.
concert *n* concierto *m*.
concession *n* concesión *f*; privilegio *m*.
concise *adj* conciso/sa.
conclude *vt* concluir.
conclusion *n* conclusión.
concord *n* concordia, armonía *f*.
concrete *n* concreto *m*.
concussion *n* concusión *f*.
condemn *vt* condenar.
condensation *n* condensación *f*.
condiment *n* condimento *m*; salsa *f*.
condition *vt* condicionar.
conditional *adj* condicional.
condom *n* condón *m*.
conduct *n* conducta *f*.
conductor *n* conductor *m*.
conduit *n* conducto *m*.
cone *n* cono *m*.
confection *n* confitura *f*.
confectioner's (shop) *n* pastelería *f*.
conference *n* conferencia *f*.
confess *vt, vi* confesar(se).
confession *n* confesión *f*.
confessional *n* confesionario *m*.
confetti *n* confeti *m*.
confidant *n* confidente.
confide *vt, vi* confiar; fiarse.
confidence *n* confianza, seguridad *f*.

confident *adj* cierto/ta, seguro/ra; confiado/da.
confine *vt* limitar; aprisionar.
confirm *vt* confirmar; ratificar.
confiscate *vt* confiscar.
conflagration *n* conflagración *f*.
conflict *n* conflicto *m*; combate *m*; pelea *f*.
conflicting *adj* contradictorio/ria.
confluence *n* confluencia *f*.
conform *vt, vi* conformar(se).
conformity *n* conformidad.
confound *vt* turbar, confundir.
confront *vt* afrontar; confrontar.
confrontation *n* enfrentamiento *m*.
confuse *vt* confundir.
congeal *vt, vi* helar, congelar(se).
congenial *adj* congenial.
congenital *adj* congénito/ta.
congested *adj* atestado/da.
congestion *n* congestión *f*; acumulación *f*.
congratulate *vt* congratular, felicitar.
congratulations *npl* felicidades *fpl*.
congratulatory *adj* congratulatorio/ria.
congregate *vt* congregar.
congress *n* congreso *m*; conferencia *f*.
congruity *n* congruencia *f*.
coniferous *adj* (*bot*) conífero/ra.
conjecture *n* conjetura.
conjugal *adj* conyugal.
conjugate *vt* (*gr*) conjugar.
conjunction *n* conjunción *f*.
conjuncture *n* coyuntura *f*.
conjure *vi* conjurar.
con man *n* timador *m*.
connect *vt* juntar, unir.
connection *n* conexión *f*.
connivance *n* connivencia *f*.
connive *vi* tolerar.

connoisseur *n* conocedor/a *m/f.*
conquer *vt* conquistar; vencer.
conqueror *n* vencedor/a, conquistador/a *m/f.*
conquest *n* conquista *f.*
conscience *n* conciencia *f.*
consciousness *n* conciencia *f.*
conscript *n* conscripto *m.*
conscription *n* reclutamiento *m.*
consecrate *vt* consagrar.
consecration *n* consagración *f.*
consecutive *adj* consecutivo/va.
consensus *n* consenso *m.*
consent *n* consentimiento *m*; aprobación *f.*
consequence *n* consecuencia *f.*
consequent *adj* consecutivo/va.
conservation *n* conservación *f.*
conservative *adj* conservativo/va.
conservatory *n* conservatorio *m.*
conserve *vt* conservar.
consider *vt* considerar.
considerable *adj* considerable.
considerate *adj* considerado/da.
consideration *n* consideración *f.*
consign *vt* consignar.
consignment *n* consignación *f.*
consist *vi* consistir.
consistency *n* consistencia *f.*
consistent *adj* consistente.
consolation *n* consolación *f*; consuelo *m.*
console *vt* consolar.
consolidate *vt, vi* consolidar(se).
consolidation *n* consolidación *f.*
consonant *adj* consonante.
consort *n* consorte, socio *m.*
conspicuous *adj* conspicuo/cua.
conspiracy *n* conspiración *f.*
conspirator *n* conspirador/a *m/f.*
conspire *vi* conspirar.
constancy *n* constancia.

constant *adj* constante.
constellation *n* constelación *f.*
constipated *adj* estreñido/da.
constituency *n* junta electoral *f.*
constituent *n* constitutivo *m.*
constitute *vt* constituir.
constitution *n* constitución *f.*
constitutional *adj* constitucional.
constrict *vt* constreñir, estrechar.
construct *vt* construir, edificar.
construction *n* construcción *f.*
consul *n* cónsul *m.*
consulate, consulship *n* consulado *m.*
consult *vt, vi* consultar(se).
consultation *n* consulta *f.*
consume *vt* consumir.
consumer *n* consumidor/a *m/f.*
consumption *n* consumo *m.*
contact *n* contacto *m.*
contact lenses *npl* lentes de contacto *mpl.*
contagious *adj* contagioso/sa.
contain *vt* contener.
container *n* recipiente *m.*
contaminate *vt* contaminar.
contamination *n* contaminación *f.*
contemplate *vt* contemplar.
contemplation *n* contemplación *f.*
contempt *n* desprecio, desdén *m.*
contend *vi* contender.
content *adj* contento/ta, satisfecho/cha.
contention *n* contención, altercación *f.*
contest *vt* contestar, disputar, litigar.
contestant *n* concursante/ta *m/f.*
context *n* contexto *m.*
continent *adj* continente.
contingency *n* contingencia *f.*
contingent *n* contingente *m*; cuota *f.*
continue *vt* continuar.

contort vt torcer.

contortion n contorsión f.

contour n contorno m.

contraband n contrabando m.

contraception n contracepción f.

contraceptive n anticonceptivo m.

contract vt contraer; abreviar; contratar.

contraction n contracción f; abreviatura f.

contradict vt contradecir.

contradiction n contradicción, oposición f.

contraption n artilugio m.

contrary adj contrario/ria, opuesto/ta.

contrast n contraste m.

contrasting adj opuesto/ta.

contributary adj contributario/ria.

contribute vt contribuir, ayudar.

contrive vt inventar, trazar.

control n control m; inspección f:—vt controlar; manejar; restringir; gobernar.

controversial adj polémico/ca.

controversy n controversia f.

conurbation n urbanización f.

convalesce vi convalecer.

convalescence n convalecencia f.

convene vt convocar; juntar, unir.

convenient adj conveniente.

convent n convento m.

convention n convención f.

converge vi converger.

conversation n conversación f.

converse vi conversar; platicar.

conversely adv mutuamente, recíprocamente.

convert vt, vi convertir(se).

convertible adj convertible.

convex adj convexo/xa.

convey vt transportar; transmitir, transferir.

conveyance n transporte m.

conveyancer n notario m.

conviction n convicción f.

convince vt convencer.

convivial adj sociable; hospitalario/ria.

convoke vt convocar, reunir.

convoy n convoy m.

convulse vt conmover, convulsionar.

convulsion n convulsión f.

convulsive adj convulsivo/va.

cook n cocinero m; cocinera f:—vt cocinar.

cool adj fresco/ca; indiferente.

cooperate vi cooperar.

cooperation n cooperación f.

coordinate vt coordinar.

coordination n coordinación f.

cop n (fam) poli m.

copier n copiadora f.

copious adj copioso/sa, abundante.

copper n cobre m.

copulate vi copularse.

copy n copia f.

copying machine n copiadora f.

coral n coral m.

cord n cuerda f; cable m.

cordial adj cordial.

corduroy n pana f.

core n cuesco m; interior m.

cork n alcornoque m; corcho m.

corkscrew n tirabuzón m.

corn n maíz m; grano m; callo m.

corncob n mazorca f.

cornea n córnea f.

corner n rincón m; esquina f.

cornet n corneta f.

cornflakes npl copos de maíz mpl.

cornice n cornisa f.

coronary n infarto m.

coronation n coronación f.

coroner n oficial que hace la inspección jurídica de los cadáveres m.

corporation *n* corporación *f.*
corps *n* cuerpo (de ejercito) *m.*
correct *vt* corregir; enmendar.
correctness *n* exactitud *f.*
correspond *vi* corresponder.
correspondence *n* correspondencia *f.*
corridor *n* pasillo *m.*
corrode *vt* corroer.
corrosive *adj, n* corrosivo *m.*
corrupt *vt* corromper; sobornar.
corruption *n* corrupción *f;* depravación *f.*
corset *n* corsé *m.*
cosily *adv* cómodamente.
cosmetic *adj* cosmético/ca.
cosmic *adj* cósmico/ca.
cosmonaut *n* cosmonauta *m.*
cosmopolitan *adj* cosmopolita.
cosset *vt* mimar.
cost *n* coste, precio *m.:—vi* costar.
costume *n* traje *m.*
cosy *adj* cómodo/da.
cottage *n* casita, casucha *f.*
cotton *n* algodón *m.*
cotton wool *n* algodón hidrófilo *m.*
couch *n* sofá *m.*
couchette *n* litera *f.*
cough *n* tos *f:—vi* toser.
council *n* concilio, consejo *m.*
counsel *n* consejo, aviso *m.*
count *vt* contar, numerar; calcular.
counter *n* mostrador *m;* ficha *f.*
counterfeit *vt* contrahacer, imitar, falsear.
counterpart *n* parte correspondiente *f.*
countersign *vt* refrendar.
countess *n* condesa *f.*
countless *adj* innumerable.
countrified *adj* rústico/ca.
country *n* país *m;* campo *m;* región *f;* patria *f.*

county *n* condado *m.*
coup *n* golpe *m.*
couple *n* par *m.*
couplet *n* copla *f;* par *m.*
coupon *n* cupón *m.*
courage *n* coraje, valor *f.*
courageous *adj* corajudo/da, valeroso/sa:—~ly *adv* valerosamente.
courier *n* correo, mensajero/ra *m/f,* expreso *m.*
course *n* curso *m;* carrera *f,* camino *m;* ruta *f.*
court *n* corte *f.*
courteous *adj* cortés.
courtesy *n* cortesía *f.*
courthouse *n* palacio de justicia *m.*
courtyard *n* patio *m.*
cousin *n* primo *m;* prima *f.*
cove *n* (*mar*) ensenada, caleta *f.*
covenant *n* contrato *m.*
cover *n* cubierta *f;* abrigo *m.*
cover letter *n* carta de explicación *f.*
covert *adj* cubierto/ta; oculto/ta, secreto/ta.
cover-up *n* encubrimiento *m.*
covet *vt* codiciar.
cow *n* vaca *f.*
coward *n* cobarde *m/f.*
cowardice *n* cobardía, timidez *f.*
cowboy *n* vaquero *m.*
cower *vi* agacharse.
cowherd *n* vaquero *m.*
crab *n* cangrejo *m.*
crab apple *n* manzana silvestre *f.*
crack *n* crujido *m;* hendedura, quebraja *f.*
cracker *n* buscapiés *m invar;* galleta *f.*
crackle *vi* crujir, chillar.
cradle *n* cuna *f.*
craft *n* arte.
craftsman *n* artífice, artesano *m.*

craftsmanship n artesanía f.
crafty adj astuto/ta, artificioso/sa.
cramp n calambre m.
cranberry n arandilla f.
crane n grulla f; grua f.
crash vi estallar.
crash helmet n casco m.
crass adj craso/sa.
crater n cráter m; boca de volcán f.
cravat n pañuelo m.
crave vt rogar, suplicar.
craving adj insaciable.
crawl vi arrastrar.
crayfish n cangrejo de río m.
crayon n lápiz m.
craze n manía f.
craziness n locura f.
crazy adj loco/ca.
cream n crema f.
creamy adj cremoso.
crease n pliegue m.
create vt crear; causar.
creation n creación f; elección f.
creator n creador/a m/f.
creature n criatura f.
credence n creencia, fe f.
credibility n credibilidad f.
credible adj creíble.
credit n crédito m.
creditable adj estimable.
credit card n tarjeta de crédito f.
creed n credo m.
creek n arroyo, rio m.
creep vi arrastrar, serpear.
creeper n (bot) enredadera f.
cremate vt incinerar cadáveres.
cremation n cremación f.
crematorium n crematorio m.
crescent adj creciente.
cress n berro m.
crest n cresta f.
crevasse n grieta (de glaciar) f.

crevice n raja, hendedura f.
crew n banda, tropa f.
crib n cuna f; pesebre m.
cricket n grillo m; criquet m.
crime n crimen m.
criminal adj criminal.
crimson adj, n carmesí m.
cripple n, adj cojo/ja m/f.
crisis n crisis f.
crisp adj crujiente.
crispness n encrespadura f.
criss-cross adj entrelazado/da.
criterion n criterio m.
critic n crítico m; crítica f.
criticize vt criticar, censurar.
crochet n ganchillo m.
crockery n loza fl.
crocodile n cocodrilo m.
crook n (fam) ladrón m.
crooked adj torcido/da; perverso/sa.
cross n cruz f.
crossbar n travesaño m.
crossbreed n raza cruzada f.
cross-country n carrera a campo traviesa f.
crossing n cruce m; paso a nivel m.
cross-reference n contrarreferencia f.
crotch n entrepierna f.
crouch vi agacharse, bajarse.
crow n cuervo m.
crowd n publico m.
crown n corona f.
crown prince n príncipe real m.
crucial adj crucial.
crucible n crisol m.
crucifix n crucifijo m.
crucifixion n crucifixión f.
crude adj crudo/da, imperfecto/ta.
cruel adj cruel.
cruelty n crueldad f.
cruet n vinagrera f.
cruiser n crucero m.

crumb n miga f.
crumble vt desmigajar.
crumple vt arrugar.
crunchy adj crujiente.
crusade n cruzada f.
crush vt apretar, oprimir.
crust n costra f; corteza f.
crutch n muleta f.
crux n lo esencial.
cry vt, vi gritar; exclamar; llorar.
crypt n cripta (bóveda subterránea) f.
cryptic adj enigmático/ca.
crystal n cristal m.
cub n cachorro m.
cube n cubo m.
cuckoo n cuclillo, cuco m.
cucumber n pepino m.
cuddle vt abrazar.
cudgel n garrote, palo m.
cue n taco (de billar) m.
cuff n puñada f; vuelta f.
cull vt escoger, elegir.
culminate vi culminar.
culpable adj culpable.
cult n culto f.
cultivate vi cultivar.
cultivation n cultivación f.
cultural adj cultural.
culture n cultura f.
cumulative adj cumulativo/va.
cunning adj astuto/ta; intrigante.
cup n taza, jícara f; (bot) cáliz m.
cupboard n armario m.
curable adj curable.
curb n freno m; bordillo m.
curd n cuajada f.
cure n cura f; remedio m.
curiosity n curiosidad f; rareza f.
curious adj curioso/sa:—**~ly** adv curiosamente.
curl n rizo de pelo m.

curly adj rizado/da.
currant n pasa f.
currency n moneda f.
current adj corriente.
current affairs npl actualidades fpl.
currently adv corrientemente; actualmente.
curry n curry m.
curse vt maldecir.
cursor n cursor m.
curt adj sucinto/ta.
curtail vt acortar.
curtain n cortina f; telón (en los teatros) m.
curvature n curvatura f.
curve vt encorvar:—n curva f.
cushion n cojín m; almohada f.
custard n natillas fpl.
custodian n custodio m.
custody n custodia f; prisión f.
custom n costumbre f, uso m.
customary adj usual, acostumbrado/da, ordinario/ria.
customer n cliente m/f.
customs npl aduana f.
customs duty n derechos de aduana mpl.
customs officer n aduanero/ra m/f.
cut vt cortar; separar.
cutback n reducción f.
cute adj lindo/da.
cutlery n cuchillería f.
cutlet n chuleta f.
cut-rate adj a precio reducido.
cut-throat n asesino m:—adj encarnizado/da.
cutting n cortadura f:—adj cortante; mordaz.
cyanide n cianuro m.
cycle n ciclo m; bicicleta f:—vi ir en bicicleta.
cycling n ciclismo m.

cyclist *n* ciclista *m/f.*
cyclone *n* ciclón *m.*
cygnet *n* pollo del cisne *m.*
cylinder *n* cilindro *m;* rollo *m.*
cylindric(al) *adj* cilíndrico/ca.
cymbals *n* címbalo *m.*

cynic(al) *adj* cínico/ca; obsceno/na:—
  n cínico *m* (*filósofo*).
cynicism *n* cinismo *m.*
cypress *n* ciprés *m.*
cyst *n* quiste *m.*
czar *n* zar *m.*

D

dad(dy) *n* papa *m.*
daddy-long-legs *n* típula *m.*
daffodil *n* narciso *m.*
dagger *n* puñal *m.*
daily *adj* diario/ria.
dainty *adj* delicado/da.
dairy *n* lechería *f.*
dairy produce *n* productos lácteos *mpl.*
daisy *n* margarita *f.*
damage *n* daño *m;* perjuicio *m.*
damask *n* damasco *m.*
damn *vt* condenar.
damnation *n* perdición *f.*
damp *adj* húmedo/da.
dampen *vt* mojar.
dampness *n* humedad *f.*
dance *n* danza *f;* baile *m.*
dandelion *n* diente de león *m.*
dandruff *n* caspa *f.*
danger *n* peligro *m.*
dare *vi* atreverse.
daredevil *n* atrevido *m.*
dark *adj* oscuro/ra.
darling *n, adj* querido *m.*
darn *vt* zurcir.
dart *n* dardo *m.*
dartboard *n* diana *f.*
dash *vi* irse de prisa.
dashboard *n* tablero de instrumentos *m.*

data *n* datos *mpl.*
database *n* base de datos *f.*
date *n* fecha *f;* cita *f.*
daughter *n* hija *f:—~ in-law* nuera *f.*
dawn *n* alba *f:—vi* amanecer.
day *n* día *m.*
dazzle *vt* deslumbrar.
deacon *n* diácono *m.*
dead *adj* muerto/ta.
deadline *n* fecha tope *f.*
deadlock *n* punto muerto *m.*
deaf *adj* sordo/da.
deal *n* convenio *m;* transacción *f.*
dean *n* deán *m.*
dear *adj* querido/da. caro/ra.
dearness *n* carestía *f.*
death *n* muerte *f.*
debacle *n* desastre *m.*
debar *vt* excluir.
debase *vt* degradar.
debate *n* debate *m;* polémica *f.*
debilitate *vt* debilitar.
debt *n* deuda *f.*
decade *n* década *f.*
decadence *n* decadencia *f.*
decaffeinated *adj* descafeinado/da.
decay *vi* decaer; pudrirse.
deceit *n* engaño *m.*
deceive *vt* engañar.
December *n* diciembre *m.*
decent *adj* decente.

decide vt, vi decidir; resolver.
deciduous adj (bot) de hoja caduca.
decimal adj decimal.
decipher vt descifrar.
decision n decisión.
declare vt declarar.
decline vt (gr) declinar; evitar.
decompose vt descomponer.
decorate vt decorar, adornar.
decoration n decoración f.
decorum n decoro m.
decrease vt disminuir.
decree n decreto m.
dedicate vt dedicar; consagrar.
dedication n dedicación f.
deduce vt deducir.
deep adj profundo/da.
deep-freeze n congeladora f.
deer n ciervo m.
defamation n difamación f.
defeat n derrota f:—vt derrotar.
defect n defecto m.
defend vt defender.
defense n defensa f.
defensive adj defensivo/va.
defer vt aplazar.
deficient adj insuficiente.
deficit n déficit m.
define vt definir.
definition n definición f.
deflate vt desinflar.
deflect vt desviar.
deform vt desfigurar.
defraud vt estafar.
defuse vt desactivar.
degenerate vi degenerar.
degrade vt degradar.
degree n grado m; título m.
dehydrated adj deshidratado/da.
deity n deidad, divinidad f.
dejection n desaliento m.
delay vt demorar:—n retraso m.

delegate vt delegar:—n delegado m.
delete vt tachar; borrar.
delicacy n delicadeza f.
delicate adj delicado/da.
delicious adj delicioso/sa.
delight n delicia f.
delinquent n delincuente m.
delirium n delirio m.
deliver vt entregar.
delivery n entrega f; parto m.
delivery truck n camioneta f.
delude vt engañar.
deluge n diluvio m.
demagog(ue) n demagogo m.
demand n demanda f.
demean vi rebajarse.
demented adj demente.
demise n desaparición f.
democracy n democracia f.
democrat n demócrata m/f.
demolish vt demoler.
demon n demonio, diablo m.
demonstrate vt demostrar.
demoralize vt desmoralizar.
demote vt degradar.
demure adj modesto/ta.
den n guarida f.
denial n negación f.
denims npl vaqueros mpl.
denomination n valor m.
denote vt denotar.
denounce vt denunciar.
dense adj denso/sa.
density n densidad f.
dental adj dental.
dentist n dentista m/f.
denture npl dentadura postiza f.
denunciation n denuncia f.
deny vt negar.
deodorant n desodorante m.
depart vi partir(se).
department n departamento m.

department store *n* gran almacén *m.*

departure lounge *n* sala de embarque *f.*

depend *vi* depender.

depict *vt* pintar, retratar; describir.

deplore *vt* deplorar, lamentar.

deport *vt* deportar.

deposit *vt* depositar.

depositor *n* depositante *m.*

depot *n* depósito *m.*

deprave *vt* depravar.

depravity *n* depravación *f.*

deprecate *vt* lamentar.

depreciate *vi* depreciarse.

depreciation *n* depreciación *f.*

depress *vt* deprimir.

depressed *adj* deprimido/da.

depression *n* depresión *f.*

deprivation *n* privación *f.*

deprive *vt* privar.

depth *n* profundidad *f.*

deputation *n* diputación *f.*

deputize *vi* suplir a.

deputy *n* diputado *m.*

derelict *adj* abandonado/da.

deride *vt* burlar.

derision *n* mofa *f.*

derivative *n* derivado *m.*

derive *vt, vi* derivar(se).

derogatory *adj* despectivo/va.

descend *vi* descender.

descendant *n* descendiente *m.*

descent *n* descenso *m.*

describe *vt* describir.

description *n* descripción *f.*

descriptive *adj* descriptivo/va.

desecrate *vt* profanar.

desert *n* desierto *m.*

deserve *vt* merecer.

design *vt* diseñar.

designate *vt* nombrar.

designedly *adv* de propósito.

designer *n* diseñador *m.*

desirable *adj* deseable.

desire *n* deseo *m.*

desk *n* escritorio *m.*

desolate *adj* desierto/ta.

despair *n* desesperación *f.*

desperado *n* bandido *m.*

desperate *adj* desesperado/da.

despise *vt* despreciar.

despite *prep* a pesar de.

despoil *vt* despojar.

despondency *n* abatimiento *m.*

despot *n* déspota *m/f.*

dessert *n* postre *m.*

destination *n* destino *m.*

destine *vt* destinar.

destiny *n* destino *m;* suerte *f.*

destitute *adj* indigente.

destroy *vt* destruir.

destruction *n* destrucción.

detach *vt* separar.

detail *n* detalle *m.*

detain *vt* retener; detener.

detect *vt* detectar.

detection *n* descubrimiento *m.*

detective *n* detective *m/f.*

deter *vt* disuadir.

detergent *n* detergente *m.*

deteriorate *vt* deteriorar.

determination *n* resolución *f.*

determine *vt* determinar.

deterrent *n* fuerza de disuasión *f.*

detest *vt* detestar.

detonate *vi* detonar.

detonation *n* detonación *f.*

detour *n* desviación *f.*

detriment *n* perjuicio *m.*

devaluation *n* devaluación *f.*

devastate *vt* devastar.

develop *vt* desarrollar.

development *n* desarrollo *m.*

deviate *vi* desviarse.

deviation n desviación f.
device n mecanismo m.
devil n diablo, demonio m.
devious adj taimado/da.
devise vt inventar.
devote vt dedicar.
devour vt devorar.
devout adj devoto/ta.
dew n rocío m.
dexterity n destreza f.
diabetes n diabetes f.
diabetic n diabético m.
diadem n diadema f.
diagnosis n (med) diagnosis f.
diagonal adj, n diagonal (f).
diagram n diagrama m.
dial n cuadrante m.
dialect n dialecto m.
dialog(ue) n dialogo m.
diameter n diámetro m.
diamond n diamante m.
diaper n pañal m.
diaphragm n diafragma m.
diarrhea n diarrea f.
diary n diario m.
dice npl dados mpl.
dictate vt dictar.
dictation n dictado m.
dictatorship n dictadura f.
diction n dicción f
dictionary n diccionario m.
didactic adj didáctico/ca.
die[1] vi morir.
die[2] n dado m.
diesel n diesel m.
diet n dieta f; régimen m.
differ vi diferenciarse.
difference n diferencia f.
different adj diferente.
difficult adj dificil.
dig vt cavar.
digest vt digerir.

digestion n digestión f.
digger n excavadora f.
digit n dígito m.
digital adj digital.
dignity n dignidad f.
dike n dique m.
dilate vt, vi dilatar(se).
dilemma n dilema m.
dilute vt diluir.
dim adj turbio/bia.
dimension n dimensión, extensión f.
diminish vt, vi disminuir(se).
dimple n hoyuelo m.
din n alboroto m.
dine vi cenar.
diner n café m, restaurante (económico) m.
dinghy n lancha neumática f.
dingy adj sombrío/ria.
dinner n cena f.
dinosaur n dinosaurio m.
diocese n diócesis f.
dip vt mojar.
diphtheria n difteria f.
diploma n diploma m.
diplomacy n diplomacia f.
diplomat n diplomático/ca m/f.
dire adj calamitoso/sa.
direct adj directo/ta:—vt dirigir.
direction n dirección f.
directly adj directamente.
director n director/a m/f.
directory n guía f.
dirt n suciedad f.
disability n incapacidad f.
disabled adj minusválido/da.
disadvantage n desventaja f:—vt perjudicar.
disagree vi no estar de acuerdo.
disappear vi desaparecer.
disappoint vt decepcionar.
disapprove vt desaprobar.

disaster *n* desastre *m*.

disbelieve *vt* desconfiar.

discard *vt* descartar.

discern *vt* discernir, percibir.

discharge *vt* descargar; pagar (una deuda).

disciple *n* discípulo *m*.

discipline *n* disciplina *f*:—*vt* disciplinar.

disclose *vi* revelar.

disco *n* discoteca *f*.

discomfort *n* incomodidad *f*.

discontent *n* descontento *m*:—*adj* malcontento/ta.

discontinue *vi* interrumpir.

discord *n* discordia *f*.

discount *n* descuento *m*; rebaja *f*.

discover *vt* descubrir.

discreet *adj* discreto/ta.

discriminate *vt* distinguir.

discuss *vt* discutir.

discussion *n* discusión *f*.

disease *n* enfermedad *f*.

disembark *vt, vi* desembarcar.

disentangle *vt* desenredar.

disfigure *vt* desfigurar.

disgrace *n* ignominia *f*.

disgruntled *adj* descontento/ta.

disguise *vt* disfrazar.

disgust *n* aversión *f*:—*vt* repugnar.

dish *n* fuente *f*; plato *m*.

disheveled *adj* desarreglado/da.

dishonest *adj* deshonesto/ta.

dishonesty *n* falta de honradez *f*.

dishonor *n* deshonra, ignominia *f*.

dishtowel *n* trapo de fregar *m*.

dishwasher *n* lavaplatos *m*.

disillusion *vt* desilusionar.

disillusioned *adj* desilusionado/da.

disincentive *n* freno *m*.

disinclination *n* aversión *f*.

disinclined *adj* reacio/cia.

disinfect *vt* desinfectar.

disinfectant *n* desinfectante *m*.

disinherit *vt* desheredar.

disintegrate *vi* disgregarse.

disinterested *adj* desinteresado/da.

disjointed *adj* inconexo/xa.

disk *n* disco, disquete *m*.

diskette *n* disco, disquete *m*.

dislike *n* aversión *f*.

dislocate *vt* dislocar.

dislocation *n* dislocación *f*.

dislodge *vt, vi* desalojar.

disloyal *adj* desleal.

disloyalty *n* deslealtad *f*.

dismal *adj* triste.

dismantle *vt* desmontar.

dismay *n* consternación *f*.

dismember *vt* despedazar.

dismiss *vt* despedir.

dismissal *n* despedida *f*.

disobedience *n* desobediencia *f*.

disobedient *adj* desobediente.

disobey *vt* desobedecer.

disorderly *adj* desarreglado/da.

disorganized *adj* desorganizado/da.

disorientated *adj* desorientado/da.

disown *vt* desconocer.

disparage *vt* despreciar.

disparaging *adj* despreciativo/va.

disparity *n* disparidad *f*.

dispassionate *adj* desapasionado/da.

dispatch *vt* enviar.

dispel *vt* disipar.

dispensary *n* dispensario *m*.

dispense *vt* dispensar; distribuir.

disperse *vt* disipersar.

dispirited *adj* desalentado/da.

displace *vt* desplazar.

display *vt* exponer.

displeased *adj* disgustado/da.

displeasure *n* disgusto *m*.

disposable *adj* desechable.

disposal n disposición f.
dispose vt disponer; arreglar.
disposition n disposición f.
dispossess vt desposeer.
disproportionate adj despropor-
cionado/da.
disprove vt refutar.
dispute n disputa, controversia f.
disqualify vt incapacitar.
disregard vt desatender:—n desdén
m.
disreputable adj de mala fama.
disrespectful adj irreverente.
disrobe vt desnudar.
disrupt vt interrumpir.
disruption n interrupción f.
dissatisfaction n descontento/ta.
dissatisfied adj insatisfecho/cha.
dissect vt disecar.
dissection n disección.
dissent vi disentir.
dissertation n disertación f.
dissident n disidente m.
dissimilar adj distinto.
dissolution n disolución f.
dissolve vt disolver.
dissuade vt disuadir.
distance n distancia f:—**at a ~** de
lejos:—vt apartar.
distant adj distante.
distillery n destilería f.
distinct adj distinto/ta.
distinction n distinción f.
distinctive adj distintivo/va.
distinguish vt distinguir.
distort vt retorcer.
distorted adj distorsionado/da.
distortion n distorción f.
distract vt distraer.
distracted adj distraído/da.
distraction n distracción f; confusión
f.

distraught adj enloquecido/da.
distress n angustia f.
distribute vt distribuir, repartir.
distribution n distribución f.
district n distrito m.
disturb vt molestar.
disturbance n disturbio m.
disturbing adj inquietante.
disused adj abandonado/da.
ditch n zanja f.
ditto adv ídem.
diuretic adj (med) diurético/ca.
diver n buzo m.
diverge vi divergir.
diverse adj diverso/sa, diferente.
diversion n diversión f.
diversity n diversidad f.
divert vt desviar; divertir.
divide vt dividir:—vi dividirse.
divine adj divino/na.
divinity n divinidad f.
divorce n divorcio m.
DJ n pinchadiscos m.
do vt hacer, obrar.
docile adj dócil, apacible.
dockyard n (mar) astillero m.
doctor n médico/ca m/f.
doctrine n doctrina f.
document n documento m.
documentary adj documental.
doe n gama f:—**~ rabbit** coneja f.
dog(ue) n perro m.
do-it-yourself n bricolaje m.
doll n muñeca f.
dollar n dólar m.
dolphin n delfín m.
dome n cúpula f.
domestic adj doméstico/ca.
domesticity n domesticidad f.
domicile n domicilio m.
dominant adj dominante.
dominate vi dominar.

domineer vi dominar.

dominion n dominio m.

dominoes npl domino m.

donate vt donar.

donation n donación f.

donkey n asno, borrico m.

donor n donante m.

door n puerta f.

doorbell n timbre m.

doorman n portero m.

doormat n felpudo m.

dormouse n lirón m.

dose n dosis f.

dossier n expediente m.

dot n punto m.

dote vi adorar.

double adj doble.

doubly adv doblemente.

doubt n duda, sospecha f.

doubtful adj dudoso/sa.

doubtless adv sin duda.

dough n masa f.

douse vt apagar.

dove n paloma f.

dovecot n palomar m.

dowdy adj mal vestido/da.

down n plumón m; flojel m:—prep abajo.

downfall n ruina f.

downhearted adj desanimado/da.

downpour n aguacero m.

downtown adv al centro (de la ciudad).

dowry n dote f.

doze vi dormitar.

dozen n docena f.

dozy adj soñoliento/ta.

drab adj gris.

draft n borrador m; quinta f; corriente de aire f.

dragon n dragón m.

dragonfly n libélula f.

drain vt desaguar.

drake n ánade macho m.

drama n drama m.

dramatic adj dramático/ca.

dramatize vt dramatizar.

dramatist n dramaturgo/ga m/f.

drape vt cubrir.

drapes npl cortinas fpl.

drastic adj drástico/ca.

draw vt tirar; dibujar.

drawback n desventaja f.

drawer n cajón m.

drawing n dibujo m.

drawing room n salón m.

dread n terror, espanto m:—vt temer.

dreadful adj espantoso/sa.

dream n sueno m:—vi sonar.

drench vt empapar.

dress vt vestir:—n vestido m.

dresser n aparador m.

dressing gown n bata f.

dressing table n tocador m.

dressmaker n modista f.

dried adj seco/ca.

drill n taladro m.

drink vt, vi beber.

drinkable adj potable.

drip vi gotear.

drive vt manejar.

driver n conductor m.

driveway n entrada f.

drizzle vi lloviznar.

droop vi decaer.

drop n gota f.

drought n seguía f.

drown vt anegar.

drowsiness n somnolencia f.

drowsy adj soñoliento/ta.

drudgery n trabajo monótono m.

drug n droga f:—vt drogar.

drug addict n drogadicto m.

drug store n farmacia f.

drum n tambor m:—vi tocar el tambor.

drummer n batería m.

drumstick n palillo de tambor m.

drunk adj borracho/cha.

drunkard n borracho m.

drunkenness n borrachera f.

dry adj seco/ca. * vt secar.

dry goods store n mercería, camisería f.

dry rot n podredumbre f.

dual adj doble.

dubbed adj doblado/da.

dubious adj dudoso/sa.

duck n pato m.

duckling n patito m.

dud adj estropeado/da.

due adj debido/da.

duel n duelo m.

duet n (mus) duo m.

dull adj lerdo/da. insípido/da.

duly adv debidamente; puntualmente.

dumb adj mudo/da.

dumbbell n pesa f.

dumbfounded adj pasmado/da.

dummy n maniquí m; imbécil m.

dumpling n bola de masa f.

dumpy adj gordito/ta.

dunce n zopenco m.

dune n duna f.

dung n estiércol m.

dungarees npl mono m.

dungeon n calabozo m.

dupe n bobo m.

duplicity n duplicidad f.

durability n durabilidad f.

durable adj duradero/ra.

duration n duración f.

during prep mientras, durante el tiempo que.

dusk n crepúsculo m.

dust n polvo m.

duster n plumero m.

dutch courage n valor fingido m.

duteous adj fiel, leal.

dutiful adj obediente.

duty n deber m; obligación f.

dwarf n enano m; enana f.

dwell vi habitar, morar.

dwelling n habitación f; domicilio m.

dwindle vi mermar, disminuirse.

dye vt teñir:—n tinte m.

dynamic adj dinámico/ca.

dynamite n dinamita f.

dynamo n dinamo f.

dynasty n dinastía f.

dysentery n disenteria f.

dyspepsia n (med) dispepsia f.

E

each pn cada uno, cada una.

eager adj entusiasmado/da.

eagle n águila f.

eaglet n aguilucho m.

ear n oreja f.

earache n dolor de oídos m.

eardrum n tímpano (del oído) m.

early adj temprano/na.

earn vt ganar; conseguir.

earnest adj serio/ria.

earth n tierra f.

earthenware n loza de barro f.

earthquake n terremoto m.
earthworm n lombriz f.
earthy adj sensual.
earwig n tijereta f.
ease n comodidad f; facilidad f.
easel n caballete m.
easily adv fácilmente.
east n este m; oriente m.
Easter n Pascua de Resurrección f.
easterly adj del este.
eastern adj del este, oriental.
easy adj fácil; cómodo/da.
easy chair n sillón m.
eat vt comer.
ebb n reflujo m.
ebony n ébano m.
eccentric adj excéntrico/ca.
echo n eco m.
eclectic adj ecléctico/ca.
eclipse n eclipse m.
ecology n ecología f.
economics npl economía f.
economy n economía f.
ecstasy n éxtasis m.
eczema n eczema m.
eddy n reflujo de agua m.
edge n filo m.
edict n edicto, mandato m.
edit vt dirigir; redactar.
edition n edición f.
editor n director m.
educate vt educar.
education n educación f.
eel n anguila f.
effect n efecto m.
effective adj eficaz..
effeminate adj afeminado/da.
effervescence n efervescencia f.
efficacy n eficacia f.
efficient adj eficaz.
effigy n efigie, imagen f.
effort n esfuerzo m.

egg n huevo m.
eggplant n berenjena f.
ego(t)ist n egoísta m/f.
eight num ocho.
eighteen num dieciocho.
eighth adj octavo.
eighty num ochenta.
either pn cualquiera.
eject vt expeler, desechar.
elastic adj elástico/ca.
elation n regocijo m.
elbow n codo m.
elder n saúco m (árbol):—adj mayor.
elect vt elegir.
election n elección f.
electrician n electricista m/f.
electricity n electricidad f.
elegance n elegancia f.
elegant adj elegante, delicado/da.
elegy n elegía f.
element n elemento m.
elephant n elefante m.
elevate vt elevar, alzar.
elevator n ascensor m.
eleven num once.
eleventh adj onceno, undécimo.
elf n duende m.
elicit vt sacar de.
eligible adj elegible.
eliminate vt eliminar, descartar.
elk n alce m.
elm n olmo m.
elocution n elocución f.
elongate vt alargar.
elope vi escapar, huir.
elopement n fuga f.
eloquence n elocuencia f.
else pn otro/ra.
elsewhere adv en otra parte.
elude vt eludir, evitar.
embargo n prohibición f.
embark vt embarcar.

embarrass vt avergonzar.

embarrassment n desconcierto m.

embassy n embajada f.

embed vt empotrar; clavar.

embellish vt hermosear.

embers npl rescoldo m.

embezzle vt desfalcar.

embitter vt amargar.

emblem n emblema m.

embrace vt abrazar.

embroider vt bordar.

embroil vt embrollar; confundir.

embryo n embrión m.

emerald n esmeralda f.

emerge vi salir, proceder.

emergency n emergencia f.

emery n esmeril m.

emigrant n emigrante m.

emigrate vi emigrar.

eminent adj eminente.

emission n emisión f.

emit vt emitir.

emotion n emoción f.

emperor n emperador m.

emphasis n énfasis m.

emphasize vt hablar con énfasis.

empire n imperio m.

employ vt emplear, ocupar.

employee n empleado m.

employer n patrón m; empresario m.

empress n emperatriz f.

empty adj vacío/cia.

emulate vt emular.

emulsion n emulsión f.

enable vt capacitar.

enact vt promulgar.

enamel n esmalte m.

enchant vt encantar.

enchanting adj encantador.

encircle vt cercar, circundar.

enclose vt cercar, circunvalar.

encore adv otra vez, de nuevo.

encounter n encuentro m.

encourage vt animar.

encouragement n estimulo, patrocinio m.

encroach vt usurpar.

encumber vt embarazar, cargar.

encyclopedia n enciclopedia f.

end n fin m.

endanger vt peligrar.

endear vt encarecer.

endeavor vi esforzarse; intentar.

endemic adj endémico/ca.

ending n conclusión.

endive n (bot) endibia f.

endless adj infinito/ta.

endorse vt endosar; aprobar.

endow vt dotar.

endure vt sufrir, soportar.

enemy n enemigo/ga.

energetic adj enérgico/ca.

energy n energía, fuerza f.

enforce vt hacer cumplir.

engine n motor m; locomotora f.

engineer n ingeniero m.

engrave vt grabar.

enhance vt aumentar.

enigma n enigma m.

enjoy vt gozar.

enjoyment n disfrute m; placer m.

enlarge vt engrandecer.

enlist vt alistar.

enliven vt animar.

enmity n enemistad f; odio m.

enormous adj enorme.

enough adv bastante; basta.

enrage vt enfurecer.

enrapture vt arrebatar.

enrich vt enriquecer.

enrol vt registrar.

enrolment n inscripción f.

ensign n (mil) bandera f.

enslave vt esclavizar.

ensue vi seguirse.

ensure vt asegurar.

entangle vt enmarañar.

enter vt entrar; admitir.

enterprise n empresa f.

entertain vt divertir; hospedar.

entertainer n artista m/f.

entertainment n entretenimiento, pasatiempo m.

enthralling adj cautivador.

enthusiasm n entusiasmo m.

entice vt tentar; seducir.

entire adj entero/ra, completo/ta.

entitle vt intitular; conferir algún derecho.

entity n entidad f.

entrance n entrada f.

entreat vt rogar, suplicar.

entrepreneur n empresario m.

entrust vt confiar.

entry n entrada f.

entwine vt entrelazar.

envelop n envolver.

envelope vt sobre m.

enviable adj envidiable.

environment n medio ambiente m.

environs npl vecindad f.

envisage vt prever; concebir.

envoy n enviado m.

envy n envidia.

ephemeral adj efímero/ra.

epic adj épico/ca.

epidemic adj epidémico/ca.

epilogue n epílogo m.

Epiphany n Epifanía f.

episcopacy n episcopado m.

episcopal adj episcopal.

episcopalian n anglicano m.

episode n episodio m.

epistle n epístola f.

epithet n epíteto m.

epoch n época f.

equal adj igual.

equalize vt igualar.

equality n igualdad, uniformidad f.

equally adv igualmente.

equate vt equiparar (con).

equation n ecuación f.

equator n ecuador m.

equatorial adj ecuatorial.

equestrian adj ecuestre.

equilibrium n equilibrio m.

equinox n equinoccio m.

equip vt equipar.

equipment n equipaje m.

equitable adj equitativo/va.

equity n equidadf.

equivalent adj, n equivalente m.

era n era f.

eradicate vt desarraigar.

eradication n extirpación f.

erase vt borrar.

eraser n goma de borrar f.

erect vt erigir; establecer.

ermine n armiño m.

erode vt erosionar.

erotic adj erótico/ca.

err vi vagar, errar.

errand n recado.

erratic adj errático/ca.

erroneous adj erróneo/nea.

error n error m.

erudite adj erudito/ta.

erupt vi entrar en erupción; hacer erupción.

eruption n erupción f.

escalate vi extenderse.

escalator n escalera móvil f.

escapade n travesura f.

escape vt evitar; escapar.

escapism n escapismo m.

escort n escolta f:—vt escoltar.

esoteric adj esotérico/ca.

especial adj especial.

essay n ensayo m.
essence n esencia f.
essential n esencia f:—adj esencial.
establish vt establecer.
establishment n establecimiento m.
estate n estado m.
esteem vt estimar, apreciar.
estimate vt estimar, apreciar.
estuary n estuario.
etch vt grabar al aguafuerte.
eternal adj eterno/na.
eternity n eternidad f.
ether n éter m.
ethical adj ético/ca.
ethics npl ética f.
ethnic adj étnico/ca.
ethos n genio m.
etiquette n etiqueta f.
etymology n etimología f.
Eucharist n Eucaristía f.
eulogy n elogio.
eunuch n eunuco m.
euphemism n eufemismo m.
evacuate vt evacuar.
evacuation n evacuación f.
evade vt evadir.
evaluate vt evaluar.
evangelical adj evangélico/ca.
evaporate vt evaporar.
evasion n evasión f.
evasive adj evasivo/va.
eve n víspera f.
even adj llano/na, igual; par, semejante:—adv aun; aun cuando, supuesto que; no obstante.
evening n tarde f.
event n acontecimiento, evento m.
eventuality n eventualidad f.
ever adv siempre.
every adj cada uno o cada una.
evict vt desahuciar.
eviction n desahucio m.

evidence n evidencia f.
evil adj malo/la, depravado/da.
evocative adj sugestivo/va.
evoke vt evocar.
evolution n evolución f.
evolve vt, vi evolucionar.
ewe n oveja f.
exacerbate vt exacerbar.
exact adj exacto/ta.
exacting adj exigente.
exaggerate vt exagerar.
exaggeration n exageración f.
exalt vt exaltar.
exaltation n exaltación.
examination n examen m.
examine vt examinar.
examiner n inspector/a m/f.
example n ejemplar m; ejemplo m.
excavate vt excavar.
excavation n excavación f.
exceed vt exceder.
exceedingly adv extremamente, en sumo grado.
excel vt sobresalir.
excellence n excelencia f.
excellent adj excelente.
except vt exceptuar, excluir:—~(ing) prep excepto, a excepción de.
exception n excepción, exclusión f.
exceptional adj excepcional.
excerpt n extracto m.
excess n exceso m.
excessive adj excesivo/va.
exchange vt cambiar; trocar.
exchange rate n tipo de cambio m.
excitability n excitabilidad f.
excitable adj excitable.
excite vt excitar; estimular.
excited adj emocionado/da.
excitement n estímulo m, excitación f.
exclaim vi exclamar.

exclamation n exclamación f.

exclamation mark n punto de admiración m.

exclamatory adj exclamatorio/ria.

exclude vt excluir; exceptuar.

exclusion n exclusión, f.

exclusive adj exclusivo/va.

excommunicate vt excomulgar.

excommunication n excomunión f.

excrement n excremento m.

excruciating adj atroz.

excursion n excursión f.

excusable adj excusable.

excuse vt disculpar.

execute vt ejecutar.

execution n ejecución f.

executioner n ejecutor/a.

executive adj ejecutivo/va.

executor n testamentario/ria, albacea m/f.

exemplary adj ejemplar.

exemplify vt ejemplificar.

exempt adj exento/ta.

exemption n exención f.

exercise n ejercicio m.

exercise book n cuaderno m.

exertion n esfuerzo m.

exhale vt exhalar.

exhaust n escape m.

exhausted adj agotado/da.

exhaustion n agotamiento m.

exhaustive adj comprensivo/va.

exhibit vt exhibir; mostrar.

exhibition n exposición f.

exhilarating adj estimulante.

exhort vt exhortar, excitar.

exhume vt exhumar.

exile n destierro m.

exist vi existir.

existence n existencia f.

exit n salida f:—vi hacer mutis.

exit ramp n vía de acceso f.

exodus n éxodo m.

exonerate vt exonerar.

exhorbitant adj exorbitante.

exorcize vt exorcizar, conjurar.

exorcism n exorcismo m.

exotic adj exótico/ca.

expand vt extender, dilatar.

expatriate vt expatriar.

expect vt esperar.

expectant mother n mujer encinta f.

expediency n conveniencia f.

expedition n expedición f.

expel vt expeler, desterrar.

expend vt expender.

expendable adj prescindible.

expenditure n gasto, desembolso m.

expense n gasto m; coste m.

experience n experiencia f; practica f.

experienced adj experimentado/da.

experiment n experimento m.

expert adj experto/ta.

expertise n pericia f.

expiration n expiración f.

expire vi expirar.

explain vt explanar, explicar.

explanation n explanación, explicación f.

expletive adj expletivo/va.

explicit adj explícito/ta.

explode vt, vi estallar, explotar.

exploit vt explotar.

exploitation n explotación f.

exploration n exploración f.

exploratory adj exploratorio/ria.

explore vt explorar.

explorer n explorador m.

explosion n explosión f.

explosive adj, n explosivo m.

exponent n (math) exponente m.

export vt exportar.

expose vt exponer; mostrar.

exposed adj expuesto/ta.

exposition *n* exposición *f.*
expostulate *vi* debatir, contender.
exposure *n* exposición *f.*
expound *vt* exponer.
express *vt* exprimir; representar.
expression *n* expresión *f.*
expressionless *adj* sin expresión (cara).
expressway *n* autopista *f.*
expulsion *n* explosión *f.*
expurgate *vt* expurgar.
exquisite *adj* exquisito/ta.
extend *vt* extender.
extension *n* extensión *f.*
extensive *adj* extenso/sa.
extent *n* extensión *f.*
extenuate *vt* extenuar.
exterior *adj, n* exterior *m.*
exterminate *vt* exterminar.
extermination *n* exterminación *f.*
external *adj* externo/na.
extinct *adj* extinto/ta.
extinction *n* extinción *f.*
extinguish *vt* extinguir.
extinguisher *n* extintor *m.*
extol *vt* alabar, magnificar.
extort *vt* sacar por fuerza.
extortion *n* extorsión *f.*

extortionate *adj* excesivo/va.
extra *adv* extra.
extract *vt* extraer.
extracurricular *adj* extraescolar.
extradition *n* (*law*) extradición *f.*
extramarital *adj* extramatrimonial.
extraneous *adj* extraño/ña.
extraordinary *adj* extraordinario/ria.
extravagance *n* extravagancia *f.*
extravagant *adj* extravagante.
extreme *adj* extremo/ma.
extremist *adj, n* extremista *m/f.*
extremity *n* extremidad *f.*
extrovert *adj, n* extrovertido *m.*
exuberance *n* exuberancia *f.*
exuberant *adj* exuberante.
exult *vt* exultar.
exultation *n* exultación *f*; regocijo *m.*
eye *n* ojo *m:—vt* ojear, contemplar, observar.
eyeball *n* globo del ojo *m.*
eyebrow *n* ceja *f.*
eyelash *n* pestaña *f.*
eyelid *n* párpado *m.*
eyesight *n* vista *f.*
eyewitness *n* testigo ocular *m.*
eyrie *n* aguilera *f.*

F

fabric *n* tejido *m.*
fabricate *vt* fabricar.
fabulous *adj* fabuloso/sa.
facade *n* fachada *f.*
face *n* cara, faz *f*; superficie *f.*
facet *n* faceta *f.*
facetious *adj* chistoso/sa.
facile *adj* fácil.
facilitate *vt* facilitar.
facility *n* facilidad *f.*

facsimile *n* facsímile *m*; telefax *m.*
fact *n* hecho *m.*
faction *n* facción *f.*
factor *n* factor *m.*
factory *n* fabrica *f.*
faculty *n* facultad *f.*
fad *n* moda , manía *f.*
fade *vi* decaer.
fail *vt* suspender, reprobar; fallar *a.*
failure *n* falta *f*; culpa *f.*

faint vi desmayarse, debilitarse.

faint-hearted adj cobarde.

fair adj hermoso/sa, bello/la; blanco/ca; rubio/bia; claro/ra, sereno/na; favorable; recto/ta, justo/ta; franco/ca:—adv limpio:—n feria f.

fairly adv justamente.

fairy n hada f.

faith n fe f; dogma de fe m.

faithfulness n fidelidad f.

fake n falsificación f.

falcon n halcón m.

fall[1] n otoño m.

fall[2] vi caer(se).

fallacy n falacia.

fallible adj falible.

false adj falso/sa.

falsify vt falsificar.

fame n fama f.

famed adj celebrado/da, famoso/sa.

familiar adj familiar.

family n familia f.

famine n hambre f; carestía f.

famous adj famoso/sa.

fan n abanico m; aficionado m.

fanatic adj, n fanático m.

fanciful adj imaginativo/va.

fancy n fantasía, imaginación f.

fanfare n (mus) fanfarria f.

fang n colmillo m.

fantastic adj fantástico/ca.

fantasy n fantasía f.

far adv lejos.

faraway adj remoto/ta.

farce n farsa f.

fare n precio m; tarifa f.

farm n finca f, granja f.

farmer n estanciero m; granjero m.

fascinate vt fascinar, encantar.

fascism n fascismo.

fashion n moda f; forma f.

fashionable adj a la moda.

fashion show n desfile de modelos m.

fast vi ayunar; adv rápidamente.

fasten vt abrochar.

fastidious adj fastidioso/sa.

fat adj gordo/da.

fatal adj fatal.

fate n hado, destino m.

fateful adj fatídico/ca.

father n padre m.

father-in-law n suegro m.

fatherland n patria f.

fathom n braza (medida) f.

fatigue n fatiga f.

fatty adj graso/sa.

faucet n espita f.

fault n falta, culpa f.

fauna n fauna f.

faux pas n plancha f.

favor n favor.

favorite n favorito m.

fawn n cervato m.

fax n facsímil(e) m; telefax m.

fear vi temer:—n miedo m.

fearful adj medroso/sa, temeroso/sa.

feasible adj factible.

feast n banquete.

feat n hecho m.

feather n pluma f.

feature n característica f; rasgo m.

February n febrero m.

federal adj federal.

federalist n federalista m/f.

federation n federación f.

fed-up adj harto/ta.

fee n honorarios mpl.

feeble adj flaco/ca, débil.

feed vt nutrir; alimentar.

feedback n reacción f.

feel vt sentir; tocar.

feign vt inventar, fingir.

feline adj gatuno/na.
fellowship n compañerismo m.
felon n criminal m/f.
felony n crimen m.
felt n fieltro m.
female n hembra f:—adj femenino/-na.
feminine adj femenino/na.
feminist n feminista m/f.
fence n cerca f; defensa f.
fennel n (bot) hinojo m.
fern n (bot) helecho m.
ferocious adj feroz.
ferret n hurón m.
ferry n barca de pasaje f.
fertile adj fértil, fecundo/da.
fester vi enconarse.
festival n fiesta f; festival m.
fetch vt ir a buscar.
fete n fiesta f.
fetus n feto m.
feud n riña, contienda f.
feudal adj feudal.
fever n fiebre f.
feverish adj febril.
few adj poco/ca.
fewer adj menor.
fewest adj los menos.
fiancé n novio m.
fiancée n novia f.
fib n mentira f.
fibre n fibra, hebra f.
fickle adj voluble.
fiction n ficción f.
fiddle n violín m; trampa f.
fidelity n fidelidad f.
field n campo m.
fieldmouse n ratón de campo m.
fierce adj fiero/ra, feroz.
fierceness n fiereza, ferocidad f.
fiery adj ardiente; apasionado/da.
fifteen adj, n quince.

fifteenth adj, n decimoquinto/ta.
fifth adj, n quinto/ta.
fiftieth adj, n quincuagésimo/ma.
fifty adj, n cincuenta.
fig n higo m.
fight vt, vi reñir; batallàr; combatir.
fig-leaf n hoja de higuera f.
figurative adj figurativo/va.
figure n figura.
filament n filamento m.
fill vt llenar; hartar.
fillet n filete m.
filling station n estación de servicio f.
fillip n (fig) estimulo m.
filly n potra f.
film n película f; film m.
filter n filtro m.
filth(iness) n inmundicia, porquería f.
fin n aleta f.
final adj final, último/ma.
finalize vt concluir.
finance n fondos mpl.
financier n financiero m.
find vt hallar, descubrir.
finesse n sutileza f.
finger n dedo m.
fingernail n uña f.
finish vt acabar, terminar, concluir.
finite adj finito/ta.
fir n abeto m.
fire n fuego m; incendio m.
firearm n arma de fuego f.
firefly n luciérnaga f.
firewood n leña f.
fireworks npl fuegos artificiales mpl.
firm adj firme, estable.
firmament n firmamento m.
firmness n firmeza f.
first adj primero/ra.
fiscal adj fiscal.
fish n pez m.
fishbone n espina f.

fisherman *n* pescador *m*.
fishy *adj* (fig) sospechoso/sa.
fist *n* puño *m*.
fitness *n* salud *f*.
five *adj, n* cinco.
fix *vt* fijar.
fixation *n* obsesión *f*.
fizzy *adj* gaseoso/sa.
flabbergasted *adj* pasmado/da.
flabby *adj* blando/da.
flaccid *adj* flojo/ja.
flag *n* bandera *f*.
flagpole *n* asta de bandera *f*.
flagrant *adj* flagrante; notorio/ria.
flagship *n* navío almirante *m*.
flair *n* aptitud especial *f*.
flake *n* copo *m*.
flamboyant *adj* vistoso/sa.
flame *n* llama *f*.
flamingo *n* flamenco *m*.
flammable *adj* inflamable.
flank *n* ijada *f*.
flannel *n* franela *f*.
flare *vi* lucir, brillar.
flash *n* flash *m*.
flashlight *n* antorcha *f*.
flask *n* frasco *m*.
flat *adj* llano/na, plano/na.
flatness *n* llanura *f*.
flatten *vt* allanar.
flatter *vt* adular.
flattery *n* adulación *f*.
flatulence *n* (med) flatulencia *f*.
flaunt *vt* ostentar.
flavor *n* sabor *m*.
flavorless *adj* soso/sa.
flaw *n* falta *m*.
flawless *adj* sin defecto.
flax *n* lino *m*.
flea *n* pulga *f*.
fleck *n* mota *f*.
flee *vt* huir de.

fleece *n* vellón *m*.
fleet *n* flota *f*.
flesh *n* carne *f*.
flex *n* cordón *m*.
flexibility *n* flexibilidad *f*.
flexible *adj* flexible.
flight *n* vuelo *m*.
flight attendant *n* tripulante auxiliar *m*.
flimsy *adj* débil; fútil.
flinch *vi* encogerse.
fling *vt* lanzar.
flint *n* pedernal *m*.
flip *vt* arrojar.
flippant *adj* petulante.
flipper *n* aleta *f*.
flirt *vi* coquetear:—*n* coqueta *f*.
flirtation *n* coquetería *f*.
flock *n* manada *f*.
flog *vt* azotar.
flogging *n* tunda, zurra *f*.
flood *n* diluvio *m*; inundación *f*.
flooding *n* inundación *f*.
floodlight *n* foco *m*.
floor *n* suelo, piso *m*.
floorboard *n* tabla *f*.
flop *n* fracaso *m*.
floppy *adj* flojo/ja.
flora *n* flora *f*.
floral *adj* floral.
florescence *n* florescencia *f*.
florid *adj* florido/da.
florist *n* florista *m/f*.
florist's (shop) *n* florería *f*.
flotilla *n* (mar) flotilla *f*.
flounder *n* platija (pez de mar) *f*.
flour *n* harina *f*.
flourish *vi* florecer.
flout *vt* burlarse de.
flow *vi* fluir.
flower *n* flor *f*.
flowerbed *n* cuadro (en un jardín) *m*.

flowerpot *n* tiesto de flores *m*.
flowery *adj* florido/da.
fluctuate *vi* fluctuar.
fluctuation *n* fluctuación *f*.
fluency *n* fluidez *f*.
fluent *adj* fluido/da.
fluff *n* pelusa *f*.
fluid *adj, n* fluido/da *m*.
fluidity *n* fluidez *f*.
fluke *n* (*sl*) chiripa *f*.
fluoride *n* fluoruro *m*.
flurry *n* ráfaga *f*; agitación *f*.
flute *n* flauta *f*.
flutter *vi* revolotear; estar en agitación.
flux *n* flujo *m*.
fly *vt* pilotar; transportar:—*vi* volar.
flying saucer *n* platillo volante *m*.
foal *n* potro *m*.
foam *n* espuma *f*.
foamy *adj* espumoso/sa.
focus *n* foco.
fodder *n* forraje *m*.
foe *n* adversario/ria *m/f*, enemigo *m*.
fog *n* niebla *f*.
foggy *adj* nebuloso/sa.
fold *n* redil *m*; pliegue *m*.
folder *n* carpeta *f*.
folding *adj* plegable.
foliage *n* follaje *m*.
folio *n* folio *m*.
folk *n* gente *f*.
folklore *n* folklore *m*.
folk song *n* canción folklórica *f*.
follow *vt* seguir; acompañar.
follower *n* seguidor/a *m/f*.
following *adj* siguiente.
folly *n* extravagancia *f*.
foment *vt* fomentar.
fond *adj* cariñoso/sa.
fondle *vt* acariciar.
fondness *n* gusto *m*; cariño *m*.

font *n* pila bautismal *f*.
food *n* comida *f*.
food mixer *n* batidora *f*.
food poisoning *n* botulismo *m*.
fool *n* loco/ca, tonto/ta *m/f*.
foolish *adj* bobo/ba, tonto/ta.
foolscap *n* papel tamaño folio *m*.
foot *n* pie *m*; pata *f*.
footage *n* imágenes *fpl*.
footnote *n* nota de pie *f*.
footpath *n* senda *f*.
footprint *n* huella *f*.
for *prep* por, a causa de; para.
forbid *vt* prohibir.
force *n* fuerza *f*; poder, vigor *m*.
forced *adj* forzado/da.
forceful *adj* enérgico/ca.
forceps *n* fórceps *m*.
ford *n* vado *m*.
fore *n:*—**to the ~** en evidencia.
forearm *n* antebrazo *m*.
foreboding *n* presentimiento *m*.
forecast *vt* pronosticar.
forecourt *n* patio *m*.
forefather *n* abuelo, antecesor *m*.
forefinger *n* índice *m*.
forefront *n:*—**in the ~ of** en la vanguardia de.
forego *vt* ceder.
foreground *n* delantera *f*.
forehead *n* frente *f*.
foreign *adj* extranjero/ra; extraño/ña.
foreigner *n* extranjero/ra, forastero/ra *m/f*.
foreign exchange *n* divisas *fpl*.
foreleg *n* pata delantera *f*.
foreman *n* capataz *m*.
foremost *adj* principal.
forensic *adj* forense.
forerunner *n* precursor/a *m/f*.
foresee *vt* prever.
foresight *n* previsión *f*.

forest *n* bosque *m;* selva *f.*
forester *n* guardabosque *m.*
forestry *n* silvicultura *f.*
foretaste *n* muestra *f.*
foretell *vt* predecir, profetizar.
forethought *n* providencia *f.*
forever *adv* para siempre.
foreword *n* prefacio *m.*
forfeit *n* confiscación *f.*
forge *n* fragua *f;* fabrica de metales *f.*
forger *n* falsificador/a *m/f.*
forgery *n* falsificación *f.*
forget *vt* olvidar.
forgetful *adj* olvidadizo/za.
forget-me-not *n* (*bot*) nomeolvides *m.*
forgive *vt* perdonar.
forgiveness *n* perdón *m.*
fork *n* tenedor *m.*
form *n* forma *f;* modelo *m;* modo *m.*
formal *adj* formal.
formality *n* formalidad *f.*
format *n* formato *m.*
formation *n* formación *f.*
formative *adj* formativo/va.
former *adj* precedente; anterior.
formidable *adj* formidable.
formula *n* fórmula *f.*
formulate *vt* formular.
forsake *vt* dejar.
fort *n* castillo *m.*
forthright *adj* franco/ca.
forthwith *adj* inmediatamente.
fortieth *adj, n* cuadragésimo *m.*
fortification *n* fortificación *f.*
fortify *vt* fortificar.
fortitude *n* fortaleza *f.*
fortnight *n* quince días *mpl.*
fortress *n* (*mil*) fortaleza *f.*
fortuitous *adj* impensado/da.
fortunate *adj* afortunado/da.
fortune *n* fortuna, suerte *f.*

fortune-teller *n* sortílego/ga.
forty *adj, n* cuarenta.
forum *n* foro *m.*
forward *adj* avanzado/da; delantero/ra.
forwardness *n* precocidad *f;* audacia *f.*
fossil *adj, n* fósil *m.*
foster *vt* criar.
foul *adj* sucio/cia, puerco/ca; impuro/ra.
found *vt* fundar, establecer.
foundation *n* fundación *f.*
founder *n* fundador/a *m/f.*
foundling *n* niño expósito *m,* niña expósita *f.*
foundry *n* fundería *f.*
fount, fountain *n* fuente *f.*
fountainhead *n* origen de fuente *m.*
four *adj, n* cuatro.
fourfold *adj* cuádruple.
fourteen *adj, n* catorce.
fourteenth *adj, n* decimocuarto/ta.
fourth *adj, n* cuarto/ta:—*n* cuarto *m:—* ~**ly** *adv* en cuarto lugar.
fowl *n* ave *f.*
fox *n* zorra *f.*
fracas *n* riña *f.*
fraction *n* fracción *f.*
fracture *n* fractura *f.*
fragile *adj* frágil; débil.
fragility *n* fragilidad *f.*
fragment *n* fragmento *m.*
fragrance *n* fragancia *f.*
fragrant *adj* fragante, oloroso/sa.
frail *adj* frágil, débil.
frailty *n* fragilidad *f;* debilidad *f.*
frame *n* armazón *m;* marco, cerco *m.*
franchise *n* sufragio *m.*
frank *adj* franco/ca, liberal.
frankly *adv* francamente.
frantic *adj* frenético/ca.

fraternize *vi* hermanarse.
fraternity *n* fraternidad *f.*
fraud *n* fraude *m.*
fraudulent *adj* fraudulento/ta.
fraught *adj* cargado/da, lleno/na.
freak *n* monstruo *m;* fenómeno *m.*
freckle *n* peca *f.*
freckled *adj* pecoso/sa.
free *adj* libre; liberal; suelto/ta.
freedom *n* libertad *f.*
freehold *n* propiedad vitalicia *f.*
free-for-all *n* riña general *f.*
freelance *adj, adv* por cuenta propia.
freemason *n* francmasón *m.*
freemasonry *n* francmasonería *f.*
freeway *n* autopista *f.*
freewheel *vi* ir en punto muerto.
freeze *vi* helar(se).
freezer *n* congeladora *f.*
freight *n* carga *f;* flete *m.*
freighter *n* fletador *m.*
frenzy *n* frenesí *m;* locura *f.*
frequency *n* frecuencia *f.*
fresco *n* fresco *m.*
fresh *adj* fresco/ca; nuevo/va.
freshly *adv* nuevamente.
freshman *n* novicio *m.*
freshwater *adj* de agua dulce.
fret *vi* agitarse.
friar *n* fraile *m.*
friction *n* fricción *f.*
Friday *n* viernes *m:—***Good ~** Viernes Santo *m.*
friend *n* amigo *m;* amiga *f.*
friendship *n* amistad *f.*
frieze *n* friso *m.*
frigate *n* (*mar*) fragata *f.*
fright *n* espanto, terror *m.*
frighten *vt* espantar.
frigid *adj* frío/ría, frígido/da.
fringe *n* franja *f.*
frisk *vt* cachear.

frivolity *n* frivolidad *f.*
frock *n* vestido *m.*
frog *n* rana *f.*
frolic *vi* juguetear.
from *prep* de; después; desde.
front *n* parte delantera *f;* fachada *f;* paseo marítimo *m;* frente *m.*
frontal *adj* de frente.
frontier *n* frontera *f.*
frost *n* helada *f;* hielo *m.*
froth *n* espuma (de algún líquido) *f.*
frown *vt* mirar con ceño.
frozen *adj* helado/da.
fruit *n* fruta *f;* fruto *m.*
fruiterer *n* frutero *m.*
fruiterer's (shop) *n* frutería *f.*
fruit juice *n* jugo de fruta *m.*
fruitless *adj* estéril; inútil.
fruit salad *n* ensalada de frutas *f.*
fruit tree *n* frutal *m.*
frustrate *vt* frustrar; anular.
fry *vt* freír.
frying pan *n* sartén *f.*
fuchsia *n* (*bot*) fucsia *f.*
fuel *n* combustible *m.*
fuel tank *n* deposito *m.*
fugitive *adj, n* fugitivo *m.*
fulcrum *n* fulcro *m.*
fulfill *vt* cumplir; realizar.
fulfillment *n* cumplimiento *m.*
full *adj* lleno/na.
full moon *n* plenilunio *m;* luna llena *f.*
fulsome *adj* exagerado/da.
fumble *vi* manejar torpemente.
fume *vi* humear; encolerizarse.
fun *n* diversión *f;* alegría *f.*
function *n* función *f.*
functional *adj* funcional.
fund *n* fondo *m.*
fundamental *adj* fundamental.
funeral *n* funerales *mpl.*

fungus n hongo m; seta f.
funnel n embudo m.
funny adj divertido/da; curioso/sa.
fur n piel f.
furious adj furioso/sa.
furnace n horno m; hornaza f.
furnish vt amueblar.
furnishings npl muebles mpl.
furniture n muebles mpl.
furrow n surco m.
furry adj peludo/da.

furthermore adv además.
fury n furor m; furia f; ira f.
fuse vt, vi fundir; derretirse.
fuse box n caja de fusibles f.
fusion n fusión f.
fuss n lío m; alboroto m.
fussy adj jactancioso/sa.
futile adj fútil, frívolo/la.
futility n futilidad f.
future adj futuro/ra.
fuzzy adj borroso/sa; muy rizado/da.

G

gable n aguilón m.
gag n mordaza f; chiste m.
gage n calibre m.
gaiety n alegría f.
gain n ganancia f.
gala n fiesta f.
galaxy n galaxia f.
gale n vendaval m.
gallant adj galante.
gallery n galería f.
gallon n galón m (medida).
gallop n galope m.
gallows n horca f.
galore adv en abundancia.
gambit n estrategia f.
gamble vi jugar; especularf.
gambler n jugador m.
game n juego m; pasatiempo m.
gamekeeper n guardabosques m.
gaming n juego m.
gammon n jamón m.
gander n ganso m.
gang n pandilla, banda f.
gangrene n gangrena f.
gangster n gangster m.
gangway n pasarela f.
gap n hueco m; claro m; intervalo m.

garage n garaje m.
garbage n basura f.
garbage can n cubo de la basura m.
garden n jardín m.
gargoyle n gárgola f.
garish adj ostentoso/sa.
garland n guirnalda f.
garlic n ajo m.
garment n prenda f.
garnish vt guarnecer m.
garter n liga f.
gas n gas m.
gasoline, gas n gasolina f.
gash n cuchillada f.
gasp vi jadear.
gastric adj gástrico/ca.
gastronomic adj gastronómico/ca.
gate n puerta f.
gateway n puerta f.
gather vt recoger.
gathering n reunión f.
gaudy adj chillón/ona.
gauze n gasa f.
gay adj alegre; vivo/va; gay.
gazelle n gacela f.
gazette n gaceta f.
gazetteer n gacetero m.

gear n atavío m; vestido m.
gearbox n caja de cambios f.
gel n gel m.
gelatin(e) n jaletina, jalea f.
gelignite n gelignita f.
gem n joya f.
Gemini n Géminis m (signo del zodiaco).
gender n género m.
gene n gen m.
genealogy n genealogía f.
general adj general, común.
generalize vt generalizar.
generation n generación f.
generic adj genérico/ca.
generosity n generosidad.
generous adj generoso/sa.
genetics npl genética f.
genial adj genial.
genitals npl genitales mpl.
genius n genio m.
genteel adj refinado, elegante.
gentile n gentil.
gentle adj suave.
gentleman n caballero m.
gentry n alta burguesía f.
gents n aseos mpl.
genuine adj genuino/na.
genus n genero m.
geographer n geógrafo/fa m/f.
geography n geografía f.
geology n geología f.
geometry n geometría f.
geranium n (bot) geranio m.
germ n (bot) germen m.
germinate vi brotar.
gesticulate vi gesticular.
gesture n gestom.
get vt ganar; conseguir, obtener.
geyser n géiser m m.
ghastly adj espantoso/sa.
gherkin n pepinillo m.

ghost n fantasma m.
ghostly adj fantasmal.
giant n gigante m.
giddy adj vertiginoso/sa.
gift n regalom.
giggle vi reírse tontamente.
gin n ginebra f.
ginger n jengibre m.
ginger-haired adj pelirrojo/ja.
giraffe n jirafa f.
girl n muchacha, chica f.
girlfriend n amiga f; novia f.
giro n giro postal m.
girth n cincha f; circunferencia f.
give vt, vi dar.
glacier n glaciar m.
glad adj alegre, contento/ta.
gladiator n gladiator m.
glamor n encantom.
gland n glándula f.
glare n deslumbramiento m.
glass n vidrio.
glean vt espigar; recoger.
glee n alegría f; gozo m.
glib adj con poca sinceridad, elocuente pero falso.
glide vi resbalar.
glimmer n vislumbre f.
glimpse n vislumbre f.
glint vi centellear.
glisten, glitter vi relucir, brillar.
gloat vi ojear con admiración.
global adj mundial.
globe n globo m; esfera f.
gloom, gloominess n oscuridad f; melancolía.
glorify vt glorificar, celebrar.
glory n gloria, fama, celebridad f.
gloss n glosa f; lustre m.
glossary n glosario m.
glove n guante m.
glow vi arder; inflamarse; relucir.

glower *vi* mirar con ceño.
glue *n* cola *f.*
glum *adj* abatido/da, triste.
glut *n* hartura, abundancia *f.*
gluttony *n* glotonería *f.*
glycerine *n* glicerina *f.*
gnarled *adj* nudoso/sa.
gnash *vt, vi* rechinar; crujir los dientes.
gnat *n* mosquito *m.*
gnaw *vt* roer.
gnome *n* gnomo *m.*
go *vi* ir, irse.
goal *n* meta *f;* fin *m.*
goaltender *n* portero *m.*
gobble *vt* engullir, tragar.
go-between *n* mediador/a *m/f.*
goblet *n* copa *f.*
goblin *n* espíritu ambulante, duende *m.*
God *n* Dios *m.*
godchild *n* ahijado, hijo de pila *m.*
goddaughter *n* ahijada, hija de pila *f.*
goddess *n* diosa *f.*
godfather *n* padrino *m.*
godmother *n* madrina *f.*
godsend *n* don del cielo *m.*
godson *n* ahijado *m.*
goggle-eyed *adj* bizco/ca.
goggles *npl* anteojos *mpl.*
gold *n* oro *m.*
goldfish *n* pez de colores *m.*
gold-plated *adj* chapado/da en oro.
golf *n* golf *m.*
golf course *n* campo de golf *m.*
golfer *n* golfista *m/f.*
gondolier *n* gondolero/ra *m/f.*
gone *adj* ido/da; perdido/da; pasado/da; gastado/da; muerto/ta.
gong *n* atabal chino *m.*
good *adj* bueno/na.
goodbye ! *excl* ¿adiós!

Good Friday *n* Viernes Santo *m.*
good-looking *adj* guapo/pa.
goodness *n* bondad *f.*
goodwill *n* benevolencia, bondad *f.*
goose *n* ganso *m; oca f.*
gooseberry *n* grosella espinosa *f.*
gorge *n* barranco *m.*
gorgeous *adj* maravilloso/sa.
gorilla *n* gorila *m.*
gorse *n* aulaga *f.*
gory *adj* sangriento/ta.
goshawk *n* azor *m.*
gospel *n* evangelio *m.*
gossamer *n* vello *m.*
gossip *n* charla *f.*
gothic *adj* gótico/ca.
gout *n* gota *f* (enfermedad).
govern *vt* gobernar, dirigir.
governess *n* gobernadora *f.*
government *n* gobierno *m.*
governor *n* gobernador *m.*
gown *n* toga *f.*
grab *vt* agarrar.
grace *n* gracia.
graceful *adj* gracioso/sa.
gracious *adj* gracioso/sa.
gradation *n* gradación *f.*
grade *n* grado *m.*
grade crossing *n* paso a nivel *m.*
gradient *n* (*rail*) pendiente.
gradual *adj* gradual.
graduate *vi* graduarse.
graduation *n* graduación *f.*
graffiti *n* pintadas *fpl.*
graft *n* injerto *m.*
grain *n* grano *m.*
gram *n* gramo *m* (peso).
grammar *n* gramática *f.*
granary *n* granero *m.*
grand *adj* grande, ilustre.
grandchild *n* nieto *m; nieta f.*
grandad *n* abuelo *m.*

granddaughter *n* nieta *f.*
grandeur *n* grandeza *f.*
grandfather *n* abuelo *m.*
grandiose *adj* grandioso/sa.
grandma *n* abuelita *f.*
grandmother *n* abuela *f.*
grandparents *npl* abuelos *mpl.*
grand piano *n* piano de cola *m.*
grandson *n* nieto *m.*
grandstand *n* tribuna *f.*
granite *n* granito *m.*
granny *n* abuelita *f.*
grant *vt* conceder.
granule *n* gránulo *m.*
grape *n* uva *f:*—**bunch of ~s** racimo de uvas *m.*
grapefruit *n* toronja *f.*
graph *n* gráfica *f.*
graphics *n* artes gráficas *fpl;* gráficos *mpl.*
grasp *vt* empuñar.
grass *n* hierba *f.*
grasshopper *n* saltamontes *m.*
grassland *n* pampa , pradera *f.*
grass snake *n* culebra *f.*
gratify *vt* contentar; gratificar.
gratifying *adj* grato/ta.
grating *n* rejado *m.*
gratis *adv* gratis.
gratitude *n* gratitud *f.*
grave *n* sepultura *f.*
gravel *n* cascajo *m.*
gravestone *n* piedra sepulcra *f.*
graveyard *n* cementerio *m.*
gravity *n* gravedad *f.*
gravy *n* jugo de la carne *f;* salsa *f.*
gray *adj* gris.
graze *vt* pastorear.
grease *n* grasa *f:*—*vt* untar.
greasy *adj* grasiento/ta.
great *adj* gran, grande.
greatcoat *n* sobretodo *m.*

greatness *n* grandeza *f.*
greedily *adv* vorazmente.
greediness, greed *n* gula *f;* codicia *f.*
Greek *n* griego (idioma) *m.*
green *adj* verde.
greengrocer *n* verdulero *m.*
greenhouse *n* invernadero *m.*
greet *vt* saludar, congratular.
greeting *n* saludo *m.*
greeting(s) card *n* tarjeta de felicitaciones *f.*
grenade *n* (*mil*) granada *f.*
grenadier *n* granadero *m.*
greyhound *n* galgo *m.*
greyish *adj* pardusco/ca.
grid *n* reja *f;* red *f.*
grief *n* dolor *m.*
grieve *vt* agraviar.
grievous *adj* doloroso/sa.
griffin *n* grifo *m.*
grill *n* parrilla *f.*
grim *adj* feo, fea.
grimace *n* visaje *m.*
grime *n* porquería *f.*
grin *n* mueca *f.*
grind *vt* moler.
grinder *n* molinero *m.*
grip *n* asimiento *m.*
grisly *adj* horroroso/sa.
gristle *n* tendón, nervio *m.*
grit *n* gravilla *f;* valor *m.*
groan *vi* gemir, suspirar.
grocer *n* tendero/ra, abarrotero/ra *m/f.*
groceries *npl* comestibles *mpl.*
groin *n* ingle *f.*
groom *n* establero *m.*
groove *n* ranura *f.*
gross *adj* grueso/sa.
grotesque *adj* grotesco/ca.
grotto *n* gruta *f.*
ground *n* tierra *f.*

ground floor n planta baja f.
group n grupo m..
grouse n urogallo m:—vi quejarse.
grove n arboleda f.
grovel vi arrastrarse.
grow vt cultivar:—vi crecer, aumentarse.
growl vi regañar, gruñir.
grown-up n adulto m.
grub n gusano m.
grubby adj sucio/cia.
grudge n rencor, odio m; envidia f:—vt, vienvidiar.
gruesome adj horrible.
gruff adj brusco/ca.
grumble vi gruñir; murmurar.
grunt vi gruñir.
G-string n taparrabo m.
guarantee n garantía f.
guard n guardia f.
guardianship n tutela f.
guerrilla n guerrillero m.
guess vt, vi conjeturar; adivinar; suponer.
guest n huésped/a.
guffaw n carcajada f.
guide vt guiar, dirigir:—n guía m.
guidebook n guía f.
guild n gremio m.
guile n astucia f.

guilt n culpabilidad f.
guilty adj reo, rea, culpable.
guinea pig n cobayo m.
guise n manera f.
guitar n guitarra f.
gulf n golfo m.
gull n gaviota f.
gullet n esófago m.
gullible adj crédulo/la.
gully n barranco m.
gulp n trago m.
gum n goma f.
gum tree n árbol gomero m.
gun n pistola f; escopeta f.
gunboat n cañonera f.
gunpowder n pólvora f.
gunshot n escopetazo m.
gurgle vi gorgotear.
guru n gurú m.
gush vi brotar.
gusset n escudete m.
gut n intestino m.
gutter n canalón m; arroyo m.
guy n tío m; tipo m.
gym(nasium) n gimnasio m.
gymnast n gimnasta m/f.
gynecologist n ginecólogo/ga m/f.
Gypsy n gitano/na m/f.
gyrate vi girar.

H

haberdasher n camisero/ra, mercero/ra m/f.
habit n costumbre f.
habitable adj habitable.
habitat n hábitat m.
habitual adj habitual.
haddock n merlango m.
hag n bruja f.

hail n granizo m.
hair n pelo; cabello m.
hairbrush n cepillo m.
haircut n corte de pelo m.
hairdresser n peluquero m.
hairdryer n secador de pelo m.
hairspray n laca f.
hairstyle n peinado m.

half *n* mitad *f.*
half-caste *adj* mestizo/za.
hall *n* vestíbulo *m.*
hallow *vt* consagrar, santificar.
hallucination *n* alucinación *f.*
halo *n* halo *m.*
halt *vi* parar.
halve *vt* partir por mitad.
ham *n* jamón *m.*
hamburger *n* hamburguesa *f.*
hamlet *n* aldea *f.*
hammer *n* martillo *m.*
hammock *n* hamaca *f.*
hamper *n* cesto *f.*
hamstring *vt* desjarretar.
hand *n* mano *f.*
handbag *n* cartera *f.*
handful *n* puñado *m.*
handicap *n* desventaja *f.*
handicraft *n* artesanía *f.*
handkerchief *n* pañuelo *m.*
handle *n* mango, puño *m;* asa; manija *f.*
handshake *n* apretón de manos *m.*
handsome *adj* guapo/pa.
handwriting *n* letra *f.*
handy *adj* practico/ca.
hang *vt* colgar.
hanger *n* percha *f.*
hangover *n* resaca *f.*
happen *vi* pasar; acontecer.
happiness *n* felicidad *f.*
happy *adj* feliz.
harass *vt* cansar, fatigar.
harbinger *n* precursor *m.*
harbor *n* puerto *m.*
hard *adj* duro/ra, firme.
harden *vt, vi* endurecer(se).
hardiness *n* robustez *f.*
hardly *adv* apenas.
hardship *n* penas *fpl.*
hard-up *adj* sin plata.

hardware store *n* ferretería *f.*
hardy *adj* fuerte.
hare *n* liebre *f.*
hare-lipped *adj* labihendido/da.
haricot *n* alubia *f.*
harlequin *n* arlequín *m.*
harm *n* mal, daño *m.*
harmful *adj* perjudicial.
harmless *adj* inocuo/cua.
harmonic *adj* armónico/ca.
harmonious *adj* armonioso/sa.
harmonize *vt* armonizar.
harmony *n* armonía *f.*
harp *n* arpa *f.*
harpoon *n* arpón *m.*
harsh *adj* duro/ra; austero/ra.
harvest *n* cosecha *f.*
harvester *n* cosechadora *f.*
hash *n* hachís *m.*
hassock *n* cojín de paja *m.*
haste *n* apuro *m.*
hasten *vt* acelerar.
hasty *adj* apresurado/da.
hat *n* sombrero *m.*
hatch *vt* incubar; tramar*f.*
hatchet *n* hacha *f.*
hatchway *n* (*mar*) escotilla *f.*
hate *n* odio.
hateful *adj* odioso/sa.
hatred *n* odio, aborrecimiento *m.*
haughty *adj* altanero/ra, orgulloso/sa.
haul *vt* tirar:—*n* botín *m.*
hauler *n* transportista *m/f.*
haunch *n* anca *f.*
haunt *vt* frecuentar, rondar.
have *vt* haber; tener, poseer.
haven *n* asilo *m.*
havoc *n* estrago *m.*
hawk *n* halcón *m.*
hawthorn *n* espino blanco *m.*
hay *n* heno *m.*
hazard *n* riesgo *m.*

haze n niebla f.

hazel n avellano m.

hazelnut n avellana f.

hazy adj oscuro/ra.

he pn el. **head** n cabeza f.

head n cakeza f.

headache n dolor de cabeza m.

headlamp n faro m.

headline n titular m.

headmaster n director m.

headphones npl auriculares mpl.

heal vt, vi curar.

health n salud f

healthy adj sano/na.

heap n montón m.

hear vt oír; escuchar.

hearing n oído m.

hearing aid n audífono m.

hearse n coche fúnebre m.

heart n corazón m.

heart attack n infarto m.

heartburn n acedia f.

hearth n hogar m.

heartily adv sinceramente.

heartless adj cruel.

hearty adj cordial.

heat n calor m.

heater n calentador m.

heathen n pagano m.

heating n calefacción f.

heatwave n ola de calor f.

heaven n cielo m.

heavily adv pesadamente.

heavy adj pesado/da.

Hebrew n hebreo m.

heckle vt interrumpir.

hectic adj agitado/da.

hedge n seto m.

hedgehog n erizo m.

heed vt hacer caso de.

heedless adj descuidado/da.

heel n talón m.

hefty adj grande.

heifer n ternera f.

height n altura f; altitud f.

heinous adj atroz.

heir n heredero/ra m/f.

heirloom n reliquia de familia f.

helicopter n helicóptero m.

hell n infierno m.

helm n (mar) timón m.

helmet n casco m.

help vt, vi ayudar, socorrer.

helper n ayudante m.

helpful adj útil.

helping n ración f.

helpless adj indefenso/sa.

hem n ribete m.

he-man n macho m.

hemisphere n hemisferio m.

hemorrhage n hemorragia f.

hemorrhoids npl hemorroides mpl.

hemp n cáñamo m.

hen n gallina f.

henchman n secuaz m.

henceforth, henceforward adv de aquí en adelante. **hepatitis** n hepatitis f.

her pn su; ella; de ella; a ella.

herald n heraldo m.

heraldry n heráldica f.

herb n hierba fl.

herbaceous adj herbáceo/cea.

herbalist n herbolario m.

herbivorous adj herbívoro/ra.

herd n rebaño m.

here adv aquí, acá.

hereabout(s) adv aquí alrededor.

hereafter adv en el futuro.

hereby adv por esto.

hereditary adj hereditario/ria.

heresy n herejía f.

heretic n hereje m/f.

heritage n patrimonio m.

hermetic *adj* hermético/ca.
hermit *n* ermitaño/ña *m/f.*
hermitage *n* ermita *f.*
hernia *n* hernia *f.*
hero *n* héroe *m.*
heroic *adj* heroico/ca.
heroine *n* heroína *f.*
heroism *n* heroísmo *m.*
heron *n* garza *f.*
herring *n* arenque *m.*
herself *pn* ella misma.
hesitant *adj* vacilante.
hesitate *vt* dudar; tardar.
heterosexual *adj, n* heterosexual *m.*
hew *vt* tajar; cortar.
heyday *n* apogeo *m.*
hi *excl* ¿hola!
hiatus *n* (gr) hiato *m.*
hibernate *vi* invernar.
hiccup *n* hipo *m.*
hickory *n* noguera americana *f.*
hide *vt* esconder*f.*
hideaway *n* escondite *m.*
hideous *adj* horrible.
hierarchy *n* jerarquía *f.*
hieroglyphic *adj* jeroglífico/ca.
hi-fi *n* estéreo, hi-fi *m.*
high *adj* alto/ta; elevado/da.
highlight *n* punto culminante *m.*
highway *n* carretera *f.*
hike *vi* ir de excursión.
hijack *vt* secuestrar.
hilarious *adj* alegre.
hill, hillock *n* colina *f.*
him *pn* le, lo, el.
himself *pn* el mismo, se, si mismo.
hinder *vt* impedir.
hindrance *n.* impedimento, obstáculo *m.*
hinge *n* bisagra *f.*
hip *n* cadera *f.*
hippopotamus *n* hipopótamo *m.*

hire *vt* alquilar.
his *pn* su, suyo, de el.
Hispanic *adj* hispano/na; hispánico/ca.
hiss *vt, vi* silbar.
historian *n* historiador *m.*
history *n* historia *f.*
hit *vt* golpear.
hitch *vt* atar.
hitch-hike *vi* hacer autostop.
hive *n* colmena *f.*
hoax *n* trampa *f.*
hobble *vi* cojear.
hobby *n* pasatiempo *m.*
hockey *n* hockey *m.*
hodge-podge *n* mezcolanza *f.*
hoe *n* azadón *m.*
hog *n* cerdo, puerco *m.*
hoist *vt* alzar.
hold *vt* tener; detener; contener.
hole *n* agujero *m.*
holiday *n* día de fiesta *m*:—~s *pl* vacaciones *fpl.*
hollow *adj* hueco/ca.
holly *n* (bot) acebo *m.*
hollyhock *n* malva hortense *f.*
holocaust *n* holocausto *m.*
holster *n* pistolera *f.*
holy *adj* santo/ta.
holy week *n* semana santa *f.*
homage *n* homenaje *m.*
home *n* casa *f.*
home address *n* domicilio *m.*
homely *adj* casero/ra.
homeopathist *n* homeopatista *m/f.*
homeopathy *n* homeopatía *f.*
homesick *adj* nostálgico/ca.
homework *n* deberes *mpl.*
homicide *n* homicidio *m*; homicida *m.*
homosexual *adj, n* homosexual *m.*
honest *adj* honrado/da.
honesty *n* honradez *f.*

honey n miel f.
honeycomb n panal m.
honeymoon n luna de miel f.
honeysuckle n (bot) madreselva f.
honor n honra f; honor m:—vt honrar.
honorary adj honorario/ria.
hood n capo m; capucha f.
hoof n pezuña f.
hook n gancho m.
hooligan n gamberro m.
hoop n aro m.
hooter n sirena f.
hop n (bot) lúpulo.
hope n esperanza f.
horde n horda f.
horizon n horizonte m.
horizontal adj horizontal.
hormone n hormona f.
horn n cuerno m.
hornet n avispón m.
horny adj calloso/sa.
horoscope n horóscopo m.
horrendous adj horrendo/da.
horrible adj horrible.
horrid adj horrible.
horrific adj horroroso/sa.
horrify vt horrorizar.
horror n horror, terror m.
hors d'oeuvre n entremeses mpl.
horse n caballo m
horse chestnut n castaño de Indias m.
horsefly n moscarda f.
horseradish n rábano silvestre m.
horticulture n horticultura, jardinería f.
horticulturist n jardinero/ra m/f.
hosepipe n manga f.
hosiery n calcetería f.
hospital n hospital m.
hospitality n hospitalidad f.
host n anfitrión m; hostia f.

hostage n rehén m.
hostess n anfitriona f.
hostile adj hostil.
hot adj caliente; cálido/da.
hotbed n semillero m.
hotel n hotel m.
hotelier n hotelero/ra m/f.
hour n hora f.
hour-glass n reloj de arena m.
house n casa f.
household n familia f.
houseless adv sin casa.
housewife n ama de casa f.
hovel n choza, cabaña f.
hover vi flotar.
how adv cómo.
howl vi aullar.
hub n centro m.
hue n color m.
hug vt abrazar:—n abrazo m.
huge adj vasto/ta, enorme.
hum vi canturrear.
human adv humano/na.
humane adv humano/na.
humanist n humanista m/f.
humanitarian adj humanitario/ria.
humanity n humanidad f.
humble adj humilde.
humid adj húmedo/da.
humidity n humedad f.
humiliate vt humillar.
humming-bird n colibrí m.
humor n sentido del humor m.
humorist n humorista m./f
humorous adj gracioso/sa.
hundred adj ciento.
hundredth adj centésimo.
hundredweight n quintal m.
hunger n hambre f.
hunt vt cazar; perseguir.
hunter n cazador/a m/f.
hurdle n valla f.

hurricane n huracán m.
hurt vt hacer daño; ofender.
hurtful adj dañoso/sa:—**~ly** adv dañosamente.
husband n marido m.
hush! excl ¡chitón!, ¡silencio!.
husk n cáscara f.
hut n cabaña f.
hutch n conejera f.
hyacinth n jacinto m.
hydraulic adj hidráulico/ca.

hydrofoil n aerodeslizador m.
hydrogen n hidroala f.
hyena n hiena f.
hygiene n higiene f.
hymn n himno m.
hypermarket n hipermercado m.
hyphen n (gr) guión m.
hypocrisy n hipocresía f.
hypocrite n hipócrita m/f.
hysterical adj histérico/ca.
hysterics npl histeria f.

I

I pn yo.
ice n hielo m:—vt helar.
ice cream n helado m.
ice rink n pista de hielo f.
icicle n carámbano m.
idea n idea f.
ideal adj ideal.
identical adj idéntico/ca.
identification n identificación f.
identify vt identificar.
identity n identidad f.
ideology n ideología f.
idiom n idioma m.
idiosyncrasy n idiosincrasia f.
idiot n idiota, necio m.
idiotic adj tonto/ta, bobo/ba.
idle adj desocupado/da.
idol n ídolo m.
idolatry n idolatría f.
idyllic adj idílico/ca.
i.e. adv esto es.
if conj si, aunque.
ignite vt encender.
ignoble adj innoble.
ignorance n ignorancia f.
ignorant adj ignorante.
ignore vt no hacer caso de.

ill adj malo/la, enfermo/ma.
ill-advised adj imprudente.
illegal adj ~**ly** adv ilegal(mente).
illegible adj ilegible.
illegitimate adj ilegítimo/ma.
ill feeling n rencor m.
illiterate adj analfabeto/ta.
illness n enfermedad f.
illogical adj ilógico/ca.
illuminate vt iluminar.
illusion n ilusión f.
illustrate vt ilustrar.
illustration n ilustración f.
image n imagen f.
imagination n imaginación f.
imagine vt imaginarse.
imbalance n desequilibrio m.
imbecile adj imbécil.
imitate vt imitar, copiar.
imitation n imitación, copia f.
immaculate adj inmaculado/da.
immature adj inmaduro/ra.
immediate adj inmediato/ta.
immense adj inmenso/sa.
immigrant n inmigrante m.
immigration n inmigración f.
imminent adj inminente.

immodest adj inmodesto/ta.
immoral adj inmoral.
immortal adj inmortal.
immune adj inmune.
imp n diablillo, duende m.
impact n impacto m.
impair vt disminuir.
impartial adj ~ly adv imparcial (mente).
impatience n impaciencia f.
impede vt estorbar.
impel vt impeler.
impending adj inminente.
imperative adj imperativo/va.
imperfect adj imperfecto/ta
imperial adj imperial.
impersonal adj, ~ly adv impersonal-(mente).
impetus n ímpetu m.
impiety n irmpiedad f.
implant vt implantar.
implement n herramienta.
implore vt suplicar.
imply vt suponer.
impolite adj maleducado/da.
import vt importar.
importance n importancia f.
important adj importante.
impose vt imponer.
impostor n impostor m.
impotence n impotencia f.
impotent adj impotente.
impound vt embargar.
impoverish vt empobrecer.
impractical adj poco práctico/ca.
imprecise adj impreciso/sa.
impress vt impresionar.
impression n impresión f; edición f.
impressive adj impresionante.
imprint n sello m:—vt imprimir; estampar.
improbable adj improbable.

improper adj impropio/pia.
improve vt, vi mejorar.
improvise vt improvisar.
impulse n impulso m.
impure adj impuro/ra.
impurity n impureza f.
in prep en.
inability n incapacidad f.
inaccessible adj inaccesible.
inaccurate adj inexacto/ta.
inadequate adj inadecuado/da, defec-tuoso/sa.
inadmissible adj inadmisible.
inadvertently adv sin querer.
inappropriate adj impropio/pia.
inaudible adj inaudible.
inaugurate vt inaugurar.
in-between adj intermedio/dia.
inborn, inbred adj innato/ta.
incapable adj incapaz.
incarcerate vt encarcelar.
incarnation n encarnación f.
incendiary n bomba incendiaria f.
incense n incienso m.
incentive n incentivo m.
incessant adj incesante.
incest n incesto m.
inch n pulgada f.
incident n incidente m.
incinerator n incinerador m.
inclination n inclinación.
incline vt, vi inclinar(se).
include vt incluir.
inclusive adj inclusivo/va.
incognito adv de incógnito.
incoherent adj incoherente.
income n renta f
incompatible adj incompatible.
incompetence n incompetencia f.
incomplete adj incompleto/ta.
incomprehensible adj incomprensi-ble.

inconceivable *adj* inconcebible.
incontinence *n* incontinencia *f.*
inconvenience *n* incomodidad *f.*
incorrect *adj* incorrecto/ta.
increase *vt* acrecentar, aumentar
incredible *adj* increíble.
incubate *vi* incubar.
incubator *n* incubadora *f.*
incurable *adj* incurable.
indecency *n* indecencia *f.*
indecent *adj* indecente:—**~ly** *adv* indecentemente.
indecisive *adj* indeciso/sa.
indeed *adv* verdaderamente, de veras.
independence *n* independencia *f.*
independent *adj* independiente.
indescribable *adj* indescriptible.
index *n* índice *m.*
indicate *vt* indicar.
indifference *n* indiferencia *f.*
indigenous *adj* indígena.
indigestion *n* indigestión *f.*
indignation *n* indignación *f.*
indigo *n* añil *m.*
indirect *adj* indirecto/ta.
indiscreet *adj* indiscreto/ta.
indispensable *adj* indispensable.
indistinguishable *adj* indistinguible.
individual *adj* individual *m.*
indoors *adv* dentro.
indulge *vt, vi* conceder; ser indulgente.
industrialist *n* industrial *m.*
industry *n* industria *f.*
inedible *adj* no comestible.
ineffective, ineffectual *adj* ineficaz.
inefficiency *n* ineficacia *f.*
ineligible *adj* ineligible.
inept *adj* incompetente.
inequality *n* desigualdad *f.*
inevitable *adj* inevitable.

inexpensive *adj* económico/ca.
inexperience *n* inexperiencia *f.*
inexpert *adj* inexperto/ta.
inexplicable *adj* inexplicable.
infallible *adj* infalible.
infamy *n* infamia *f.*
infancy *n* infancia *f.*
infant *n* niño/ña *m/f.*
infantile *adj* infantil.
infantry *n* infantería *f.*
infatuation *n* infatuación *f.*
infect *vt* infectar.
infection *n* infección *f.*
inferior *adj* inferior.
infernal *adj* infernal.
inferno *n* infierno *m.*
infest *vt* infestar.
infidelity *n* infidelidad *f.*
infinite *adj* infinito/ta.
infinitive *n* infinitivo *m.*
infinity *n* infinito *m; infinidad *f.*
infirm *adj* enfermo/ma.
infirmary *n* enfermería *f.*
infirmity *n* fragilidad, enfermedad *f.*
inflammation *n* inflamación *f.*
inflatable *adj* inflable.
inflate *vt* inflar, hinchar.
inflation *n* inflación *f.*
inflict *vt* imponer.
influence *n* influencia *f.*
influenza *n* gripe *f.*
inform *vt* informar.
informal *adj* informal.
information *n* información *f.*
infrastructure *n* infraestructura *f.*
infuriate *vt* enfurecer.
infusion *n* infusión *f.*
ingenious *adj* ingenioso/sa.
ingenuity *n* ingeniosidad *f.*
ingot *n* barra de metal *f.*
ingrained *adj* inveterado/da.
ingratitude *n* ingratitud *f.*

ingredient n ingrediente m.
inhabit vt, vi habitar.
inhabitant n habitante m.
inhale vt inhalar.
inherent adj inherente.
inherit vt heredar.
inheritance n herencia f.
inhibit vt inhibir.
inhospitable adj inhospitalario/ria.
inhuman adj inhumano/na.
inhumanity n inhumanidad, crueldad f.
initial adj inicial.
initiate vt iniciar.
initiative n iniciativa f.
inject vt inyectar.
injection n inyección f.
injure vt herir.
injury n daño m.
injustice n injusticia f.
ink n tinta f.
inkling n sospecha f.
inlaid adj taraceado/da.
in-laws npl suegros mpl.
inlay vt taracear.
inlet n entsenada f.
inmate n preso m.
inn n posada f; mesón m.
innkeeper n posadero/ra, mesonero/ra m/f.
innocence n inocencia f.
innocent adj inocente.
innovate vt innovar.
innovation n innovación f.
innuendo n indirecta, insinuación f.
inoffensive adj inofensivo/va.
inorganic adj inorgánico/ca.
inpatient n paciente interno m.
input n entrada f.
inquest n encuesta judicial f.
inquire vt, vi preguntar.
inquiry n pesquisa f.

inquisition n inquisición f.
inquisitive adj curioso/sa.
insane adj loco/ca, demente.
insanity n locura f.
inscription n inscripción f.
inscrutable adj inescrutable.
insect n insecto m.
insecticide n insecticida m.
insecure adj inseguro/ra.
insensitive adj insensible.
inseparable adj inseparable.
insert vt introducir.
insertion n inserción f.
inside n interior m:—adv dentro.
inside out adv al revés; a fondo.
insignia npl insignias fpl.
insignificant adj insignificante.
insincere adj poco sincero/ra.
insipid adj insípido/da.
insist vi insistir.
insole n plantilla f.
insolence n insolencia f.
insoluble adj insoluble.
insomnia n insomnio m.
insomuch conj puesto que.
inspect vt examinar, inspeccionar.
inspection n inspección f.
inspire vt inspirar.
instability n inestabilidad f.
instance n ejemplo m.
instant adj inmediato/ta.
instead (of) pr por, en lugar de, en vez de.
instill vt inculcar.
instinct n instinto m.
instinctive adj instintivo/va.
institute vt establecer:—n instituto m.
institution n institución f.
instruct vt instruir, enseñar.
instruction n instrucción f.
instrument n instrumento m.
instrumental adj instrumental.

insufferable adj insoportable.
insufficient adj insuficiente.
insulate vt aislar.
insulin n insulina f.
insult vt insultar:—n insulto m.
insurance n (com) seguro m.
insure vt asegurar.
intact adj intacto/ta.
integral adj íntegro/gra.
integrate vt integrar.
integrity n integridad f.
intellect n intelecto m.
intelligence n inteligencia f.
intend vi tener intención.
intense adj intenso/sa.
intensity n intensidad f.
intention n intención f.
inter vt enterrar.
interaction n interacción f.
intercourse n relaciones sexuales fpl.
interest vt interesar.
interesting adj interesante.
interest rate n tipo de interés m.
interfere vi entrometerse.
interference n interferencia f.
interior adj interior.
interlude n intermedio m.
intermediate adj intermedio/dia.
interment n entierro m; sepultura f.
intermission n descanso m.
intermittent adj intermitente.
internal adj interno/na.
international adj internacional.
interpret vt interpretar.
interpretation n interpretación f.
interpreter n intérprete m/f.
interregnum n interregno m.
interrelated adj interrelacionado/da.
interrogate vt interrogar.
interrogation n interrogatorio m.
interrogative adj interrogativo/va.
interrupt vt interrumpir.

interruption n interrupción f.
intersect vi cruzarse.
intersection n cruce m.
intersperse vt esparcir.
intertwine vt entretejer.
interval n intervalo m.
intervene vi intervenir.
intervention n intervención f.
interview n entrevista f.
interviewer n entrevistador/a m/f.
intestine n intestino m.
intimacy n intimidad f.
intimate n amigo/ga íntimo/ma.
intimidate vt intimidar.
into prep en, dentro, adentro.
intolerable adj intolerable.
intolerance n intolerancia f.
intoxicate vt embriagar.
intravenous adj intravenoso/sa.
intrepid adj intrépido/da.
intricate adj intricado/da.
intrigue n intriga f:—vi intrigar.
intriguing adj fascinante.
intrinsic adj intrínseco/ca.
introduce vt introducir.
introduction n introducción f.
introvert n introvertido m.
intrude vi entrometerse.
intruder n intruso/sa m/f.
intuition n intuición f.
intuitive adj intuitivo/va.
inundate vt inundar.
inundation n inundación f.
invade vt invadir.
invalid adj inválido/da.
invalidate vt invalidar, anular.
invaluable adj inapreciable.
invariable adj invariable.
invariably adv invariablemente.
invasion n invasión f.
invent vt inventar.
invention n invento m.

inventor n inventor m.
inventory n inventario m.
inversion n inversión f.
invert vt invertir.
invest vt invertir.
investigate vt investigar.
investment n inversión f.
invigilate vt vigilar.
invigorating adj vigorizante.
invincible adj invencible.
invisible adj invisible.
invitation n invitación f.
invite vt invitar.
invoice n (com) factura f.
involuntarily adv involuntariamente.
involve vt implicar.
involvement n compromiso m.
iodine n (chem) yodo m.
IOU (I owe you) n vale m.
irate, ireful adj enojado/da.
iris n iris m.
irksome adj fastidioso/sa.
iron n hierro m:—adj férreo/rea:—vt planchar.
ironic adj irónico/ca:—~ly adv con ironía.
ironwork n herraje m:—~s pl herrería f.

irony n ironía f.
irradiate vt irradiar.
irrational adj irracional.
irreconcilable adj irreconciliable.
irregular adj ~ly adv irregular (mente).
irrelevant adj impertinente.
irreparable adj irreparable.
irresistible adj irresistible.
irresponsible adj irresponsable.
irrigate vt regar.
irrigation n riego m.
irritable adj irritable.
irritant n (med) irritante m.
irritate vt irritar.
island n isla f.
isle n isla f.
isolate vt aislar.
issue n asunto m.
it pn el, ella, ello, lo, la, le.
italic n cursiva f.
itch n picazón f:—vi picar.
item n artículo m.
itemize vt detallar.
itinerary n itinerario m.
its pn su, suyo.
itself pn el mismo, la misma, lo mismo.
ivory n marfil m.
ivy n hiedra f.

J

jab vt clavar.
jabber vi farfullar.
jack n gato m; sota f.
jackal n chacal m.
jackboots npl botas militares fpl.
jackdaw n grajo m.
jacket n chaqueta f.
jack-knife vi colear.
jackpot n premio gordo m.
jade n jade m.

jagged adj dentado/da.
jaguar n jaguar m.
jail n cárcel f.
jailer n carcelero/ra m/f.
jam n conserva f; mermelada de frutas f.
jangle vi sonar.
January n enero m.
jargon n jerigonza f.
jasmine n jazmín m.

jaundice n ictericia f.
jaunt n excursión f.
jaunty adj alegre.
javelin n jabalina f.
jaw n mandíbula f.
jay n arrendajo m.
jazz n jazz m.
jealous adj celoso/sa.
jealousy n celos mpl; envidia f.
jeans npl vaqueros mpl.
jeep n jeep m.
jeer vi befar.
jelly n jalea, gelatina f.
jellyfish n aguamar m; medusa f.
jeopardize vt arriesgar.
jersey n jersey m.
jest n broma f.
jester n bufón/ona m/f.
Jesuit n jesuita m.
Jesus n Jesús m.
jet n avión a reacción m
jettison vt desechar.
jetty n muelle m.
Jew n judío/día m/f.
jewel n joya f.
jewelry n joyería f.
Jewish adj judío/día.
jib n (mar) foque m.
jibe n mofa f.
jig n giga f.
jigsaw n rompecabezas m.
jilt vt dejar.
job n trabajo m.
jockey n jinete m/f.
jocular adj jocoso/sa, alegre.
jog vi hacer footing.
jogging n footing m.
join vt juntar, unir.
joiner n carpintero/ra m/f.
joinery n carpintería f.
joint n articulación f.
jointly adv conjuntamente.

joke n broma f:—vi bromear.
joker n comodín m.
jollity n alegría f.
jolly adj alegre.
jolt vt sacudir:—n sacudida f.
jostle vt codear.
journal n revista f.
journalism n periodismo m.
journalist n periodista m/f.
journey n viaje m:—vt viajar.
jovial adj jovial.
joy n alegría f; jubilo m.
jubilant adj jubiloso/sa.
jubilation n jubilo/la, regocijo m.
jubilee n jubileo m.
Judaism n judaísmo m.
judge n juez/a m/f:—vt juzgar.
judgment n juicio m.
judicial adj ~ly adv judicial(mente).
judiciary n judicatura m.
judicious adj prudente.
judo n judo m.
juggle vi hacer juegos malabares.
juggler n malabarista m/f.
juice n jugo m; suco m.
juicy adj jugoso/sa.
jukebox n gramola f.
July n julio m.
jumble vt mezclar
jump vi saltar
jumper n suéter m.
jumpy adj nervioso/sa.
juncture n coyuntura f.
June n junio m.
jungle n selva f.
junior adj más joven.
juniper n (bot) enebro m.
junk n basura f; baratijas fpl.
junta n junta f.
jurisdiction n jurisdicción f.
jurisprudence n jurisprudencia f.
jurist n jurista m/f.

jury *n* jurado *m*.
just *adj* justo/ta.
justice *n* justicia *f*.
justification *n* justificación *f*.
justify *vt* justificar.
justly *adv* justamente.

justness *n* justicia *f*.
jut *vi*:—**to ~ out** sobresalir.
jute *n* yute *m*.
juvenile *adj* juvenil.
juxtaposition *n* yuxtaposición *f*.

K

kaleidoscope *n* calidoscopio *m*.
kangaroo *n* canguro *m*.
karate *n* karate *m*.
kebab *n* pincho *m*.
keel *n* (*mar*) quilla *f*.
keen *adj* agudo/da; vivo/va.
keep *vt* mantener; guardar; conservar.
keeper *n* guardián/ana *m/f*.
keepsake *n* recuerdo *m*.
keg *n* barril *m*.
kennel *n* perrera *f*.
kernel *n* fruta *f*; meollo *m*.
kerosene *n* kerosene *m*.
ketchup *n* catsup *m*.
kettle *n* hervidor *m*.
key *n* llave *f*; (*mus*) clave *f*; tecla *f*.
keyboard *n* teclado *m*.
keyhole *n* ojo de la cerradura *m*.
key ring *n* llavero *m*.
khaki *n* caqui *m*.
kick *vt, vi* patear.
kid *n* chico *m*.
kidnap *vt* secuestrar.
kidnapper *n* secuestrador/a *m/f*.
kidney *n* riñón *m*.
killer *n* asesino/na *m/f*.
killing *n* asesinato *m*.
kiln *n* horno *m*.
kilo *n* kilo *m*.
kilobyte *n* kiloocteto *m*.
kilogram *n* kilo *m*.

kilometer *n* kilómetro *m*.
kilt *n* falda escocesa *f*.
kin *n* parientes *mpl*.
kind *adj* cariñoso/sa:—*n* genero *m*.
kind-hearted *adj* bondadoso/sa.
kindle *vt, vi* encender.
kindly *adj* bondadoso/sa.
kindness *n* bondad *f*.
kindred *adj* emparentado/da.
kinetic *adj* cinético/ca.
king *n* rey *m*.
kingdom *n* reino *m*.
kingfisher *n* martín pescador *m*.
kiosk *n* quiosco *m*.
kiss *n* beso *m*:—*vt* besar.
kit *n* equipo *m*.
kitchen *n* cocina *f*.
kite *n* cometa *f*.
kitten *n* gatillo *m*.
knack *n* don *m*.
knapsack *n* mochila *f*.
knave *n* bribón
knead *vt* amasar.
knee *n* rodilla *f*.
kneel *vi* arrodillarse.
knell *n* toque de difuntos *m*.
knife *n* cuchillo *m*.
knight *n* caballero *m*.
knit *vt, vi* tejer.
knitting needle *n* aguja de tejer *f*.
knitwear *n* prendas de punto *fpl*.
knob *n* bulto *m*.

knock *vt, vi* golpear.
knocker *n* aldaba *f.*
knock-kneed *adj* patizambo/ba.
knock-out *n* K.O. *m.*
knoll *n* cima de una colina *f.*
knot *n* nudo *m;* lazo *m:—vt* anudar.
knotty *adj* escabroso/sa.
know *vt, vi* conocer; saber.

know-all *n* sabelotodo *m/f.*
know-how *n* conocimientos *mpl.*
knowing *adj* entendido/da:—**~ly** *adv*
a sabiendas.
knowledge *n* conocimiento *m.*
knowledgeable *adj* bien informado/
da.
knuckle *n* nudillo *m.*

L

label *n* etiqueta *f.*
laboratory *n* laboratorio *m.*
laborious *adj* laborioso/sa.
labor *n* trabajo *m.*
laborer *n* peón *m.*
labyrinth *n* laberinto *m.*
lace *n* cordón.
lacerate *vt* lacerar.
lack *vt, vi* faltar.
lacquer *n* laca *f.*
lad *n* muchacho *m.*
ladder *n* escalera *f.*
ladle *n* cucharón *m.*
lady *n* señora *f.*
lag *vi* quedarse atrás.
lager *n* cerveza (rubia) *f.*
lagoon *n* laguna *f.*
lake *n* lago *m.*
lamb *n* cordero *m:—vi* parir.
lame *adj* cojo/ja.
lament *vt, vi* lamentar(se).
lamp *n* lámpara *f.*
lampoon *n* sátira *f.*
lampshade *n* pantalla *f.*
lance *n* lanza *f.*
lancet *n* lanceta *f.*
land *n* país *m;* tierra *f.*
landing *n* desembarco *m.*
landmark *n* lugar conocido *m.*
landscape *n* paisaje *m.*

lane *n* callejuela *f.*
language *n* lengua *f;* lenguaje *m.*
lank *adj* lacio/cia.
lanky *adj* larguirucho.
lantern *n* linterna *f;* farol *m.*
lap *n* regazo *m.*
lapel *n* solapa *f.*
lapse *n* lapso *m.*
larceny *n* latrocinio *m.*
larch *n* alerce *m.*
lard *n* manteca de cerdo *f.*
larder *n* despensa *f.*
large *adj* grande.
lark *n* alondra *f.*
larva *n* larva, oruga *f.*
laryngitis *n* laringitis *f.*
larynx *n* laringe *f.*
lascivious *adj* lascivo/va.
laser *n* láser *m.*
lash *n* latigazo *m.*
lasso *n* lazo *m.*
last *adj* último/ma.
lasting *adj* duradero/ra, permanente.
latch *n* picaporte *m.*
late *adj* tarde; difunto/ta.
latent *adj* latente.
lathe *n* torno *m.*
lather *n* espuma *f.*
latitude *n* latitud *f.*
latter *adj* último/ma.

lattice n celosía f.
laugh vi reir.
laughter n risa f.
launch vt, vi lanzar(se):—n (mar) lancha f.
launching n lanzamiento m.
launder vt lavar.
laundry n lavandería f.
laurel n laurel m.
lava n lava f.
lavatory n water m.
lavender n (bot) espliego m, lavándula f.
lavish adj pródigo/ga:—~ly adv pródigamente:—vt disipar.
law n ley f; derecho m.
law court n tribunal m.
lawn n pasto m.
lawnmower n cortacésped m.
law suit n proceso m.
lawyer n abogado/da m/f.
laxative n laxante m.
lay vt poner.
layabout n vago/ga m/f.
layer n capa f.
layout n composición f.
laze vi holgazanear.
laziness n pereza f.
lazy adj perezoso/sa.
lead n plomo m.
leader n jefe/fa m/f.
leaf n hoja f.
leaflet n folleto m.
league n liga, alianza f.
leak n escape m.
lean vt, vi apoyar(se).
leap vi saltar
leap year n año bisiesto m.
learn vt, vi aprender.
lease n arriendo m:—vt arrendar.
leash n correa f.
least adj mínimo/ma.

leather n cuero m.
leave n licencia f; permiso m.
lecherous adj lascivo/va.
lecture n conferencia f.
ledge n reborde m.
ledger n (com) libro mayor m.
leech n sanguijuela f.
leek n (bot) puerro m.
left adj izquierdo/da.
left-handed adj zurdo/da.
leftovers npl sobras fpl.
leg n pierna f
legacy n herencia f.
legal adj legal.
legalize vt legalizar.
legend n leyenda f.
legendary adj legendario/ria.
legible adj legible.
legion n legión f.
legislate vt legislar.
legislation n legislación f.
leisure n ocio m:—~ly adj sin prisa:—at ~ desocupado/da.
lemon n limón m.
lemonade n limonada f.
lend vt prestar.
length n largo m; duración f.
lenient adj indulgente.
lens n lente f.
Lent n Cuaresma f.
lentil n lenteja f.
leopard n leopardo m.
leotard n leotardo m.
leper n leproso/sa m/f.
leprosy n lepra f.
lesbian n lesbiana f.
less adj menor.
lesson n lección f.
let vt dejar, permitir.
lethal adj mortal.
lethargy n letargo m.
letter n letra f; carta f.

lettuce n lechuga f.
leukemia n leucemia f.
level adj llano/na, igual.
lever n palanca f.
leverage n influencia f.
levy n leva (de tropas) f.
lexicon n léxico m.
liability n responsabilidad f.
liable adj sujeto/ta; responsable.
liaise vi enlazar.
liaison n enlace m.
liar n embustero m.
libel n difamación f:—vt difamar.
liberal adj liberal.
liberate vt libertar.
liberation n liberación f.
liberty n libertad f.
Libra n Libra f.
librarian n bibliotecario m.
library n biblioteca f.
license n licencia f.
lick vt lamer.
lid n tapa f.
lie n mentira f.
life n vida f.
lifelike adj natural.
life preserver n chaleco salvavidas m.
lift vt levantar.
ligament n ligamento m.
light n luz f.
light bulb n foco m; bombilla f.
lighter n encendedor m.
lighthouse n (mar) faro m.
lightning n relámpago m.
like adj semejante; igual.
likeness n semejanza f.
lilac n lila f.
lily n lirio m.
lima beans npl haba gruesa f.
limb n miembro m.
lime n cal f; lima f.
limestone n piedra caliza f.

limit n limitem.
line n línea f.
linen n lino m.
liner n transatlántico m.
linger vi persistir.
lingerie n ropa interior f.
linguist n lingüista m.
lining n forro m.
link n eslabón m.
linoleum n linóleo m.
lintel n dintel m.
lion n león m.
lip n labio m.
liqueur n licor m.
liquid adj líquido/da
liquor n licor m.
liquorice n orozuz m; regalicia f.
lisp vi cecear.
list n lista f.
listen vi escuchar.
literature n literatura f.
lithe adj ágil.
lithograph n litografía f.
litigation n litigio m.
liter n litro m.
litter n litera f.
little adj pequeño/ña, poco/ca
live vi vivir; habitar.
liver n hígado m.
livestock n ganado m.
living n vida f:—adj vivo/va.
living room n sala de estar f.
lizard n lagarto m.
load vt cargar
loaf n pan m.
loam n marga f.
loan n préstamo m.
loathe vt aborrecer.
loathing n aversión f.
lobby n vestíbulo m.
lobe n lóbulo m.
lobster n langosta f.

local *adj* local.
locality *n* localidad *f.*
locate *vt* localizar.
location *n* situación *f.*
loch *n* lago *m.*
lock *n* cerradura *f.*
locker *n* vestuario *m.*
locket *n* medallón *m.*
locomotive *n* locomotora *f.*
locust *n* langosta *f.*
loft *n* desván *m.*
lofty *adj* alto/ta.
log *n* leño *m.*
logic *n* lógica *f.*
logo *n* logotipo *m.*
loiter *vi* merodear.
lollipop *n* pirulí *m.*
loneliness *n* soledad *f.*
long *adj* largo/ga.
longitude *n* longitud *f.*
look *vi* mirar *f.*
looking glass *n* espejo *m.*
loop *n* lazo *m.*
loose *adj* suelto/ta.
loot *vt* saquear:—*n* botín *m.*
lop *vt* desmochar.
lord *n* señor *m.*
lose *vt* perder.
loss *n* perdida *f.*
lotion *n* loción *f.*
lottery *n* lotería *f.*
loud *adj* fuerte:—~**ly** *adv* fuerte.
loudspeaker *n* altavoz *m.*
lounge *n* salón *m.*
louse *n* piojo (*pl* **lice**) *m.*

lout *n* gamberro *m.*
love *n* amor, cariño *m.*
lovely *adj* hermoso/sa.
lover *n* amante *m.*
low *adj* bajo/ja.
loyal *adj* leal; fiel.
lozenge *n* pastilla *f.*
lubricant *n* lubricante *m.*
lubricate *vt* lubricar.
luck *n* suerte *f;* fortuna *f.*
lucrative *adj* lucrativo/va.
ludricrous *adj* absurdo/da.
lug *vt* arrastrar.
luggage *n* equipaje *m.*
lull *vt* acunar:—*n* tregua *f.*
lullaby *n* nana *f.*
lumbago *n* lumbago *m.*
lumber *n* madera de construccion *f*
luminous *adj* luminoso/sa.
lump *n* terrón *m.*
lunacy *n* locura *f.*
lunar *adj* lunar.
lunatic *adj* loco/ca.
lunch, luncheon *n* merienda *f.*
lungs *npl* pulmones *mpl.*
luscious *adj* delicioso/sa.
lush *adj* exuberante.
lust *n* lujuria, sensualidad *f.*
luster *n* lustre *m.*
luxurious *adj* lujoso/sa.
luxury *n* lujo *m.*
lymph *n* linfa *f.*
lynx *n* lince *m.*
lyrical *adj* lírico/ca.
lyrics *npl* letra *f.*

M

macaroni *n* macarrones *mpl.*
macaroon *n* almendrado *m.*
mace *n* maza *f;* macis *f.*

machine *n* maquina *f.*
machinery *n* maquinaria, mecanica *f.*
mackerel *n* escombro *m.*

mad *adj* loco, furioso, rabioso.

madam *n* madama, senora *f.*

madhouse *n* casa de locos *f.*

madness *n* locura *f.*

magazine *n* revista *f.*

maggot *n* gusano *m.*

magic *n* magia *f.*

magician *n* mago *m*

magistrate *n* magistrado *m.*

magnet *n* iman *m.*

magnetic *adj* magnetico.

magnificent *adj* magnifico.

magnify *vt* aumentar.

magnifying glass *n* lupa *f.*

magnitude *n* magnitud *f.*

magpie *n* urraca *f.*

mahogany *n* caoba *f.*

mail *n* correo *m.*

mailman *n* cartero *m.*

maim *vt* mutilar.

main *adj* principal.

maintain *vt* mantener.

maintenance *n* mantenimiento *m.*

maize *n* maiz *m.*

majesty *n* majestad *f.*

major *adj* principal

make *vt* hacer, crear.

make-up *n* maquillaje *m.*

malaria *n* malaria *f.*

male *adj* masculino:—*n* macho *m.*

malice *n* malicia *f.*

malicious *adj* malicioso.

mall *n* centro comercial *m.*

malleable *adj* maleable.

mallet *n* mazo *m.*

mallows *n* (*bot*) malva *f.*

malnutrition *n* desnutricion *f.*

malpractice *n* negligencia *f.*

malt *n* malta *f.*

maltreat *vt* maltratar.

mammal *n* mamifero *m.*

mammoth *adj* gigantesco.

man *n* hombre *m.*

manage *vt, vi* manejar, dirigir.

management *n* direccion *f.*

manager *n* director *m.*

mandate *n* mandato *m.*

mane *n* crines del caballo *fpl.*

maneuvre *n* maniobra *f.*

mangle *n* rodillo *m.*

mangy *adj* sarnoso.

manhood *n* edad viril *f.*

mania *n* mania *f.*

maniac *n* maniaco *m.*

manipulate *vt* manejar.

mankind *n* genero humano *m.*

man-made *n* artificial.

manner *n* manera *f; modo *m*

mansion *n* palacio *m.*

mantelpiece *n* repisa de chimenea *f.*

manual *adj, n* manual *m.*

manufacture *n* fabricacion *f.*

manufacturer *n* fabricante *m.*

manuscript *n* manuscrito *m.*

many *adj* muchos, muchas.

map *n* mapa *m.*

maple *n* arce *m.*

mar *vt* estropear.

marathon *n* maraton *m.*

marble *n* marmol *m.*

March *n* marzo *m.*

mare *n* yegua *f.*

margarine *n* margarina *f.*

margin *n* margen *m; borde *m.*

marigold *n* (*bot*) calendula *f.*

marijuana *n* marijuana *f.*

marine *adj* marino*m.*

marital *adj* marital.

mark *n* marca *f.*

market *n* mercado *m.*

marmalade *n* mermelada de naranja *f.*

maroon *adj* marron.

marquee *n* entoldado *m.*

marriage *n* matrimonio *m*

marrow *n* medula *f.*

marry *vi* casar(se).

marsh *n* pantano *m.*

marshy *adj* pantanoso.

martyr *n* martir *m.*

marvel *n* maravilla *f.*

marvelous *adj* maravilloso.

marzipan *n* mazapan *m.*

mascara *n* rimel *m.*

masculine *adj* masculino.

mask *n* mascara *f.*

masochist *n* masoquista *m.*

mason *n* albanil *m.*

mass *n* masa *f;* misa *f;*

massacre *n* carniceria, matanza *f.*

massage *n* masaje *m.*

massive *adj* enorme.

mast *n* mastil *m.*

masterpiece *n* obra maestra *f.*

masticate *vt* masticar.

mat *n* estera *f.*

match *n* fosforo *m,* cerilla *f.*

mate *n* companero *m:—vt* acoplar.

mathematics *npl* matematicas *fpl.*

matinee *n* funcion de la tarde *f.*

mating *n* aparejamiento *m.*

matriculate *vt* matricular.

matriculation *n* matriculacion *f.*

matt *adj* mate.

matter *n* materia, substancia *f.*

mattress *n* colchon *m.*

mature *adj* maduro.

mauve *adj* de color malva.

maximum *n* maximo *m.*

May *n* mayo *m.*

mayonnaise *n* mayonesa *f.*

mayor *n* alcalde *m.*

maze *n* laberinto *m.*

me *pn* me; mi.

meal *n* comida *f;* harina *f.*

mean *adj* tacano.

meander *vi* serpentear.

meaning *n* sentido, significado *m.*

meantime, meanwhile *adv* mientras tanto.

measles *npl* sarampion *m.*

measurement *n* medida *f.*

meat *n* carne *f.*

mechanic *n* mecanico *m.*

mechanism *n* mecanismo *m.*

medal *n* medalla *f.*

media *npl* medios de comunicacion *mpl.*

medical *adj* medico.

medicate *vt* medicinar.

medicine *n* medicina *f.*

medieval *adj* medieval.

mediocre *adj* mediocre.

meditate *vi* meditar.

meditation *n* meditacion *f.*

Mediterranean *adj* mediterraneo.

medium *n* medio *m.*

meet *vt* encontrar.

meeting *n* reunion *f.*

megaphone *n* megafono *m.*

melancholy *n* melancolia *f.*

mellow *adj* maduro.

mellowness *n* madurez *f.*

melody *n* melodia *f.*

melon *n* melon *m.*

melt *vt* derretir.

member *n* miembro *m.*

membrane *n* membrana *f.*

memento *n* memento *m.*

memoir *n* memoria *f.*

memorandum *n* memorandum *m.*

memorial *n* monumento conmemorativo *m.*

memory *n* memoria *f;* recuerdo *m.*

menace *n* amenaza *f.*

menagerie *n* casa de fieras *f.*

mend *vt* reparar.

menial *adj* domestico.

meningitis n meningitis f.
menopause n menopausia f.
menstruation n menstruacion f.
mental adj mental.
mention n mencion f.
mentor n mentor m.
menu n menu m; carta f.
merchandise n mercancia f.
merchant n comerciante m.
mercury n mercurio m.
mercy n compasion f.
mere adj mero.
meridian n meridiano m.
merit n merito m.
mermaid n sirena f.
merry adj alegre.
merry-go-round n tiovivo m.
mesh n malla f.
mesmerize vt hipnotizar.
mess n lio m.
message n mensaje m.
metabolism n metabolismo n.
metal n metal m.
metallic adj metalico.
metamorphosis n metamorfosis f.
metaphor n metafora f.
meteor n meteoro m.
meteorological adj meteorológico.
meteorology n meteorologia f.
meter[1] n medidor m.
meter[2] n metro m.
method n metodo m.
methodical adj metodico.
Methodist n metodista m.
metric adj metrico.
metropolis n metropoli f.
metropolitan adj metropolitano.
mettle n valor m.
mew vi maullar.
mezzanine n entresuelo m.
microbe n microbio m.
microphone n microfono m.

microchip n microplaqueta f.
microscope n microscopio m.
microwave n horno microondas m.
mid adj medio.
midday n mediodia m.
middle adj mediom.
midge n mosca f.
midget n enano m.
midnight n medianoche f.
midst n medio, centro m.
midsummer n pleno verano m.
midwife n partera f.
might n poder m; fuerza f.
mighty adj fuerte.
migraine n jaqueca f.
migrate vi emigrar.
migration n emigracion f.
mike n microfono m.
mild adj apacible; suave.
mildew n moho m.
mileage n kilometraje m.
milieu n ambiente m.
militant adj militante.
military adj militar.
milk n leche f.
milkshake n batido m
milky adj lechoso:—**M~ Way** n Via
  Lactea f.
mill n molino m.
millennium n milenio m.
miller n molinero m.
milligram n miligramo m.
milliliter n mililitro m.
millimeter n milimetro m.
milliner n sombrerero.
million n millon m.
millionaire n millonario m.
millionth adj n millonésimo.
mime n mimo m.
mimic vt imitar.
mince vt picar.
mind n mente f.

mine *pn* mio, mia, mi:—*n* mina:—*vi* minar.

miner *n* minero *m*.

mineral *adj, n* mineral *m*.

mineral water *n* agua mineral *f*.

mingle *vt* mezclar.

miniature *n* miniatura *f*.

minimal *adj* minimo.

minimum *n* minimum *m*.

mining *n* explotacion minera *f*.

minister *n* ministro *m*.

mink *n* vison *m*.

minnow *n* pecicillo *m* (pez).

minor *adj* menor

mint *n* (*bot*) menta *f*.

minus *adv* menos.

minute *adj* diminuto.

minute *n* minuto *m*.

miracle *n* milagro *m*.

mirage *n* espejismo *m*.

mire *n* fango *m*.

mirror *n* espejo *m*.

mirth *n* alegria *f*.

misbehave *vi* portarse mal.

miscarry *vi* abortar.

miscellaneous *adj* varios, varias.

miser *n* avaro *m*.

miserable *adj* miserable.

miserly *adj* mezquino, tacano.

misery *n* miseria *f*.

mislay *vt* extraviar.

mislead *vt* enganar.

misogynist *n* misogino *m*.

Miss *n* senorita *f*.

miss *vt* perder; echar de menos.

missile *n* misil *m*.

mission *n* mision *f*.

missionary *n* misionero *m*.

mist *n* niebla *f*.

mistake *vt* entender mal

Mister *n* Senor *m*.

mistletoe *n* (*bot*) muerdago *m*.

mistress *n* amante *f*.

mistrust *vt* desconfiar.

mitigate *vt* mitigar.

mitigation *n* mitigacion *f*.

miter *n* mitra *f*.

mittens *npl* manoplas *fpl*.

mix *vt* mezclar.

mixer *n* licuadora *f*.

mixture *n* mezcla *f*.

moan *n* gemido *m*.

moat *n* foso *m*.

mob *n* multitud *f*.

mobile *adj* movil.

mode *n* modo *m*.

model *n* modelo *m*.

moderate *adj* moderado.

moderation *n* moderacion *f*.

modern *adj* moderno.

modernize *vt* modernizar.

modest *adj* modesto.

modesty *n* modestia *f*.

modify *vt* modificar.

module *n* modulo *m*.

mogul *n* magnate *m*.

mohair *n* mohair *m*.

moist *adj* humedo.

moisture *n* humedad *f*.

mold *n* molde *m*.

mole *n* topo *m*.

molecule *n* molecula *f*.

molest *vt* importunar.

mom *n* mama *f*.

moment *n* momento *m*.

momentum *n* impetu *m*.

mommy *n* mama *f*.

monarch *n* monarca *m*.

monarchy *n* monarquia *f*.

monastery *n* monasterio *m*.

Monday *n* lunes *m*.

monetary *adj* monetario.

money *n* moneda *f*; dinero *m*.

mongol *n* mongolico *m*.

mongrel *adj, n* mestizo *m*.
monk *n* monje *m*.
monkey *n* mono *m*.
monopoly *n* monopolio *m*.
monotonous *adj* monotono.
monsoon *n* (*mar*) monzon *m*.
monster *n* monstruo *m*.
month *n* mes *m*.
monthly *adj, adv* mensual (mente).
monument *n* monumento *m*.
mood *n* humor *m*.
moody *adj* malhumorado.
moon *n* luna *f*.
moor *n* paramo.
moorland *n* paramo *m*.
moose *n* alce *m*.
mop *n* fregona *f*.
mope *vi* estar triste.
moped *n* ciclomotor *m*.
morality *n* etica, moralidad *f*.
morbid *adj* morboso.
more *adj, adv* mas.
moreover *adv* ademas.
morgue *n* deposito de cadaveres *m*.
morning *n* manana *f*:—**good ~**
buenos dias *mpl*.
moron *n* imbecil *m*.
morphine *n* morfina *f*.
morse *n* morse *m*.
morsel *n* bocado *m*.
mortal *adj* mortal
mortality *n* mortalidad *f*.
mortar *n* mortero *m*.
mortgage *n* hipoteca *f*.
mortify *vt* mortificar.
mortuary *n* deposito de cadaveres *m*.
mosaic *n* mosaico *m*.
mosque *n* mezquita *f*.
mosquito *n* mosquito *m*.
moss *n* (*bot*) musgo *m*.
most *adj* la mayoria de.
motel *n* motel *m*.

moth *n* polilla *f*.
mother *n* madre *f*.
mother-in-law *n* suegra *f*.
mother-of-pearl *n* nacar *m*.
motif *n* tema *m*.
motion *n* movimiento *m*.
motive *n* motivo *m*.
motor *n* motor *m*.
motorbike *n* moto *f*.
motorcycle *n* motocicleta *f*.
motor vehicle *n* automovil *m*.
motto *n* lema *m*.
mount *n* monte *m*.
mountain *n* montana *f*.
mountaineering *n* montañismo *m*.
mourn *vt* lamentar.
mourner *n* doliente *m*.
mourning *n* luto *m*.
mouse *n* (*pl* mice) raton *m*.
mousse *n* mousse *f*.
mouth *n* boca *f*;
mouthful *n* bocado *m*.
mouthwash *n* enjuague *m*.
mouthwatering *adj* apetitoso.
move *vt* mover.
movement *n* movimiento *m*.
movies *n* pelicula *f*; el cine
moving *adj* conmovedor.
mow *vt* segar.
mower *n* cortacesped *m*; mocion *f*.
Mrs *n* senora *f*.
much *adj, adv* mucho.
muck *n* suciedad *f*.
mucous *adj* mocoso.
mud *n* barro *m*.
muddle *vt* confundir *m*; confusion *f*.
muffle *vt* embozar.
mug *n* jarra *f*.
mulberry *n* mora *f*.
mule *n* mulo *m*, mula *f*.
multiple *adj* multiplo *m*.
multiplication *n* multiplicacion *f*.

multiply vt multiplicar.
multitude n multitud f.
mumble vt, vi refunfunar.
mummy n momia f.
mumps npl paperas fpl.
munch vt mascar.
mundane adj trivial.
municipal adj municipal.
municipality n municipalidad f.
mural n mural m.
murder n asesinato m; homicidio m.
murky adj sombrio.
murmur n murmullo.
muscle n musculo m.
muse vi meditar.
museum n museo m.
mushroom n (bot) seta f; champinon m.
music n musica f.
musician n musico m.
musk n musco m.
muslin n muselina f.

mussel n marisco m.
must v aux estar obligado.
mustache n bigote m.
mustard n mostaza f.
mute adj mudo, silencioso.
mutilate vt mutilar.
mutter vt, vi murmurar.
mutton n carnero m.
mutual adj mutuo, mutual.
muzzle n bozal m.
my pn mi, mis; mio, mia; mios, mias.
myriad n miriada f.
myrrh n mirra f.
myrtle n mirto, arrayan m.
myself pn yo mismo.
mysterious adj misterioso.
mystery n misterio m.
mystic(al) adj mistico.
mystify vt dejar perplejo.
mystique n misterio m.
myth n mito m.
mythology n mitologia f.

N

nag n jaca f:—vt reganar.
nagging adj persistente.
nail n una f; garra f; clavo m.
naive adj ingenuo.
naked adj desnudo.
name n nombre m.
nameless adj anonimo.
namely adv a saber.
namesake n tocayo m.
nanny n ninera f.
nap n sueno ligero m.
nape n nuca f.
napkin n servilleta f.
narcissus n (bot) narciso m.
narcotic adj, n narcotico m.

narrate vt narrar.
narrative adj narrativo.
narrow adj angosto, estrecho.
nasal adj nasal.
nasty adj sucio, puerco.
natal adj nativo; natal.
nation n nacion f.
nationalize vt nacionalizar.
nationalism n nacionalismo m.
nationalist adj, n nacionalista m.
nationality n nacionalidad f.
native adj nativo m.
native language n lengua materna f.
Nativity n Navidad f.
natural adj natural.

naturalize *vt* naturalizar.

naturalist *n* naturalista *m*.

nature *n* naturaleza *f*.

naught *n* cero *m*.

naughty *adj* malo.

nausea *n* nausea.

nauseous *adj* fastidioso.

nautic(al), naval *adj* nautico, naval.

nave *n* nave (de la iglesia) *f*.

navel *n* ombligo *m*.

navigate *vi* navegar.

navigation *n* navegacion *f*.

navy *n* marina *f*.

Nazi *n* nazi *m*.

near *prep* cerca de.

nearby *adj* cercano.

nearly *adv* casi.

near-sighted *adj* miope.

nebulous *adj* nebuloso.

necessarily *adv* necesariamente.

necessary *adj* necesario.

necessity *n* necesidad *f*.

neck *n* cuello *m*.

necklace *n* collar *m*.

necktie *n* corbata *f*.

nectar *n* nectar *m*.

need *n* necesidad *f*.

needle *n* aguja *f*.

needless *adj* superfluo.

needlework *n* costura *f*

needy *adj* necesitado, pobre.

negation *n* negacion *f*.

negative *adj* negativo.

neglect *vt* descuidar.

negligee *n* salto de cama *m*.

negligence *n* negligencia *f*

negligible *adj* insignificante.

negotiate *vt, vi* negociar (con).

negotiation *n* negociacion *f*; negocio *m*.

Negress *n* negra *f*.

Negro *adj, n* negro *m*.

neighbor *n* vecino *m*.

neighborhood *n* vecindad *f*; vecindariom.

neither *conj* ni:—*pn* ninguno.

neon *n* neon *m*.

neon light *n* luz de neon *f*.

nephew *n* sobrino *m*.

nepotism *n* nepotismo *m*.

nerve *n* nervio *m*; valor *m*.

nerve-racking *adj* espantoso.

nervous *adj* nervioso; nervudo.

nervous breakdown *n* crisis nerviosa *f*.

nest *n* nido *m*.

nest egg *n* (fig) ahorros *mpl*.

nestle *vt* anidarse.

net *n* red *f*.

netball *n* basquet *m*.

nettle *n* ortiga *f*.

network *n* red *f*.

neurosis *n* neurosis *f* invar.

neurotic *adj, n* neurotico *m*.

neuter *adj* (gr) neutro.

neutral *adj* neutral.

neutrality *n* neutralidad *f*.

neutron *n* neutron *m*.

never *adv* nunca, jamas.

nevertheless *adv* no obstante.

new *adj* nuevo.

news *npl* novedad, noticias *fpl*.

newscaster *n* presentador *m*.

newspaper *n* periodico *m*.

next *adj* proximo.

nib *n* pico *m*.

nibble *vt* picar.

nice *adj* simpatico.

niche *n* nicho *m*.

nickel *n* niquel *m*

nickname *n* mote.

nicotine *n* nicotina *f*.

niece *n* sobrina *f*.

niggling *adj* insignificante.

night *n* noche *f*.

nightclub n cabaret m.
nightfall n anochecer m.
nightingale n ruisenor m.
nightmare n pesadilla f.
nihilist n nihilista m.
nimble adj ligero, activo, listo, agil.
nine adj, n nueve.
nineteen adj, n diecinueve.
nineteenth adj, n decimonono.
ninetieth adj, n nonagesimo.
ninety adj, n noventa.
ninth adj, n nono, noveno.
nip vt pellizcar; morder.
nipple n pezon m; tetilla f.
nit n liendre f.
nitrogen n nitrogeno m.
no adv no.
nobility n nobleza f.
noble adj noble.
nobleman n noble m.
nobody n nadie, ninguna persona f.
nocturnal adj nocturnal.
noise n ruido m.
noisy adj ruidoso, turbulento.
nominate vt nombrar.
nomination n nominacion f.
nominee n candidato m.
non-alcoholic adj no alcoholico.
nonchalant adj indiferente.
nondescript adj no descrito.
none adj nadie, ninguno.
nonentity n nulidad f.
nonetheless adv sin embargo.
nonsense n disparate m.
noodles npl fideos mpl.
noon n mediodia m.
noose n lazo corredizo m.
nor conj ni.
normal adj normal.
north n norte m.
North America n America del Norte f.

northeast n nor(d)este m.
northerly, northern adj norteno.
North Pole n polo artico m.
northwest n nor(d)oeste m.
nose n nariz f
nosebleed n hemorragia nasal f.
nostalgia n nostalgia f.
nostril n ventana de la nariz f.
not adv no.
notable adj notable.
notably adv especialmente.
notary n notario m.
notch n muesca f.
note n nota, marca f.
notebook n librito de apuntes m.
noted adj afamado, celebre.
nothing n nada f.
notice n noticia f; aviso m.
notification n notificacion f.
notify vt notificar.
notion n nocion f.
notoriety n notoriedad f.
notwithstanding conj no obstante, aunque.
nougat n turron m.
nought n cero m.
noun n (gr) sustantivo m.
nourish vt nutrir, alimentar.
novel n novela f.
novelist n novelista m.
novelty n novedad f.
November n noviembre m.
novice n novicio m.
now adv ahora.
nowadays adv hoy (en) dia.
nowhere adv en ninguna parte.
noxious adj nocivo, danoso.
nozzle n boquilla f.
nuance n matiz m.
nuclear adj nuclear.
nucleus n nucleo m.
nude adj desnudo.

nudge vt dar un codazo a.
nudist n nudista m.
nudity n desnudez f.
null adj nulo.
nullify vt anular.
numb adj entorpecido.
number n numero m.
numerous adj numeroso.
nun n monja f.
nunnery n convento de monjas m.
nuptial adj nupcial fpl.
nurse n enfermera f.

nursery n guarderia infantil f
nursery rhyme n cancion infantil f.
nursery school n parvulario m.
nursing home n clinica de reposo f.
nurture vt criar.
nut n nuez f.
nutcrackers npl cascanueces m.
nutmeg n nuez moscada f.
nutritious adj nutritivo.
nut shell n cascara de nuez f.
nylon n nilon m.

O

oak n roble m.
oar n remo m.
oasis n oasis f.
oat n avena f.
oath n juramento m.
obedience n obediencia f.
obese adj obeso, gordo.
obey vt obedecer.
obituary n necrologia f.
object n objeto m:—vt objetar.
objective adj, n objetivo m.
oblige vt obligar.
obliterate vt borrar.
oblivion n olvido m.
oblong adj oblongo.
obnoxious adj odioso.
oboe n oboe m.
obscene adj obsceno.
obscenity n obscenidad f.
obscure adj oscuro.
observatory n observatorio m.
observe vt observar, mirar.
obsess vt obsesionar.
obsolete adj en desuso.
obstacle n obstaculo m.

obstinate adj obstinado.
obstruct vt obstruir; impedir.
obtain vt obtener, adquirir.
obvious adj obvio, evidente.
occasion n ocasion f.
occupant, occupier n ocupador m
occupation n ocupacion f; empleo m.
occupy vt ocupar.
occur vi pasar.
ocean n oceano m; alta mar f.
ocher n ocre m.
octave n octava f.
October n octubre m.
octopus n pulpo m.
odd adj impar.
oddity n singularidad.
odious adj odioso.
odor n olor m.
of prep de.
off adv desconectado; apagado.
offence n ofensa f.
offend vt ofender.
offensive adj ofensivo.
offer vt ofrecer.

offering n sacrificio m.

office n oficina f.

officer n oficial, empleado m.

official adj oficial.

offspring n prole f.

ogle vt comerse con los ojos.

oil n aceite m.

oil painting n pintura al oleo f.

oil rig n torre de perforacion f.

oil tanker n petrolero m.

ointment n unguento m.

OK, okay excl vale.

old adj viejo; antiguo.

old age n vejez f.

olive n olivo m.

omelet n tortilla de huevos f.

omen n agüero.

ominous adj ominoso.

omission n omisión f.

omit vt omitir.

omnipotence n omnipotencia f.

on prep sobre, encima, en; de; a.

one adj un, uno.

oneself pn si mismo; si misma.

ongoing adj continuo.

onion n cebolla f.

onlooker n espectador m.

only adj unico, solo.

onus n responsabilidad f.

onwards adv adelante.

opaque adj opaco.

open adj abierto; vi abrirse.

open-minded adj imparcial.

opera n opera f.

operate vi obrar.

operation n operacion f.

operational adj operacional.

operative adj operativo.

operator n operario m; operador m.

ophthalmic adj oftálmico.

opinion n opinion f.

opinion poll n sondeo m.

opponent n antagonista m.

opportune adj oportuno.

opportunity n oportunidad f.

oppose vt oponerse.

opposite adj opuesto; contrario.

opposition n oposicion f.

oppress vt oprimir.

oppression n opresion f.

optic(al) adj optico f.

optician n optico m.

optimist n optimista m.

optimum adj optimum.

option n opcion f; deseo m.

opulent adj opulento.

or conj o; u.

oracle n oraculo m.

oral adj oral.

orange n naranja f.

orbit n orbita f.

orchard n huerto m.

orchestra n orquesta f.

orchid n orquidea f.

order n orden mf; regla f; mandar.

ordinary adj ordinario.

ore n mineral m.

organ n organo m.

organic adj organico.

organization n organizacion f.

organize vt organizar.

organism n organismo m.

organist n organista m.

orgasm n orgasmo m.

orgy n orgia f.

oriental adj oriental.

orifice n orificio m.

origin n origen m.

original adj original.

originate vi originar.

ornament n ornamento m.

ornate adj adornado.

orphan *adj, n* huerfano *m.*
orphanage *n* orfanato *m.*
orthodox *adj* ortodoxo.
orthopedic *adj* ortopedico.
oscillate *vi* oscilar.
osprey *n* aguila marina *f.*
ostensibly *adv* aparentemente.
ostentatious *adj* ostentoso.
osteopath *n* osteopata *m.*
ostrich *n* avestruz *m.*
other *pn* otro.
otter *n* nutria *f.*
ouch *excl* ¡ay!
ought *v aux* deber, ser menester.
ounce *n* onza *f.*
our, ours *pn* nuestro, nuestra, nuestros, nuestras.
ourselves *pn pl* nosotros mismos.
out *adv* fuera.
outbreak *n* erupcion *f.*
outcast *n* paria *m.*
outcome *n* resultado *m.*
outcry *n* clamor *m.*
outdo *vt* exceder a otro, sobrepujar.
outer *adj* exterior.
outermost *adj* extremo; lo mas exterior.
outfit *n* vestidos *mpl;* ropa *f.*
outlet *n* enchufe *m.*
outline *n* contorno *m*
outlook *n* perspectiva *f.*
out-of-date *adj* caducado; pasado de moda.
outpatient *n* paciente externo *m.*
output *n* rendimiento *m.*
outrage *n* ultraje *m.*
outrageous *adj* ultrajoso.
outside *n* superficie *f;* exterior *m.*
outsider *n* forastero *m.*
outskirts *npl* alrededores *mpl.*

outstanding *adj* excepcional.
outwit *vt* enganar a uno a fuerza de tretas.
oval *n* ovalo *m:—adj* oval.
ovary *n* ovario *m.*
oven *n* horno *m.*
ovenproof *adj* resistente al horno.
over *prep* sobre, encima.
overbearing *adj* despotico.
overcharge *vt* sobrecargar.
overcoat *n* abrigo *m.*
overdose *n* sobredosis *f.*
overdue *adj* retrasado.
overeat *vi* atracarse.
overflow *vt, vi* inundar.
overhaul *vt* revisar.
overkill *n* exceso de medios *m.*
overlap *vi* traslaparse.
overleaf *adv* al dorso.
overload *vt* sobrecargar.
overpower *vt* predominar, oprimir.
overseas *adv* en ultramar:—*adj* extranjero.
oversee *vt* inspeccionar.
overshadow *vt* eclipsar.
overstate *vi* exagerar.
overstep *vt* exceder, pasar de.
overtake *vt* sobrepasar.
overtime *n* horas extra *fpl.*
overtone *n* tono *m.*
owe *vt* deber.
owl *n* buho *m.*
own *adj* propio.
owner *n* dueno, propietario *m.*
ownership *n* posesion *f.*
ox *n* buey *m.*
oxidize *vt* oxidar.
oxygen *n* oxigeno *m.*
oyster *n* ostra *f.*
ozone *n* ozono *m.*

P

pa n papa m.

pace n paso m.

pacemaker n marcapasos m.

pacific(al) adj pacifico.

pacify vt pacificar.

package n paquete m.

packet n paquete m.

packing n embalaje m.

pact n pacto m.

pad n bloc m.

paddle vi remar

paddock n corral m.

paddy n arrozal m.

pagan adj, n pagano m.

page n pagina f.

pain n pena f; castigo m; dolor m.

painkiller n analgesico m.

paint vt pintar.

paintbrush n pincel m.

painter n pintor m.

painting n pintura f.

pair n par m.

pajamas npl pijama m.

palatial adj palatino.

pale adj palido; claro.

pallet n pallet m.

palliative adj, n paliativo m.

pallid adj palido.

pallor n palidez f.

palm n (bot) palma f.

Palm Sunday n Domingo de Ramos m.

palpable adj palpable.

paltry adj irrisorio; mezquino.

pamphlet n folleto m.

pan n cazuela f.

pancake n bunuelo m.

pandemonium n jaleo m.

pane n cristal m.

panel n panel m

panic adj, n panico m.

pansy n (bot) pensamiento m.

pant vi jadear.

panther n pantera f.

pantry n despensa f.

pants npl pantalones mpl.

papacy n papado m.

papal adj papal.

paper n papel m.

paperback n libro de bolsillo m.

paper clip n clip m.

paperweight n sujetapapeles m.

paprika n pimienta hungara f.

parachute n paracaidas m.

paradise n paraiso m.

paradox n paradoja f.

paragon n modelo perfecto m.

paragraph n parrafo m.

parallel adj paralelo.

paralysis n paralisis f.

paralytic(al) adj paralitico.

paralyze vt paralizar.

paramedic n ambulanciero m.

paramount adj supremo.

paranoid adj paranoico.

parasite n parásito m.

parasol n parasol m.

parcel n paquete m.

parch vt resecar.

pardon n perdon m.

parent n padre m; madre f.

parentage n parentela f.

parental adj paternal.

parenthesis n parentesis m.

parish n parroquia f.

parity n paridad f.

park n parque m.

parliament n parlamento m.

parlor n sala de recibimiento f.

pang n angustia f. **parody** n parodia f.

parrot n papagayo m.
parsley n (bot) perejil m.
parsnip n (bot) chirivia f.
part n parte f.
participate vi participar (en).
particle n particula f.
particular adj particular.
parting n separacion f.
partition n particion.
partner n socio, companero m.
partridge n perdiz f.
party n partido m; fiesta f.
pass vt pasar.
passage n pasaje m
passbook n libreta de depositos f.
passenger n pasajero m.
passion n pasion f
passionate adj apasionado.
passive adj pasivo.
Passover n Pascua f.
passport n pasaporte m.
password n contrasena f.
past adj pasado.
pasta n pasta f.
paste n pasta f.
pastime n pasatiempo m f.
pastor n pastor m.
pastry n pasteleria f.
pasture n pasto m.
patch n remiendo m; parche m.
patent adj patente.
pathetic adj patetico.
patience n paciencia f.
patient adj paciente.
patio n patio m.
patriot n patriota m.
patriotism n patriotismo m.
patrol n patrulla f.
patron n patron m.
patronize vt patrocinar.
pattern n patron m; dibujo m.
pauper n pobre m.

pause n pausa f.
pave vt empedrar.
pavilion n pabellon m.
paw n pata f.
pay vt pagar.
pea n guisante m.
peace n paz f.
peach n melocoton m.
peacock n pavon, pavo real m.
peak n cima f.
peanut n cacahuete m.
pear n pera f.
pearl n perla f.
peasant n campesino m.
pebble n guija f.
peculiar adj peculiar.
pedal n pedal m.
pedestal n pedestal m.
pedestrian n peaton m.
pedigree n genealogia f.
peel vt pelar.
peg n clavija f.
pelican n pelicano m.
pen n boligrafo m; pluma f
penal adj penal.
pence n d pl of penny.
pencil n lapiz m.
pendulum n pendulo m.
penetrate vt penetrar.
penguin n pinguino m.
penicillin n penicilina f.
peninsula n peninsula f.
penis n pene m.
penitence n penitencia f.
penitentiary n encierro m.
penknife n navaja f.
penny n penique m.
pension n pension f.
pensive adj pensativo.
Pentecost n Pentecostes m.
penthouse n atico m.
people n pueblo m; nacion f; gente f.

pepper *n* pimienta *f.*
peppermint *n* menta *f.*
perceive *vt* percibir.
percentage *n* porcentaje *m.*
perception *n* percepcion *f.*
percolator *n* cafetera de filtro *f.*
percussion *n* percusion *f;* golpe *m.*
perennial *adj* perenne; perpetuo.
perfect *adj* perfecto.
perform *vt* ejecutar.
performance *n* ejecucion *f.*
perfume *n* perfume *m;* fragancia *f:—*
   vt perfumar.
perhaps *adv* quiza, quizas.
peril *n* peligro *m.*
period *n* periodo *m.*
periodical *n* jornal, periodico *m.*
perk *n* extra *m.*
perm *n* permanente *f.*
permanent *adj,* ~**ly** *adv* permanente
   (mente).
permissible *adj* licito.
permission *n* permiso *m.*
permit *vt* permitir.
perplex *vt* confundir.
persecute *vt* perseguir.
persevere *vi* perseverar.
persist *vi* persistir.
person *n* persona *f.*
personality *n* personalidad *f.*
personnel *n* personal *m.*
perspective *n* perspectiva *f.*
perspiration *n* transpiracion *f.*
perspire *vi* transpirar.
persuade *vt* persuadir.
perturb *vt* perturbar.
peruse *vt* leer.
perverse *adj* perverso.
pessimist *n* pesimista *m.*
pester *vt* molestar.
pet *n* animal domestico *m.*
petal *n* (*bot*) petalo *m.*

petition *n* presentacion, peticion *f.*
petroleum *n* petroleo *m.*
petticoat *n* enaguas *fpl.*
petty *adj* mezquino.
pewter *n* peltre *m.*
phantom *n* fantasma *m.*
pharmacist *n* farmacéutico *m.*
pharmacy *n* farmacia *f.*
phase *n* fase *f.*
pheasant *n* faisan *m.*
phenomenon *n* fenomeno *m.*
phial *n* redomilla *f.*
philosopher *n* filosofo *m.*
philosophy *n* filosofia *f.*
phlegm *n* flema *f.*
phobia *n* fobia *f.*
phone *n* telefono *m.*
photocopier *n* fotocopiadora *f.*
photocopy *n* fotocopia *f.*
photograph *n* fotografia *f:—vt*
   fotografiar.
photographic *adj* fotografico.
photography *n* fotografia *f.*
phrase *n* frase *f.*
physical *adj* fisico.
physician *n* medico *m.*
physicist *n* fisico *m.*
physiotherapy *n* fisioterapia *f.*
physique *n* fisico *m.*
pianist *n* pianista *m, f.*
piano *n* piano *m.*
piccolo *n* flautin *m.*
pick *vt* escoger, elegir.
pickle *n* escabeche *m.*
picnic *n* comida, merienda *f.*
picture *n* pintura *f.*
picturesque *adj* pintoresco.
pie *n* pastel *m;* tarta *f.*
piece *n* pedazo *m;* pieza *f.*
pierce *vt* penetrar, agujerear.
pig *n* cerdo *m.*
pigeon *n* paloma *f.*

pigtail n trenza f.
pike n lucio m; pica f.
pile n estaca f; pila f; monton m.
pilgrim n peregrino m.
pill n pildora f.
pillar n pilar m.
pillow n almohada f.
pilot n piloto m.
pimple n grano m.
pin n alfiler m.
pinball n fliper m.
pincers n pinzas fpl.
pinch vt pellizcar.
pine n (bot) pino m.
pineapple n pina f, ananas m.
pink n rosa f.
pinnacle n cumbre f.
pint n pinta f.
pioneer n pionero m.
pious adj pio.
pip n pepita f.
pipe n tubo.
pirate n pirata m.
pirouette n pirueta.
Pisces n Piscis m (signo del zodiaco).
piss n (sl) meados mpl.
pistol n pistola f.
piston n embolo m.
pit n hoyo m; mina f.
pitcher n cantaro, jarro m.
pitchfork n horca f.
pity n piedad, compasion f.
pivot n eje m.
pizza n pizza f.
placard n pancarta f.
placate vt apaciguar.
place n lugar, sitio m.
placid adj placido.
plagiarism n plagio m.
plague n peste, plaga f.
plaice n platija f (pez).
plaid n tartan m.

plain adj liso, llano
plaintiff n (law) demandador m.
plan n plano m.
plane n avion m; plano m.
planet n planeta m.
plank n tabla f.
plant n planta f.
plantation n plantacion f.
plaque n placa f.
plaster n yeso m.
plastic adj plastico.
plate n plato m.
plateau n meseta f.
platform n plataforma f.
platinum n platino m.
platoon n (mil) peloton m.
play n juego m.
playboy n playboy m.
player n jugador m
plea n defensa f.
pleasant adj agradable.
please vt agradar.
pleasure n gusto, placer m.
pleat n pliegue m.
plentiful adj copioso.
plethora n pletora, replecion f.
pleurisy n pleuresia f.
pliers npl alicates mpl.
plinth n plinto m.
plough n arado m.
ploy n truco m.
plug n tapon m.
plum n ciruela f.
plumage n plumaje m.
plumb n plomada f.
plumber n plomero m.
plume n pluma f.
plump adj gordo.
plunder vt saquear.
plunge vi sumergir(se), precipitarse.
pluperfect n (gr) pluscuamperfecto m.
plural adj, n plural m.

plus *n* signo de mas *m*.
plush *adj* de felpa.
plutonium *n* plutonio *m*.
plywood *n* madera contrachapada *f*.
pneumatic *adj* neumatico.
pneumonia *n* pulmonia *f*.
poach *vt* escalfar.
pocket *n* bolsillo *m*.
pod *n* vaina *f*.
poem *n* poema *m*.
poet *n* poeta *m*.
poetry *n* poesia *f*.
poignant *adj* punzante.
point *n* punta *f*; punto *m*.
point-blank *adv* directamente.
poise *n* peso *m*; equilibrio *m*.
poison *n* veneno *m*.
poker *n* atizador *m*; poker *m*.
polar *adj* polar.
pole *n* polo *m*.
police *n* policia *f*.
policy *n* politica *f*.
polio *n* polio *f*.
polish *vt* pulir, alisar.
polite *adj* pulido, cortes.
politician *n* politico *m*.
politics *npl* politica *f*.
polka *n* polca *f*.
pollen *n* (*bot*) polen *m*.
pollute *vt* ensuciar.
pollution *n* polucion, contaminacion *f*.
polo *n* polo *m*.
polyester *n* poliester *m*.
polytechnic *n* politecnico *m*.
pomegranate *n* granada *f*.
pomp *n* pompa *f*; esplendor *m*.
pompom *n* borla *f*.
pompous *adj* pomposo.
pond *n* estanque *m*.
ponder *vt* ponderar, considerar.
ponderous *adj* ponderoso, pesado.

pontoon *n* ponton *m*.
pony *n* jaca *f*.
pool *n* charca *f*; piscina.
poor *adj* pobre.
pop *n* papá *m*.
popcorn *n* palomitas *fpl*.
Pope *n* papa *m*.
poplar *n* alamo *m*.
poppy *n* (*bot*) amapola *f*.
popular *adj*, **~ly** *adv* popular(mente).
populate *vi* poblar.
population *n* poblacion *f*.
porcelain *n* porcelana *f*.
porch *n* portico *m*.
porcupine *n* puerco espin *m*.
pore *n* poro *m*.
pork *n* carne de puerco *f*.
pornography *n* pornografia *f*.
porous *adj* poroso.
porpoise *n* marsopa *f*.
porridge *n* gachas de avena *fpl*.
port *n* puerto *m m*.
portable *adj* portatil.
portal *n* portal *m f*.
porter *n* portero *m*.
portfolio *n* cartera *f*.
porthole *n* portilla *f*.
portico *n* portico *m*.
portion *n* porcion*f*.
portly *adj* rollizo.
portrait *n* retrato *m*.
portray *vt* retratar.
pose *n* postura *f*; pose *f*.
posh *adj* elegante.
position *n* posicion *f*.
positive *adj* positivo.
posse *n* peloton *m*.
possess *vt* poseer.
possession *n* posesion *f*.
possibility *n* posibilidad *f*.
possible *adj* posible.
post *n* correo *m*; puesto *m*.

postage stamp n sello m.
postcard n tarjeta postal f.
poster n cartel m.
posterior n trasero m.
posterity n posteridad f.
postgraduate n posgraduado m.
posthumous adj postumo.
post office n correos m.
postpone vt diferir.
posture n postura f.
posy n ramillete de flores m.
pot n marmita f.
potato n patata f; papa f.
potent adj potente.
potential adj potencial.
pothole n bache m.
potion n pocion f.
potter n alfarero m.
pottery n cerámica f.
pouch n bolsa f.
poultice n cataplasma f.
poultry n aves caseras fpl.
pound n libra f; libra esterlina f.
pour vt echar; servir.
pout vi ponerse cenudo.
poverty n pobreza f.
powder n polvo m.
power n poder m.
practicable adj practicable; hacedero.
practical adj práctico:—**~ly** adv prácticamente.
practicality n factibilidad f.
practice n practica f.
pragmatic adj pragmático.
prairie n pampa f.
praise n renombre m.
prattle vi charlar:—n charla f.
prawn n gamba f.
pray vi rezar.
prayer n oracion f.
preach vi predicar.

preacher n pastor m.
precaution n precaucion f.
precede vt anteceder.
precious adj precioso.
precise n preciso.
precision n precision f.
preconception n preocupacion f.
predator n animal de rapina m.
predict vt predecir.
prediction n prediccion f.
predominant adj predominante.
predominate vt predominar.
preface n prefacio m.
prefer vt preferir.
preference n preferencia f.
prefix vt prefijar.
pregnancy n embarazo m.
pregnant adj embarazada.
prehistoric adj prehistorico.
prejudice n perjuicio m.
preliminary adj preliminar.
prelude n preludio m.
premature adj prematuro.
premier n primer ministro m.
premises npl establecimiento m.
premium n premio m.
premonition n presentimiento m.
prepare vt preparar(se).
preposition n preposicion f.
preposterous adj prepostero; absurdo.
prerequisite n requisito m.
prerogative n prerrogativa f.
prescribe vi prescribir; recetar.
prescription n prescripcion f.
present n regalo m.
presentation n presentacion f.
preservation n preservacion f.
preservative n preservativo m.
preserve vt preservar.
preside vi presidir.
presidency n presidencia f.

president n presidente m.
press vt empujar n prensa.
pressure n presion f.
prestige n prestigio m.
presume vt presumir, suponer.
pretence n pretexto m; pretension f.
pretend vi pretender.
preterite n preterito m.
pretext n pretexto m.
pretty adj lindo.
prevent vt prevenir.
preview n preestreno m.
previous adj previo.
prey n presa f.
price n precio m; premio m.
prick vt punzar, picar.
pride n orgullo m.
priest n sacerdote m.
priggish adj afectado.
prim adj peripuesto.
primary adj primario.
primate n primado m.
primeval adj primitivo.
primitive adj primitivo.
primrose n (bot) primula f.
prince n principe m.
princess n princesa f.
principle n principio m.
printer n impresor m.
prior adj anterior.
priority n prioridad f.
priory n priorato m.
prism n prisma m.
prison n prision, carcel f.
prisoner n prisionero m.
pristine adj pristino.
privacy n soledad f.
private adj secreto, privado; particular.
private eye n detective privado m.
privet n alhena f.

privilege n privilegio m.
prize n premio m.
probability n probabilidad f.
probable adj probable.
probation n prueba f.
problem n problema m.
procedure n procedimiento
proceed vi proceder.
process n proceso m.
procession n procesion f.
proclaim vt proclamar.
proclamation n proclamacion f.
procure vt procurar.
prod vt empujar.
prodigal adj prodigo.
prodigious adj prodigioso.
prodigy n prodigio m.
produce vt producir
product n producto m; obra f; efecto m.
production n produccion f.
profane adj profano.
profess vt profesar.
profession n profesion f.
professor n profesor, catedrático m.
proficient adj proficiente.
profile n perfil m.
profit n ganancia f.
profound adj profundo.
profuse adj profuso.
program n programa m.
progress n progreso m.
prohibit vt prohibir.
project vt proyectar
prominent adj prominente, saledizo.
promiscuous adj promiscuo.
promise n promesa f.
promontory n promontorio m.
promote vt promover.
promotion n promocion f.
prone adj inclinado.

prong n diente m.
pronoun n pronombre m.
pronounce vt pronunciar.
proof n prueba f.
propaganda n propaganda f.
propel vt impeler.
propeller n helice f.
propensity n propension f.
proper adj propio.
property n propiedad f.
prophecy n profecia f.
prophesy vt profetizar.
prophet n profeta m.
prophetic adj profetico.
proportion n proporcion f.
proportional adj proporcional.
proposal n propuesta f.
propose vt proponer.
proposition n proposicion f.
proprietor n propietario m.
propriety n propiedad f.
pro rata adv a prorrateo.
prosaic adj prosaico.
prose n prosa f.
prosecute vt proseguir.
prosecution n prosecucion f.
prosecutor n acusador m.
prospect n perspectiva f.
prospectus n prospecto m.
prosper vi prosperar.
prosperity n prosperidad f.
prostitute n prostituta f.
prostitution n prostitucion f.
prostrate adj postrado.
protagonist n protagonista m.
protect vt proteger.
protection n proteccion f.
protective adj protectorio.
protector n protector, patrono m.
protege n protegido m.
protein n proteina f.

protest vi protestar.
Protestant n protestante m.
protester n manifestante m.
protocol n protocolo m.
prototype n prototipo m.
protracted adj prolongado.
protrude vi sobresalir.
proud adj soberbio, orgulloso.
prove vt probar.
proverb n proverbio m.
provide vt proveer.
provided conj:—~ **that** con tal que.
providence n providencia f.
province n provincia f
provincial adj, n provincial m.
provision n provision f.
proviso n estipulacion f.
provocation n provocacion f.
provocative adj provocativo.
provoke vt provocar.
prowess n proeza f.
prowl vi rondar.
proximity n proximidad f.
proxy n poder m; apoderado m.
prudence n prudencia f.
prudent adj prudente.
prudish adj gazmono.
prussic acid n acido prúsico m.
pry vi espiar, acechar.
psalm n salmo m.
pseudonym n seudonimo m.
psyche n psique f.
psychiatrist n psiquiatra m.
psychiatry n psiquiatria f.
psychic adj psiquico.
psychoanalysis n psicoanalisis m.
psychoanalyst n psicoanalista m.
psychological adj psicologico.
psychologist n psicologo m.
psychology n psicologia f.
puberty n pubertad f.

public adj publico
publicize vt publicitar.
publicity n publicidad f.
publish vt publicar.
publisher n publicador m.
pucker vt arrugar, hacer pliegues.
puddle n charco m.
puff n soplo m.
pull vt tirar.
pulley n polea f.
pullover n jersey m.
pulp n pulpa f.
pulpit n pulpito m.
pulsate vi pulsar.
pulse n pulso m; legumbres fpl.
pumice n piedra pomez f.
pummel vt aporrear.
pump n bomba f.
pumpkin n calabaza f.
pun n equivoco, chiste m.
punch n punetazo m.
punctual adj puntual.
punctuate vi puntuar.
punctuation n puntuacion f.
pungent adj picante.
punish vt castigar.
punishment n castigo m.
punk n punki m.
punt n barco llano m.

pup n cachorro m.
pupil n alumno m.
puppet n titere m.
puppy n perrito m.
purchase vt comprar.
pure adj puro.
puree n pure m.
purification n purificacion f.
purify vt purificar.
puritan n puritano m.
purity n pureza f.
purple adj purpureo.
purpose n intencion f.
purr vi ronronear.
purse n bolsa f; cartera f.
pursue vi perseguir.
pursuit n perseguimiento m.
purveyor n abastecedor m.
push vt empujar
pusher n traficante de drogas m.
push-up n plancha f.
put vt poner, colocar.
putrid adj podrido.
putty n masilla f.
puzzle n acertijo m.
puzzling adj extrano.
pylon n torre de conduccion electrica f.
pyramid n piramide f.
python n piton atigrado m.

Q

quack vi graznar.
quadrangle n cuadrangulo m.
quadrant n cuadrante m.
quadrilateral adj cuadrilatero.
quadruped n cuadrupedo m.
quadruple adj cuadruplo.
quadruplet n cuatrillizo m.
quagmire n tremedal m.
quail n codorniz f.

quaint adj pulido; exquisito.
quake vi temblar; tiritar.
qualification n calificacion f.
qualify vt calificar.
quality n calidad f.
qualm n escrupulo m.
quandary n incertidumbref.
quantitative adj cuantitativo.
quantity n cantidad f.

quarantine n cuarentena f.
quarrel n rina, contienda f.
quarrelsome adj pendenciero.
quarry n cantera f.
quarter n cuarto mr.
quarterly adj trimestral.
quartermaster n (mil) comisario m.
quartet n (mus) cuarteto m.
quartz n (min) cuarzo m.
quash vt fracasar; anular.
quay n muelle m.
queasy adj nauseabundo.
queen n reina f.
queer adj extrano.
quell vt calmar.
quench vt apagar.
query n cuestion.
quest n pesquisa f.
question n pregunta f; cuestion f.
questionable adj cuestionable.
question mark n punto de interrogación m.
questionnaire n cuestionario m.
quibble vi buscar evasivas.

quick adj rapido.
quicken vt apresurar.
quicksand n arena movediza f.
quicksilver n azogue, mercurio m.
quick-witted adj agudo, perspicaz.
quiet adj callado.
quinine n quinina f.
quintet n (mus) quinteto m.
quintuple adj quintuplo.
quintuplet n quintillizo m.
quip n indirecta f:—vt echar pullas.
quirk n peculiaridad f.
quit vt dejar.
quite adv bastante.
quits adv ien paz!.
quiver vi temblar.
quixotic adj quijotesco.
quiz n concurso m.
quizzical adj burlon.
quota n cuota f.
quotation n citacion, cita f.
quotation marks npl comillas fpl.
quote vt citar.
quotient n cociente m.

R

rabbi n rabi m.
rabbit n conejo m.
rabble n gentuza f.
rabid adj rabioso.
rabies n rabia f.
race n raza.
rack n rejilla f.
racket n ruido m; raqueta f.
racy adj picante.
radiance n brillantez f.
radiant adj radiante.
radiate vt, vi radiar.
radiation n radiacion f.
radiator n radiador m.

radical adj, ~ly adv radical(mente).
radio n radio f.
radioactive adj radioactivo.
radish n rabano m.
radius n radio f.
raffle n rifa f.
raft n balsa f.
rafter n par m; viga f.
rag n trapo m.
rage n rabia f.
raid n incursion f.
rail n baranda, barandilla f.
railroad, railway n ferrocarril m.
rain n lluvia f.

rainbow *n* arco iris *m.*
raise *vt* levantar, alzar.
raisin *n* pasa *f.*
rake *n* rastro *m.*
ram *n* carnero *m.*
ramble *vi* divagar.
ramification *n* ramificacion *f.*
ramp *n* rampa *f.*
rampant *adj* exuberante.
ramshackle *adj* en ruina.
ranch *n* hacienda *f.*
rancid *adj* rancio.
rancor *n* rencor *m.*
random *adj* fortuito, sin orden.
range *vt* colocar, ordenar.
ransack *vt* saquear.
ransom *n* rescate *m.*
rape *n* violacion *f.*
rapid *adj* rapido.
rapist *n* violador *m.*
rapture *n* rapto *m.*
rare *adj* raro.
rascal *n* picaro *m.*
rash *adj* precipitado *m;* erupción (cutánea) *f.*
raspberry *n* frambuesa *f.*
rat *n* rata *f.*
rate *n* tasa *f,* precio, valor *m.*
rather *adv* mas bien; antes.
ratification *n* ratificacion *f.*
ratify *vt* ratificar.
ratio *n* razon *f.*
ration *n* racion *f.*
rational *adj* racional.
ravage *vt* saquear.
rave *vi* delirar.
raven *n* cuervo *m.*
ravine *n* barranco *m.*
ravish *vt* encantar.
ravishing *adj* encantador.
raw *adj* crudo.
ray *n* rayo de luz *m;* raya *f* (pez).

raze *vt* arrasar.
razor *n* navaja.
reach *vt* alcanzar.
react *vi* reaccionar.
reaction *n* reaccion *f.*
read *vt* leer.
readable *adj* legible.
reader *n* lector *m.*
readjust *vt* reajustar.
ready *adj* listo, pronto.
real *adj* real.
realization *n* realizacion *f.*
realize *adv* darse cuenta de; realizar.
reality *n* realidad *f.*
realm *n* reino *m.*
ream *n* resma *f.*
reap *vt* segar.
reappear *vi* reaparecer.
rear *n* parte trasera *fr.*
rearmament *n* rearme *m.*
reason *n* razon *f;* causa *f:—vt, vi* razonar.
reassure *vt* tranquilizar, alentar; (*com*) asegurar.
rebel *n* rebelde *m/f.*
rebellion *n* rebelion *f.*
rebound *vi* rebotar.
rebuke *vt* reprender.
rebut *vi* repercutir.
recede *vi* retroceder.
receipt *n* recibo *m.*
receive *vt* recibir.
recent *adj* reciente.
reception *n* recepcion *f.*
recess *n* descanso *m.*
recession *n* retirada *f;* (*com*) recesion *f.*
recipe *n* receta *f.*
recipient *n* recipiente *m.*
recital *n* recital *m.*
recite *vt* recitar.
reckless *adj* temerario.

reckon *vt* contar.

recline *vt, vi* reclinar(se).

recluse *n* recluso/a *m/f.*

recognize *vt* reconocer.

recommend *vt* recomendar.

recommendation *n* recomendacion *f.*

recompense *n* recompensa *f.*

reconcile *vt* reconciliar.

reconsider *vt* considerar de nuevo.

record *vt* registrar; grabar.

recourse *n* recurso *m.*

recover *vt* recobrar; recuperar.

recovery *n* convalecencia *f;* recobro *m.*

recreation *n* recreacion *f;* recreo *m.*

recruit *vt* reclutar.

rectangle *n* rectangulo *m.*

rectify *vt* rectificar.

rectilinear *adj* rectilineo.

rector *n* rector *m.*

recur *vi* repetirse.

red *adj* rojo; tinto:—*n* rojo *m.*

redeem *vt* redimir.

redemption *n* redencion *f.*

redhot *adj* candente, ardiente.

redress *vt* corregir.

reduce *vt* reducir.

reduction *n* reduccion *f.*

reed *n* cana *f.*

reek *n* mal olor.

refectory *n* refectorio *m.*

refer *vt, vi* referir.

referee *n* arbitro *m.*

reference *n* referencia.

refine *vt* refinar.

refit *vt* reparar.

reflect *vt, vi* reflejar.

reflection *n* reflexion *f.*

reflex *adj* reflejo.

reform *vt, vi* reformar(se).

refresh *vt* refrescar.

refreshment *n* refresco.

refrigerator *n* nevera *f.*

refuge *n* refugio, asilo *m.*

refugee *n* refugiado *m/f.*

refund *vt* devolver.

refurbish *vt* restaurar.

refusal *n* negativa *f.*

refuse *vt* rehusar.

refute *vt* refutar.

regal *adj* real.

regard *vt* estimar.

regardless *adv* a pesar de todo.

regatta *n* regata *f.*

regime *n* regimen *m.*

region *n* region *f.*

register *n* registro *m.*

registrar *n* registrador *m.*

registration *n* registro *m.*

registry *n* registro *m.*

regular *adj* regular.

regulation *n* regulacion *f.*

reign *n* reinado, reino *m.*

reinforce *vt* reforzar.

reinstate *vt* reintegrar.

reject *vt* rechazar.

rejection *n* rechazo *m.*

rejoice *vt, vi* regocijar(se).

relapse *vi* recaer.

relate *vt, vi* relatar.

relation *n* relacion *f.*

relationship *n* parentesco *m;* relacion *f.*

relative *adj* relativo.

relax *vt, vi* relajar.

release *vt* soltar, libertar.

relic *n* reliquia *f.*

relief *n* relieve *m.*

relieve *vt* aliviar.

religion *n* religion *f.*

rely *vi* confiar en; contar con.

remain *vi* quedar.

remains *npl* restos *mpl.*

remark *n* observacion, nota *f.*

remedial *adv* curativo.
remedy *n* remedio *m*.
remember *vt* acordarse de; recordar.
remind *vt* recordar.
remit *vt, vi* remitir.
remorse *n* remordimiento *m*.
remote *adj* remoto.
remove *vt* quitar.
renew *vt* renovar.
renovate *vt* renovar.
rent *n* renta *f*.
rental *n* alquiler *m*.
repair *vt* reparar.
repeat *vt* repetir.
repel *vt* repeler.
repetition *n* repeticion *f*.
replace *vt* reemplazar.
reply *n* respuesta *f*.
repose *vt, vi* reposar.
represent *vt* representar.
reproduce *vt* reproducir.
reproduction *n* reproduccion *f*.
reptile *n* reptil *m*.
republic *n* republica *f*.
repugnance *n* repugnancia *f*.
repulse *vt* repulsar.
request *n* peticion.
require *vt* requerir.
rescue *vt* librar.
research *vt* investigar.
resemble *vt* asemejarse.
resent *vt* resentirse.
reserve *vt* reservar.
residence *n* residencia *f*.
resign *vt, vi* resignar.
resin *n* resina *f*.
resist *vt* resistir, oponerse.
resolve *vt, vr* resolver(se).
resort *vi* recurrir.
resource *n* recurso *m*.
respect *n* respecto *m*.
respite *n* suspension *f*.

respond *vt* responder.
rest *n* reposo *m*.
restless *adj* insomne.
restore *vt* restaurar.
restrict *vt* restringir.
result *vi* resultar.
resume *vt* resumir.
résumé *n* currículum *m*.
resurrection *n* resurreccion *f*.
resuscitate *vt* resucitar.
retail *vt* revender *f*.
retain *vt* retener.
reticence *n* reticencia *f*.
retina *n* retina *f*.
retire *vt, vi* retirar(se).
retreat *n* retirada *f*.
return *vt* retribuir; restituir; devolver.
reveal *vt* revelar.
revenge *vt* vengar:—*n* venganza *f*.
revenue *n* renta *f* .
revere *vt* reverenciar.
reverse *vt* trastrocar.
review *vt* rever.
revise *vt* rever; repasar.
revival *n* restauracion *f*.
revolt *vi* rebelarse.
revolution *n* revolucion *f*.
revolve *vt* revolver.
revue *n* revista *f*.
reward *n* recompensa *f*.
rheumatism *n* reumatismo *m*.
rhinoceros *n* rinoceronte *m*.
rhombus *n* rombo *m*.
rhubarb *n* ruibarbo *m*.
rhyme *n* rima *f*.
rhythm *n* ritmo *m*.
rib *n* costilla *f*.
ribbon *n* liston *m*.
rice *n* arroz *m*.
rich *adj* rico.
riches *npl* riqueza *f*.
rickets *n* raquitis *f*.

rid vt librar.

riddle n enigma m.

ride vi cabalgar.

ridge n espinazo.

ridiculous adj ridiculoso.

rifle n rifle m.

right adj derecho, recto; justo.—n derecho m; título m; privilegio m.

rigid adj rigido.

rigor n rigor m.

rind n corteza f.

rinse vt lavar, limpiar.

rise vi levantarse.

risk n riesgo, peligro m.

rite n rito m.

ritual adj, n ritual m.

rival adj emulo.

river n rio m.

road n camino m.

roadsign n senal de trafico f.

roar vi rugir.

roast vt asar.

rob vt robar.

robber n robador, ladron m.

robbery n robo m.

robust adj robusto.

rock n roca f.

rocket n cohete m.

rodent n roedor m.

rogue n bribon m.

roll vt rodar.

Roman Catholic adj, n catolico/a m/f (romano/a).

romance n romance m.

roof n tejado m.

room n habitacion, sala f.

roomy adj espacioso.

root n raiz f.

rope n cuerda f.

rosary n rosario m.

rose n rosa f.

rosebed n campo de rosales m.

rosebud n capullo de rosa m.

rosemary n (bot) romero m.

rosette n roseta f.

rot vi pudrirse.

rotten adj podrido.

rouble n rublo m.

rouge n arrebol m.

rough adj aspero.

roulette n ruleta f.

round adj redondo.

rouse vt despertar.

route n ruta f.

routine adj rutinario.

row n camorra f.

row n (line) hilera, fila f:—vt (mar) remar, bogar.

royal adj real.

royalty n realeza, dignidad real f.

rub vt estregar, fregar, frotar.

rubber n caucho m; goma f.

rubber-band n goma, gomita f.

rubric n rubrica f.

ruby n rubi m.

rudder n timon m.

rude adj rudo, brutal.

rudiment n rudimentos mpl.

rue vi compadecerse.

rug n alfombra f.

rugby n rugby m.

ruin n ruina f.

ruinous adj ruinoso.

rule n mando m; regla f.

ruler n gobernador m; regla f.

rum n ron m.

rumor n rumor m.

run vt dirigir; organizar, vi correr.

runaway n fugitivo.

rung n escalon.

runway n pista de aterrizaje f.

rupture n rotura f.

rural adj rural.

ruse n astucia f.

rush n junco m; rafaga f.
rusk n galleta f.
russet adj bermejo.
rust n herrumbre f.
rustic adj rustico.

rustle vi crujir.
rut n celo m.
ruthless adj cruel.
rye n (bot) centeno m.

S

Sabbath n sabado m.
sabotage n sabotaje m.
saccharin n sacarina f.
sachet n sobrecito m.
sack n saco m:—vt despedir.
sacrament n sacramento m.
sacred adj sagrado.
sacredness n santidad f.
sacrifice n sacrificio m.
sacrilege n sacrilegio m.
sad adj triste.
saddle n silla f.
sadness n tristeza f.
safari n safari m.
safe adj seguro; n caja fuerte f.
safety n seguridad f
saffron n azafran m.
sage n (bot) salvia f.
Sagittarius n Sagitario m (signo del zodiaco).
sago n (bot) zagu m.
sail n vela f.
sailor n marinero m.
saint n santo m; santa f.
sake n causa, razon f.
salad n ensalada f.
salamander n salamandra f.
salary n sueldo m.
sale n venta f.
sales clerk n dependiente m.
salient adj saliente.
saline adj salino.
saliva n saliva f.

salmon n salmon m.
salmon trout n trucha salmonada f.
saloon n bar m.
salt n sal f.
salubrious adj salubre.
salutation n salutacion f.
salute vt saludar.
same adj mismo, idéntico/a
sample n muestra f; ejemplo m.
sanctify vt santificar.
sanctuary n santuario m.
sand n arena f.
sandal n sandalia f.
sandstone n piedra arenisca f.
sandwich n bocadillo m.
sane adj sapo.
sanitarium n sanatorio m.
sanity n juicio sano m.
sap n savia f.
sapling n arbolito m.
sapphire n zafir m.
sarcasm n sarcasmo m.
sarcophagus n sarcofago.
sardine n sardina f.
Satan n Satanas m.
satchel n mochila f.
satellite n satelite m.
satin n raso m.
satire n satira f.
satisfaction n satisfaccion f.
satisfy vt satisfacer.
Saturday n sabado m.
satyr n satiro m.

sauce n salsa f.

saucepan n cazo m.

saucer n platillo m.

sausage n salchicha f.

savage adj salvaje

savagery n crueldad f.

savannah n sabana f.

save vt salvar.

saveloy n chorizo m.

Savior n Salvador m.

savory adj sabroso.

saw n sierra f.

saxophone n saxofono m.

say vt decir.

saying n dicho m.

scab n rona f.

scald vt escaldar.

scale n balanza f.

scalp n cabellera f.

scamp n bribon.

scampi npl gambas fpl.

scan vt escudrinar.

scandal n escandalo m.

scandalize vt escandalizar.

scar n cicatriz f.

scarce adj raro.

scare vt espantar.

scarf n bufanda f.

scarlet n escarlata f.

scarp n escarpa f.

scene n escena f.

scenery n vista f.

schedule n horario m.

scheme n proyecto, plan m.

schism n cisma m.

scholar n estudiante m

school n escuela f.

schoolteacher n maestro, tra m/f; profesor, ra m/f.

science n ciencia f.

scientist n cientifico, ca m/f.

scissors npl tijeras fpl.

scooter n moto f.

scorch vt quemar.

scorn vt, vi despreciar.

Scorpio n Escorpion m (signo del zodiaco).

scorpion n escorpion m.

Scotch n whisky escoces m.

scoundrel n picaro m.

scramble vi arrapar.

scrap n migaja f; sobras fpl.

scrape vt, vi raer, raspar.

scraper n rascador m.

scratch vt rascar.

scrawl vt, vi garrapatear.

scream, screech vi chillar.

screen n pantalla f.

screenplay n guion m.

screw n tornillo m.

screwdriver n destornillador m.

scribble vt escarabajear.

scribe n escritor m.

script n guion m; letra f.

Scripture n Escritura sagrada f.

scruffy adj desalinado.

scruple n escrupulo m.

scullery n fregadero m.

sculptor n escultor, ra m/f.

sculpture n escultura f.

scum n espuma f; escoria f.

scurvy n escorbuto m.

scythe n guadana f.

sea n mar m/f:—adj de mar.

sea breeze n viento de mar m.

seafood n mariscos mpl.

sea front n paseo maritimo m.

seagull n gaviota f.

sea horse n hipocampo m.

seal n sello m; foca f.

seam n costura f.

seaman n marinero m.

sea plane n hidroavion m.

sear vt cauterizar.

search vt examinar, buscar.
seashore n ribera f, litoral m.
seasick adj mareado.
season n estacion f.
seasoning n condimento m.
seat n asiento m; silla f.
seat belt n cinturon de seguridad m.
seaweed n alga marina f.
seclude vt apartar.
seclusion n separacion f.
second adj segundo.
secondary adj secundario.
secondhand n segunda mano f.
secret adj, n secreto m.
secretary n secretario, ria m/f.
sect n secta f.
section n seccion f.
sector n sector m.
secular adj secular.
secure adj seguro.
security n seguridad f.
sedate adj sosegado.
sedative n sedativo m.
sedge n (bot) junco m.
sediment n sedimento m
sedition n sedicion f.
seduce vt seducir.
seducer n seductor m.
seduction n seduccion f.
seductive adj seductivo.
see vt, vi ver
seed n semilla.
seedy adj desaseado.
seek vt, vi buscar.
seem vi parecer.
seemliness n decensia f.
seesaw n vaiven m.
seethe vi hervir.
segment n segmento m.
seize vt asir.
seizure n captura f.
seldom adv raramente.

select vt elegir.
selection n seleccion f.
self n uno mismo.
selfish adj egoista.
self-portrait n autorretrato m.
selfsame adj identico.
sell vt, vi vender.
semen n semen m.
semester n semestre m.
semicircle n semicirculo m.
semicircular adj semicircular.
semicolon n punto y coma m.
seminary n seminario m.
senate n senado m.
senator n senador, ra m/f.
send vt enviar.
sender n remitente m.
senile adj senil.
senior n mayor m.
senna n (bot) sena f.
sensation n sensacion f.
sense n sentido m.
sensibility n sensibilidad f.
sensible adj sensato/a, juicioso/a..
sensitive adj sensitivo.
sensual, sensuous adj sensual.
sensuality n sensualidad f.
sentence n oracion f; sentencia f.
sentiment n sentimiento m.
sentinel, sentry n centinela m.
separate vt (vi) separar(se).
separation n separacion f.
September n se(p)tiembre m.
sepulcher n sepulcro m.
sequel n continuacion f.
sequence n serie f.
seraph n serafin m.
serenade n serenata f.
serene adj seneno.
serenity n serenidad f.
serf n siervo m.
sergeant n sargento m.

serial *adj* consecutivo.
series *n* serie *f.*
serious *adj* serio, grave.
sermon *n* sermon *f.*
serious *adj* seroso.
serpent *n* serpiente *f.*
serpentine *adj* serpentino.
serrated *adj* serrado.
serum *n* suero *m.*
servant *n* criado *m;* criada *f.*
serve *vt, vi* servir.
service *n* servicio *m.*
servile *adj* servil.
session *n* junta *f;* sesion *f.*
set *vt* poner, colocar, fijar.
setter *n* perro de muestra *m.*
seven *adj, n* siete.
seventeen *adj, n* diez y siete, diecisiete.
seventeenth *adj, n* decimoseptimo.
seventh *adj, n* septimo.
seventieth *adj, n* septuagesimo.
seventy *adj, n* setenta.
sever *vt, vi* separar.
several *adj, pn* varios.
severance *n* separacion *f.*
severe *adj* severo.
severity *n* severidad *f.*
sew *vt, vi* coser.
sewer *n* albanal *m.*
sex *n* sexo *m.*
sexist *adj n* sexista *m/f.*
sexual *adj* sexual.
sexy *adj* sexy.
shade *n* sombra.
shadow *n* sombra *f.*
shaft *n* flecha, saeta *f.*
shake *vt* sacudir; agitar.
shallow *adj* somero.
sham *vt* enganar.
shame *n* verguenza *f.*
shamefaced *adj* vergonzoso.

shampoo champu *m.*
shamrock *n* trebol *m.*
shank *n* pierna *f.*
shanty *n* chabola *f.*
shantytown *n* barrio de chabolas *m.*
shape *vt, vi* formar; *n* forma *m.*
shapeless *adj* informe.
shapely *adj* bien hecho.
share *n* parte, porcion *f;* compartir.
shark *n* tiburon *m.*
sharp *adj* agudo.
shatter *vt* destrozar.
shave *vt* afeitar.
shaver *n* maquina de afeitar *f.*
shawl *n* chal *m.*
she *pn* ella.
sheaf *n* gavilla *f*
shear *vt* atusar.
sheath *n* vaina *f.*
shed *vt* verter; cabana *f.*
sheen *n* resplandor *m.*
sheep *n* oveja *f.*
sheer *adj* puro, claro.
sheet *n* sabana *f.*
sheet lightning *n* relampagueamiento
m.
shelf *n* anaquel *m.*
shell *n* cascara *f;* concha *f.*
shelter *n* guardia *f;* amparo *m.*
shepherd *n* pastor *m.*
sherbet *n* sorbete *m.*
sheriff *n* sherif *m.*
sherry *n* jerez *m.*
shield *n* escudo *m.*
shift *vi* cambiarse.
shinbone *n* espinilla *f.*
shine *vi* lucir, brillar.
shiny *adj* brillante.
ship *n* nave *f;* barco *m.*
shipwreck *n* naufragio *m.*
shirt *n* camisa *f.*
shit *excl (sl)* imierda!

shiver *vi* tiritar de frio.
shoal *n* banco *m*.
shock *n* choque *m*.
shock absorber *n* amortiguador *m*.
shoddy *adj* de pacotilla.
shoe *n* zapato *m*.
shoelace *n* correa de zapato *f*.
shoemaker *n* zapatero *m*.
shoot *vt* tirar.
shopper *n* comprador, ra *m/f*.
shopping *n* compras *fpl*.
shopping mall *n* centro comercial *m*.
shore *n* costa, ribera *f*.
short *adj* corto breve.
short-sighted *adj* corto de vista.
shot *n* tiro *m*.
shotgun *n* escopeta *f*.
shoulder *n* hombro *m*.
shout *vi* gritar, aclamar.
shove *vt, vi* empujar.
shovel *n* pala *f*.
show *vt* mostrar.
shower *n* nubada *f*; llovizna *f*; ducha *f*.
showy *adj* ostentoso.
shred *n* cacho, pedazo.
shrewd *adj* astuto.
shriek *vt, vi* chillar
shrimp *n* camaron *m*.
shrine *n* relicario *m*.
shrink *vi* encogerse.
shroud *n* cubierta *f*.
Shrove Tuesday *n* martes de carnaval *m*.
shrub *n* arbusto *m*.
shrug *vt* encogerse de hombros.
shun *vt* huir, evitar.
shut *vt* cerrar.
shutter *n* contraventana *f*.
shuttle *n* lanzadera *f*.
shuttlecock *n* volante *m*.
shy *adj* timido.

shyness *n* timidez *f*.
sick *adj* malo, enfermo.
sickle *n* hoz *f*.
sickness *n* enfermedad *f*.
side *n* lado *m*.
sideboard *n* aparador *m*; alacena *f*.
sidewalk *n* calzada *f*.
siege *n* (*mil*) sitio *m*.
sieve *n* tamiz *m*.
sift *vt* cerner.
sigh *vi* suspirar.
sight *n* vista *f*.
sightseeing *n* excursionismo, turismo *m*.
sign *n* senal *f*.
signal *n* senal *f*.
signature *n* firma *f*.
significance *n* importancia *f*.
signify *vt* significar.
signpost *n* indicador *m*.
silence *n* silencio *m*.
silk *n* seda *f*.
silky *adj* hecho de seda; sedeno.
sill *n* repisa *f*.
silly *adj* tonto.
silver *n* plata *f*.
similar *adj* similar; semejante.
similarity *n* semejanza *f*.
simile *n* simil *m*.
simmer *vi* hervir a fuego lento.
simple *adj* simple.
simplicity *n* sencillez *ff*.
simulate *vt* simular.
simulation *n* simulacion *f*.
sin *n* pecado *m*.
since *adv* desde.
sincerity *n* sinceridad *f*.
sinew *n* tendon *m*; nervio *m*.
sing *vi, vt* cantar.
singe *vt* chamuscar.
singer *n* cantor *m*; cantora *f*.

single *adj* solo; soltero, soltera.

singly *adv* separadamente.

singular *adj* singular.

sinister *adj* siniestro.

sink *vi* hundirse.

sinner *n* pecador *m*; pecadora *f.*

sinus *n* seno *m.*

sip *vt* sorber:—*n* sorbo *m.*

siphon *n* sifon *m.*

sir *n* senor *m.*

siren *n* sirena *f.*

sister *n* hermana *f.*

sister-in-law *n* cunada *f.*

sisterly *adj* con hermandad.

sit *vi* sentarse.

site *n* sitio *m*; situacion *f.*

sit-in *n* ocupacion *f.*

sitting room *n* sala de estar *f.*

situation *n* situacion *f.*

six *adj, n* seis.

sixteen *adj, n* diez y seis, dieciseis.

sixteenth *adj, n* decimosexto.

sixth *adj, n* sexto.

sixtieth *adj, n* sexagesimo.

sixty *adj, n* sesenta.

size *n* tamano *m.*

skate *n* patin *m*:—*vi* patinar.

skeleton *n* esqueleto *m.*

skeptic *n* esceptico.

skepticism *n* escepticismo *m.*

sketch *n* esbozo *m.*

ski *n* esqui *m*:—*vi* esquiar.

skid *n* patinazo *m.*

skill *n* destreza *f.*

skim *vt* espumar.

skin *n* piel *f*; cutis *m/f.*

skip *vi* saltar, brincar.

skirt *n* falda.

skittle *n* bolo *m.*

skulk *vi* escuchar, acechar.

skull *n* craneo *m.*

sky *n* cielo *m.*

skyscraper *n* rascacielos *m invar.*

slab *n* losa *f.*

slack *adj* flojo.

slag *n* escoria *f.*

slander *vt* calumniar *f.*

slang *n* argot *m f.*

slap *n* manotada *f.*

slate *n* pizarra *f.*

slave *n* esclavo *m.*

slaver *n* baba *f*:—*vi* babosear.

slay *vt* matar.

sled, sleigh *n* trineo *m.*

sleek *adj* liso.

sleep *vi* dormir.

sleeping bag *n* saco de dormir *m.*

sleeping pill *n* somnifero *m.*

sleepwalking *n* sonambulismo *m.*

sleet *n* aguanieve *f.*

sleeve *n* manga *f.*

slender *adj* delgado.

slice *n* rebanada *f.*

slide *vi* resbalar, deslizarse.

slight *adj* ligero.

slim *adj* delgado.

slime *n* lodo *m/f.*

slimy *adj* viscoso, pegajoso.

sling *n* honda *f*; cabestrillo *m.*

slingshot *n* catapulta *f.*

slip *vi* resbalar; escapar.

slipper *n* zapatilla *f.*

slogan *n* eslogan, lema *m.*

slope *n* cuesta *f.*

slow *adj* tardio, lento, torpe.

slum *n* tugurio *m.*

slump *n* depresion *f.*

slur *vt* ensuciar; calumniar.

slut *n* marrana *f.*

sly *adj* astuto.

smack *n* sabor, gusto *m*; chasquido de latigo *m.*

small *adj* pequeno.

smallpox *n* viruelas *fpl*.

smalltalk *n* charla, prosa *f*.

smart *adj* elegante; listo.

smash *vt* romper, quebrantar

smell *vt, vi* oler.

smile *vi* sonreirse:—*n* sonrisa *f*.

smoke *n* humo *m; fumar.

smoker *n* fumador, ra *m/f*.

smooth *adj* liso.

smug *adj* presumido.

smut *n* tiznon *m*.

snack *n* bocadom.

snag *n* problema *m*.

snail *n* caracol *m*.

snake *n* culebra *f*.

snap *vt, vi* romper.

snapdragon *n* (*bot*) antirrino *m*.

snatch *vt* arrebatar.

sneeze *vi* estornudar.

sniff *vt* oler:—*vi* resollar con fuerza.

snob *n* (e)snob *m/f*.

snore *vi* roncar.

snow *n* nieve *f*.

snowdrop *n* (*bot*) campanilla blanca *f*.

snowman *n* figura de nieve *f*.

snub *vt* reprender.

snuff *n* rape *m*.

so *adv* asi; de este modo; tan.

soap *n* jabon *m*.

soap opera *n* telenovela *f*.

soar *vi* remontarse.

sob *n* sollozo *m*:—*vi* sollozar.

soccer *n* balón *m; fútbol *m*.

soccer player *n* futbolista *m/f*.

sociable *adj* sociable.

social *adj* social.

socialism *n* socialismo *m*.

society *n* sociedad *f*.

sociologist *n* sociologo, ga *m/f*.

sociology *n* sociologia *f*.

sock *n* calcetin *m*.

sod *n* cesped *m*.

soda *n* sosa *f*.

sofa *n* sofa *m*.

soft *adj* blando.

soil *vt* ensuciar, tierra *f*.

solar *adj* solar.

soldier *n* soldado *m*.

sole *n* planta del pie *f*.

solemn *adj*, **~ly** *adv* solemne (mente).

solicitor *n* representante, agente *m/f*.

solid *adj* solido.

solitaire *n* solitario *m;* grueso diamante *m*.

solitude *n* soledad *f*.

solo *n* (*mus*) solo *m*.

solstice *n* solsticio *m*.

soluble *adj* soluble.

solution *n* solucion *f*.

solve *vt* resolver.

some *adj* algo de, un poco, algun, alguno, alguna, unos, pocos, ciertos.

somebody *n* alguien *m*.

something *n* alguna cosa, algo.

sometimes *adv* a veces.

somnambulism *n* somnambulismo *m*.

somnambulist *n* somnambulo *m*.

somnolence *n* somnolencia *f*.

son *n* hijo *m*.

sonata *n* (*mus*) sonata *f*.

song *n* cancion.

son-in-law *n* yerno *m*.

sonnet *n* soneto *m*.

soon *adv* pronto.

soot *n* hollin *m*.

soothe *vt* adular; calmar.

sop *n* sopa *f*.

sophisticate *vt* sofisticar.

sophisticated *adj* sofisticado.

sorcerer n hechicero m.
sorcery n hechizom.
sordid adj sordido.
sore n llaga, ulcera f.
sorrow n pesar m; tristeza f.
sorry adj triste.
soul n alma f.
sound adj sano; sonido,vi sonar.
soup n sopa f.
sour adj agrio.
souvenir n recuerdo m.
south n sur m.
sovereign adj, n soberano, na (m/f).
sovereignty n soberania f.
sow n puerca f.
sow vt sembrar.
space n espacio m.
spacious adj espacioso.
spade n laya.
spaghetti n espaguetis mpl.
span n palmo m.
spangle n lentejuela f.
spaniel n perro de aguas m.
Spanish adj espanol(a)
spar n palo m.
spark n chispa f.
sparkle n centella.
sparrow n gorrion m.
sparse adj delgado.
spasm n espasmo m.
spatula n espatula f.
spawn n freza f.
speak vt, vi hablar.
spear n lanza f.
special adj especial.
species n especie f.
specific adj especifico m.
specimen n muestra f.
spectacle n espectaculo m.
spectator n espectador, ra m/f.
specter n espectro m.
speculate vi especular.

speculation n especulacion f.
speed n prisa f; velocidad f.
spell n hechizom.
spelling n ortografia f.
spend vt gastar.
sperm n esperma f.
spew vi (sl) vomitar.
sphere n esfera f.
spherical adj esferico.
spice n especia f.
spicy adj aromatico.
spider n arana f.
spike n espigon m.
spill vt derramar.
spin vt hilar.
spinach n espinaca f.
spinal adj espinal.
spine n espinazo m.
spinster n soltera f.
spiral adj espiral.
spire n espira f.
spirit n aliento m; espiritu m.
spiritual adj, ~ly adv espiritual (mente).
spiritualist n espiritualista m.
spit n asador m; saliva f.
spite n rencor m.
splash vt salpicar.
spleen n bazo m.
splendid adj esplendido.
splendor n esplendor m.
splint n tablilla f.
splinter n cacho m.
split n hendedura f.
spoil vt despojar.
spoke n rayo de la rueda m.
spokesman n portavoz m.
sponge n esponja f.
sponsor n fiador m.
spontaneity n espontaneidad f.
spool n carrete m.
spoon n cuchara f.

spoonful n cucharada f.

sport n deporte m

spot n mancha f.

spouse n esposo m; esposa f.

sprain adj descoyuntar.

sprat n meleta, nuesa f (pez).

sprawl vi revolcarse.

spray n rociada f; espray m.

spread vt extender

spree n fiesta f; juerga f.

sprig n ramito m.

sprinkle vt rociar.

spur n espuela f.

spurn vt despreciar.

spy n espia m.

squad n escuadra f.

squadron n (mil) escuadron m.

squalid adj sucio.

squall n rafaga f.

squalor n porqueria f.

squander vt malgastar.

square adj cuadrado m; plaza f.

squash vt aplastar.

squaw n hembra de un indiano f.

squeak vi planir.

squeamish adj fastidioso.

squeeze vt apretar.

squid n calamar m.

squint adj bizco.

squirrel n ardilla f.

stable n establo m.

stack n pila f.

staff n personal m.

stag n ciervo m.

stage n etapa f; escena f.

stagnate vi estancarse.

stain vt manchar.

stair n escalon m.

staircase n escalera f.

stale adj anejo.

stalk, tronco m.

stall n pesebre m; tienda portatil f.

stallion n semental m.

stamina n resistencia f.

stammer vi tartamudear.

stamp estampar, imprimir; sello m.

stampede n estampida f.

stand vi estar de pie o derecho; stand m.

standard n estandarte m.

staple n grapa f.

star n estrella f.

starch n almidon m.

stark adj fuerte, aspero.

starling n estornino m.

start vi empezar.

startle vt sobresaltar.

starvation n hambre f.

state n estado m; condicion f.

statement n afirmacion f.

static adj estatico.

station n estacion f.

stationary adj estacionario, fijo.

stationery n papeleria f.

statistics npl estadistica f.

statuary n estatuario m.

statue n estatua f.

stature n estatura f.

statute n estatuto m.

stay n estancia f.

steak n filete m; bistec m.

steal vt, vi robar.

stealth n hurto m.

steam n vapor m.

steel n acero m.

steep adj escarpado.

steeple n torre f; campanario m.

steer n novillo m:—vt manejar, conducir.

steering wheel n volante m.

stem n vastago.

stench n hedor m.

stencil n cliche m.

stenographer n taquigrafo, fa m/f.

stenography n taquigrafia f.

step n paso, escalon m.

stepbrother n hermanastro m.

stepdaughter n hijastra f.

stepfather n padrastro m.

stepmother n madrastra f.

stepsister n hermanastra f.

stepson n hijastro m.

stereo n estereo m.

stereotype n estereotipo m.

sterile adj esteril.

sterling n libras esterlinas fpl.

stethoscope n (med) estetoscopio m.

stew vt estofar f.

steward n mayordomo m

stick n palo, pegarse.

stiff adj tieso.

stifle vt sufocar.

stigma n estigma m.

stigmatize vt infamar.

stiletto n estilete m

still tranquilo; adv todavia.

stillborn adj nacido muerto.

stilts npl zancos mpl.

stimulant n estimulante m.

stimulate vt estimular.

stimulus n estimulo m.

sting vt picar o morder (un insecto).

stingy adj mezquino.

stink vi heder.

stint n tarea f.

stipulate vt estipular.

stipulation n estipulacion f.

stir vt agitar.

stirrup n estribo m.

stitch vt coser.

stoat n comadreja f.

stock n ganado m; caldo m.

stockbroker n agente de bolsa m/f.

stock exchange n bolsa f.

stocking n media f.

stock market n bolsa f.

stoic n estoico m.

stoical adj estoico.

stole n estola f.

stomach n estomago m.

stone n piedra f.

stop vt detener, parar.

stopwatch n cronometro m.

store n provision f; almacen m.

stork n ciguena f.

storm n tempestad.

story n historia f.

stout adj robusto.

stove n estufa f.

straight adj derecho.

strain vt colar, filtrar; n tension f.

strainer n colador m.

strange adj raro/a, extranjero.

stranger n desconocido m; extranjero, ra m/f.

strangle vt ahogar.

strap n correa.

strapping adj abultado.

stratagem n estratagema f; astucia f.

strategic adj estrategico m.

strategy n estrategia f.

stratum n estrato m.

straw n paja m; pajita f.

strawberry n fresa f.

stray vi extraviarse.

streak n raya.

street n calle f.

streetcar n tranvia f.

strength n fuerza.

strenuous adj arduo.

stress n presion f; estres m.

stretch vt, vi extender.

stretcher n camilla f.

strew vt esparcir.

strict adj estricto.

stride n tranco m.

string n cordon m.

stringent adj astringente.

strip vt desnudar.

stripe n raya.

strive vi esforzarse.

stroll n paseo.

strong adj fuerte.

strongbox n cofre fuerte m.

structure n estructura f.

struggle vi esforzarse.

strum vt (mus) rasguear.

strut vi pavonearse.

stubborn adj obstinado.

stucco n estuco m.

stud n corchete m.

student n estudiante m/f.

studio n estudio de un artista m.

studious adj estudioso.

study n estudio m.

stuff n materia f.

stuffing n relleno m.

stumble vi tropezar.

stump n tronco m.

stun vt aturdir.

stunt n vuelo acrobático m; truco publicitario m.

stuntman n especialista m.

stupid adj estupido.

sturdy adj fuerte.

sturgeon n esturion m.

stutter vi tartamudear.

sty n zahurda f.

stye n orzuelo m.

style n estilo m.

stylish adj elegante.

suave adj afable.

subdivide vt subdividir.

subdue vt sojuzgar, sujetar.

subject adj sujeto.

subjunctive n subjuntivo m.

sublime adj sublime.

submarine adj submarino.

submerge vt sumergir.

submit vt, (vi) someter(se).

subordinate adj subordinado, inferior:—vt subordinar.

subscribe vt, vi suscribir.

subsequent adj, ~ly adv subsiguiente (mente).

subservient adj subordinado.

subside vi sumergirse.

subsidence n derrumbamiento m.

subsidiary adj subsidiario.

subsidize vt subvencionar.

subsidy n subvencion f.

substance n substancia f.

substitute vt sustituir.

substratum n lecho m.

subterranean adj subterraneo.

subtitle n subtitulo m.

subtle adj sutil.

suburb n suburbio m.

subversion n subversion f.

subway n metro m.

succeed vt, vi seguir; conseguir, lograr, tener exito.

success n exito m.

succumb vi sucumbir.

such adj tal.

suck vt, vi chupar.

sudden adj repentino, no previsto.

sue vt poner por justicia; suplicar.

suede n ante m.

suffer vt, vi sufrir, padecer.

sufficient adj suficiente.

suffocate vt sufocar.

suffrage n sufragio.

sugar n azucar m.

sugar cane n cana de azucar f.

suggest vt sugerir.

suggestion n sugestion f.

suicide n suicidio m.

suit n conjunto m; traje m.

suitcase n maleta f.

suitor n suplicante m.

sultan n sultan m.

sultana n sultana f.

sum n suma f.

summary adj, n sumario (m).

summer n verano m.

summit n apice m.

summon vt citar.

summons n citacion f.

sumptuous adj suntuoso.

sun n sol m.

sunbathe vi tomar el sol.

Sunday n domingo m.

sundial n reloj de sol m.

sundry adj varios.

sunflower n girasol m.

sunglasses npl gafas o antojos de sol mpl.

sunlight n luz del sol f.

sunrise n salida del sol f.

sunset n puesta del sol f.

sunshade n quitasol m.

sunstroke n insolacion f.

suntan n bronceado m.

suntan oil n aceite bronceador m.

superb adj magnifico.

superficial adj superficial.

superfluity n superfluidad f.

superior adj, n superior (m).

supermarket n supermercado m.

supernatural n sobrenatural.

superpower n superpotencia f.

superstition n supersticion f.

supertanker n superpetrolero m.

supervise vt inspeccionar.

supper n cena f.

supple adj flexible.

supplement n suplemento m.

supplementary adj adicional.

suppleness n flexibilidad f.

suppli(c)ant n suplicante m.

supplicate vt suplicar.

supplication n suplica, suplicacion f.

supplier n distribuidor, ra m/f.

supply vt suministrar; suplir, completar; surtir:—n provision f; suministro m.

support vt sostener; soportar, asistir:—n apoyo m.

supportable adj soportable.

supporter n partidario, ria; aficionado, da m/f.

suppose vt, vi suponer.

supposition n suposicion f.

suppress vt suprimir.

suppression n supresion f.

supremacy n supremacia f.

supreme adj supremo:—~ly adv supremamente.

surcharge vt sobrecargar:—n sobretasa f.

sure adj seguro, cierto; firme; estable:—**to be** ~ sin duda; ya se ve:—~ly adv ciertamente, seguramente, sin duda.

sureness n certeza, seguridad f.

surety n seguridad f; fiador m.

surf n (mar) resaca f.

surface n superficie f:—vt revestir:—vi salir a la superficie.

surfboard n plancha (de surf) f.

surfeit n exceso m.

surge n ola, onda f:—vi avanzar en tropel.

surgeon n cirujano, na m/f.

surgery n cirujia m.

surgical adj quirurgico.

surliness n mal humor m.

surly adj aspero de genio.

surmise vt sospechar:—n sospecha f.

surmount vt sobrepujar.

surmountable adj superable.

surname n apellido, sobrenombre m.

surpass vt sobresalir, sobrepujar, exceder, aventajar.

surpassing adj sobresaliente.

surplice *n* sobrepelliz *f.*

surplus *n* excedente *m;* sobrante *m:—adj* sobrante.

surprise *vt* sorprender:—*n* sorpresa *f.*

surprising *adj* sorprendente.

surrender *vt, vi* rendir; ceder; rendirse:—*n* rendicion *f.*

surreptitious *adj* subrepticio:—**~ly** *adv* subrepticiamente.

surrogate *vt* subrogar:—*n* subrogado *m.*

surrogate mother *n* madre portadora *f.*

surround *vt* circundar, cercar, rodear.

survey *vt* inspeccionar, examinar; apear:—*n* inspeccion *f;* apeo (de tierras) *m.*

survive *vi* sobrevivir:—*vt* sobrevivir a.

survivor *n* sobreviviente *m/f.*

susceptibility *n* susceptibilidad *f.*

susceptible *adj* susceptible.

suspect *vt, vi* sospechar:—*n* sospechoso, sa *m/f.*

suspend *vt* suspender.

suspense *n* suspense *m;* detencion *f;* incertidumbre *f.*

suspension *n* suspension *f.*

suspension bridge *n* puente colgante o colgado *m.*

suspicion *n* sospecha *f.*

suspicious *adj* suspicaz:—**~ly** *adv* sospechosamente.

suspiciousness *n* suspicacia *f.*

sustain *vt* sostener, sustentar, mantener; apoyar; sufrir.

sustenance *n* sostenimiento, sustento *m.*

suture *n* sutura, costura *f.*

swab *n* algodon *m;* frotis *m* invar.

swaddle *vt* fajar.

swaddling-clothes *npl* panales *mpl.*

swagger *vi* baladronear.

swallow *n* golondrina *f:—vt* tragar, engullir.

swamp *n* pantano *m.*

swampy *adj* pantanoso.

swan *n* cisne *m.*

swap *vt* canjear:—*n* intercambio *m.*

swarm *n* enjambre *m;* gentio *m;* hormiguero *m:—vi* enjam brar; hormiguear de gente; abundar.

swarthy *adj* atezado.

swarthiness *n* tez morena *f.*

swashbuckling *adj* fanfarron.

swath *n* tranco *m.*

swathe *vt* fajar:—*n* faja *f.*

sway *vt* mover:—*vi* ladearse, inclinarse:—*n* balanceo *m;* poder, imperio, influjo *m.*

swear *vt, vi* jurar; hacer jurar; juramentar.

sweat *n* sudor *m:—vi* sudar; trabajar con fatiga.

sweater, sweatshirt *n* sueter *m.*

sweep *vt, vi* barrer; arrebatar; deshollinar; pasar o tocar liger amente; oscilar:—*n* barredura *f;* vuelta *f;* giro *m.*

sweeping *adj* rapido:—**~s** *pl* barreduras *fpl.*

sweepstake *n* loteria *f.*

sweet *adj* dulce, grato, gustoso; suave; oloroso; melodioso; hermoso; amable:—*adv* dulcemente, suavemente.

sweetbread *n* mellejas de ternera *fpl.*

sweeten *vt* endulzar; suavizar; aplacar; perfumar.

sweetener *n* edulcorante *m.*

sweetheart *n* novio, via *m/f;* querida *f.*

sweetmeats *npl* dulces secos *mpl.*

sweetness *n* dulzura, suavidad *f.*

swell *vi* hincharse; ensoberbecerse; embravecerse:—*vt* hin char, inflar, agravar:—*n* marejada *f:*—*adj* (*fam*) estupendo, fenomenal.

swelling *n* hinchazon *f*; tumor *m*.

swelter *vi* ahogarse de calor.

swerve *vi* vagar; desviarse.

swift *adj* veloz, ligero, rapido:—*n* vencejo, *m*.

swiftly *adv* velozmente.

swiftness *n* velocidad, rapidez *f*.

swill *vt* beber con exceso:—*n* bazofia *f*.

swim *vi* nadar; abundar en:—*vt* pasar a nado:—*n* nadada *f*.

swimming *n* natacion *f*; vertigo *m*.

swimming pool *n* piscina *f*.

swimsuit *n* traje de bano *m*.

swindle *vt* estafar.

swindler *n* trampista *m*.

swine *n* puerco, cochino *m*.

swing *vi* balancear, columpiarse; vibrar; agitarse:—*vt* colum piar; balancear; girar:—*n* vibracion *f*; balanceo *m*.

swinging *adj* (*fam*) alegre.

swinging door *n* puerta giratoria *f*.

swirl *n* hacer remolinos (en el agua).

switch *n* varilla *f*; interruptor *m*; (*rail*) aguja *f:*—*vt* cambiar de:—**to ~ off** apagar; parar:—**to ~ on** encender, prender.

switchboard *n* centralita (de teléfonos) *f*.

swivel *vt* girar.

swoon *vi* desmayarse:—*n* desmayo, deliquio, pasmo *m*.

swoop *vi* calarse:—*n* calada; redada *f:*—**in one ~** de un golpe.

sword *n* espada *f*.

swordfish *n* pez espada *f*.

swordsman *n* guerrero *m*.

sycamore *n* sicomoro *m* (arbol).

sycophant *n* sicofante *m*.

syllabic *adj* silabico.

syllable *n* silaba *f*.

syllabus *n* programa de estudios *m*.

syllogism *n* silogismo *m*.

sylph *n* silfio *m*; silfida *f*.

symbol *n* simbolo *m*.

symbolic(al) *adj* simbolico.

symbolize *vt* simbolizar.

symmetrical *adj* simetrico:—**~ly** *adv* con simetria.

symmetry *n* simetria *f*.

sympathetic *adj* simpatico:—**~ally** *adv* simpaticamente.

sympathize *vi* compadecerse.

sympathy *n* simpatia *f*.

symphony *n* sinfonia *f*.

symposium *n* simposio *m*.

symptom *n* sintoma *m*.

synagogue *n* sinagoga *f*.

synchronism *n* sincronismo *m*.

syndicate *n* sindicato *m*.

syndrome *n* sindrome *m*.

synod *n* sinodo *m*.

synonym *n* sinonimo *m*.

synonymous *adj* sinonimo:—**~ly** *adv* con sinonimia.

synopsis *n* sinopsis *f*; sumario *m*.

synoptical *adj* sinoptico.

syntax *n* sintaxis *f*.

synthesis *n* sintesis *f*.

syringe *n* jeringa, lavativa *f:*—*vt* jeringar.

system *n* sistema *m*.

systematic *adj* sistematico:—**~ally** *adv* sistematicamente.

systems analyst *n* analista de sistemas *m/f*.

table 240 teddy

T

table *n* mesa *f* m.
tablecloth *n* mantel *m.*
tablespoon *n* cuchara para comer *f.*
tablet *n* tableta *f* m.
table tennis *n* ping-pong *m.*
taboo *adj* tabu.
tacit *adj* tacito.
taciturn *adj* taciturno.
tack *n* tachuela *f.*
tact *n* tacto *m.*
tactician *n* tactico *m.*
tactics *npl* tactica *f.*
tadpole *n* ranilla *f.*
taffeta *n* tafetan *m.*
tag *n* herrete *m.*
tail *n* cola *f.*
tailor *n* sastre *m.*
tailor-made *adj* hecho a la medida.
taint *vt* tachar.
take *vt* tomar, coger.
takeoff *n* despegue *m.*
takings *npl* ingresos *mpl.*
talc *n* talco *m.*
talent *n* talento *m.*
talisman *n* talisman *m.*
talk *vi* hablar.
talkative *adj* locuaz.
tall *adj* alto.
talon *n* garra de ave de rapina *f.*
tambourine *n* pandereta *f.*
tame *adj* amansado.
tamper *vi* tocar.
tampon *n* tampon *m.*
tan *vt* broncear.
tang *n* sabor fuerte *m.*
tangerine *n* mandarina *f.*
tangle *vt* enredar.
tank *n* cisterna *f*; aljibe *m.*
tanned *adj* bronceado.

tantrum *n* rabieta *f.*
tape *n* cinta *f.*
tape measure *n* metro *m.*
tapestry *n* tapiz *mf.*
tar *n* brea *f.*
target *n* blanco *m* (para tirar).
tariff *n* tarifa *f.*
tarmac *n* pista *f.*
tarnish *vt* deslustrar.
tarpaulin *n* alquitranado *m.*
tarragon *n* (*bot*) estragon *m.*
tartan *n* tela escocesa *f.*
tartar *n* tartaro *m.*
task *n* tarea *f.*
tassel *n* borlita *f.*
taste *n* gusto *m*; sabor *m.*
tasty *adj* sabroso.
tattoo *n* tatuaje *m.*
taunt *vt* mofar.
Taurus *n* Tauro *m.*
tax *n* impuesto *m.*
taxi *n* taxi *m.*
tea *n* te *m.*
teach *vt* ensenar.
teacher *n* profesor, ra *m/f.*
teak *n* teca *f* (arbol).
team *n* equipo *m.*
teamster *n* camionero *m.*
teapot *n* tetera *f.*
tear *vt* despedazar, rasgar.
tear *n* lagrima *f.*
tease *vt* tomar el pelo.
teaspoon *n* cucharita *f.*
teat *n* ubre, teta *f.*
technical *adj* tecnico.
technician *n* tecnico *m.*
technique *n* tecnica *f.*
technology *n* tecnologia *f.*
teddy (bear) *n* osito de felpa *m.*

tedious *adj* tedioso.

tedium *n* tedio *m*.

tee-shirt *n* camiseta *f*.

teeth *npl*·de tooth.

telegraph *n* telegrafo *m*.

telegraphic *adj* telegrafico.

telepathy *n* telepatia *f*.

telephone *n* telefono *m*.

telescope *n* telescopio *m*.

telescopic *adj* telescopico.

television *n* television *f*.

tell *vi* decir.

teller *n* cajero *m*.

temper *vt* templar:—*n* mal genio *m*.

temperament *n* temperamento *m*.

temperate *adj* templado.

temperature *n* temperatura *f*.

template *n* plantilla *f*.

temple *n* templo *m*.

temporary *adj* temporal.

tempt *vt* tentar.

temptation *n* tentacion *f*.

ten *adj, n* diez.

tenacity *n* tenacidad *f*.

tenancy *n* tenencia *f*.

tenant *n* arrendador *m*.

tend *vt* guardar.

tendency *n* tendencia *f*.

tender *adj* tierno, estimar.

tendon *n* tendon *m*.

tennis *n* tenis *m*.

tense *adj* tieso, tenso.

tension *n* tension *f*.

tent *n* tienda de campana *f*.

tentacle *n* tentaculo *m*.

tenth *adj, n* decimo.

tenure *n* tenencia *f*.

tepid *adj* tibio.

term *n* termino *m*.

terminal *adj* mortal.

termination *n* terminacion *f*.

terminus *n* terminal *f*.

terrace *n* terraza *f*.

terrain *n* terreno *m*.

terrestrial *adj* terrestre.

terrible *adj* terrible.

terrier *n* terrier *m*.

terrific *adj* fantastico.

terrify *vt* aterrar.

territorial *adj* territorial.

territory *n* territorio, distrito *m*.

terror *n* terror *m*.

terrorism *n* terrorismo *m*.

test *n* examen *m*.

testament *n* testamento *m*.

testicles *npl* testiculos *mpl*.

testify *vt* testificar.

testimony *n* testimonio *m*.

tetanus *n* tetano *m*.

tether *vt* atar.

text *n* texto *m*.

textiles *npl* textiles *mpl*.

texture *n* textura *f*.

than *adv* que, de.

thank *vt* agradecer.

thanks *npl* gracias *fpl*.

that *pn* aquel, aquello, aquella; que; este.

thaw *n* deshielo *m*.

the *art* el, la, lo; los, las.

theater *n* teatro *m*.

theft *n* robo *m*.

their *pn* su, suyo, suya; de ellos, de ellas:—~**s** el suyo, la suya, los suyos, las suyas; de ellos, de ellas.

them *pn* los, las, les; ellos, ellas.

theme *n* tema *m*.

themselves *pn pl* ellos mismos, ellas mismas; si mismos; se.

then *adv* entonces, despues.

theology *n* teologia *f*.

theory *n* teoria *f*.

therapist *n* terapeuta *m*.
therapy *n* terapia *f*.
there *adv* alli, alla.
thermal *adj* termal.
thermometer *n* termometro *m*.
thesaurus *n* tesoro *m*.
these *pn pl* estos, estas.
thesis *n* tesis *f*.
they *pn pl* ellos, ellas.
thick *adj* espeso.
thicken *vi* espesar.
thief *n* ladron *m*.
thigh *n* muslo *m*.
thimble *n* dedal *m*.
thin *adj* delgado.
thing *n* cosa *f*.
think *vi* pensar.
third *adj* tercero.
thirst *n* sed *f*.
thirteen *adj, n* trece.
thirteenth *adj, n* decimotercio.
thirtieth *adj, n* trigesimo.
thirty *adj, n* treinta.
this *adj* este, esta, esto:—*pn* este, esta, esto.
thorn *n* espino *m;* espina *f*.
those *pn pl* esos, esas; aquellos, aquellas:—*adj* esos, esas; aquellos, aquellas.
thought *n* pensamiento *m*.
thousand *adj, n* mil.
thousandth *adj, n* milesimo.
thrash *vt* golpear.
thread *n* hilo *m*.
threat *n* amenaza *f*.
threaten *vt* amenazar.
three *adj, n* tres.
threshold *n* umbral *m*.
thrifty *adj* economico.
thrill *vt* emocionar.
thrive *vi* prosperar.
throat *n* garganta *f*.

throb *vi* palpitar.
throne *n* trono *m*.
through *prep* por; durante; mediante.
throw *vt* echar.
thrush *n* tordo *m* (ave).
thrust *vt* empujar.
thug *n* gamberro *m*.
thumb *n* pulgar *m*.
thump *n* golpe *m*.
thunder *n* trueno *m*.
Thursday *n* jueves *m*.
thus *adv* asi, de este modo.
thyme *n* (*bot*) tomillo *m*.
thyroid *n* tiroides *m*.
tiara *n* tiara *f*.
tic *n* tic *m*.
ticket *n* billete *m* .
tickle *vt* hacer cosquillas.
tidal *adj* (*mar*) de marea.
tide *n* marea *f*.
tidy *adj* ordenado.
tie *vt* anudar, atar
tiger *n* tigre *m*.
tight *adj* tirante, apretado/a.
tile *n* azulejo *m*.
till *n* caja *f*:—*vt* cultivar.
time *n* tiempo; epoca *f*.
timer *n* interruptor *m*.
timid *adj* timido.
timidity *n* timidez *f*.
tin *n* estano *m*.
tinfoil *n* papel de estano *m*.
tinsel *n* oropel *m*.
tint *n* tinte *m*.
tiny *adj* pequeno, chico.
tip *n* punta, extremidad *f;* propina *f*.
tire *vt* cansar, fatigar:—*n* neumático *m*.
tissue *n* tejido *m*.
title *n* titulo *m*.
titular *adj* titular.

to *prep* a; para; por; de; hasta; en; con; que.

toad *n* sapo *m*.

toadstool *n* (*bot*) hongovejin *m*.

toast *vt* tostar; brindar.

toaster *n* tostadora *f*.

tobacco *n* tabaco *m*.

tobacco shop *n* tabaqueria *f*.

today *adv* hoy.

toe *n* dedo del pie *m*.

together *adv* juntamente.

toilet paper *n* papel higienico *m*.

token *n* senal *f*.

tolerate *vt* tolerar.

tomato *n* tomate *m*.

tomb *n* tumba *f*.

tomboy *n* muchachota *f*.

tombstone *n* piedra sepulcral *f*.

tomcat *n* gato *m*.

tomorrow *adv, n* manana *f*.

ton *n* tonelada *f*.

tongs *npl* tenacillas *fpl*.

tongue *n* lengua *f*.

tonic *n* (*med*) tonico.

tonight *adv, n* esta tarde (*f*).

tonsil *n* amigdala *f*.

too *adv* demasiado; tambien.

tool *n* herramienta *f*.

tooth *n* diente *m*.

toothache *n* dolor de muelas *m*.

top *n* cima.

topaz *n* topacio *m*.

topic *n* tema *m*.

topless *adj* topless.

topographic(al) *adj* topografico.

topography *n* topografia *f*.

torment *vt* atormentar.

tornado *n* tornado *m*.

torrent *n* torrente *m*.

torrid *adj* apasionado.

tortoise *n* tortuga *f*.

tortoiseshell *adj* de carey.

tortuous *adj* tortuoso.

torture *n* tortura *f*.

toss *vt* tirar, lanzar.

total *adj* total.

totalitarian *adj* totalitario.

totality *n* totalidad *f*.

totter *vi* vacilar.

touch *vt* tocar.

touchdown *n* aterrizaje *m*.

touching *adj* patetico, conmovedor.

tough *adj* duro.

toupee *n* tupe *m*.

tour *n* viaje *m*.

touring *n* viajes turisticos *mpl*.

tourism *n* turismo *m*.

tourist *n* turista *m/f*.

tourist office *n* oficina de turismo *f*.

tournament *n* torneo *m*.

tow *n* remolque *m*.

toward(s) *prep, adv* hacia.

towel *n* toalla *f*.

tower *n* torre *m*.

town *n* ciudad *f*.

town hall *n* ayuntamiento *m*.

toy *n* juguete *m*.

toy store *n* jugueteria *f*.

trace *n* huella *f*:—*vt* trazar.

trade *n* comercio *m*; ocupacion *f*.

trade(s) union *n* sindicato *m*.

tradition *n* tradicion *f*.

traditional *adj* tradicional.

traffic *n* trafico *m*.

traffic lights *npl* semaforo *m*.

tragedy *n* tragedia *f*.

tragic *adj* tragico.

trail *vt, vi* rastrear:—*n* senda *f*.

trailer *n* caravana *f*.

train *vt* entrenar * *n* tren *m*.

trainee *n* aprendiz *m*.

trainer *n* entrenador *m*.

trait *n* rasgo *m*.

traitor *n* traidor *m*.

tramp *n* vagabundo *m*.
trample *vt* pisotear.
trampoline *n* trampolin *m*.
trance *n* rapto *m*.
tranquil *adj* tranquilo.
tranquillizer *n* tranquilizante *m*.
transact *vt* negociar.
transaction *n* transaccion *f*.
transatlantic *adj* transatlántico.
transcription *n* traslado *m*.
transfer *vt* transferir.
transform *vt* transformar.
transformation *n* transformacion *f*.
transfusion *n* transfusion *f*.
transit *n* transito *m*.
transition *n* transito *m*; transicion *f*.
translate *vt* traducir.
translation *n* traduccion *f*.
translator *n* traductor, ra *m/f*.
transmit *vt* transmitir.
transparent *adj* transparente.
transpire *vi* resultar.
transplant *vt* trasplantar.
transport *vt* transportar.
trap *n* trampa *f*.
trapeze *n* trapecio *m*.
trappings *npl* adornos *mpl*.
trash *n* pacotilla *f*; basura *f*.
travel *vi* viajar.
trawler *n* pesquero de arrastre *m*.
tray *n* bandeja *f*
treachery *n* traicion *f*.
tread *vi* pisar.
treason *n* traicion *n*.
treasure *n* tesoro *m*.
treasurer *n* tesorero *m*.
treat *vt* tratar.
treatise *n* tratado *m*.
treatment *n* trato *m*.
treaty *n* tratado *m*.
treble *adj* triple.

treble clef *n* clave de sol *f*.
tree *n* arbol *m*.
trellis *n* enrejado *m*.
tremble *vi* temblar.
tremendous *adj* tremendo.
tremor *n* temblor *m*.
trench *n* foso *m*.
trend *n* tendencia *f*.
trendy *adj* de moda.
trespass *vt* transpasar.
tress *n* trenza *f*.
trestle *n* caballete de serrador *m*.
trial *n* proceso *m*.
triangle *n* triangulo *m*.
triangular *adj* triangular.
tribal *adj* tribal.
tribe *n* tribu *f*.
tribunal *n* tribunal *m*.
tributary *adj, n* tributario *m*.
tribute *n* tributo *m*.
trice *n* momento, tris *m*.
trick *n* engano.
trickle *vi* gotear.
tricky *adj* dificil.
tricycle *n* triciclo *m*.
trifle *n* bagatela.
trigger *n* gatillo *m*.
trigonometry *n* trigonometria *f*.
trim *adj* aseado.
Trinity *n* Trinidad *f*.
trinket *n* joya.
trio *n* (*mus*) trio *m*.
trip *vt* hacer caer; viaje corto *m*.
tripe *n* callos *mpl*.
triple *adj* triple.
triplets *npl* trillizos *mpl*.
triplicate *n* triplicado *m*.
tripod *n* tripode *m*.
triumph *n* triunfo *m*.
triumphal *adj* triunfal.
triumphant *adj* triunfante.

trivia *npl* trivialidades *fpl.*
trivial *adj* trivial.
trolley *n* carrito *m.*
trombone *n* trombon *m.*
trophy *n* trofeo *m.*
tropical *adj* tropico.
trot *n* trote *m.*
trouble *vt* afligir.
trough *n* abrevadero *m.*
trout *n* trucha *f.*
trowel *n* paleta *f.*
truce *n* tregua *f.*
truck *n* camion *m*
true *adj* verdadero.
truffle *n* trufa *f.*
truly *adv* en verdad.
trumpet *n* trompeta *f.*
trunk *n* baul, cofre *m*; trompa *f.*
trust *n* confianza *f.*
truth *n* verdad *f.*
try *vt* examinar, tentar.
tub *n* balde, cubo *m.*
tuba *n* tuba *f.*
tube *n* tubo *m.*
tuberculosis *n* tuberculosis *f.*
Tuesday *n* martes *m.*
tuition *n* enseñanza. *f.*
tulip *n* tulipan *m.*
tumble *vi* caer.
tumbler *n* vaso *m.*
tummy *n* barriga *f.*
tumor *n* tumor *m.*
tumultuous *adj* tumultuoso.
tuna *n* atun *m.*
tune *n* tono *m.*
tunic *n* tunica *f.*
tunnel *n* tunel *m.*
turban *n* turbante *m.*
turbine *n* turbina *f.*
turbulence *n* turbulencia *f.*
tureen *n* sopera *f.*

turf *n* cesped *m.*
turgid *adj* pesado.
turkey *n* pavo *m.*
turmoil *n* disturbio *m.*
turn *vi* volver.
turncoat *n* desertor *m.*
turnip *n* nabo *m.*
turnover *n* facturacion *f.*
turnstile *n* torniquete *m.*
turpentine *n* trementina *f.*
turquoise *n* turquesa *f.*
turret *n* torrecilla *f.*
turtle *n* galapago *m.*
turtledove *n* tortola *f.*
tusk *n* colmillo *m.*
tussle *n* pelea *f.*
tutor *n* tutor *m.*
tuxedo *n* smoking *m.*
twang *n* gangueo *m.*
tweezers *npl* tenacillas *fpl.*
twelfth *adj, n* duodecimo.
twelve *adj, n* doce.
twentieth *adj, n* vigesimo.
twenty *adj, n* veinte.
twice *adv* dos veces.
twig *n* ramita *f:—vi* caer en la cuenta.
twilight *n* crepusculo *m.*
twin *n* gemelo *m.*
twist *vt* torcer.
twit *n* (*col*) tonto *m.*
twitch *vi* moverse nerviosamente.
two *adj, n* dos.
two-faced *adj* falso.
tycoon *n* magnate *m.*
type *n* tipo *m*; letra *f*; modelo *m:—vt*
escribir a maquina.
typewriter *n* maquina de escribir *f.*
typical *adj* tipico.
tyrannical *adj* tiranico.
tyranny *n* tirania *f.*
tyrant *n* tirano *m.*

U

ubiquitous *adj* ubicuo.

udder *n* ubre *f*.

ugh *excl* ¡uf!

ugliness *n* fealdad *f*.

ugly *adj* feo; peligroso.

ulcer *n* ulcera *f*.

ulterior *adj* ulterior.

ultimate *adj* ultimo.

ultimatum *n* ultimatum *m*.

umbrella *n* paraguas *m invar*.

umpire *n* arbitro *m*.

unable *adj* incapaz.

unaccompanied *adj* solo.

unaccustomed *adj* desacostumbrado.

unanimity *n* unanimidad *f*.

unanimous *adj* unanime.

unanswerable *adj* incontrovertible.

unapproachable *adj* inaccesible.

unbearable *adj* intolerable.

unbecoming *adj* indecente.

unbutton *vt* desabotonar.

uncanny *adj* extraordinario.

unchanged *adj* no alterado.

uncharitable *adj* nada caritativo.

uncle *n* tio.

uncomfortable *adj* incomodo.

uncommon *adj* raro.

uncompromising *adj* irreconciliable.

unconscious *adj* inconsciente.

unconventional *adj* poco convencional.

uncork *vt* destapar.

uncouth *adj* grosero.

uncover *vt* descubrir.

undaunted *adj* intrepido.

under *prep* debajo de.

under-age *adj* menor de edad.

underclothing *n* ropa intima *f*.

underdeveloped *adj* subdesarrollado.

underdog *n* desvalido *m*.

underestimate *vt* subestimar.

undergo *vt* sufrir.

undergraduate *n* estudiante *m*.

underground *n* movimiento clandestino *m*.

underline *vt* subrayar.

underpaid *adj* mal pagado.

undershirt *n* camiseta *f*.

understand *vt* entender, comprender.

understatement *n* subestimacion *f*.

underwear *n* ropa intima *f*.

underworld *n* hampa *f*.

undetermined *adj* indeterminado, indeciso.

undigested *adj* indigesto.

undisciplined *adj* indisciplinado.

undismayed *adj* intrepido.

undisputed *adj* incontestable.

undisturbed *adj* quieto, tranquilo.

undivided *adj* indiviso, entero.

undo *vt* deshacer, destar.

undoubted *adj* indudable.

undress *vi* desnudarse.

undue *adj* indebido.

undulating *adj* ondulante.

unduly *adv* indebidamente.

undying *adj* inmortal.

unearth *vt* desenterrar.

uneasy *adj* inquieto.

uneducated *adj* ignorante.

unemployed *adj* parado.

unemployment *n* paro *m*.

unenlightened *adj* no iluminado.

unenviable *adj* poco envidiable.

unequal *adj* desigual.

unequaled *adj* incomparable.

uneven *adj* desigual.

unexpected *adj* inesperado.

unexplored *adj* inexplorado.

unfair *adj* injusto.

unfaithful adj infiel.
unfamiliar adj desacostumbrado.
unfashionable adj pasado de moda.
unfasten vt desatar.
unfavorable adj desfavorable.
unfeeling adj insensible.
unfit adj indispuesto.
unfold vt desplegar.
unforeseen adj imprevisto.
unforgettable adj inolvidable.
unforgivable adj imperdonable.
unforgiving adj implacable.
unfortunate adj desafortunado.
unfounded adj sin fundamento.
unfriendly adj antipatico.
unfruitful adj esteril; infructuoso.
unfurnished adj sin muebles.
ungrateful adj ingrato.
unhappily adv infelizmente.
unhappy adj infeliz.
unhealthy adj malsano.
unhook vt desenganchar; descolgar; desabrochar.
unhoped(-for) adj inesperado.
unhurt adj ileso.
unicorn n unicornio m.
uniform adj uniforme:—n uniforme m.
uniformity adj uniformidad f.
unify vt unificar.
unimaginable adj inimaginable.
unimportant adj nada importante.
uninformed adj ignorante.
uninhabitable adj inhabitable.
uninhabited adj inhabitado, desierto.
uninjured adj ileso, no danado.
unintelligible adj ininteligible.
unintentional adj involuntario.
uninterested adj desinteresado.
uninteresting adj poco interesante.
uninvited adj no convivado.
union n union f; sindicato m.

unionist n unitario m.
unique adj unico, uno, singular.
unit n unidad f.
unite vt vi unir(se), juntarse.
United States (of America) npl Estados Unidos (de América) mpl.
unity n unidad f.
universal adj universal.
universe n universo m.
university n universidad f.
unjust adj injusto.
unkind adj poco amable.
unknown adj incognito.
unlawful adj ilícito/a.
unless conj a menos que, si no.
unload vt descargar.
unluckily adv desafortunadamente.
unlucky adj desafortunado.
unmarried adj soltero; soltera.
unmerited adj desmerecido.
unmistakable adj evidente.
unmoved adj inmoto, firme.
unnatural adj antinatural.
unnecessary adj inutil, innecesario.
unnoticed adj no observado.
unobserved adj invertido/a.
unobtainable adj inconseguible.
unobtrusive adj modesto.
unoccupied adj desocupado.
unofficial adj no oficial.
unpack vt desempacar; desenvolver.
unpaid adj no pagado.
unpleasant adj desagradable.
unpopular adj no popular.
unpracticed adj inexperto.
unprecedented adj sin ejemplo.
unpredictable adj imprevisible.
unprepared adj no preparado.
unprofitable adj inútil, vano; poco lucrativo.
unpunished adj impune.
unqualified adj sin titulos; total.

unquestionable *adj* indubitable.

unravel *vt* desenredar.

unrealistic *adj* poco realista.

unreasonable *adv* irracionalmente.

unrelated *adj* sin relacion; inconexo.

unrelenting *adj* incompasivo, inflexible.

unreliable *adj* poco fiable.

unrestrained *adj* desenfrenado; ilimitado.

unripe *adj* inmaduro.

unrivaled *adj* sin rival.

unroll *vt* desenrollar.

unsafe *adj* inseguro.

unsatisfactory *adj* insatisfactorio.

unscrew *vt* destornillar.

unscrupulous *adj* sin escrupulos.

unseemly *adj* indecente.

unseen *adj* invisible.

unselfish *adj* desinteresado.

unsettle *vt* perturbar.

unshaken *adj* firme, estable.

unskilled *adj* inhabil.

unsociable *adj* insociable.

unspeakable *adj* inefable.

unstable *adj* instable, inconstante.

unsteady *adj* inestable.

unsuccessful *adj* infeliz, desafortunado.

unsuitable *adj* inapropiado; inoportuno.

unsure *adj* inseguro.

unsympathetic *adj* inompasivo.

untapped *adj* sin explotar.

untenable *adj* insostenible.

unthinkable *adj* inconcebible.

unthinking *adj* desatento, irreflexivo.

untidiness *n* desalino *m*.

untidy *adj* desordenado; sucio.

untie *vt* desatar, deshacer, soltar.

until *prep* hasta:—*conj* hasta que.

untimely *adj* intempestivo.

untiring *adj* incansable.

untold *adj* nunca dicho; indecible; incalculable.

untouched *adj* intacto.

untoward *adj* impropio; adverso.

untried *adj* no ensayado o probado.

untroubled *adj* no perturbado, tranquilo.

untrue *adj* falso.

untrustworthy *adj* indigno de confianza.

untruth *n* falsedad, mentira *f*.

unused *adj* isin usar, no usado.

unusual *adj* inusitado, raro:—**~ly** *adv* inusitadamente, raramente.

unveil *vt* quitar el velo, descubrir.

unwavering *adj* inquebrantable.

unwelcome *adj* desagradable, inoportuno.

unwell *adj* enfermizo, malo.

unwieldy *adj* pesado.

unwilling *adj* desinclinado:—**~ly** *adv* de mala gana.

unwillingness *n* mala gana, repugnancia *f*.

unwind *vt* desenredar, desenmaranar:—*vi* relajarse.

unwise *adj* imprudente.

unwitting *adj* inconsciente.

unworkable *adj* poco practico.

unworthy *adj* indigno.

unwrap *vt* desenvolver.

unwritten *adj* no escrito.

up *adv* arriba, en lo alto; levantado:—*prep* hacia; hasta.

upbringing *n* educacion *f*.

update *vt* poner al dia.

upheaval *n* agitacion *f*.

uphill *adj* dificil, penoso:—*adv* cuesta arriba.

uphold *vt* sos tener, apoyar.

upholstery *n* tapiceria *f*.

upkeep *n* manteniniento *m*.
uplift *vt* levantar.
upon *prep* sobre, encima.
upper *adj* superior; mas elevado.
upper-class *adj* de la clase alta.
upper-hand *n* (fig) superioridad *f*.
uppermost *adj* mas alto, supremo:—
  to be ~ predominar.
upright *adj* derecho, perpendicular,
  recto; puesto en pie; hon rado.
uprising *n* sublevacion *f*.
uproar *n* tumulto, alboroto *m*.
uproot *vt* desarraigar.
upset *vt* trastornar; derramar, volcar:—*n* reves *m*; trastorno *m*:—*adj*
  molesto; revuelto.
upshot *n* remate *m*; fin *m*; conclusion *f*.
upside-down *adv* de arriba abajo.
upstairs *adv* de arriba.
upstart *n* advenedizo *m*.
uptight *adj* nervioso.
up-to-date *adj* al dia.
upturn *n* mejora *f*.
upward *adj* ascendente:—**~s** *adv*
  hacia arriba.
urban *adj* urbano.
urbane *adj* cortes.
urchin *n* golfillo *m*.
urge *vt* animar:—*n* impulso *m*; deseo
  m.
urgency *n* urgencia *f*.

urgent *adj* urgente.
urinal *n* orinal *m*.
urinate *vi* orinar.
urine *n* orina *f*.
urn *n* urna *f*.
us *pn* nos; nosotros.
usage *n* tratamiento *m*; uso *m*.
use *n* uso *m*; utilidad, practica *f*:—*vt*
  usar, emplear.
used *adj* usado.
useful *adj* , **~ly** *adv* util(mente).
usefulness *n* utilidad *f*.
useless *adj* inútil:—**~ly** *adv* inútil-
  mente.
uselessness *n* inutilidad *f*.
user-friendly *adj* amistoso.
usher *n* ujier *m*; acomodador *m*.
usherette *n* acomodadora *f*.
usual *adj* usual, comun, normal:—
  ~ly *adv* normalmente.
usurer *n* usurero *m*.
usurp *vt* usurpar.
usury *n* usura *f*.
utensil *n* utensilio *m*.
uterus *n* utero *m*.
utilize *vt* utilizar.
utility *n* utilidad *f*.
utmost *adj* extremo, sumo; ultimo.
utter *adj* total; todo; entero:—*vt* pro-
  ferir; expresar; publicar.
utterance *n* expresion *f*.
utterly *adv* enteramente, del todo.

V

vacancy *n* cuarto libre *m*.
vacant *adj* vacio; desocupado.
vacate *vt* desocupar.
vacation *n* vacaciones *fpl*.

vaccinate *vt* vacunar.
vaccination *n* vacunacion *f*.
vaccine *n* vacuna *f*.
vacuous *adj* necio/a, bobo/a.

vacuum n vacio m.
vagina n vagina f.
vagrant n vagabundo.
vague adj vago.
vain adj vano.
valet n criado m.
valiant adj valiente.
valid adj valido.
valley n valle m.
valor n valor m.
valuable adj precioso.
valuation n tasa, valuacion f.
value n valor.
valued adj apreciado.
valve n valvula f.
vampire n vampiro m.
vandal n gamberro m.
vandalize vt danar.
vandalism n vandalismo m.
vanguard n vanguardia f.
vanilla n vainilla f.
vanish vi desvanecerse.
vanity n vanidad f.
vanquish vt vencer.
vantage point n punto panoramico m.
vapor n vapor m.
variable adj variable.
variance n discordia f.
variation n variacion f.
varicose vein n variz f.
varied adj variado.
variety n variedad f.
various adj vario.
varnish n barniz m.
vary vt, vi variar.
vase n florero m.
vast adj vasto.
vat n tina f.
vault n boveda f.
veal n ternera f.
veer vi (mar) virar.

vegetable adj vegetal, n ~s pl legumbres fpl.
vegetable garden n huerta f.
vegetarian n vegetariano, na m/f.
vegetate vi vegetar.
vegetation n vegetacion f.
vehemence n vehemencia f.
vehement adj vehemente.
vehicle n vehiculo m.
veil n velo m.
vein n vena f.
velocity n velocidad f.
velvet n terciopelo m.
vendor n vendedor m.
veneer n chapa f.
venerable adj venerable.
venerate vt venerar.
veneration n veneracion f.
venereal adj venereo.
vengeance n venganza f.
venial adj venial.
venison n (carne de) venado f.
venom n veneno m.
venomous adj venenoso.
vent n respiradero m; salida f.
ventilate vt ventilar.
ventilation n ventilacion f.
ventilator n ventilador m.
ventriloquist n ventrilocuo m.
venture n empresa f:—vi aventurarse.
venue n lugar de reunion m.
veranda(h) n terraza f.
verb n (gr) verbo m.
verbal adj verbal.
verdict n (law) veredicto m.
verification n verificacion f.
verify vt verificar.
veritable adj verdadero.
vermin n bichos mpl.
vermouth n vermut m.
versatile adj versatil.
verse n verso m.

versed *adj* versado.

version *n* version *f.*

versus *prep* contra.

vertebra *n* vertebra *f.*

vertebral, vertebrate *adj* vertebral.

vertical *adj*, **~ly** *adv* vertical (mente).

vertigo *n* vertigo *m.*

very *adj adv* muy, mucho.

vessel *n* vasija *f.*

vest *n* chaleco *m.*

vestibule *n* vestibulo *m.*

vestige *n* vestigio *m.*

vestry *n* sacristia *f.*

veteran *adj, n* veterano (*m*).

veterinary *adj* veterinario.

veto *n* veto *m.*

vex *vt* molestar.

via *prep* por.

viaduct *n* viaducto *m.*

vial *n* redoma *f.*

vibrate *vi* vibrar.

vibration *n* vibracion *f.*

vicarious *adj* sustituto.

vice *n* vicio *m.*

vice versa *adv* viceversa.

vicinity *n* vecindad *f.*

vicious *adj* vicioso.

victim *n* victima *f.*

victimize *vt* victimizar.

victor *n* vencedor *m.*

victorious *adj* victorioso.

victory *n* victoria *f.*

video *n* videofilm *m;* video cassette *f;* videograbadora *f.*

video tape *n* cinta de video *f.*

vie *vi* competir.

view *n* vista *f.*

viewpoint *n* punto de vista *m.*

vigilance *n* vigilancia *f.*

vigilant *adj* vigilante.

vigorous *adj* vigoroso.

vigor *n* vigor *m.*

vile *adj* vil.

vilify *vt* envilecer.

villa *n* chalet *m.*

village *n* aldea *f.*

villain *n* malvado *m.*

vindicate *vt* vindicar.

vindication *n* vindicacion *f.*

vindictive *adj* vengativo.

vine *n* vid *f.*

vinegar *n* vinagre *m.*

vineyard *n* vina *f.*

vintage *n* vendimia *f.*

vinyl *n* vinilo *m.*

viola *n* (*mus*) viola *f.*

violate *vt* violar.

violation *n* violacion *f.*

violence *n* violencia *f.*

violent *adj* violento.

violet *n* (*bot*) violeta *f.*

violin *n* (*mus*) violin *m.*

viper *n* vibora *f.*

virgin *n* virgen *f.*

virginity *n* virginidad *f.*

Virgo *n* Virgo *f* (signo del zodiaco).

virile *adj* viril.

virility *n* virilidad *f.*

virtual *adj* , **~ly** *adv* virtual(mente).

virtue *n* virtud *f.*

virtuous *adj* virtuoso.

virulent *adj* virulento.

virus *n* virus *m.*

visa *n* visado *m*, visa *f.*

vis-a-vis *prep* con respecto a.

visibility *n* visibilidad *f.*

visible *adj* visible.

vision *n* vista *f.*

visit *vt* visitar:—*n* visita *f.*

visitor *n* visitante *m/f.*

visor *n* visera *f.*

vista *n* vista, perspectiva *f.*

visual *adj* visual.

visualize *vt* imaginarse.

vital adj vital.
vitality n vitalidad f.
vitamin n vitamina f.
vitiate vt viciar.
vivacious adj vivaz.
vivid adj vivo.
vivisection n viviseccion f.
vocabulary n vocabulario m.
vocal adj vocal.
vocation n vocacion f.
vociferous adj vocinglero.
vodka n vodka m.
vogue n moda f; boga f.
voice n voz f:—vt expresar.
void adj nulo:—n vacio m.
volatile adj volatil; voluble.
volcanic adj volcanico.
volcano n volcan m.
volition n voluntad f.
volley n descarga f; salva f; rociada f; volea f.
volleyball n voleibol m.

volt n voltio m.
voltage n voltaje m.
voluble adj locuaz.
volume n volumen m.
voluntarily adv voluntariamente.
voluntary adj voluntario.
volunteer n voluntario m.
voluptuous adj voluptuoso.
vomit vt, vi vomitar.
vortex n remolino m.
vote n voto.
voter n votante m/f.
voting n votacion f.
voucher n vale m.
vow n voto m.
vowel n vocal f.
voyage n viaje m.
vulgar adj ordinario.
vulgarity n groseria.
vulnerable adj vulnerable.
vulture n buitre m.

W

wad n fajo m.
waddle vi anadear.
wade vi vadear.
wafer n galleta f.
waffle n gofre m.
wag vt menear.
wage n salario m.
waggon n carro m.
wail n lamento m.
waist n cintura f.
wait vi esperar.
waiter n camarero m.
waiting list n lista de espera f.
waiting room n sala de espera f.
waive vt suspender.

wake vi despertarse.
waken vt, (vi) despertar(se).
walk vt, vi pasear; andar.
walking stick n baston m.
wall n pared f; muralla f; muro m.
wallflower n (bot) aleli m.
wallpaper n papel pintado m.
walnut n nogal m; nuez f.
walrus n morsa f.
waltz n vals m (baile).
wan adj palido.
wand n varita magica f.
wane vi menguar.
want vt querer.
wanton adj lascivo.

war *n* guerra *f.*
ward *n* sala *f*
wardrobe *n* guardarropa *f.*
warehouse *n* almacen *m.*
warm *adj* calido; caliente.
warm-hearted *adj* afectuoso.
warmth *n* calor *m.*
warn *vt* avisar.
warning *n* aviso *m.*
warp *vi* torcerse.
warrant *n* orden judicial *f.*
warranty *n* garantia *f.*
warren *n* conejero *m.*
warrior *n* guerrero *m.*
wart *n* verruga *f.*
wary *adj* cauto.
wash *vt* lavar.
washbowl *n* lavabo *m.*
washing machine *n* lavadora *f.*
washing-up *n* fregado *m.*
washroom *n* servicios *mpl.*
wasp *n* avispa *f.*
waste *vt* malgastar.
watch *n* reloj *m;* vigilar.
watchdog *n* perro guardian *m.*
water *n* agua *f.*
watercolor *n* acuarela *f.*
waterfall *n* cascada *f.*
watering-can *n* regadera *f.*
waterlily *n* ninfea *f.*
water melon *n* sandia *f.*
watertight *adj* impermeable.
watt *n* vatio *m.*
wave *n* ola, onda *f.*
waver *vi* vacilar.
wax *n* cera *f.*
way *n* camino *m;* via *f.*
we *pn* nosotros, nosotras.
weak *adj* , **~ly** *adv* debil(mente).
wealth *n* riqueza *f.*
wealthy *adj* rico.

weapon *n* arma *f.*
wear *vt* gastar, consumir; usar, llevar.
weary *adj* cansado.
weasel *n* comadreja *f.*
weather *n* tiempo *m.*
weave *vt* tejer; trenzar.
weaving *n* tejido *m.*
web *n* telarana *f.*
wed *vt, vi* casar(se).
wedge *n* cuna *f.*
Wednesday *n* miercoles *m.*
wee *adj* pequenito.
weed *n* mala hierba *f.*
week *n* semana *f.*
weekend *n* fin de semana *m.*
weekly *adj* semanal.
weep *vt, vi* llorar.
weeping willow *n* sauce lloron *m.*
weigh *vt, vi* pesar.
weight *n* peso *m.*
welcome *adj* recibido con agrado:—
~! ¡bienvenido!.
weld *vt* soldar.
welfare *n* prosperidad *f*
well *n* fuente *f adv* bien.
wench *n* mozuela *f.*
west *n* oeste, occidente *m.*
wet *adj* humedo, mojado.
whale *n* ballena *f.*
wharf *n* muelle *m.*
what *pn* que, qué?, el que, la que, lo que.
whatever *pn* cualquier o cualquiera cosa que.
wheat *n* trigo *m.*
wheel *n* rueda *f.*
wheelbarrow *n* carretilla *f.*
wheelchair *n* sillita de ruedas *f.*
wheeze *vi* jadear.
when *adv* cuando.
whenever *adv* cuando; cada vez que.

where adv dónde? conj donde.

whether conj si.

which pn que; lo que; el que, el cual; cual:—adj qué?; cuyo.

while n rato m; vez f:—conj durante; mientras; aunque.

whim n antojo m.

whine vi llorar, lamentar

whinny vi relinchar.

whip n azote m; latigo m.

whirlpool n vortice m.

whirlwind n torbellino m.

whiskey n whisky m.

whisper vi cuchichear.

whistle vi silbar.

white adj blanco.

who pn quién?, que.

whoever pn quienquiera, cualquiera.

whole adj todo.

wholemeal adj integral.

wholly adv enteramente.

whom pn quién? que.

whooping cough n tos ferina f.

whore n puta f.

why n por qué?

wick n mecha f.

wicked adj malvado.

wide adj ancho.

widen vt ensanchar.

widow n viuda f.

widower n viudo m.

width n anchura f.

wield vt manejar.

wife n esposa f.

wig n peluca f.

wild adj silvestre.

wilderness n desierto m.

wild life n fauna f.

will n voluntad f.

willful adj deliberado; testarudo.

willow n sauce m (arbol).

willpower n fuerza de voluntad f.

wilt vi marchitarse.

wily adj astuto.

win vt ganar.

wince vi encogerse, estremecerse.

winch n torno m.

wind n viento m.

wind vt enrollar.

windfall n golpe de suerte m.

winding adj tortuoso.

windmill n molino de viento m.

window n ventana f.

window box n jardinera de ventana f.

window ledge n repisa f.

window pane n cristal m.

window sill n repisa f.

windpipe n traquea f.

windshield n parabrisas m invar.

windy adj de mucho viento.

wine n vino m.

wine cellar n bodega f.

wine glass n copa f.

wing n ala f.

winged adj alado.

wink vi guinar.

winner n ganador.

winter n invierno m.

wintry adj invernal.

wipe vt limpiar.

wire n telegrama m.

wisdom n sabiduria f.

wisdom teeth npl muelas de juicio fpl.

wise adj sabio.

wisecrack n broma f.

wish vt querer.

wishful adj deseoso.

wit n entendimiento m.

witch n bruja f.

witchcraft n brujeria f.

with prep con; por, de, a.

withdraw vt quitar.

withdrawal n retirada f.

withdrawn adj reservado.

withhold *vt* detener.
within *prep* dentro de.
without *prep* sin.
withstand *vt* resistir.
witless *adj* necio.
witness *n* testigo *m.*
witticism *n* ocurrencia *f.*
wittily *adv* ingeniosamente.
witty *adj* ingenioso.
wizard *n* brujo *m.*
woe *n* dolor *m;* miseria *f.*
woeful *adj* triste.
wolf *n* lobo *m.*
woman *n* mujer *f.*
womb *n* utero *m.*
wonder *n* milagro *m.*
wonderful *adj* maravilloso.
won't *abrev* de will not.
woo *vt* cortejar.
wood *n* bosque *m;* selva *f;* madera *f;* lena *f.*
woodland *n* arbolado *m.*
woodlouse *n* cochinilla *f.*
woodpecker *n* picamaderos *m* invar.
woodworm *n* carcoma *f.*
wool *n* lana *f.*
woolen *adj* de lana.
word *n* palabra *f.*
wordy *adj* verboso.
work *vi* trabajar; obrar.
world *n* mundo *m.*
worm *n* gusano *m.*
worn-out *adj* gastado.
worried *adj* preocupado.
worry *vt* preocupar.

worse *adj, adv* peor.
worship *n* culto *m;* adoracion *f.*
worst *adj* el/la peor.
worth *n* valor *m.*
worthwhile *adj* que vale la pena; valioso.
worthy *adj* digno.
wound *n* herida *f.*
wrangle *vi* renir *f.*
wrap *vt* envolver.
wrath *n* ira *f.*
wreath *n* corona *f.*
wreck *n* naufragio *m;* ruina *f.*
wreckage *n* restos *mpl.*
wren *n* reyezuelo *m* (avecilla).
wrestle *vi* luchar; disputar.
wrestling *n* lucha *f.*
wretched *adj* infeliz, miserable.
wring *vt* torcer.
wrinkle *n* arruga *f.*
wrist *n* muneca *f.*
wristband *n* puno de camisa *m.*
wristwatch *n* reloj de pulsera *m.*
writ *n* escrito *m;* escritura *f.*
write *vt* escribir.
write-off *n* perdida total *f.*
writer *n* escritor, ra, *m/f;* autor, ra *m/f.*
writhe *vi* retorcerse.
writing *n* escritura *f*
writing desk *n* escritorio *m.*
writing paper *n* papel para escribir *m.*
wrong *n* injuria *f;* injusticia *f.*
wrongful *adj* injusto.
wrongly *adv* injustamente.
wry *adj* ironico.

XYZ

Xmas *n* Navidad *f.*
X-ray *n* radiografia *f.*
xylophone *n* xilofano *m.*

yacht *n* yate *m.*
yachting *n* balandrismo *m.*
Yankee *n* yanqui *m.*

yard *n* corral *m*; yarda *f*.

yardstick *n* criterio *m*.

yarn *n* estambre *m*; hilo de lino *m*.

yawn *vi* bostezar

yeah *adv* si.

year *n* ano *m*.

yearling *n* primal *m*, ala *f*.

yearly *adj* anual.

yearn *vi* anorar.

yearning *n* anoranza *f*.

yeast *n* levadura *f*.

yell *vi* aullar.

yellow *adj* amarillo.

yelp *vi* latir, ganir.

yes *adv, n* si (*m*).

yesterday *adv, n* ayer (*m*).

yet *conj* sin embargo; pero:—*adv* todavia.

yew *n* tejo *m*.

yield *vt* dar, producir.

yoga *n* yoga *m*.

yog(h)urt *n* yogur *m*.

yoke *n* yugo *m*.

yolk *n* yema de huevo *f*.

yonder *adv* alla.

you *pn* vosotros, tu, usted, ustedes.

young *adj* joven.

youngster *n* jovencito, ta *m/f*.

your(s) *pn* tuyo, vuestro, suyo:—**sincerely** ~**s** su seguro ser vidor.

yourself *pn* tu mismo, usted mismo, vosotros mismos, ustedes mismos.

youth *n* juventud *f*.

youthful *adj* juvenil.

youthfulness *n* juventud *f*.

yuppie *adj, n* yuppie *m/f*.

zany *adj* estrafalario.

zap *vt* borrar.

zeal *n* celo *m*; ardor *m*.

zealous *adj* celoso.

zebra *n* cebra *f*.

zenith *n* cenit *m*.

zero *n* zero, cero *m*.

zest *n* animo *m*.

zigzag *n* zigzag *m*.

zinc *n* zinc *m*.

zip, zipper *n* cremallera *f*.

zodiac *n* zodiaco *m*.

zone *n* banda, faja *f*; zona *f*.

zoo *n* zoo *m*.

zoological *adj* zoologico.

zoologist *n* zoologo, ga *m/f*.

zoology *n* zoologia *f*.

zoom *vi* zumbar.

zoom lens *n* zoom *m*.